THE FATHERS
OF THE CHURCH

A NEW TRANSLATION

VOLUME 130

THE FATHERS
OF THE CHURCH

A NEW TRANSLATION

ST. EPHREM THE SYRIAN

THE HYMNS ON FAITH

Translated by

JEFFREY T. WICKES

Saint Louis University

THE CATHOLIC UNIVERSITY OF AMERICA PRESS
Washington, D.C.

The paper used in this publication meets the minimum requirements of
the American National Standards for Information Science—Permanence
of Paper for Printed Library Materials, ANSI z39.48-1984.
∞

Library of Congress Cataloging-in-Publication Data
Ephraem, Syrus, Saint, 303-373.
[Hymni de fide. English]
Hymns on faith / St. Ephrem the Syrian ; translated by
Jeffrey Thomas Wickes, St. Louis University.
pages cm. — (The fathers of the church, a new translation ; volume 130)
Includes bibliographical references and index.
ISBN 978-0-8132-3012-2 (pbk : alk. paper)   1. Hymns, Syriac.   2. Hymns,
Syriac–Translations into English.   I. Wickes, Jeffrey Thomas, 1978–
translator.   II. Title.
BR65.E633H9513 2015
264'.014023—dc23
2014042752

CONTENTS

INDICES

ACKNOWLEDGMENTS

The present translation has developed slowly, in a variety of places, and in conversation with a number of different people. It is my great pleasure to thank them here.

Joseph Amar guided my study of Syriac during my doctoral studies at the University of Notre Dame. I read many of these hymns in Syriac with him, and he has offered continuous feedback and friendship, at no small inconvenience to himself. *Malfono*, thank you.

Robin Darling Young has been a constant source of encouragement from the time I began graduate studies. She has read Syriac and Armenian with me and challenged me to ask bigger questions and to read more sources.

I initially began studying this particular hymn cycle for a seminar with Brian Daley, SJ. Fr. Daley encouraged my work then and has repeatedly answered long e-mails about the fourth-century controversies.

M. Tzvi Novick served on my dissertation committee, and, in that capacity, read significant portions of this translation. His eye for detail is surpassed only by his kindness.

Susan Ashbrook Harvey originally suggested I submit this translation to the Catholic University of America Press. She has kindly promoted my work and offered feedback as often as I have asked.

Robert Kitchen read the entirety of this translation and checked it for accuracy against the Syriac. He noticed many errors and, beyond that, offered many helpful suggestions for improving my English.

Carole Monica Burnett, the editor of the Fathers of the Church series, has been prompt and clear in answering my questions, as well as encouraging and kind throughout the publishing process.

James Ginther, my department chair at Saint Louis University, has supported my work and shown a consistent appreciation for the scholarly contributions that translations make.

Blake Hartung, my research assistant from 2012 to 2014, typed up my handwritten translation, read through it at least three times, and began the process of indexing these hymns.

My research has been supported by a fellowship from the Dumbarton Oaks Research Library, by a dissertation grant from the Dolores Zorhab Liebmann fund, and by two Mellon Faculty Development grants through the Saint Louis University College of Arts and Sciences.

I have discussed these translations and the ideas behind them with a number of other people: Daniel Galadza, Carl Griffin, Sidney Griffith, ST, Kristian Heal, Scott Johnson, Joel Kalvesmaki, Derek Krueger, Joshua Lollar, Peter Martens, Geoffrey Miller, Margaret Mullet, Joshua Robinson, Daniel Smith, Matthew Thiessen, and Jack Tannous.

In spite of the help I have received from all these people, I am sure that outright errors and subtle misinterpretations remain. These are my fault, not theirs.

My wife, Julia, and my two daughters, Esme and Elsa, have shared their lives with these translations. I thank them above all.

SYRIAC
TRANSLITERATION
CHART

ܐ	' or vowel	ܠ	l
ܒ	b	ܡ	m
ܓ	g	ܢ	n
ܕ	d	ܣ	s
ܗ	h	ܥ	ʻ
ܘ	w or vowel	ܦ	p
ܙ	z	ܨ	ṣ
ܚ	ḥ	ܩ	q
ܛ	ṭ	ܪ	r
ܝ	y or vowel	ܫ	š
ܟ	k	ܬ	t

ABBREVIATIONS
AND SIGLA

Critical Editions of Ephrem's Works

ER   Assemani, J. S., ed. *Sancti Patris Nostri Ephraem Syri Op-
          era Omnia quae exstant graece, syriace, latine, in sex tomos
          distributa.* Rome, 1732–43.

HF (S) *Des heiligen Ephraem des Syrers Hymnen de fide,*
          volume 154.

HF (G) *Des heiligen Ephraem des Syrers Hymnen de fide,*
          volume 155.

Ephrem's Works

CJ   *Contra Julianum*

CDia   *Commentary on the Diatessaron*

CEx   *Commentary on Exodus*

CGen.   *Commentary on Genesis*

CH   *Hymns* Contra Haereses

CNis   *Carmina Nisibena*

HE   *Hymns on the Church*

HEpi   *Hymns on Epiphany*

HF   *Hymns on Faith*

HPar   *Hymns on Paradise*

HUB   *Hymns on Unleavened Bread*

PR   *Prose Refutations*

SF   *Sermons on Faith*

General

P	Peshitta
Syr	Syriac

Manuscripts

A	Br. Mus. add. 12 176
B	Cod. vat. sir. 111
C	Cod. vat. sir. 113
D	Br. mus. add. 14571

Periodicals and Serials

ARAM	*ARAM Periodical.* ARAM Society for Syro-Mesopotamian Studies
CSCO	*Corpus Scriptorum Christianorum Orientalium*
FOTC	Fathers of the Church. Washington, DC: The Catholic University of America Press, 1947–
OC	*Oriens Christianus*
OCA	*Orientalia Christiana Analecta*
OCP	*Orientalia Christiana Periodica*
PBC	*The Patristic and Byzantine Review*
PdO	*Parole de l'Orient*
PO	*Patrologia Orientalis*
SA	*Studia Anselmiana*
SP	*Studia Patristica*
SVTQ	*St Vladimir's Theological Quarterly*
VC	*Vigiliae Christianae*
ZTC	*Zeitschrift für Kirchengeschichte*

Lexica

DJBA	Michael Sokoloff. *A Dictionary of Jewish Babylonian Aramaic of the Talmudic and Geonic Periods.* Baltimore and London: The Johns Hopkins University Press, 2002.

LS   Michael Sokoloff. *A Syriac Lexicon: A Translation
            from the Latin, Correction, Expansion, and Update of
            C. Brockelmann's* Lexicon Syriacum. Winona Lake, IN:
            Eisenbrauns; and Piscataway, NJ: Gorgias Press, 2009.

Thes. Syr. R. Payne Smith. *Thesaurus Syriacus.* With New Fore-
            word by K. C. Hanson. Two Volumes. Eugene, OR:
            Wipf and Stock Publishers, 2007.

Sigla

{ }   A reading substituted from a ms other than A, not
            used by Beck

[ ]   Words supplied by the translator of the present
            volume

BIBLIOGRAPHY

Select Editions of the Works of Ephrem the Syrian

Assemani, J. S., ed. *Sancti Patris Nostri Ephraem Syri Opera Omnia quae exstant graece, syriace, latine, in sex tomos distributa.* Rome, 1732–43.

Beck, E., ed. *Des heiligen Ephraem des Syrers Carmina Nisibena.* CSCO 218–19, 240–41. Louvain, 1961.

———, ed. *Des heiligen Ephraem des Syrers Hymnen auf Abraham Kidunaya und Julianos Saba.* CSCO 322–23. Louvain, 1972.

———, ed. *Des heiligen Ephraem des Syrers Hymnen contra haereses.* CSCO 169–70. Louvain, 1957.

———, ed. *Des heiligen Ephraem des Syrers Hymnen de ecclesia.* 2 vols. CSCO 198–99. Louvain, 1960.

———, ed. *Des heiligen Ephraem des Syrers Hymnen de fide.* CSCO 154–55. Louvain, 1955.

———, ed. *Des Heiligen Ephraem des Syrers Hymnen de Ieiunio.* CSCO 246–47. Louvain, 1964.

———, ed. *Des heiligen Ephraem des Syrers Hymnen de Nativitate (Epiphania).* CSCO 186–87. Louvain, 1959.

———, ed. *Des heiligen Ephraem des Syrers Hymnen de Paradiso und Contra Julianum.* CSCO 174–75. Louvain, 1957.

———, ed. *Des Heiligen Ephraem des Syrers Hymnen de Virginitate.* CSCO 223–24. Louvain, 1962.

———, ed. *Des Heiligen Ephraem des Syrers Paschahymnen.* CSCO 247–48. Louvain, 1962.

———, ed. *Des Heiligen Ephraem des Syrers Sermo de Domino Nostro.* CSCO 270–71. Louvain, 1966.

———, ed. *Des Heiligen Ephraem des Syrers Sermones de Fide.* CSCO 212–13. Louvain, 1961.

———, ed. *Des Heiligen Ephraem des Syrers Sermones,* Vol. 1. CSCO 305–6. Louvain, 1969.

———, ed. *Des Heiligen Ephraem des Syrers Sermones,* Vol. 2. CSCO 311–12. Louvain, 1970.

———, ed. *Des Heiligen Ephraem des Syrers Sermones,* Vol. 3. CSCO 320–21. Louvain, 1972.

———, ed. *Des Heiligen Ephraem des Syrers Sermones,* Vol. 4. CSCO 334–35. Louvain, 1973.

——, ed. *Ephraem Syrus. Sermones in Hebdomadam Sanctam. CSCO* 412–13. Louvain, 1979.

——, ed. *Nachträge zu Ephraem Syrus. CSCO* 363–64. Louvain, 1975.

Bevan, E. A., and F. C. Burkitt. S. *Ephraim's Prose Refutations of Mani, Marcion and Bardaisan.* Volume 1. Oxford, 1912. Reprint, Piscataway, NJ: Gorgias Press, 2008.

Leloir, L., ed. *Saint Ephrem Commentaire de l'évangile concordant.* Chester Beatty Monographs, no. 8. Dublin, 1963.

——, ed. *Saint Ephrem Commentaire de l'évangile concordant texte syriaque (Manuscript Chester Beatty 709), Folios Additionnels.* Chester Beatty Monographs, no. 8. Louvain, 1990.

Maries, L., and C. Mercier, eds. *Hymnes de S. Ephrem conservés en version arménienne. PO* 30. Paris, 1961.

Mitchell, C. W. S. *Ephraim's Prose Refutations of Mani, Marcion, and Bardaisan,* volume 1. London, 1912. Reprint, Piscataway, NJ: Gorgias Press, 2008.

Renoux, C., ed. *Ephrem de Nisibe Mêmrê sur Nicomidie. PO* 37. Paris, 1975.

Tounneau, R. M., ed. *Sancti Ephraem Syri in Genesim et in Exodum commentarii. CSCO* 152–53. Louvain, 1955.

Select Secondary Sources

Amar, Joseph P., and Edward G. Mathews, trans. *St. Ephrem the Syrian: Selected Prose Works.* FOTC 91. Washington, DC: The Catholic University of America Press, 1994.

Anatolios, Khaled. *Retrieving Nicaea: The Development and Meaning of Trinitarian Doctrine.* Grand Rapids, MI: Baker Academic, 2011.

Ayres, Lewis. *Nicaea and its Legacy: An Approach to Fourth-Century Trinitarian Theology.* Oxford: Oxford University Press, 2004.

Beck, Edmund. "Das Bild vom Weg mit Meilensteinen und Herbergen bei Ephraem." *Oriens Christianus* 65 (1981): 1–39.

——. *Die Theologie des hl Ephraem in seinen Hymnen über den Glauben.* *Studia Anselmiana* 21. Rome: Pontificium Institutum S. Anselmi, 1949.

——. "Ephräms des Syrers Hymnik." In *Liturgie und Dichtung: Ein interdisziplinäres Kompendium: Gualtero Duerig annum vitae septuagesimum feliciter complenti,* volume 1. Edited by H. Becker and R. Kaczynski, 345–79. St Ottilien, 1983.

——. *Ephräms Reden über den Glauben: Ihr theologischer Lehregehalt und ihr geschichtlicher Rahmen.* Rome, 1953.

——. *Ephräms Trinitätslehre im Bild von Sonne/Feuer, Licht und Wärme.* *CSCO Subsidia,* volume 425. Louvain, 1981.

Behr, John. *The Nicene Faith. The Formation of Christian Theology,* volume 2. Crestwood, NY: St Vladimir's Seminary Press, 2004.

Botha, Philippus J. "Antithesis and Argument in the Hymns of Ephrem the Syrian." *Hervormde Teologiese Studies* 44 (1988): 581–95.

―――. "Argument and Art in Ephrem the Syrian's Hymn *De Fide* 78." *Acta Patristica et Byzantina* 7 (1996): 21–36.

―――. "Christology and Apology in Ephrem the Syrian." *Hervormde Teologiese Studies* 45 (1989): 19–29.

―――. "Ephrem's Comparison of the Father/Son Relationship to the Relationship Between a Tree and Its Fruit in His Hymns *on Faith*." *Acta Patristica et Byzantina* 4 (1993): 23–32.

―――. "God in a Garment of Words: The Metaphor of Metaphoric Language in Ephrem the Syrian's Hymn 'on Faith' 31." *Acta Patristica et Byzantina* 3 (1992): 63–79.

―――. "The Structure and Function of Paradox in the Hymns of Ephrem the Syrian." *Ekklesiastikos Pharos* 68 (1990): 50–62.

Bou Mansour, Tanios. *La pensée symbolique de Saint Ephrem le Syrien.* Kaslik, Lebanon: Université Saint-Esprit, 1988.

Brock, Sebastian P. "A Brief Guide to the Main Editions and Translations of the Works of St Ephrem." *The Harp* 3:1–2 (June, 1990), 7–25.

―――. "Clothing Metaphors as a Means of Theological Expression in Syriac Tradition." In *Typus, Symbol, Allegorie bei den östlichen Vätern und ihren Parallelen im Mittelalter.* Edited by M. Schmidt, 11–40. Regensburg: Pustet, 1982.

―――. *The Holy Spirit in the Syrian Baptismal Tradition.* Reprint Edition. Piscataway, NJ: Gorgias Press, 2008.

―――. *St Ephrem the Syrian: Hymns on Paradise.* Crestwood, NY: St Vladimir's Seminary Press, 1990.

―――. "Jewish Traditions in Syriac Sources." *Journal of Jewish Studies* 30 (1979): 212–32.

―――. *The Luminous Eye: The Spiritual World Vision of Saint Ephrem the Syrian.* Kalamazoo, MI: Cistercian Publications, 1985.

―――. "The Poetic Artistry of St Ephrem: An Analysis of H.Azym. III." *Parole de l'Orient* 6/7 (1975–1976): 21–28.

―――. *St Ephrem: A Hymn on the Eucharist (Hymns on Faith, no.10).* Lancaster, UK: J. F. Coakley at the Department of Religious Studies, University of Lancaster, 1986.

―――. "The Transmission of Ephrem's *madrashe* in the Syriac Liturgical Tradition." In *Studia Patristica* 33. Edited by E. A. Livingstone, 490–505. Leuven: Peeters, 1997.

Bruns, Peter. "*Aithallaha's Brief über den Glauben*: Ein bedeutendes Dokument frühsyrischer Theologie." *Oriens Christianus* 76 (1992): 46–73.

―――. "Arius hellenizans?—Ephräm der Syrer und die neoarianischen Kontroversen seiner Zeit." *Zeitschrift für Kirchengeschichte* 101 (1990): 21–57.

Bundy, David. "Language and the Knowledge of God in Ephrem Syrus." *The Patristic and Byzantine Review* 5 (1986): 91–103.

―――. "The Letter of Aithallaha [CPG 3340]: Theology, Purpose, Date." In *Symposium Syriacum III, 1980.* Edited by R. Lavenant, 135–42. Rome: Pontifical Institute, 1983.

Daley, Brian. "The Enigma of Meletius of Antioch." In *Tradition and the Rule of Faith in the Early Church: Essays in Honor of Joseph T. Lienhard.* Edited by Ronnie J. Rombs and Alexander Y. Hwang, 128–50. Washington, DC: The Catholic University of America Press, 2010.

den Biesen, Kees. *Annotated Bibliography of Ephrem the Syrian* (Self-published, 2012).

———. *Simple and Bold: Ephrem's Art of Symbolic Thought.* Piscataway, NJ: Gorgias Press, 2006.

Griffith, Sidney H. "Ephraem, the Deacon of Edessa, and the Church of the Empire." In *Diakonia: Studies in Honor of Robert T. Meyer.* Edited by T. Halton, 22–52.Washington, DC: The Catholic University of America Press, 1986.

———. "Ephraem the Syrian's Hymns 'Against Julian': Meditations on History and Imperial Power." *Vigiliae Christianae* 41:3 (September, 1987): 245–46.

———. *"Faith Adoring the Mystery": Reading the Bible With Ephrem the Syrian.* Milwaukee, WI: Marquette University Press, 1997.

———. "Faith Seeking Understanding in the Thought of Saint Ephrem the Syrian." In *Faith Seeking Understanding.* Edited by George C. Berthold, 35–55. New York: St. Anselm College Press, 1991.

———. "The Marks of the 'True Church' according to Ephraem's *Hymns Against Heresies.*" In *After Bardaisan: Change and Continuity in Syriac Christianity, in Honour of Professor Han J. W. Drijvers.* Edited by G. J. Reinink and A. C. Klugkist, 125–40. Leuven: Peeters, 1999.

———. "Setting Right the Church of Syria: Saint Ephraem's *Hymns Against Heresies.*" In *The Limits of Ancient Christianity: Essays on Late Antique Thought and Culture in Honor of R. A. Markus,* 97–114. Ann Arbor, MI: The University of Michigan Press, 1999.

———. "St. Ephraem, Bar Dayṣān and the Clash of Madrāshê in Aram: Readings in St. Ephraem's *Hymni contra haereses.*" *The Harp* 21 (2006): 447–72.

Hanson, R. P. C. *The Search for the Christian Doctrine of God: The Arian Controversies, 318–381.* New York: T & T Clark, 1998. Reprint, Grand Rapids, MI: Baker Academic, 2005.

Harvey, Susan Ashbrook. *Song and Memory: Biblical Women in Syriac Tradition.* Milwaukee, WI: Marquette University Press, 2010.

Lange, Christian. *The Portrayal of Christ in the Syriac Commentary on the Diatessaron. CSCO* Subsidia. Volume 616. Louvain: Peeters, 2005.

McVey, Kathleen E. *Ephrem the Syrian: Hymns.* Mahwah, NJ: Paulist Press, 1989.

———. "Were the Earliest Madrāšē Songs or Recitations?" In *After Bardaisan: Studies on Continuity and Change in Syriac Christianity in Honour of Professor Han J. W. Drijvers.* Orientalia Lovaniensia Analecta 89. Edited by G. J. Reinink and A. C. Klugkist, 185–99. Leuven: Peeters, 1999.

Morris, John Brande, trans. *The Rhythms of Saint Ephrem the Syrian: Select*

Works of S. Ephrem the Syrian. Oxford, 1847. Reprint, Piscataway, NJ: Gorgias Press, 2006.

Murray, Robert. *Symbols of Church and Kingdom: A Study in Early Syriac Tradition.* Revised Edition. Piscataway, NJ: Gorgias Press, 2004.

———. "The Theory of Symbolism in St. Ephrem's Theology." *Parole de l'Orient* 6/7 (1975): 1–20.

Palmer, Andrew. "Akrostich Poems: Restoring Ephrem's *Madroshe.*" *The Harp* 15 (2002): 275–87.

———. "Interpolated Stanzas in Ephraim's Madroshe III–VII on Faith." *Oriens Christianus* 93 (2009): 1–27.

———. "Interpolated Stanzas in Ephraim's Madroshe LXVI–LXVIII on Faith." *Oriens Christianus* 90 (2006): 1–22.

———. "'A Lyre Without a Voice': The Poetics and the Politics of Ephrem the Syrian." *ARAM* 5 (1993): 371–99.

———. "Restoring the ABC in Ephraim's Cycles on *Faith* and *Paradise.*" *The Journal of Eastern Christian Studies* 55 (2003): 147–94.

———. "A Single Human Being Divided in Himself: Ephraim the Syrian, the Man in the Middle." *Hugoye: Journal of Syriac Studies* 1:2 (1998). Accessed on Dec. 21, 2012. http://syrcom.cua.edu/Hugoye/Vol1No2/HV1N2Palmer.html.

———. "Words, Silences, and the Silent Word: Acrostics and Empty Columns in Saint Ephrem's *Hymns on Faith.*" *Parole de l'Orient* 20 (1995): 129–200.

Possekel, Ute. *Evidence of Greek Philosophical Concepts in the Writings of Ephrem the Syrian.* CSCO Subsidia. Volume 102. Louvain, 1999.

Russell, Paul S. *St. Ephraem the Syrian and St. Gregory the Theologian Confront the Arians.* Kottayam: St. Ephrem Ecumenical Research Institute, 1994.

Shepardson, Christine C. *Anti-Judaism and Christian Orthodoxy: Ephrem's Hymns in Fourth-Century Syria.* Washington, DC: The Catholic University of America Press, 2008.

———. "'Exchanging Reed for Reed': Mapping Contemporary Heretics onto Biblical Jews in Ephrem's *Hymns on Faith.*" *Hugoye: Journal of Syriac Studies* 5:1 (2002). Accessed on Dec. 21, 2012. http://www.bethmardutho.org/index.php/hugoye/hugoye-author-index/137.html.

INTRODUCTION

INTRODUCTION

I. Ephrem and Syriac Christianity

We can see Syriac Christianity's earliest development only in shadowy form: through the scattered pieces of inscriptions,[1] biblical translations,[2] obscure religious poems,[3] speculative treatises,[4] and fantastical narratives.[5] Syriac itself is the dialect of Aramaic that was spoken east of Palestine, in and around the city of Edessa (modern-day Urfa in southeast Turkey).[6] But in regard to the questions of precisely *who* made up the earliest Syriac-speaking Christians, how these communities related to

1. See H. J. W. Drijvers and J. F. Healey, *The Old Syriac Inscriptions of Edessa and Osrhoene* (Leiden: E. J. Brill, 1999).

2. On the Syriac translations of the Old and New Testaments, see S. Brock, *The Bible in the Syriac Tradition,* 2d rev. ed. (Piscataway, NJ: Gorgias Press, 2006).

3. Such as the *Odes of Solomon* and the *Song of the Pearl.* On the *Odes,* see J. Charlesworth, *The Odes of Solomon: The Syriac Texts* (Missoula, MT: Scholars Press, 1978), and M. Lattke, *Oden Salomos: Text, Übersetzung, Kommentar,* Vol. 41, *Novum Testamentum et Orbis Antiquus* (Freiburg: Universitätsverlag Freiburg Schweiz, 1999). On the *Song of the Pearl,* which is preserved within the longer *Acts of Judas Thomas,* see J. Ferreira, *The Hymns of the Pearl: The Syriac and Greek Texts with Introduction, Translations, and Notes* (Sydney: St Paul's Publications, 2002).

4. See H. J. W. Drijvers, *The Book of the Laws of Countries: Dialogue on Fate of Bardaisan of Edessa* (Assen: Van Gorcum & Comp., 1965).

5. Such as the *Acts of Judas Thomas.* See H. J. W. Drijvers, "The Acts of Thomas," in W. Schneemelcher, ed., *New Testament Apocrypha, Vol. II: Writings Relating to the Apostles; Apocalypses and Related Subjects,* rev. ed. (Louisville, KY: Westminster John Knox Press, 1992), 1–22. Syriac text in W. Wright, *Apocryphal Acts of the Apostles, Edited from Syriac Manuscripts in the British Museum and Other Libraries, With English Translation and Notes, Volume I: The Syriac Texts* (Amsterdam: Philo Press, 1968; reprint of 1871 edition), 172–333.

6. For an introduction to the place of Syriac within the family of Aramaic dialects, see S. Brock, *An Introduction to Syriac Studies,* 2d ed. (Piscataway, NJ: Gorgias Press, 2006), 19–23.

their Jewish and pagan neighbors, how they related to Greek-
and Latin-speaking Christians to the West, and how the early
Syriac church developed, we can only speculate.[7] However earliest Syriac Christianity developed, we can say this with certainty:
by the fourth century CE there existed a fully functioning Syriac Christian church with buildings,[8] bishops in contact with
other bishops in the West,[9] and a sizeable body of theological
literature.[10] It is within the milieu of this slowly emerging Syriac
Christian culture that we find Ephrem the Syrian (d. 373).

Ephrem lived and wrote for Christian communities on the
border of the Roman and Persian Empires, and was recognized
among Syriac-, Greek-, and Latin-speaking Christians as a saint
almost immediately following his death. His corpus is large:
over four hundred hymns, three extant biblical commentaries,
and smaller collections of simple, metrical homilies. Among
fourth-century Christian theologians, in terms of literary out-
put, he stands alongside those names familiar from textbooks
of the Christianity of the period—Athanasius, Gregory Nazianzen, Gregory of Nyssa, Ambrose, and Basil the Great. Cul-
turally, however, his is a voice shaped outside the Greco-Roman
rhetorical and philosophical traditions so crucial for these
other authors. There was no standard Syriac educational cur-
riculum of which we are aware, and the exegetical traditions

7. For a recent general introduction to early Syriac Christianity, see L. Van
Rompay, "The East (3): Syria and Mesopotamia," in *The Oxford Handbook of
Early Christian Studies* (Oxford: Oxford University Press, 2008), 362–86.

8. An early fourth-century baptismal font, albeit with a Greek inscription, is
still extant in Ephrem's hometown of Nisibis. For the inscription, see Friedrich
Sarre and Ernst Herzfeld, *Archäologische Reise im Euphrat- und Tigris-Gebiet* (Ber-
lin: Reimer, 1920). See also M. M. Mango, "The Continuity of the Classical Tradition in the Art and Architecture of Northern Mesopotamia," in N. Garsoian,
T. F. Matthews, and R. W. Thomson, eds., *East of Byzantium: Syria and Armenia in
the Formative Period* (Washington, DC: Dumbarton Oaks, 1982), 115–34.

9. See below, p. 19.

10. In addition to Ephrem's corpus, his younger contemporary Aphrahat
wrote twenty-three sermons ("Demonstrations") that have come down to us.
Syriac text ed. by R. Graffin in *Patrologia Syriaca*, 1:1–2. The hymns have recently been re-translated into English by Adam Lehto, *The Demonstrations of
Aphrahat, the Persian Sage* (Piscataway, NJ: Gorgias Press, 2010).

he wove into his biblical commentaries share as much with the Jewish Targums as they do with Christian philosophers.[11]

The collection of hymns here translated, the *Hymns on Faith* (*madrāšê d-ʿal haymānûtâ*), is his longest hymn collection, and the collection in which he most explicitly deals with the so-called "Arian" controversies of the fourth century.[12] As such, these hymns provide our earliest evidence for how the Council of Nicaea was received among non-Greek- and non-Latin-speaking Christians. Yet, despite the importance of this collection to our understanding of fourth-century Christianity, no English translation of these hymns, based upon the 1955 critical edition of the Syriac text (*HF [S]*), has been previously offered.

This introduction proceeds in three parts. First, I offer a general picture of what can be known of the life of Ephrem and the community for which he wrote these hymns. Then I turn to the vexing question of the context of the *HF* themselves, specifically as they relate to the broader Christological controversies of the fourth century. Finally, I present the theological vision of these hymns.

II. Ephrem's Life and Works

While detailed sources for the life of Ephrem abound, their credibility has been seriously challenged over the last eighty

11. See S. Brock, "Jewish Traditions in Syriac Sources," *Journal of Jewish Studies* 30 (1979): 212–32, and P. Féghali, "Influence des Targums sur la pensée exégétique d'Ephrem," *OCA* 229 (1987): 71–82.

12. The characterization of these controversies as "Arian" has come under scrutiny in the last thirty years, as scholars have recognized that none of the post-Nicene writers who would later be tabbed "Arian" identified themselves as such. Thus, while in the past Ephrem's *HF* would have been called his "anti-Arian" hymns, scholars now recognize that such a title is anachronistic. Throughout this work, I refer to Ephrem's opponents as "subordinationists," to suggest that these thinkers (as he characterizes them) share a tendency to subordinate the Son to the Father. They do not, however, think of themselves as "Arian," and Ephrem himself never calls them "Arian." For a recent synopsis of these issues, see J. Rebecca Lyman, "Arius and Arians," in *Oxford Handbook of Early Christian Studies*, ed. S. Ashbrook Harvey and D. Hunter (Oxford: Oxford University Press, 2008), 237–57.

years.[13] The Syriac *Life* depicts Ephrem as having spent most or all of his life in Edessa,[14] and emphasizes his meetings with Basil the Great,[15] his travels to the Egyptian desert,[16] and his adoption of a solitary monastic life on a hilltop outside of that city.[17] In fact, there is little or no reliable evidence to suggest that Ephrem ever met Basil,[18] traveled to Egypt, or lived a reclusive and severely ascetic life outside Edessa.

What we do know is that Ephrem was born in the early fourth century (usually dated around 307–309)[19] in the east-

---

13. All references to the *Life of Ephrem* (hereafter, *Life*) are to the chapter divisions of the recently edited Syriac text and translation in *The Syriac* Vita *Tradition of Ephrem the Syrian,* ed. and trans. Joseph P. Amar, *CSCO* 629/630 (Louvain: Peeters, 2011). See also the critical discussion of this life and its sources therein. For general introductions to his life and thought, see Sebastian P. Brock, *St Ephrem the Syrian: Hymns on Paradise* (Crestwood, NY: St. Vladimir's Seminary Press, 1990), 7–75; Christian Lange, *The Portrayal of Christ in the Syriac Commentary on the Diatessaron* (Louvain: Peeters, 2005), 13–27; Edward G. Mathews and Joseph P. Amar, *St. Ephrem the Syrian: Selected Prose Works* (Washington, DC: The Catholic University of America Press, 1994), 12–56; Kathleen E. McVey, *Ephrem the Syrian: Hymns* (Mahwah, NJ: Paulist Press), 1–48. The two classic studies of Ephrem's life are A. de Halleux, "Saint Éphrem le Syrien," *Revue Théologique de Louvain* 14 (1983): 328–55, and B. Outtier, "Saint Éphrem d'après ses biographies et ses oeuvres," *PdO* 4 (1973): 11–33.

14. While the *Life* identifies Nisibis as his birthplace, only the first nine chapters are devoted to his life there, while the following thirty-two are devoted to his life in Edessa.

15. The meeting of Basil and Ephrem occurs in *Life* 25–28, but episodes involving Basil are also found in 20, 34, 39, and 40.

16. *Life* 21–24.

17. *Life* 13.

18. The legend of the encounter of Ephrem and Basil develops slowly. Its kernel appears in Sozomen (writing ca. 425), who says that "Basil ... was a great admirer of Ephrem, and was astonished at his erudition" (*Ecclesiastical History* 3.16, trans. C. D. Hartranft, in ANPF, ser. 2, vol. 2 [New York, 1891]). Sozomen does not suggest that the two ever met. Given Basil's well-known travels, however, as well as his correspondence with figures such as Eusebius of Samosata (about 75 miles NW of Edessa), it is entirely possible that Ephrem's reputation reached Basil, and vice versa; see Basil's *Epistle* 30, in R. Deferrari, *Saint Basil: The Letters,* vol. 1, Loeb Classical Library (Cambridge, MA: Harvard University Press, 1950).

19. Ephrem's *CNis* show familiarity with Bishop Jacob of Nisibis (ca. 308–338), so an early fourth-century date seems likely. See de Halleux, "Saint Éphrem le Syrien," 331.

ern Roman city of Nisibis (modern-day Nusaybin). It was here that he lived most of his life, albeit in the midst of recurrent political and military unrest. Shapur II of Persia unsuccessfully besieged Nisibis three times during Ephrem's lifetime (in 338, 346, and 350), before finally taking the city in 363.[20] Following the loss of Nisibis, Jovian (Julian's successor) and Shapur negotiated a treaty that ensured that Nisibis would remain Persian for 120 years and that granted the city's Christian inhabitants peaceful travel to Amid.[21]

Whether or not Ephrem initially traveled to Amid (modern-day Diyarbakir), we do not know. Eventually, however, he made his way to the eastern Roman city of Edessa (modern-day Urfa), about a hundred miles west of Nisibis.[22] Perhaps because he spent such a short time in Edessa, or because the city was less politically fraught,[23] it is very difficult to construct a narrative of these years. Much has been written about Edessa and its religiously diverse make-up: the city housed Jews, Manichees, Marcionites, Daysanites, and a host of other religious and phil-

20. On the loss of Nisibis, see *CJ* (English translation in McVey, *Hymns,* 219–57). For the general history of the Sassanian empire, see R. N. Frye, "The Political History of Iran under the Sassanians," in *The Cambridge History of Iran,* ed. E. Yarshater, vol. 3.1, *The Seleucid, Parthian and Sassanian Periods* (Cambridge: Cambridge University Press, 2000), esp. 116–80. For the specific history of Nisibis in this period, see Mathews and Amar, *Selected Prose Works,* 26–33, and Paul Russell, "Nisibis as the Background to the Life of Ephrem the Syrian," *Hugoye* 8:2 (2005): 179–235. On Julian's campaign, see G. W. Bowersock, *Julian the Apostate* (Cambridge, MA: Harvard University Press, 1978), chapter 10.

21. According to Ammianus Marcellinus, in J. C. Rolfe, ed., *Ammianus Marcellinus* (Cambridge, 1930), 25:9.

22. There are questions about his travels to Edessa. The portion of *CNis* that dealt with this period (hymns 22–25) is now lost. Equally, in *CJ* 2:26, Ephrem, speaking of Nisibis, writes: "The Just One ... did not render us captive and cast us away, [but] made us to dwell in our own place" (*'atrâ*). McVey takes this as a reference to "the Syriac-speaking region of the Roman Empire" (*Hymns,* 241, n. 104), as does Beck (*Des heiligen Ephraem des Syrers Hymnen de Paradiso und Contra Julianum,* vol. 175, 75, n. 37). De Halleux ("Saint Éphrem le Syrien," 331), however, suggests the possibility that Christians were not banned from Nisibis, or that Ephrem spent time in Amid before heading to Edessa. The *Life* also says that Ephrem went first to Amid (chapter 10).

23. But see below on Valens.

osophical sects.[24] It also played host to the well-known theological debates familiar to students of the fourth-century Greek and
Latin worlds, about which I will speak in greater detail below.[25]
The issues and ideas raised by these groups certainly left a mark
on Ephrem's writings, especially his *HF, CH,* and *PR.* After only
about a decade in Edessa, Ephrem died in 373.[26]

The basic chronological details of his life are thus simple and
few. The character of his religious upbringing is equally difficult
to ascertain with much precision, as is the formal nature of his
role in the churches of Nisibis and Edessa. Nevertheless, we can
sketch a broad outline. Though the *Life* claims that his father
was a pagan priest,[27] references in his authentic works suggest a
Christian upbringing. In this regard, scholars frequently cite *CH*
26:10—"In the way of truth was I born, even if my childishness
did not recognize [it]"—and *Hymns on Virginity* 37:10—"Your
truth was in my youth; your truth is in my old age." While the
evidence of these passages is itself inconclusive,[28] *CNis* 16:16–22
indicates that Ephrem had a close relationship with Nisibis's first
four bishops, Jacob (d. 338), Babu (d. 346), Vologeses (d. 361),
and Abraham (361–?).[29] Specifically, Ephrem gives the impression of having been a child when Jacob was the bishop.[30] It is
thus likely that Ephrem was a Christian from a very young age.

His later biographers would further remember him as a reclu-

24. On Edessan religious life, see H. J. W. Drijvers, *Bardaisan of Edessa* (As-
sen: Van Gorcum & Comp., 1966); idem, *Cults and Beliefs at Edessa* (Leiden:
Brill, 1980), as well as the articles collected in his *East of Antioch: Studies in Early
Syriac Christianity* (London: Variorum, 1984) and *History and Religion in Late
Antique Syria* (London: Variorum, 1994).

25. See below, pp. 19–43.

26. The 6th-century *Chronicle of Edessa* dates his death to June 9. See L. Ha-
lier, *Untersuchungen über die Edessenische Chronik: Mit dem syrischen Text und einer
übersetzung* (Leipzig: J. C. Hinrichs, 1892), 149.

27. *Life,* ch. 1, version P.

28. That is, while these lines could imply that Ephrem was raised a Christian, they could also imply some sort of basic sense that Ephrem was destined
to find the truth of Christianity (regardless of his initial religious environ-
ment), or even that he was raised in some other religious community that enabled him eventually to convert to Christianity.

29. On these four, see J. M. Fiey, "Les évêques de Nisibe au temps de saint
Ephrem," *Parole de l'Orient* 4 (1973): 122–35.

30. In *CNis* 16:16–20, he depicts the character of the three bishops as

sive ascetic, in the vein of Antony the Great. In fact, Ephrem's authentic writings bear the marks of a public persona and teacher, intimately concerned and connected with the life and theological pulse of the cities in which he lived. There is thus nothing in these writings to suggest that he was a recluse, or that he himself practiced the sort of lifestyle characteristic of the Egyptian monks of his day (and which would become increasingly common in northern Mesopotamia soon after Ephrem's death).[31]

Nevertheless, the scholarly consensus is that Ephrem's communities in both Nisibis and Edessa privileged a celibate lifestyle, and that the celibates, the so-called *îḥîdāyâ(ê)*—"single one(s)"—occupied a unique status within these communities.[32] Collectively, these celibates were known as the *bnay/bnāt qyāmâ*, that is, "sons/daughters of the covenant."[33] Our most exten-

---

corresponding to the first three stages of his life. Thus, in his childhood (*ṭalyûtâ*), he was fearful, and Jacob likewise struck fear in him (16:16–17). In his youth (*'laymûtâ*), he was both childish and mature, so Babu was stern, yet humble (16:18). Vologeses, then, becomes the fullness of the three, giving him "interpretations" (*tûrgāmaw[hy]*), "meekness" (*makkîkûteh*), "pleasantness" (*bassîmûteh*), and "sobriety" (*yaqqîrûteh*) (16:19).

31. One can see this tendency to read later monastic standards back into Ephrem in the nineteenth-century English translation of his *CNis*. In *CNis* 15:9, Ephrem refers to his bishop as *îḥîdāyâ*, literally, "single one." John Gwynn, the *Hymns'* translator in the ANF translation, renders the term "solitary recluse" (ANPF Ser. 2, vol. 13, p. 184).

32. The literature on these communities, as well as on the nuances of this ascetic terminology, is quite large. On the terminology, the classic works are two articles by E. Beck, "Asketentum und Monchtum bei Ephraem," in *Il monachesimo orientale*, OCA 153 (Rome, 1958) and "Ein Beitrag zur Terminologie des altesten syrischen Monchtums," SA 38 (1956): 254–67. Though now dated, these still are very valuable for providing references to the relevant portions of Ephrem's works. On the social organization of these communities, G. Nedungatt's "The Covenanters of the Early Syriac-Speaking Church," OCP 39 (1973): 419–44, remains indispensable. See also R. Murray, "The Exhortation to Candidates for Ascetical Vows at Baptism in the Ancient Syriac Church," *New Testament Studies* 21 (1974): 59–80. For a more recent discussion of older literature, as well as a nuanced assessment of the terminology involved, see S. Griffith's "Asceticism in the Church of Syria: The Hermeneutics of Early Syrian Monasticism," in *Asceticism,* ed. V. L. Wimbush and R. Valantasis (New York: Oxford University Press, 1995), 220–48.

33. On *qyāmâ*, see Griffith, "Asceticism in the Church of Syria: The Hermeneutics of Early Syrian Monasticism," 229–34.

sive early source for these "single ones," as well as the "sons and daughters of the covenant," is the sixth *Demonstration* of Aphrahat, Ephrem's older Persian contemporary (d. ca. 345).[34] Much of the scholarship on Ephrem's community, therefore, has used Aphrahat as an interpretive guide to Ephrem's otherwise somewhat elusive use of terms such as "single one," "sons/daughters of the covenant," and "virginity" (*btûlûtâ*). For the purposes of this introduction, however, I will simply focus on Ephrem's own writings, however ambiguous they may at times be.

On a most basic level, it is clear that Ephrem privileged many of the virtues that would later be deemed monastic: fasting,[35] keeping of vigil,[36] chastity,[37] poverty,[38] and especially virginity.[39] Moreover, he clearly regards *îḥîdāyâ* as a term of praise, one that he bestows upon virtuous paragons of his own day.[40] This term, *îḥîdāyâ*, would eventually take on the formal connotations of the Greek *monachos* ("monk"),[41] but in Ephrem's writings, it is much broader in its signification and more poetic. We should note especially that, unlike *monachos*, *îḥîdāyâ* is a scriptural term,[42] and its primary reference is to Christ, the archetypal "single one," who is the "only-begotten"—*îḥîdāyâ*—of his Father, and who lived his life in singular devotion to his Father.[43] By extension,

34. See Adam Lehto, *Demonstrations*, 169–98.
35. See *HF* 6:3; *CH* 6:20.   36. See *HF* 6:3.
37. Syr., *nakpê*. See *CH* 6:19.   38. E.g., *CNis* 19:15.
39. The term he uses is *btûlûtâ*, but *îḥîdāyâ*—single one—is closely related. The two terms often appear together. Ephrem's writings are replete with references to virginity. See, for example, *HPar* 7:15; *CH* 45:9–10; *CNis* 1:9, 19:3, 21:5.

40. See, for example, *CNis* 15.9. It is not entirely clear which of the bishops this hymn is devoted to, though Beck and Fiey both identify Vologeses as its subject. See E. Beck, ed. and trans., *CNis*, vol. 219, 47, and J. M. Fiey, "Les évêques de Nisibe au temps de saint Ephrem," *Parole de l'Orient* 4 (1973): 129.

41. See E. Beck, "Asketentum und Monchtum bei Ephraem," as well as J. P. Amar, "Byzantine Ascetic Monachism and Greek Bias in the *Vita* Tradition of Ephrem the Syrian," *OCP* 58 (1992): 123–56.

42. Though *monachos* is practically synonymous with the scriptural term *monogenês*, "only-begotten," which *îḥîdāyâ* translates.

43. For a thorough explication of the theological significance of the term *îḥîdāyâ*, see Brock, *Hymns on Paradise*, 25–33, as well as Griffith's "Asceticism in the Church of Syria: The Hermeneutics of Early Syrian Monasticism," 223–29.

its application to a celibate person (woman or man) theologically connotes the close relationship between that person and
Christ. In this respect, the *HEpi*, although probably written just
after Ephrem, speak of all Christians (not just celibates) as having put on Christ, the *Îḥîdāyâ* ("single one"), thus becoming, in
some sense, *iḥîdāyê* ("single ones").⁴⁴

As for how these celibates fit within Ephrem's community, it
seems most likely that in Ephrem's own day there were celibates
within the church who were esteemed as *iḥîdāyê* in a particular
way, who probably took some sort of ascetic vows at baptism,
and who, because of their more rigorous devotion, held, *ipso
facto*, a primary place within the community.⁴⁵ Yet baptism was
certainly open to celibates and non-celibates alike, and there
seem to have been no other features separating the celibates
from the non-celibates within the community: there is no evidence that *iḥîdāyê* wore distinctive clothing or that their celibate status entailed formal ecclesial duties. They lived, moreover, in the midst of the local church community and made
their own living arrangements.⁴⁶ Finally, though Ephrem never
identifies himself as one of these *iḥîdāyê*, there is little doubt
that he was one, an assumption that is supported by all the tes-
timonies we have about him and by the clear privileging of virginity evidenced in his writings.⁴⁷

44. *HEpi* 8:17: "For, whoever has been baptized and has put on / the *Îḥîdāyâ*
..." On the authenticity of the *HEpi*, see Beck, *Des Heiligen Ephraem des Syrers
Hymnen de Nativitate* (*Epiphania*), CSCO 186 (Louvain, 1959), v–vii. As Beck
points out, the *HEpi* appear in a liturgical manuscript that clearly presumes
that Nativity and Epiphany are two different feasts, and Epiphany is an occasion for baptism. Ephrem's authentic writings, however, counter both of these
positions.

45. See Griffith, "Asceticism in the Church of Syria: The Hermeneutics of
Early Syrian Monasticism," 227.

46. This is implied in *HPar* 7:15, where Ephrem writes, "The virgin who
rejected / the marriage crown that fades / now has the radiant marriage chamber.... To her who was alone / in a lonely house / the wedding feast now grants
tranquility." The reference to this widow living in a "lonely house" suggests
she did not reside in a larger monastic community or in a residence provided
to her on the basis of her celibate state. See also Aphrahat's warning against
abuse of this freedom in *Demonstration* 1.272.

47. There may also be a tacit assumption that he would have had to be

The earliest sources further present Ephrem as a deacon.[48] Though Ephrem suggests the existence of such an office, however, he never applies the term "deacon" to himself.[49] A term that Ephrem does claim, however, is *'allānâ*, variously translated as "steward," "herdsman," or even "shepherd boy."[50] In the *CH* 56:10, Ephrem declares, "O Lord, let the labors of your *'allānâ* not be despised." This title appears also in *CNis* 17:3, where Ephrem describes his bishop as a "shepherd" (*rā'yâ*) who governed his flock (*mar'îtâ*) with a "fold of herdsmen" (*daryâ d-'allānê*). It is thus entirely possible that *'allānâ* is a poetic term which Ephrem has adopted to speak of the office of deacon, and, in *CH*, of himself as a deacon.

Two fairly early Syriac sources, which emerge apart from the rest of the hagiographical tradition, emphasize Ephrem's role as teacher in the Christian communities of Nisibis and Edessa.[51] While Jacob of Serugh's metrical homily (ca. 500) does this in a more eulogistic manner, the *Foundation of the Schools* (late sixth-century) alleges that Ephrem was appointed head (*mpaššqānâ*)[52] of the Christian schools in Nisibis and Edessa.

---

celibate in order to occupy the position he did. As an aside, however, we should note that, on the evidence of Gregory of Nyssa's *On Virginity*, a fourth-century married person could still privilege virginity in writing.

48. The report that Ephrem was a deacon first appears in Jerome's *On Famous Men* 115, which is also the earliest external witness to Ephrem. See St. Jerome, *On Illustrious Men,* trans. Thomas P. Halton, FOTC 100 (Washington, DC: The Catholic University of America Press, 1999), 149.

49. "Office" is perhaps anachronistic. At *CNis* 18:5 Ephrem exhorts his bishop to direct the "deacons" (*šammāšê*), alongside the "elders," or "priests" (*qaššîšê*), the young and the old (literally, "youth" and "old age," *šabrûtâ* and *saybûtâ*), and the "virgins" (*nakpâtâ*). The term *šammāšê*, here translated as "deacon," is not the term typically used for deacon in the Syriac-speaking churches, though it is derived from the same root (*šammeš*, "to serve"). Rather, deacons are called *mšammšānê*. Also, note that throughout the *CNis*, "bishops" are called *kāhnê*, "priests." It is thus likely that the terminology and the rites of ordination are still in flux at the time of Ephrem.

50. See Amar, *The Syriac Vita Tradition,* vol. 630, xvi–xvii.

51. Jacob of Serugh, *A Metrical Homily on Mar Ephrem,* ed. and trans. J. P. Amar (Turnhout: Brepols, 1995), and Barḥadbeshabbâ of Ḥalwan, *The Cause of the Foundation of the Schools,* ed. and trans. A. Scher (Turnhout: Brepols, 1971), and in Adam H. Becker, *Sources for the Study of the School of Nisibis* (Liverpool: Liverpool University Press, 2009), esp. 144–45.

52. Literally, "interpreter," or "exegete."

Though opinion varies regarding the exact nature of these schools, or if any such thing existed *per se*,[53] it is easy to envision a "classroom" setting for Ephrem's prose commentaries on Genesis and Exodus. Exactly what this school might have looked like, and whether Ephrem was a teacher in any formal sense, we cannot know, but the image of teacher is one perfectly consonant with his extant works.

Finally, our very earliest external source for Ephrem tells us that he "wrote a great deal in the Syriac language."[54] This is a report we can confirm without any doubt. In addition to the works falsely attributed to him and a host of works apparently lost, the extant genuine works of Ephrem are quite vast. Ephrem wrote in three genres: hymns (*madrāšê*), verse homilies (*mêmrê*), and commentaries (*pûšāqâ* and *turgāmâ*).[55] Though rumored to have written commentaries on every book of the Bible, we have only his commentaries *On Genesis, On Exodus,* and *On the Diatessaron* in Syriac. The verse homilies (*mêmrê*) are metered didactic works, arranged in isosyllabic couplets, and while there are independent *mêmrê* collections, *mêmrê* are also included within the larger *madrāšê* collections.[56]

Predominantly, however, Ephrem wrote hymns (*madrāšê*), and it is these for which he is best known.[57] The hymns treat

53. R. Murray notes that "Nisibis was almost the first place in the east to have a Jewish school, and probably by early in the fourth century there was a Christian counterpart where Ephrem taught." See his *Symbols of Church and Kingdom: A Study in Early Syriac Tradition*, rev. ed. (Piscataway, NJ: Gorgias Press, 2004), 18. U. Possekel nevertheless notes that no such school is attested before the fifth century. See her *Evidence of Greek Philosophical Concepts in the Writings of Ephrem the Syrian*, CSCO 580, subs.102 (1999), 19. Indeed, it seems that if a school existed in Ephrem's lifetime, there would be some trace of it in the *CNis*.

54. Jerome, *On Famous Men* 115.

55. The heading of *CGen.* identifies it as a *pûšāqâ*, while that of the *CEx* names it a *turgāmâ*, words which are basically synonymous. These headings, however, are likely later than the commentaries themselves.

56. See, for example, *HF* 2–3.

57. There is debate as to whether the English word "hymn" adequately translates the Syriac *madrāšê*. K. den Biesen translates the term as "Teaching Song" (*Simple and Bold: Ephrem's Art of Symbolic Thought* [Piscataway, NJ: Gorgias Press, 2006], esp. xxii). See also M. Lattke, "Sind Ephraems Madrāšê Hymnen?" *OC* 73 (1983): 38–43, who argues that only those parts of Ephrem's

an array of topics and were most likely performed publicly by all-female choirs.[58] The hymn was a metrical composition, and its meters ranged from isosyllabic stichs to highly complicated metrical patterns.[59] These metered lines were further divided into stanzas of anywhere from three to eleven lines, and each stanza was followed by a repeated refrain.[60] While all the manuscripts of Ephrem's hymns include names of accompanying melodies, we no longer know the melodic patterns that these names represented. Around four hundred of Ephrem's authentic hymns survive in Syriac, divided into eleven collections, with the *CJ* being the shortest collection (containing four hymns), and the *HF*, here translated, being the longest (containing eighty-seven hymns). It is to the specific collection called *Hymns on Faith* that I now turn.

---

corpus that are strictly doxological can properly be called "hymns." Nevertheless, I have retained "hymn" because it is recognizable in English. On the genre of the *madrāšê*, see E. Beck, "Ephräms des Syrers Hymnik," in *Liturgie und Dichtung. Ein interdisziplinäres Kompendium. Gualtero Duerig annum vitae septuagesimum feliciter complenti*, vol.1, ed. H. Becker and R. Kaczynski (St Ottilien, 1983), 345–79, S. Brock, "Poetry and Hymnography (3): Syriac," in S. Ashbrook Harvey and D. Hunter, eds., *The Oxford Handbook of Early Christian Studies* (Oxford: Oxford University Press, 2008), 657–71, and K. McVey, "Were the Earliest *Madrāšê* Songs or Recitations?" in *After Bardaisan: Studies on Continuity and Change in Syriac Christianity in Honour of Professor Han J. W. Drijvers*, Orientalia Lovaniensia Analecta 89, ed. G. J. Reinink and A. C. Klugkist (Louvain, 1999), 185–99.

58. The earliest reference to these female choirs appears in Jacob of Serugh's *Homily on Mar Ephrem*, 96–99. On these choirs, see Susan Ashbrook Harvey, *Song and Memory: Biblical Women in Syriac Tradition* (Milwaukee, WI: Marquette University Press, 2010), 17–39, and eadem, "Revisiting the Daughters of the Covenants: Women's Choirs and Sacred Song in Ancient Syriac Christianity," *Hugoye* 8:2 (July 2005), at http://syrcom.cua.edu/Hugoye/Vol-8No2/HV8N2Harvey.html.

59. Ephrem composed in roughly forty-five different meters; see Brock, "Poetry and Hymnography (3): Syriac," 661.

60. The refrains that have come down to us in the manuscripts likely date from after Ephrem's life, and they differ significantly between different manuscripts.

III. The Collection of the Hymns on Faith

We know very little about how Ephrem wrote his hymn cycles, how the performances and the written compositions af-
fected one another, and how the compositional and editing
processes overlapped. Even in Ephrem's shorter hymn collections, however, there is still evidence of a compositional and
editorial process.[61] This is even more the case with Ephrem's
longer hymn cycles. While Ephrem may well have had a hand
in their editing, none of them appears to have been composed
as a unified whole. Indeed, in cycles such as the *HVir* and the
HE, there does not appear to be any organizing principle gov-
erning the entirety of the collection.

Ephrem's *HF* form his longest extant hymn cycle. Even more
than the shorter cycles, the *HF* have clearly been formed out
of the compilation of various smaller cycles. Unlike the *HVir* or
the *HE*, however, the *HF* display a notable overlap in vocabulary, theme, and structure. The collection comprises eighty-sev-
en hymns and evinces thirteen different meters and melodies.[62]
There can be little doubt that the collection as it has come down
to us has been composed of smaller collections that, predating
the *HF* as such, were written independently of one another and
may well have once circulated independently. "The Hymns on
the Pearl," spanning hymns 81–85 of the *HF*, form the most
well-known example of a smaller hymn cycle embedded within
the larger *HF*.[63] Aside from the thematic and lexical integrity
of the pearl hymns, the clearest indicator of their unity is the

61. In the *CJ*, for example, hymns 3 and 4 are noticeably different from 1
and 2; 3 and 4 take a suddenly personal turn, and lack the scriptural focus
that 1 and 2 display. Regarding the *HPar*, Andrew Palmer has even argued for
the evidence of later interpolations. See his "Restoring the ABC in Ephraim's
Cycles on *Faith* and *Paradise*," *The Journal of Eastern Christian Studies* 55 (2003):
147–94.

62. I have included melodic and metric information within the translation,
at the beginning of each new melody and meter.

63. On the "Hymns on the Pearl," see Beck, *HF* (*S*), v–vi; J. Melki, "Saint
Ephrem le syrien, un bilan de l'édition critique," *PdO* 11 (1983): 24; E. G.
Mathews, Jr., "St. Ephrem, Madrase on Faith, 81–85, Hymns on the Pearl I–V,"
SVTQ 38 (1994): 55–56.

introductory title and concluding colophon: the hymns begin
with the words "On the pearl," and conclude with the words
"completed are [the hymns] on the pearl." While the five pearl
hymns are the only subset within the *HF* that have their own
title, three other subsets within the collection have colophons:
hymns 10–25,[64] hymns 49–65,[65] and hymns 66–78.[66]

The question, then, is not whether Ephrem wrote the *HF* as
a single, coherent, and intentionally sequenced hymn cycle—
clearly, he did not—but whether he had a hand in their editing,
and, even more, whether they represent an entirely authentic
work. Andrew Palmer, in a series of articles published over the
last fifteen years, has argued that large parts of the *HF* are, in
fact, inauthentic.[67] He discerns these inauthentic passages on
the basis of broken acrostics,[68] in which case a stanza that does
not fit within the acrostic pattern constitutes an interpolation,
or on the basis of acrostics that repeat letters,[69] in which the
stanzas beginning with a repeated letter are inauthentic.

But there are problems with taking these points as axiomatic.
For example, *HF* 53 stands in the midst of an acrostic that has
been frozen on the letter *M* since 50:2, and continues as such
until 65:13. According to one of Palmer's basic criteria, these
stanzas would all have to be deemed inauthentic, derived as
glosses upon 50:1.[70] All other internal criteria, however, suggest

64. Concluding with "the end of the sixteen *madrāšê* in one melody."

65. "Completed are the sixteen *madrāšê* according to the melody 'The
Herd of Bardaisan.'"

66. "Completed are the thirteen *madrāšê* [according to the melody] 'If you
Investigate Being.'"

67. I have already alluded to his "Restoring the ABC in Ephraim's Cycles
on *Faith* and *Paradise*." See also his "Akrostich Poems: Restoring Ephrem's *Madroshe*," *The Harp* 15 (2002): 275–87; idem, "Interpolated Stanzas in Ephraim's
Madroshe III–VII on Faith," *OC* 93 (2009): 1–27; idem, "Interpolated Stanzas
in Ephraim's Madroshe LXVI–LXVIII on Faith," *OC* 90 (2006): 1–22; idem,
"Words, Silences, and the Silent Word: Acrostics and Empty Columns in Saint
Ephrem's *Hymns on Faith*," *PdO* 20 (1995): 129–200.

68. See, for example, *HF* 4:6–9. Palmer's theory is articulated repeatedly
in the articles cited above.

69. E.g., see *HF* 50:2–65:13.

70. Unless compelling literary reasons could be given to show that Ephrem
had intentionally repeated letters.

53's authenticity: it fits well with what we know of "anti-Arian" literature of the mid-late fourth century; it uses vocabulary and themes characteristic of Ephrem; it contains no obvious anachronisms; and there is a discernible structure within it. In short, aside from the fact that it violates Palmer's rule of "one stanza per letter," there is no reason to assume it inauthentic.

For the sake of the present translation, therefore, my working hypothesis is that Ephrem did compose, for a public context, the majority of the hymns that were later collected as the *HF*. While he may not have intended all these hymns to form a single unit, and in fact may not have written all the stanzas included, their eventual grouping makes sense. For the most part, all the hymns deal with the limits of human knowledge as it relates to divine matters—specifically matters related to Christ's divinity and the Father's begetting of him. My sense is thus that the *HF* represent a posthumously edited collection of Ephremic hymns related to the fourth-century Christological controversies.

Regardless of the original shape of the *HF*, we do know that within 150 years of Ephrem's death, the eighty-seven hymns were traveling as a single unit (including the five "Hymns on the Pearl"),[71] and with little divergence between the different manuscripts.[72] The collection survives completely in only two manuscripts—Br. Mus. add. 12 176[73] and Cod. vat. sir. 111[74]—and is partially contained in two others. Br. Mus. add. 12 176 offers the most consistently legible of the complete manuscripts, and forms the base text for Edmund Beck's critical edition. This 5th/6th-century vellum codex is written in an Estrangelo script and begins with a work entitled *Sermo Admonitionis,* which is then followed by the *HF* in their entirety, and then a complete text of the hymns *CH*.

71. Br. mus. add. 1457 providing the exception (on which manuscript, see below). Even with Br. mus. add. 1457, however, there is no sense that it represents an earlier form or edition of the collection.
72. As attested by the manuscripts listed below, but also attested in Sinai Syr. 10, a 6th-century manuscript that refers to the *HF* as including 87 hymns.
73. A.
74. B.

Cod. vat. sir. 111, albeit water-damaged and illegible in many places, forms the other complete manuscript of the *HF*. It is also a vellum codex written in three columns in an Estrangelo script, and from its colophon can be dated to the year 522. Cod. vat. sir. 111 places the *HF* and the *CH* together, and also includes the *HE, HVir,* and *HPar.*

In addition to these two complete manuscripts, the *HF* are partially contained in two other manuscripts. Cod. vat. sir. 113,[75] a single-column vellum codex dating from 552, contains only the *HF,* but hymns 1:1–1:3, 18:7–31:7, 59:4–67:2, and 85:2–87:9 are illegible due to water damage. Br. mus. add. 1457,[76] dating from 519, provides excerpted hymns from the collection, and, as such, is the only manuscript (that we know of) that attests to hymns from the *HF* circulating independently of the larger collection. These are *HF* 10, 11, 12, 14, 21, 23 (in fol. 60–67), and 32.

The *HF* were first edited in 1743 as the third volume of the *Editio Romana* (ER), based upon Cod. vat. sir. 111 and 113.[77] According to Beck, Assemani was "very free" in his copying of the manuscripts, especially in places where Cod. vat. sir. 111 and 113 were illegible or missing.[78] It was on the basis of this edition that John Morris in 1847 produced the first (and only) English translation of the *HF.* Not surprisingly, his translation mirrors the errors contained in the ER,[79] and, aside from these errors, its English is often unintelligible.

In 1955, Edmund Beck produced the first and only critical edition of the *HF,* which took into account all four available manuscripts, and accompanied these with a German transla-

75. C.

76. D.

77. On this edition, see J. Melki, "Saint Ephrem, bilan de l'édition critique," 16.

78. Beck, I–II.

79. This translation has recently been reprinted as *The Rhythms of Saint Ephrem the Syrian: Select Works of S. Ephrem the Syrian,* trans. John Brande Morris (Piscataway, NJ: Gorgias Press, 2006). For a complete list of all translations of various hymns from the *HF* (though now dated), see S. P. Brock, "A Brief Guide to the Main Editions and Translations of the Works of St Ephrem," *The Harp* 3:1–2 (June, 1990): 7–25.

tion. Beck used Br. mus. add. 12 176 as his base text, but supplemented it frequently with the three other manuscripts. While Beck's edition has been criticized in some areas,[80] it still provides a reliable witness to the extant manuscripts as we have them. It thus forms the basis of this translation.

IV. The Audience and Context
of the Hymns on Faith

In his 1949 study of the *HF*, Edmund Beck stated that "[t]he major theme of all ... the *Hymns on Faith* is the defense of the Church's teaching against the innovation of Arianism."[81] Unfortunately, we know only the broadest outlines of the process by which the teachings and canons of Nicaea came to Syriac-speaking Christians. The earliest lists of attendees of the Council include five bishops from Mesopotamia, namely, Aithallaha of Edessa, Antiochus of Reshaina, Mareas of Macedonopolis, John of Persia, and Jacob of Nisibis.[82] The last of these was Ephrem's bishop and one of the subjects of Ephrem's *CNis*. It was presumably from Jacob that Ephrem first learned

80. Brock faults Beck for always printing, in the body of the text, his primary manuscript (Br. mus. add. 12 176), "even when it is clearly erroneous"; see *St Ephrem: A Hymn on the Eucharist (Hymns on Faith, no. 10)* (Lancaster, UK: J. F. Coakley at the Department of Religious Studies, University of Lancaster, 1986), 2. Palmer notes that while Beck "collects and organizes the ancient MSS, he does not make a systematic search for excerpts from this cycle in later liturgical compilations" ("Interpolated Stanzas in Ephraim's Madroshe LXVI–LXVIII on Faith," 2). On this point, see also Brock's "The Transmission of Ephrem's *madrashe* in the Syriac Liturgical Tradition," *SP* 33, ed. E. A. Livingstone (Leuven, 1997), 490–505. Throughout this translation, I have noted where Beck divides the Syriac text incorrectly, and have reflected the correct line divisions both in my translation and in the notes.

81. "Das Hauptthema aller achtzig Hymnen über den Glauben ist die Verteidigung der kirchlichen Lehre gegenüber der Neuerung des Arianismus," *Die Theologie des hl Ephraem in seinen Hymnen über den Glauben*, vol. 21, *SA* (Rome: Pontificium Institutum S. Anselmi, 1949), 62. Beck wrote this sentence before completing his critical edition of the *HF*, in which he includes hymns 81–87.

82. See E. Honigmann, "La liste originale des Pères de Nicée," *Byzantion* 14 (1939): 17–76; H. Kaufhold, "Griechisch-Syrische Väterlisten der frühen Griechischen Synoden," *OC* 77 (1993): 1–96.

of the Council, and it is assumed that Ephrem refers to Nicaea
in *CH* 22:20.[83] The passage reads:[84]

> The voice of our Lord counted them out,
> And their dwellings were lifted up—
> The Aetians, and Arians;
> Sabellians[85] and Cathars;[86]
> Photinians,[87] and Audians[88]—
> They who accepted ordination from our Church,
> And some of whom signed onto[89]
> The faith which was written down
> At that glorious Synod.
> Memorable is the King who convened it!

In the note to his German translation of this passage, Beck
glosses the penultimate line with the words "undoubtedly Nicaea."[90] The reference, however, is not so clear. While "Nicaea"
is perhaps the most likely candidate, recent scholarship has
emphasized that the path by which Nicaea came to represent

83. On the later report that Ephrem accompanied Jacob to Nicaea, see *The Syriac* Vita *Tradition of Ephrem the Syrian,* ed. and trans. Joseph P. Amar, *CSCO* 629/630 (Louvain: Peeters, 2011), 16, n. 1.

84. All translations are my own.

85. Little is known about the historical Sabellius, but during the course of the fourth-century Trinitarian controversies his name came to be associated negatively with a radical insistence on the unity of Father and Son (to the exclusion of any distinction). See John Behr, *Formation of Christian Theology, Volume 1: The Way to Nicaea* (Crestwood, NY: St Vladimir's Seminary Press), 151–53.

86. As far as I know, this group has not been identified.

87. Photinus, bishop of Sirmium, was condemned at the Council of Antioch in 344 and at a council in Milan in 345. He was thought to hold an adoptionist Christology. See Hanson, *Search,* 235–38.

88. The "Audians" are mentioned in the *Theodosian Code,* "On Religion," 5:65 (cited in *Christianity in Late Antiquity 300–450 C.E.: A Reader,* ed. Bart D. Ehrman and Andrew S. Jacobs [Oxford: Oxford University Press, 2004], 72).

89. Translated literally, lines 6 and 7 would read, "They accepted a hand from our Church, / And some of them placed a hand / on ..."

90. In Griffith's translation of this hymn he simply adds to the line, in brackets, "i.e., Nicaea." See his "Setting Right the Church of Syria: Saint Ephraem's *Hymns Against Heresies,*" in *The Limits of Ancient Christianity: Essays on Late Antique Thought and Culture in Honor of R. A. Markus* (Ann Arbor, MI: The University of Michigan Press, 1999), 102.

the measuring stick for all Orthodoxy was a circuitous one.[91] Ephrem never mentions it by name, and this is the only passage in which he appears to allude to it in any way.[92] Nor does the reference to "the King" demand an identification with Constantine: Ephrem praises a series of emperors throughout his corpus, including Constantine, as well as Constantius and Valens.[93] During the 350s, moreover, Constantius was affiliated with several synods.[94] It is thus worth at least entertaining the possibility that Ephrem is referring to one of these councils.

Moreover, even if we affirm that the above passage demonstrates Ephrem's embrace of Nicaea, we have no other contemporaneous Syriac documents to demonstrate the process by which Syriac Christians came to understand and accept the teachings of the Council. We do have a letter, extant only

91. For a narrative of the period as a whole, R. P. C. Hanson's *The Search for the Christian Doctrine of God: The Arian Controversies, 318–381* (New York: T & T Clark, 1998; Grand Rapids, MI: Baker Academic, 2005) is still indispensable, although it has been seriously nuanced by Lewis Ayres, *Nicaea and its Legacy: An Approach to Fourth-Century Trinitarian Theology* (Oxford: Oxford University Press, 2004). On this issue, see especially 85–88. See also Khaled Anatolios, *Retrieving Nicaea: The Development and Meaning of Trinitarian Doctrine* (Grand Rapids, MI: Baker Academic, 2011), and John Behr, *The Nicene Faith*, vol. 2 of *Formation of Christian Theology* (Crestwood, NY: SVS Press), 2004.

92. It is curious that Ephrem mentions Photinians and Aetians, both of whom came into existence and prominence after the Council. We can, however, take the first six lines as referring to general activity *after* Nicaea, with lines seven and eight narrowing the focus to Nicaea itself. On Photinus, who was condemned repeatedly throughout the fourth century, beginning in 344, see Hanson, *Search*, 235–38. I will discuss Aetius in more detail below. For now, see Ayres, *Nicaea*, 144–49, and Hanson, *Search*, 598–611.

93. On Ephrem's imperial references, see Sidney H. Griffith, "Ephraem, the Deacon of Edessa, and the Church of the Empire," in *Diakonia: Studies in Honor of Robert T. Meyer*, ed. T. Halton (Washington, DC: The Catholic University of America Press, 1986), 22–52.

94. He is affiliated with, and indeed attended, the Council of Antioch in 341 and the Council of Sirmium in 351, though he did not convene either of these. He actually convened the Council of Ariminum in 359, in preparation for which the "Dated" Creed (of 359) was produced. This creed sought to exclude both radical Arians (such as Aetius and Eunomius), as well as radical Nicenes (such as Athanasius). See Hanson, *Search*, 274–380; Ayres, *Nicaea*, 157–66.

in an Armenian translation, which purports to be from the
above-mentioned Aithallaha of Edessa, and which advises Persian Christians on the finer points of Nicene theology, over
against subordinationist theological tendencies.[95] While Peter
Bruns has argued for the letter's authenticity, dating it to the
340s, David Bundy argues convincingly that the highly developed pneumatology of the letter places it much later, probably after 381.[96] It thus turns out that to garner an impression
of the theological and ecclesiastical discourse that developed
in response to Nicaea among fourth-century Syriac-speaking
Christianity, Ephrem, though never mentioning the Council
by name, is really our first and most extensive witness.[97] Along
with his brief *SF,* the *HF* are the writings most relevant to the
theological issues addressed at the Council of Nicaea and debated throughout the entirety of the fourth century in all corners of the eastern and western Mediterranean. But, as this discussion of *CH* 22:20 has suggested, and as we shall see below,
he does not emerge in these hymns as the Nicene enforcer that
recent literature has depicted him as being.[98]

Following in the wake of Edmund Beck's characterization of
the *HF* as representing a Syriac Nicene rebuttal of Arian theology, most scholars of Ephrem, and, more recently, scholars of

95. On "subordinationists," see p. 5, n. 12. As for Aithallaha's letter, the
Armenian text, with accompanying Italian translation, is edited in I. Thoros-
sian, ed., *Aithallaha Episcopi Edesseni Epistola Ad Christianos in Persarum Regione
De Fide* (Venice: Typis S. Lazari in Insula, 1942). There is a German transla-
tion and study in P. Bruns, "*Aithallaha's Brief über den Glauben:* Ein bedeutendes
Dokument frühsyrischer Theologie," *OC* 76 (1992): 46–73. See also D. Bundy,
"The Letter of Aithallaha [CPG 3340]: Theology, Purpose, Date," in R. Lav-
enant, ed., *III Symposium Syriacum 1980* (1983), 135–42.

96. Bundy in Lavenant, ed. See p. 22, n. 95

97. In spite of his early dating of Aithallaha's *Letter,* Bruns willingly admits this fact in his "Arius hellenizans?—Ephräm der Syrer und die neoarianischen Kontroversen seiner Zeit," *ZTC* 101 (1990): 22. This, of course, brackets
Aphrahat simply because he appears to have had no knowledge of Nicaea.

98. Sidney Griffith has promoted this picture of Ephrem in a series of articles. In his "Setting Right the Church of Syria," he states that "it is clear from
his works that Ephraem was a staunch, even insistent, supporter of an ecclesi-
ology reminiscent of that of Eusebius of Caesarea, along with an unwavering
Nicene orthodoxy" (97–98; full reference, p. 20, n. 90).

the fourth-century Trinitarian controversies generally, have approached the *HF* through this lens, reading the work as unambiguously "anti-Arian." Yet we should note a very basic feature of the *HF*: unlike, for example, Athanasius's *Contra Arianos*, whose project very much involves the rhetorical construction and defeat of a named enemy, Ephrem's *HF* never mention Arius or any of the figures later writers would tab "Arian."[99] Nor, as we have already seen, does Ephrem ever mention Nicaea by name.[100] The earliest Western edition of Ephrem's works, the *ER*,[101] refers to the *HF* as *Sermones adversus scrutatores* ("Sermons against the Investigators"). While the name was entirely the editors' own invention, it bespeaks a basic insight into the works' contents. For, far more than any discussion of "Father" and "Son" or of "Begetter" and "Begotten," Ephrem develops in the *HF* an extensive vocabulary for condemning inappropriate inquiry into divine matters and recommends in its place recourse to silence. A brief excerpt from the hymns illustrates this. In the first stanza of *HF* 4, Ephrem writes:

> A thousand thousands stand;
> Ten thousand ten thousands hasten—
> Thousands and ten thousands—
> To the One they cannot investigate.
> All of them in silence
> Stand to serve.
> No one shares his throne
> Except the Child who is from him.
> Investigation of him exists within silence.
> Whenever the watchers go to investigate,
> They arrive at silence and are kept back.

This language is characteristic of the theological approach of the *HF*. Rather than offering positive and straightforwardly didactic statements regarding the divinity of the Son and the relationship of this divinity to that of the Father, Ephrem locates

---

99. A point noted by Christine Shepardson, *Anti-Judaism and Christian Orthodoxy: Ephrem's Hymns in Fourth-Century Syria* (Washington, DC: The Catholic University of America Press, 2008), 113, n. 21.

100. And in the *HF* he never even alludes to it.

101. On the *ER*, see p. 18.

them both beyond the reach of human discourse. It is by iden-
tifying their mutual hiddenness within silence that Ephrem affirms the relationship of the Father and Child. All of this is set,
moreover, within a dramatic scene of angelic worship, in which
an inviolable wall of silence keeps "the watchers" at a distance.

These condemnations of investigation and debate, and the
concomitant insistence upon silence, form one of the most consistent lexical and thematic features of the *HF*. Beck argued
that this anti-investigative language should be connected with
other passages where Ephrem mockingly condemns "Greek wisdom."[102] Peter Bruns has developed Beck's insight and argued
that Ephrem's anti-Arian polemic derives from a "deep aversion
to everything Greek in theology."[103] In *HF* 47:11, for example,
Ephrem poetically represents Paul's preaching at the Athe-
nian Areopagus (Acts 17.16–34) and says that "the apostle was
more subtle than the presumptuous ones"; they did not receive
his teaching, "for they had been sick a long time with the illness of debating." This term "subtle"—*qaṭṭîn*—is the same term
Ephrem identifies as characteristic of the Aetians in *CH* 22:4.

Based upon these condemnations of inappropriate investigation, combined with Ephrem's strong distrust of so-called
"Greek wisdom," Beck initially suggested that the *HF* developed in response to what Ephrem saw as overly philosophical
tendencies that had infected the Church's proclamation of the
faith.[104] Bruns and several others have followed Beck in identi-
fying these features, but have taken it a step further and suggested that Ephrem's criticisms are reminiscent of Cappado-
cian criticisms of Eunomius and Aetius, so-called "neo-Arians,"
or "heterousians."[105]

102. E. Beck, *Die Theologie des hl Ephraem in seinen Hymnen über den Glauben,*
SA 21 (Rome: Pontificium Institutum S. Anselmi, 1949): 63–64.

103. "Arius hellenizans?—Ephräm der Syrer und die neoarianischen Kontroversen seiner Zeit," 47.

104. Beck, *Die Theologie,* 63–64.

105. For this reading of the *HF,* see S. Griffith, "Faith Seeking Understanding in the Thought of Saint Ephrem the Syrian," in *Faith Seeking Understanding,* ed. George C. Berthold (New York: St. Anselm College Press, 1991), esp.
40–43. Elsewhere Griffith states in a footnote that "Ephraem's arguments
seem often to be directed against those 'Arians' who are more properly called

Indeed, the prevalence of Ephrem's condemnations of investigation, coupled with the fact that Aetius is one of only two figures relevant to the Arian controversy whom Ephrem mentions by name (albeit not in the *HF*),[106] lends weight to this suggestion. While it is highly unlikely that Ephrem knew any of the treatises written against Aetius's pupil Eunomius—Ephrem knew little or no Greek, and the earliest anti-Eunomian treatise, Basil's, derives from the 360s[107]—Ephrem apparently had at least a basic idea of these characterizations of Aetius's theological tendencies, and this may well have influenced his mistrust of gratuitous theological debate. Yet, on their own, these two characteristics—a condemnation of "investigation" and a mistrust of "Greek wisdom"—do not tell us much about the specific context of Ephrem's anti-Arian polemic.[108]

Recently Lewis Ayres has disputed the anti-Eunomian characterization of Ephrem's polemics.[109] Ayres suggests instead that

---

'Homoeans,' the group in favor with the emperor Valens and his court bishop Eudoxius" ("Setting Right the Church of Syria," 104, n. 28). He references no aspect of the *HF* in support of this statement. The "neo-Arian" hypothesis is far more frequently suggested. See P. Bruns, "Arius hellenizans?—Ephräm der Syrer und die neoarianischen Kontroversen seiner Zeit," esp. 47–52; U. Possekel, "Ephrem's Doctrine of God," in *God in Early Christian Thought: Essays in Memory of Lloyd G. Patterson*, ed. A. B. McGowan et al. (Leiden: Brill, 2010), 202; P. Russell, "An Anti-Neo-Arian Interpolation in Ephraem of Nisibis' Hymn 46 *on Faith*," *SP* 33, ed. Elizabeth Livingstone (Louvain: Peeters, 1997): 568–72.

106. The other being Arius himself.

107. See F. M. Young and A. Teal, *From Nicaea to Chalcedon: A Guide to the Literature and Its Background* (Grand Rapids, MI: Baker Academic, 2010), 156–59. Of course, a date in the 360s does not preclude Ephrem from knowing the work: though there is no evidence of it, it could have been quickly translated into Syriac, or Ephrem could have gained familiarity with Basil's general ideas through bilingual contacts. Yet Ephrem's theology and especially his linguistics show no influence of the theological path Basil took in response to Eunomius.

108. Note that Alexander of Alexandria accuses Arius of "the impious doctrine of the Greeks" ("Letter to Alexander of Constantinople," English translation by Andrew S. Jacobs in *Christianity in Late Antiquity, 300–450 C.E.: A Reader*, ed. Bart Ehrman and Andrew S. Jacobs [Oxford: Oxford University Press], 160).

109. *Nicaea and its Legacy*, 230–31. Ayres's reading of the polemical context of the hymns draws upon a NAPS paper by Mark Weedman, in which Ayres's arguments are explained more fully. Professor Weedman graciously supplied me with the original seminar paper upon which his NAPS paper was based. While I disagree with his conclusions, his approach to the context of

Ephrem is writing against "the Homoian theology promoted by
Valens," albeit a Homoian theology that "included some radical
Homoian trends influenced by Aetius's teaching in Antioch."[110]
The emperor Valens ruled over the eastern half of the Empire
from 364 to 378.[111] Several sources suggest that he engaged in
hostile treatment of pro-Nicene Christians in Edessa, under
the advisement of a certain Bishop Eudoxius.[112] Among the few
things we know about Eudoxius was that he claimed that the Son
was "like in substance" (κατ' οὐσίαν ὅμοιον) to the Father, hence
the name "homoian" (literally, "like").[113] Thus, if we assume that
Ephrem lived in Edessa during Valens's persecutions there, and
that he knew Valens was advised by a homoian bishop, we would
expect Ephrem to have a personal stake in refuting such views.[114]

Regarding the narrative of Valens's persecution, however,
there are problems. First, all of our sources for the persecution
at Edessa are late, and there are aspects of their presentation of
Christianity in Edessa that we know to be inaccurate.[115] Their

---

the *HF* has been a huge help to me, especially his reflections on Ephrem's
understanding of language.

110. Ibid.

111. On Valens, see Noel Lenski, *Failure of Empire: Valens and the Roman State
in the Fourth Century A.D.* (Berkeley, CA: University of California Press, 2003),
esp. 242–63.

112. See Socrates, *Ecclesiastical History* 4:18; Sozomen, *Ecclesiastical History*
6:18; Theodoret, *Ecclesiastical History* 4:14 and 15. The *Chronicle of Edessa* says
that "in the month Elul (September) of that year [i.e., 684 = 373], the people
departed from the church of Edessa, through the persecution of the Arians."
This would, however, have been after Ephrem's death. Griffith refers to Valens's practice of installing "Arian" bishops in Syriac-speaking regions of the
Empire in "Setting Right the Church of Syria," 105.

113. Behr, *The Nicene Faith*, 87; Ayres, *Nicaea and its Legacy,* 138.

114. Lenski (*Failure of Empire*) finds the reports of late ecclesiastical histori-
ans about the violence of the reign of Valens overstated. He does mention the
exile of Barses, which he dates to 373 (the year of Ephrem's death), and also
reports the tradition that Nicenes were expelled from the city following Barses's exile (p. 257). If, however, this occurred in 373, we do not know whether
Ephrem experienced it. According to the only Syriac source, this exile occurred a few months after his death.

115. Namely, those related to Ephrem's biography. See *The Syriac* Vita
Tradition of Ephrem the Syrian, ed. and trans. Joseph P. Amar, *CSCO* 629/630
(Louvain: Peeters, 2011), v–xxix of vol. 630, and J. P. Amar, "Byzantine Ascetic

reports about fourth-century Edessan religious life, therefore, should probably be taken with a grain of salt. Second, if we turn to Ephrem's own writings, it is difficult to discern whether he alludes to any of these events.[116] To be sure, the *HF*, especially hymn 87, are peppered with allusions to ecclesial strife and politicking, and it may be that *CNis* 26–30 reflect these struggles with Valens.[117] Griffith, in fact, finds an allusion to Valens's persecution in *HF* 87:21,[118] where Ephrem writes: "The crown is absolved, for priests have placed stumbling blocks before kings." It is, however, difficult to identify accurately the historical references of these lines. They *may* refer to Valens, or they could refer to Constantius,[119] or Ephrem could be simply stating a general perspective on the whole thrust of fourth-century ecclesiastical politics. Moreover, even if we could prove that Ephrem is referring to Valens's persecutions, these passages are too general to tell us much about his experience of the persecution: Ephrem never mentions the alleged exile of Bishop Barsai, the removal of Nicene Christians from the Church in Edessa, the association of Valens with "Homoian theology," or Bishop Eudoxius.[120]

It is thus very difficult to attach the *HF* to a specific context

Monachism and Greek Bias in the *Vita* Tradition of Ephrem the Syrian," *OCP* 58 (1992): 123–56.

116. It is also striking that none of the historical sources mentioned (38, n. 47) connects Ephrem to the Edessan persecutions.

117. As suggested by Beck in *Des heiligen Ephraem des Syrers Carmina Nisibena,* ed. E. Beck, *CSCO* 218 (Louvain: Peeters, 1961), IV. As with so many of Ephrem's writings, however, their elliptical nature makes it difficult to locate the precise historical context. E.g., see *CarNis* 27:4: "How long, indeed, shall you chasten your church, which, lo, is despised! / Even passers on the road turn aside when they see its shame. / You have chastened the passerby, and exposed Your bride." It is very difficult to situate such a line in a specific historical context.

118. S. H. Griffith, "Ephraem, the Deacon of Edessa, and the Church of the Empire," 34.

119. Constantius, though "Arian," is praised in *De Ecclesia* 15, the single hymn prefixed to the *CJ*.

120. It is also difficult to argue for the context of the *HF* as a whole on the basis of hymn 87 alone. The latter is noticeably different from the rest of the *HF* in terms of its anti-Jewish language and obvious ecclesio-political references. It is possible that it derives from later than the rest of the *HF,* or even soon after Ephrem's death.

on the basis of political allusions. Yet Ayres's discussion reveals
two other aspects of the *HF,* the second of which helps us better
contextualize these hymns. First, Ayres suggests that Ephrem
is concerned with whether the Son was begotten willingly or
unwillingly,[121] a concern shared by "homoians all across the
empire."[122] Second, Ayres suggests that Ephrem has in mind
figures who are "taking literally scriptural statements which
appear to subordinate the Son," a critique for which "Heterousians need not be understood."[123]

Regarding the first point, that Ephrem is concerned with
whether the Son was begotten willingly or unwillingly, there is
very little in the authentic *HF* to indicate that this was a crucial
concern for Ephrem. Ayres himself does not point to a specific
passage, but the confusion most likely comes from an interpolation in the *ER,* which was repeated in Morris's 1847 translation.[124] At *HF* 46:3, the editors added to a very difficult passage
of Syriac the following line: "If the True One begot, it was either willingly or not willingly. If it was willingly, then that which
he begot was not God." In fact, there is no manuscript evidence
for this reading prior to the eighteenth century.[125] The Syriac
itself reads as follows:

> A fool, angered, [asks], "Why does the Father have a Son?
> And if the True One begets, the ruler has impugned
>   himself."
> Is your eye evil because he has truly begotten?
> You have become envious of the one who is without envy.
> Leave all of these [things] and find out what his will is:
> The Father wills that you believe that his Son is from him.

When we examine the way Ephrem actually does use "will"
(*ṣebyānâ*) in the *HF,* it is clear that, as is the case in 46:3, it refers
predominantly to the human or divine will, with respect to human behavior (that is, "may I do your will," or, "may I not follow

121. *Nicaea and its Legacy,* 231.   122. Ibid.
123. Ibid.   124. Morris, *Rhythms,* 253.
125. *Pace* Russell, "An Anti-Neo-Arian Interpolation in Ephraem of Nisibis'
Hymn 46 *on Faith.*" For a discussion of this interpolation, as well as a broader discussion of the notion of willing or unwilling begetting in Ephrem, see
Beck, *Die Theologie,* 68–70.

my own will"). Two passages, however, potentially contribute to our understanding of these issues, but in conflicting ways.

The first of these appears in 40:7 and emphasizes the role of the Father's will in the begetting of the Son. Using the metaphor of fire, Ephrem in 40:6 affirms its triune nature and then in 40:7 asserts: "The first one gathers all of itself to itself. / After it is another, which proceeds according to its will, / And the third is poured out abundantly." Here, Ephrem emphasizes the role of the will in the begetting of the Son. Second, in a brief stanza, Ephrem affirms the unity of the will of the three: "United names, an equal procession. / One will, like one yoke, / They come bearing" (*HF* 77:21). These two stanzas, then, help us little in situating Ephrem within the fourth century. If we are to work from the stereotypes developed in secondary treatments of this period, we can say that the first sounds more like a "homoian" position, and the second a pro-Nicene.[126]

Ayres's second point, that Ephrem's polemic is directed against a too-literal reading of "scriptural statements which appear to subordinate the Son," deserves further attention.[127] *HF* 53:11 supports this characterization. There, Ephrem suggests that Prv 8.22 should be taken in reference to Christ's humanity. Yet Ephrem's view of Scripture in relation to subordinationist christologies is more complex than this single passage suggests. In fact, within hymn 53 as a whole, this particular interpretation is minimized. Though Ephrem does emphasize establishing the correct referent of Prv 8.22, this style of reading does not particularly appeal to him: "Let us abandon interpretations," he writes in 53:9, "And seek clearly and openly the names / 'Son' and 'creature.'" He expands this in 53:13, suggesting that we "count, therefore, how many times he is called 'Son' and 'Begotten,' / And then add up how often he is called 'creature.'" We have here two reading styles juxtaposed—two hermeneutic paths to discerning Christ's appropriate name:

126. *HF* 55:7 may well prove relevant to these issues, but it is very difficult to assess precisely what it means and how it relates to these controversies.

127. Kees den Biesen and Paul Russell support this interpretation. See den Biesen, *Simple and Bold,* 296, and Russell, *St. Ephraem the Syrian and St. Gregory the Theologian Confront the Arians* (Kottayam: St. Ephraem Ecumenical Research Institute, 1994), 33–75.

one seeks layers of meaning and the appropriate referents of various passages; the other places texts side by side, and merely admits the name that outnumbers the other. Ephrem acknowledges the former style of reading, but prefers the latter.

These hermeneutical reflections offer a clue for discerning the context of the *HF*. As Ayres and others have noted, overly literal and subordinationist reading tendencies, especially with respect to Prv 8.22, are characteristic of those figures labeled "homoian."[128] What is interesting here, though, is that Ephrem himself emphasizes a literal manner of reading Scripture, albeit one applied in a different way: he is not interested in a metaphoric reading of Prv 8.22, but rather in balancing Prv 8.22 with other passages (passages that affirm Christ as "Son") and setting these as the control of apparently subordinationist passages. The metaphoric depth of these passages, however, does not interest him; their meaning he takes to be self-evident.

Ephrem thus actually endorses a literal reading of Scripture, but with the aim of rebutting subordinationist readings. There are two explanations for this approach. First, it could be the case that Ephrem's employment of these literal reading strategies represents a rhetorical twisting of his opponents' position for the sake of an apologetic against them. Here Ephrem uses his opponents' methods, but to arrive at a conclusion opposite theirs: he does not condemn literal readings of Scripture, but rather proposes his own literal reading, albeit one that equally discounts subordinationist readings of Prv 8.22. A second option is that Ephrem's manner of reading these subordinationist passages actually betrays the influence of "homoian" hermeneutic tendencies, but does not necessarily assume that such a hermeneutic leads inevitably to subordinationism. Here we would simply argue that "homoian" need not always imply subordinationism.[129]

On the basis of previous scholarship, then, we can identify three characteristics that provide insight into the polemical context within which Ephrem wrote the *HF*:[130]

128. Hanson says that homoians insisted "upon the actual meaning of metaphorical or analogical language used of God, scarcely recognizing its equivocal nature" (*Search,* 559).

129. On this, see pp. 41–43.

130. I am not counting the emphasis on will, which tells us very little, or

(1) A condemnation of what Ephrem terms, *inter alia*, "investigation," by which he presumably means overly logical modes of theological discourse, or a mistaken estimation of the capacity of human knowledge (a characteristic that may well reflect his knowledge of the theological styles of Aetius and Eunomius);

(2) A distrust of so-called "Greek wisdom," also potentially suggesting the philosophical and syllogistic style of Aetius and Eunomius;

(3) Various hermeneutic tendencies, including, on the one hand, an insistence that Prv 8.22 should be read in reference to Christ's humanity, but, on the other hand, an arrival at the name "Son" through a relatively literal manner of reading (either adding up the preponderance of usages of "Son" or simply pointing to passages where Christ is called "Son").

To these three we can add six others:

(4) A knowledge of counter-readings of Prv 8.22 and Mt 24.36 / Mk13.32;

(5) An apparent knowledge of the Arian formula, "there was [a time] when he was not";

(6) A repeated emphasis on the names "Son" and "Begotten" over against "creature," potentially reflecting a polemic against Aetius's and Eunomius's insistence on "Unbegotten" as God's proper title;[131]

---

the context of Valens's persecutions, which Ephrem never references unambiguously.

131. For Aetius, God is defined by being "Ingenerate" or "Unbegotten" (*agennētos*). Therefore, whatever is generate (i.e., the Son) cannot be God. As for Eunomius, DelCogliano argues that he "accepted Aetius' understanding of 'unbegotten' and its centrality to his theory of names, but significantly improved upon his teacher's argumentation for it" (*Basil of Caesarea's Anti-Eunomian Theory of Names: Christian Theology and Late-Antique Philosophy in the Fourth Century Trinitarian Controversy* [Leiden: Brill, 2010], 32). On Eunomius, see Richard Paul Vaggione, *Eunomius: The Extant Works* (Oxford: Clarendon Press, 1987), and idem, *Eunomius of Cyzicus and the Nicene Revolution* (Oxford: Oxford University Press, 2000). On his linguistics, see Ayres, *Nicaea and its Legacy*, 144–49; Behr, *Nicene Faith*, 267–81; DelCogliano, *Basil*, ch.1; Hanson, *Search*,

(7) A theology of names that divides scriptural titles into
    "true" and "borrowed," and, in describing "true" names
    as "perfect" and "accurate," suggests a familiarity with,
    and reversal of, Aetius's and Eunomius's linguistics (by
    positing "Father" and "Son" as accurate names, rather
    than "Unbegotten");[132]

(8) A distrust of the Nicene language of *homoousios;*

(9) An emphasis on the divinity of the Holy Spirit.

We will consider these latter six points one by one.

Point (4): Prv 8.22 and Mt 24.36 / Mk 13.32

Ephrem devotes four hymns in their entirety to the issue of
the subordinationist christologies associated with Arius: hymn
53 (which takes up subordinationist interpretations of Prv 8.22),
and hymns 77–79 (which deal similarly with Mt 24.36 / Mk
13.32).[133] We have already mentioned Ephrem's rebuttal of subordinationist readings of Prv 8.22, but we can step back here
and make the more basic point that this rebuttal shows that he
knew of subordinationist readings of Prv 8.22. This knowledge
situates him within the fourth-century anti-Arian movement,
but only in the broadest way: it cannot tell us much about when
he wrote hymn 53 (much less the rest of the *HF*), except that it
was probably after Athanasius's *Contra Arianos,* in which Athanasius began to focus anti-Arian polemic on this verse.[134]

Likewise, in hymns 77–79, Ephrem counters readings of
Mt 24.36 / Mk 13.32 that would point to that verse as evidence
for the Son's creaturely status (see, for example, *HF* 77:4). In

---

603–36. See more recently Tarmo Toom, "Hilary of Poitier's *De Trinitate* and
the Name(s) of God," *VC* 64 (2010): 456–79. Though dealing with Hilary,
Toom gives a helpful synopsis of his linguistic precedent.

132. See preceding note.

133. Mt 24.36 and Mk 13.32. For the sake of historical accuracy, however, it
should be noted that Ephrem draws upon Matthew far more than Mark, and
so it is much more likely that his knowledge of this verse came from Matthew.

134. See Anatolios, *Retrieving Nicaea,* 109. Ayres dates the *Contra Arianos* to
ca. 345 (*Nicaea,* 110).

response, he suggests that Christ's ignorance derives from his having put on a body (77:23–25). Contextually, we can say this: refutations of Mt 24.36/Mk 13.32 appear almost exclusively among pro-Nicene authors, and there is no textual evidence of an anti-Nicene author ever having cited the verse in support of his case. Basil cites it as a particularly heterousian text,[135] whereas Gregory Nazianzen alludes to it much more generally in the midst of a litany of anti-Nicene proof-texts.[136] It is also cited by Athanasius,[137] Didymus the Blind,[138] and Epiphanius.[139] This littering of anti-Arian refutations of the verse, without concomitant Arian uses, suggests that it was a text on which authors focused as possessing a potentially subordinationist meaning, not necessarily one that their opponents were actually using. This suggests, then, that Ephrem should be placed within the broad contours of anti-Arian thought, and tells us that he had some knowledge of the shape of debates further west.

Point (5): The Arian formula

Ephrem seems to know the famous Arian dictum, "there was [a time] when he was not" (ἦν ποτε ὅτε οὐκ ἦν), a statement that, while not quoted in any of Arius's surviving works, does appear in the original Creed of Nicaea[140] and was repeated in creeds (both "Arian" and "Nicene") thereafter.[141] Ephrem never quotes this exactly, but in the *HF* 40:1, while using the metaphor of the sun and its rays as a way to discuss the Father and the Son, he writes, "The sun's shining is no younger than [the sun itself], / And there is no time when it was not" (*w-lâ 'ît leh zabnâ / d-layt-[h]û*).[142] While not conclusive, it seems very likely

135. *Epistle* 8.6.1–2, 12–13; Ayres, *Nicaea*, 231.

136. *Oration* 29:18.   137. *Contra Arianos* 3:26, 42.

138. *De Trinitate* 3:22.   139. *Adversus haereses* 69:15.5; 43.1.

140. Τοὺς δὲ λέγοντας· ἦν ποτε ὅτε οὐκ ἦν ... ἀναθεματίζει ἡ καθολικὴ καὶ ἀποστολικὴ ἐκκλησία. Quoted in J. N. D. Kelly, *Early Christian Creeds*, 3d ed. (New York: Continuum International Publishing Group), 216.

141. See, for example, the "Fourth" Creed of the Council of Antioch, 344. See Hanson, *Search*, 309; J. N. D. Kelly, *Early Christian Creeds*, 3d ed., 272.

142. Further, in *CH* 55:2, Ephrem states, "How pure must have been [our

that Ephrem is here alluding to the Arian formula. Yet, like so much else of the material in the *HF,* this fact alone can do no more than alert us to his general familiarity with these issues.

Point (6): "Son" and "Begotten" versus "thing-made"

In Ephrem's identification of Prv 8.22 as a reference to Christ's humanity, he reveals an important part of his polemic. Namely, the crucial issue is not how various passages refer to Christ, but, more specifically, that the appropriate names for Christ be established. "Son" (*brâ*),[143] Ephrem suggests, occurs much more frequently than "thing-made" (*'bādâ*)[144] and thus should be taken as determinative for Christ's identity.

This emphasis on "Son" over against "thing-made" reverberates throughout the *HF.* Other than this basic observation, however, it is difficult to assess the importance that Ephrem attaches to it. This difficulty is due, on the one hand, to its sheer prevalence in the *HF* and, on the other hand, to the fact that Ephrem never outlines its content in a discursive way. Given Ephrem's literary style, this lack of discursive explanation is probably to be expected, but the absence of any such explanations makes it difficult to situate precisely this aspect of his thought. Nevertheless, we can make some basic observations.

Lord's] divine nature, which is light from light!" Possekel suggests this may be a reference to the Nicene Creed. See her "Ephrem's Doctrine of God," 200, n. 24. Lange (*Portrayal of Christ,* 148–49) compiles several passages from throughout Ephrem's corpus that he takes as references to the Nicene Creed. On the basis of these passages, he suggests that "it seems likely that Ephraem was … acquainted with the creed of Nicaea." His compilation of these phrases is impressive, but given that the phrases are often very short, very general, and woven together from throughout Ephrem's large corpus, I am skeptical.

143. Ephrem also frequently uses *yaldâ,* "child" or "thing-begotten."

144. I distinguish the Syriac term *'bādâ* ("work" or "thing-made") from *brîtâ* ("creature"), which, though occurring in Prv 8.22, Ephrem does not reference. *'bādâ* is derived from the verb *'bad*—"to do, make." I use "thing-made" to evoke its connection to Prv 8.22. In P, the latter reads, "The Lord created me as the beginning of his creations, before all his works" (*māryâ brān[y] b-rîš baryāteh. w-men qdām 'abdaw[hy] kullhôn*). The penultimate word—*'abdaw[hy],* "works"—is what I have translated as "thing-made" or "things-made," to bring out its potentially subordinationist echoes.

First, "Son" is privileged because the Father himself utters it in Scripture (at the scenes of the Baptism and Transfiguration, as well as in Ps 2.7, where it is specifically connected with being begotten), and because, more generally, it occurs so often in Scripture (as opposed to "thing-made").[145] Second, Ephrem's privileging of the name "Son" probably derives from the first word of the Syriac text of Prv 8.22: *brān[y]*. The verb *brâ*, "to create," is the root for both the noun "son" (also *brâ*) and "creature" (*brîtâ*). Especially in *HF* 61, Ephrem demonstrates an awareness of the linguistic similarity of these two disputed terms and rhetorically exploits the ambiguity. Third, Ephrem frequently argues for the importance of the names "Father," "Son," and "Spirit" due to their prominent role in baptism.[146] Finally, as names for Christ, "Son" (*brâ*) and "Begotten" (*yaldâ*) are privileged precisely in place of "thing-made" (*'bādâ*): Ephrem clearly conceives of "Son"/"begotten" and "thing-made" as mutually exclusive,[147] and assumes that the use of the correct name will ensure a correct theology.

While "Son" and "Begotten" are interchanged freely within the *HF*, Ephrem's emphasis on the name "Begotten" suggests that he has the anti-Aetian and Eunomian "Unbegotten" in mind.[148] For example, at 62:3 Ephrem writes, "How much his name agrees with and corresponds to his Begetter: / If he is Son, he is Begotten!" Ephrem seems intent to demonstrate the importance of both "Begetter" and "Begotten," and suggests likewise that "Begotten" follows from "Son." If we are to use this data to suggest a specific polemical context for the *HF*, an anti-Eunomian context seems most likely.

This same polemic seems to stand behind Ephrem's juxtaposition of "Son" and "thing-made" in hymn 53. While Ephrem never mentions the term "Unbegotten" as a potential divine name (even to refute it), this emphasis on the importance of divine names in Christological discourse is nevertheless striking in comparison with Aetius and Eunomius. Specifically, it is plausible that Ephrem's emphasis on "Son" and "thing-made"

145. See *HF* 53:13–14.
146. See, e.g., *HF* 13:6.
147. E.g., *HF* 60:8.
148. See p. 31, n. 131.

as two mutually exclusive names reflects a rhetorical twisting
of their position: rather than emphasizing "Unbegotten" and
"Father," Ephrem, reading Aetius's and Eunomius's theology
through the lens of Prv 8.22, emphasizes its logical outcomes: if
"Unbegotten" is the primary title for God, then the Son, as begotten, can only be "thing-made." On the other hand, if "Son"
is the primary name for Christ, then "Father" must be a proper
divine name. This connection to Aetian and Eunomian views
of language brings us to the following point.

Point (7): "True" and "borrowed" names

Ephrem divides scriptural "names" (by which he can mean
an actual description of God, names—adjectives, nouns—or
whole narrative scenes) into categories of "true" and "borrowed."[149] "Borrowed" names are generally those which are either simply unbefitting of God (for example, that he repents or
grows weary) or which appear to subordinate the Son to the Father (for example, Prv 8.22). "True" names, on the other hand,
which can include denominators such as "good" or "judge," but
which Ephrem predominantly uses to refer to the names "Fa-
ther/Son" (*'abbâ/brâ*) and "Begetter/Begotten" (*yālûdâ/yaldâ*),
refer to God "accurately" (*ḥattîtâ*) or "perfectly" (*gmîrâ*).

This emphasis on the "accuracy" of true names will inevitably seem redolent of Eunomian theories of language. As is well
known, Eunomius claimed that divine names either must be
"accurate," and thus transparent to the divine essence, or are
merely human, fallible, and ultimately misleading constructs.[150]
Indeed, on one level, Ephrem's notion of "true" names seems

---

149. On Ephrem's linguistics, see Beck, *Die Theologie*, 62–80; Brock, *The Luminous Eye: The Spiritual World Vision of Saint Ephrem the Syrian* (Kalamazoo, MI: Cistercian Publications, 1985), pp. 60–66; D. Bundy, "Language and the Knowledge of God in Ephrem Syrus," *PBC* 5 (1986): 91–103; K. den Biesen, *Simple and Bold*, 301–11; C. Molenberg, "An Invincible Weapon: Names in the Christological Passages in Ephrem's 'Hymns on Faith' 44–55," *Symposium Syriacum* V (1990): 135–42; R. Murray, "The Theory of Symbolism in St Ephrem's Theology," *Parole de l'Orient* 6/7 (1975–76), esp. 10–12.

150. DelCogliano writes, "The Heteroousian theory that names specifically disclose substance is the basis of their theological epistemology" (*Basil*, 34). See also Ayres, *Nicaea and its Legacy*, 149; Behr, *The Nicene Faith*, 272–73.

similar: by all accounts, he envisions the true names as the unfailing product of divine revelation and describes them as "accurate" and "perfect." There are, however, some important differences. First of all, Ephrem never suggests that "true" names reveal God's essence. In fact, his emphasis on the absolute hiddenness of God's essence is one of the most characteristic aspects of his theology. Thus, though true names represent genuine, non-negotiable revelations, Ephrem never defines their actual content, or even suggests that they possess content accessible to human knowledge. "True" names, instead, form necessary boundary markers, which must be observed, but the true content of which cannot be known.

Though Ephrem's understanding of "true" names bears significant differences from Eunomian linguistics, his theology of names as a whole does suggest an anti-Eunomian context for these hymns. In fact, it seems likely that Ephrem knew of the Eunomian emphasis on "accurate" speech, and of "Unbegotten" as an accurate revealer of God's essence. In response, he has simply shifted the "accurate" name from "Unbegotten" to "Begetter" and "Begotten," and rejected the notion that these names reveal God's essence.

Point (8): Distrust of Nicene language of essence

While hymn 53 provides some of our most straightforward data for situating Ephrem within broader anti-Arian polemics, it is remarkable for what it lacks, namely, a terminology for expressing the likeness or sameness of Father and Son *on the level of essence*.[151] That is, we have nothing equivalent to the Nicene *homoousios* (*bar kyānâ/bar 'îtûtâ*).[152] In fact, the only place in that hymn where Ephrem does articulate the relationship between Father and Son seems to suggest a homoian position. In 53:12, Ephrem tells his audience to "look upon him [that is, the Son] and look upon his Father, and see [the Son] entirely / Like his Begetter." This reference to the Son being "entirely like his Be-

151. As will become clear, Ephrem certainly does express the likeness of Father and Son; he just does not couple this likeness-language with essence-language.

152. See p. 38, n. 153.

getter" (*dāmê kulleh l-yāludeh*), coupled with the fact that it is modified by no language relating to "being," "essence," or "nature," suggests that while Ephrem is unequivocally condemning subordinationist readings of Scripture, he is doing so without the specific essence-language of Nicaea.

Indeed, this tendency is evident throughout the majority of the *HF*. Nevertheless, toward the very end of the cycle, in 73:11, Ephrem uses the Syriac phrase "one essence" (*ḥda 'îtûtâ*), which, while not translating *homoousios* (the latter can be translated as *bar 'îtûtâ*, or *bar kyānâ*),[153] does clearly indicate a willingness to use essence language to express the relationship of Father and Son. This single citation, however, forms simply one piece of a fairly complex puzzle as it relates to this sort of Christological language.

The first difficulty comes in a passage in which Ephrem seems to refer negatively to *homoousios*. He writes in 52:14:

> Why would we introduce some other thing into that
> Truth he dictated to us? The names that we have added,
> These, brothers, have become an excuse for the presumptuous.

---

153. *bar 'îtûtâ* appears in *CDia* 13:8, and Christian Lange argues that there it resembles *homoousios*, though he takes it to be a latter interpolation (*The Portrayal of Christ*, 73–74). In the earliest Syriac translations of the Nicene Creed, however, *bar kyānâ* translates *homoousios;* see A. de Halleux, "Le symbole des évêques perses au synode de Séleucie-Ctésiphon (410)," in *Erkenntnisse und Meinungen: Festschrift W. Strothmann* (Wiesbaden, 1978), 163; Arthur Vööbus, "New Sources for the Symbol in Early Syrian Christianity," *VC* 26 (1972): 295. This phrase does appear once in Ephrem's corpus: in *CGen.* prol. 5, Ephrem says that the earth was created by a "Mediator who was of the same nature and equal in skill to the Maker" (*d-'îtaw[hy] bar kyāneh w-bar 'ûmānûteh d-'ābûdâ*). Here Ephrem clearly uses *bar kyānâ* to describe Christ. One can interpret this datum in at least three ways: (1) The easiest explanation is that at some point Ephrem made peace with *bar kyānâ*, and became willing to use it in writing; (2) connected to this, given that the *CGen.* is generally taken to have been written for a small, scholastic audience, it could be that Ephrem was comfortable using *bar kyānâ* in that setting, even as he refused to use the term in public, liturgical settings; (3) it could also be the case that the introduction to the *CGen.*, which is literarily quite different from the rest of the work, was added by a later scribe.

Ephrem identifies his audience in this passage as "my brothers," and distinguishes them from "the presumptuous." It is
this first group—identified with the first person—that has introduced a "thing" that has "become an excuse" for this other
group, "the presumptuous." It is difficult to imagine a target
more likely than the Nicene *homoousios*.[154] We know that many
anti-Arian authors distrusted the Nicene formula as introducing an unscriptural term into theological discourse.[155] Ephrem
here identifies Scripture as "that / Truth he dictated to us,"
which suggests he has this same criticism in mind. It seems very
likely that Ephrem is here faulting the Nicene *homoousios* for
the theological emphases of figures such as Eunomius, whose
own "Unbegotten" was challenged precisely on the basis of its
absence in Scripture.

We have, then, a fairly complex picture of Ephrem's Christology: in the passage just cited, Ephrem expresses distrust for
the Nicene *homoousios*. In 73:11, however, Ephrem refers to the
"one essence" of the Trinity, which sounds closer to *homoousios*. Nevertheless, the latter seems to be the outlier, and is any-
way not the Syriac for *homoousios*. More frequently in the *HF*
Ephrem repeatedly finds ways to speak about the Father and
the Son without the language of essence. At 40:6, he speaks of
the Father and Son being "equal to" or "worthy of" one another, and in 53:12, as we saw above, Ephrem uses the language
of "like." This evidence suggests a twofold interpretation: first,
it seems to be the case that Ephrem distrusted *homoousios*, although, like many authors in the fourth century, he wanted to
affirm the likeness of Father and Son and went about doing
so in a variety of ways. Second, the single occurrence of "one
essence" suggests that, at some point, Ephrem made peace with
the language of essence, though he was still unwilling to use
the Nicene *homoousios*.

---

154. In the note to his German translation of this passage, Beck asks,
"Richtet sich das auch gegen das nizänische *homoūsios*?" (*HF [G]*, 140, n. 6).
155. On this general hermeneutic aspect of the debates, see F. Young, *Biblical Exegesis and the Formation of Christian Culture* (Peabody, MA: Hendrickson,
2002), 31.

Point (9): The divinity of the Holy Spirit

While Ephrem's *SF* provide our earliest window onto the thinking that would emerge in the *HF*, those sermons rarely address the divinity of the Holy Spirit, focusing instead on the relationship between Father and Son.[156] In the *HF*, however, Ephrem is clearly interested in affirming the divinity of the Holy Spirit. While there are scattered references to the Holy Spirit throughout the work,[157] he most frequently implies the divinity of the Spirit by situating it alongside the Father and the Son in doxological formulas.[158] Ephrem also insists upon the Spirit's inscrutability,[159] affirms that its nature is distinct from that of the angels,[160] and denies that it is a "thing-made."[161] Finally, Ephrem hints that there are people calling the Spirit's divinity into question.[162]

This emphasis on the Holy Spirit's divinity could suggest a late 360s–early 370s date for these parts of the collection.[163] It is during this time that there emerges in Egypt an outright denial of the Holy Spirit's divinity, and a concomitant affirmation of its divinity among, especially, the Cappadocians.[164] While Ephrem shares certain characteristics with Basil's defense of the Spirit's divinity,[165] however, there is also no substantial difference be-

156. Even here, though, the picture is not so simple. While the Spirit is conspicuously absent from sermons 1–3 and 5–6, sermon 4 speaks of the Holy Spirit in ways very similar to the *HF*.

157. See *HF* 5:2, where Ephrem seems to articulate an angelomorphic pneumatology.

158. See *HF* 13:2; 15:10; 18:3; 23:13; 43:10; 51:8; 52:10; 59:4, 6; 62:12; 65:3, 6; 67:9, 24; 73:1.

159. *HF* 29:5; 33:7; 37:19; 74:2.

160. *HF* 46:7.   161. *HF* 59:3.

162. *HF* 59:8.

163. While we cannot assume that the hymns' ordering represents the order in which they were composed, it is interesting that most of the more explicit references to the Holy Spirit's divinity come in the later hymns.

164. See Ayres, *Nicaea*, 215–17.

165. For example, Ephrem affirms the order of the Trinitarian names in *HF* 23:13 and connects it with baptism throughout. Note, however, that Basil's *On the Holy Spirit* was not composed until 375, after Ephrem's death (see Ayres, *Nicaea*, 215).

tween Ephrem's manner of articulating the Spirit's divinity and
that found in Cyril of Jerusalem around 350.[166]

Taken together, the *HF* exhibit these nine characteristics, situating the hymns within the fourth-century controversies: (1) a
condemnation of "investigation"; (2) a mistrust of "Greek wisdom"; (3) a particular hermeneutic (rebutting subordinationist readings of Scripture, but pursuing a fairly literal means of
reading scriptural titles); (4) a knowledge of basic "Arian" and
anti-Arian texts (namely, Prv 8.22 and Mt 24.36 / Mk 13.32);
(5) an apparent knowledge of the formula "there was [a time]
when he was not"; (6) a juxtaposition of the names "Son" and
"Begotten" with "creature"; (7) a theology of names, which divides scriptural titles into categories of "true" and "borrowed";
(8) a distrust of the Nicene *homoousios,* but an eventual willingness to use a possible Syriac equivalent; and (9) an insistence
on the divinity of the Holy Spirit. To this list of nine characteristics present within the *HF,* we can add one that is notable for
its absence: Ephrem, though by all accounts intending the *HF*
as anti-Arian polemical literature, never names any specific opponents. This latter characteristic makes Ephrem fairly unique
within the currents of fourth-century Arian literature.[167]

These nine characteristics provide the most obvious means
for attaching the *HF* in a concrete way to the fourth-century
controversies. But they are by no means present in all of the
HF, and some (for example, characteristics 3, 4, 5, and 8) occur
infrequently in the collection. By far the most common feature
of the aforementioned is Ephrem's condemnation of investigation, and, after that, his repeated positing of the names "Son"
and "Begotten." This conglomeration suggests that a general
anti-Eunomian/Aetian context of the 360s seems most likely.

Ephrem's distrust of Nicene language, however, and his

166. See Hanson, *Search,* 743.
167. In his *Catechetical Homilies,* Cyril of Jerusalem also leaves his opponents unmentioned, thus providing one parallel for Ephrem. Athanasius's
Against the Pagans provides another parallel. Traditionally, Athanasius's failure
to name opponents in this work has been taken as evidence for its early date;
Anatolios suggests that it reflects Athanasius's own precarious position within
the eastern Empire (*Retrieving Nicaea,* 100–101).

preference for language of "like" situates him alongside other fourth-century figures who fit fourth-century categories less clearly, figures such as Cyril of Jerusalem and Meletius of Antioch. Recently, in a brief study of Meletius, Brian Daley has suggested a model that is compelling in trying to contextualize the *HF*.[168] We have already suggested that Ephrem's use of a literalist reading of Scripture against a subordinationist reading (that is, adding up the uses of "Son" and "creature") potentially resembled a homoian hermeneutic tendency (albeit one that Ephrem could be utilizing *against* homoians).[169] Daley presents Meletius of Antioch as a representative of a fourth-century theological option that carved a path between the Nicene *homoousios,* on the one hand, and the neo-Arian insistence on radical difference, on the other hand.[170] Daley characterizes the movement in this way:

Many Church leaders at that time ... whom we now refer to as "Homoeans," because they emphasized that Jesus is "like" ... the Father, refused to identify themselves either with Arius and his followers or with the defenders of the Nicene formula, and were even more opposed to the highly rationalized anti-Nicene polemic developed in the 350s by "Neo-Arians" such as Eunomius and Aetius.[171]

According to H. C. Brennecke, figures of this ilk tended to "avoid theological speculation," endorsed "simple Biblicism," and evidenced "a zeal that sometimes [turned] into fanaticism against all things pagan."[172] When we think of the characteristics manifested by the *HF,* this description fits Ephrem quite well: Ephrem uses the language of "like," his condemnation of theological speculation forms one of the collection's most salient characteristics, and his dismissal of "Greek wisdom" could be read as zeal "against all things pagan."[173] Given, moreover, that Meletius

168. In *Tradition and the Rule of Faith in the Early Church: Essays in Honor of Joseph T. Lienhard,* ed. Ronnie J. Rombs and Alexander Y. Hwang (Washington, DC: The Catholic University of America Press, 2010), 128–50.

169. See pp. 29–30.

170. "The Enigma of Meletius of Antioch," 130.

171. Ibid., 131.

172. H. C. Brennecke, *Studien zur Geschichte der Homöer. Der Osten bis zum Ende der homöischen Reichskirche* (Tübingen: Mohr, 1988), 2–3, quoted in Daley, "Enigma," 131.

173. It is interesting to note as well that, in his *CJ,* Ephrem refers to Julian

(like Aetius) worked and lived in Antioch, his ideas could have reached Ephrem (and Ephrem's bishops) in either Edessa or Nisibis.

All of this exploration results in a complex picture: aspects of the *HF* betray a "homoian" or "homoiousian" position, and suggest a date in the 350s. Others—the apparently anti-Eunomian language and the language affirming the Spirit's divinity—suggest an anti-Eunomian position of the late 360s. Given Ephrem's status as a "doctor of the Church," there is perhaps a desire to see in him an unambiguously anti-Arian, pro-Nicene author—a veritable Syriac Athanasius. Yet, if we read Ephrem on his own terms, what emerges is much less predictable and much more interesting: he is virulently anti-subordinationist, but his writings also suggest a real ambivalence about Nicaea and its *homoousios*. Ephrem, like Cyril of Jerusalem or Meletius of Antioch, refuses "to be located on an anachronistic map in which a clear frontier runs between Nicene Orthodoxy and everything else."[174]

V. The Language of Investigation and Ephrem's Theological Voice

As we have looked at the fourth-century ideas and movements that gave rise to the *HF*, and within which the *HF* can be situated, we have returned again and again to Ephrem's condemnations of "investigation." As already stated, one of the most fascinating features of the *HF* is that, though their anti-subordinationist intent is clear, Ephrem never identifies his opponents by name, but instead develops a symbolic language with which to identify them. Thus we have not "Arians," "Aetians," or "Eunomians," but "investigators," "debaters," "presumptuous ones," and so on.

Because of this consistent symbolic naming and the absence

---

the Apostate as the "King of Greece" (*CJ* 1:18:3 and 1:20:4) and speaks of Julian's having "revered all the Greeks" (*CJ* 4:6:2). This suggests a direct link within Ephrem between Hellenism and paganism.

174. Rowan Williams, "Baptism and the Arian Controversy," in *Arianism after Arius: Essays on the Development of the Fourth Century Trinitarian Controversies,* ed. Michel R. Barnes and Daniel H. Williams (Edinburgh: T & T Clark, 1993), 162. For a similar reading of this data, see Lange, *Portrayal of Christ,* 146–49.

of clear references to historical figures or events, the polemical language of the *HF* comes to transcend the fourth-century concerns that gave rise to it: because Ephrem's opponents are all cloaked in symbols, these hymns come across less as simply anti-"Arian," and more as an attempt to articulate the boundaries and parameters of theology writ large. From this perspective, the hymns do not represent a simple polemical rebuttal of subordinationist christologies, or a catechetical guide to their orthodox responses. Rather, they provide us with highly metaphoric, stylized, poetic reflections upon basic questions (about God, belief, human knowledge, Scripture, and the world), questions that are, in turn, refracted through the particular problems occasioned by these fourth-century subordinationist christologies. The *HF* thus do not aim to refute these christologies, but seek to establish the limits of human knowledge, the means by which knowledge can (or, more often, cannot) be established, and a reading of Scripture and the world as dramatically acting out the consequences of this (errant or virtuous) pursuit of knowledge. On the basis of this critique of a false epistemology (that is, one that believes humans can understand divine matters), the *HF* further aim to construct an opponent and, particularly, to persuade a presumably diverse audience that whatever Ephrem's opponents claim to be doing, their manner of speaking about God amounts to a prideful and presumptuous objectification of him.

Historical arguments can be made for why Ephrem would refuse to name any opponents. Foremost among these arguments is the hypothesis that the hymns are written in the context of Valens's persecution of Nicene Christians. If this is the case, Ephrem's refusal to name Arius, Aetius, or Eunomius represents a political move: he employs the anti-investigative language as a political code that his audience would recognize, but that the emperor would not.[175] As we have already stated,

---

175. On this, see James C. Scott, *Domination and the Arts of Resistance: Hidden Transcripts* (New Haven: Yale University Press, 1992). To the best of my knowledge, no one has actually made this argument, though it is similar to the argument Anatolios makes regarding Athanasius's *Against the Pagans* (*Retrieving Nicaea*, 100–101).

however, contextualizing the *HF* within the persecution of Valens in Edessa demands reliance upon a historiographical tradition that emerges after Ephrem's life and that in other known cases proves ignorant of Edessan religious life.

On another level, this style of naming, in which Ephrem refers to real, contemporary people by symbolic titles, is simply characteristic of his poetics.[176] Ephrem tends throughout his corpus to "metaphorize" things. That is to say, whether his topic is Scripture or the emperor Julian or the world, he talks about these things in a way that makes them symbolic of other things, and thus transcendent of their limited historical contexts.[177]

Thus far, we have sought to contextualize the *HF* within the confines of the ecclesio-political debates of the fourth century. Here, however, it is worth considering these hymns' more immediate context—the context of the liturgies of Nisibis and Edessa. As theorists of performative language have noted, language works differently in these ritual contexts.[178] In such contexts, language seeks to transcend the function of strictly communicative meaning and establishes instead "a state of affairs ... *in* communicating."[179] Applying this to Ephrem, if we are to read his language of investigation simply as code for some concrete, historically identifiable fourth-century group, we will miss the performative nature of the language. Rather, the goal of such language is to transcend the mundane structures of fourth-century life.

Within this context of performance, an "investigator" is not simply an "Arian" disguised. Rather, Ephrem's language creates

176. See, for example, *CJ* 1, in which Ephrem cloaks the emperor Julian in similarly metaphoric language.

177. On this, see my article "The Poetics of Self-Presentation in Ephrem the Syrian's *Hymns on Faith* 10," in *Syriac Encounters: Papers presented at the Sixth North American Syriac Symposium, 2011* (Leuven: Peeters, forthcoming).

178. See Joseph J. Schaller, "Performative Language Theory: An Exercise in the Analysis of Ritual," *Worship* 62 (1988): 415–32. For an application of Schaller's insights to *piyyutim*, see L. Lieber, "The Rhetoric of Participation: Experiential Elements of Early Hebrew Liturgical Poetry," *Journal of Religion* 90 (2010): 119–47.

179. Schaller, 416.

categories and types that transcend the historical particularities that gave rise to them. "Investigator," or "debater," comes to refer to a *way* of doing theology, as much as, or even more than, the theological conclusions to which someone came by means of that way. For Ephrem the various theological tendencies of the fourth century (whether non-, pro-, or anti-Nicene) trigger questions about who God is and how he can be known. He then addresses these questions within a performative context. The *HF* provide the traces of that performance, and, in so doing, represent a dramatic retelling, using narratives and signs from Scripture and the world, of a basic struggle to know and to believe in God. Thus, whereas Athanasius in his *Contra Arianos* sought to construct a group called "Arians," Ephrem seeks to construct a theological category called "investigation": he says nothing about the social make-up of this group, its figurehead, or historical lineage. "Investigation," rather, represents a way of approaching or avoiding God, and stands at the heart of Ephrem's understanding of God, belief, and the world.

Ephrem develops in these hymns an extensive lexicon to delineate these activities. I have identified thirteen terms that Ephrem uses to denote a family of meanings, ranging from, most commonly, "investigation" or "debating" to, less frequently, "assault." Within this group of thirteen, however, four predominate. I will discuss these four in some detail before briefly delineating the remaining nine. Though I offer individual treatments of this vocabulary, it seems to me (as will be made clear below) that there is little difference between the various terms, and a philological study of them sheds little light on Ephrem's own usage. Rather, in the *HF* Ephrem seems to work with a fairly consistent notion of "investigation," "debate," or "discussion," and uses a variety of words to communicate this basic idea. Where there are differences (for example, in the words that mean "to assault"), these will be noted.

A. *bṣâ* ("to investigate")[180]

The hymns' most common term for investigation, *bṣâ*, appears first in *HF* 1:11, and in most of the hymns thereafter. While its basic meaning is simply "to search" or "to examine," it takes on a life of its own in Ephrem's hymns, appearing in its basic verbal form, *bṣâ*, and in two noun forms, *bṣātâ*, "investigation," and, less frequently, *bāṣûyâ*, "investigator." Its use in 2:3 is typical:

> Blessed is the one, my Lord, who has become the salt of truth in this generation,
> And whose faith has not lost its taste among the tasteless who investigate you.

One can see clearly the term's polemical valence as well as its connection with faith. Indeed, Ephrem elsewhere identifies the presence of investigation as an indicator of the absence of faith.[181] Moreover, while its predominance in Ephrem is possibly influenced by the highly technical discourse of Aetius and other non-Nicenes of the time, in these hymns it has become detached from its original impetus and transformed into a fundamental feature of Ephrem's view of God, humanity, and the world: humanity is essentially limited in its outlook, and investigation seeks to know what exists beyond the purview of human limitedness, primarily God (and his begetting of a Son), but also certain aspects of humanity itself.[182]

It is especially in its noun form, *bṣātâ*, that "investigation" appears as an identifiable object or activity that transcends its mundane meaning. Ephrem, for example, will speak about "investigation" in a historical sense, as if present-day "investigation" is something concrete and identifiable, which both he and his audience recognize. For example, at 9:1 he writes, "In-

180. For each of these terms, the English that immediately follows in parentheses indicates the term I have typically used to translate the Syriac. On a few occasions I depart from the indicated term, when the context makes clear that it does not fit. I have tried, however, to be as consistent as possible.

181. See *HF* 7:9; 65:12.

182. While this theme echoes throughout the *HF*, it is probably articulated most succinctly in *SF* 1:1–21.

vestigation was upright / But it has changed in our generation."
Here, "investigation" is a concrete activity, though its precise
character is left unstated.

B. *b'â* ("to investigate")

On a most basic level, *b'â* means simply "to desire," or "to request," with no obvious negative connotations. Yet within these
hymns it too takes on the negative sense of "to investigate," and,
in its more frequently attested noun form, *b'ātâ,* "investigation."
As it is used in the hymns, *b'â* is, for the most part, interchange-
able with *bṣâ,* albeit with some slight differences. Most significant of these is that *b'ātâ* carries a more neutral valence, representing an activity that can be negative or positive.[183] While
the former predominates, the latter does appear. For example,
at 2:12, Ephrem writes, "Blessed is the one who weighed his
investigation (*b'ātâ*) with the benefits of his hearers," thus suggesting a positive role for such investigation, provided it is balanced with audience needs. And at 2:18 Ephrem states similarly: "Blessed is the one who has polished his investigation (*b'ātâ*)
like a mirror." In these instances, *b'ātâ,* while left undefined in
any concrete sense, suggests a permissible inquisitiveness about
matters related to God. Moreover, while these stanzas give us
some basic criteria for what might qualify as permissible investigation, 8:9 suggests another: "In the Church there is / Investigation which discusses revealed things. / There is no investigation
of hidden things." *b'ātâ* can thus be permitted when it treats of
"revealed things," that is, aspects of Christ's humanity.

C. *draš* ("to debate")

Of the terms thus far examined, *draš* stands as the most familiar from literature beyond the *HF.* In its root form, *draš* conveys
a wide variety of meanings, ranging from "to tread" or "trample" (as in Jb 19.12, "His messengers come upon me as one; they
trample their roads upon me") to "to converse," "to dispute,"

183. Ephrem uses it with an explicitly positive valence throughout hymn
72 (specifically, stanzas 8, 11, 12, 23).

or "to debate." It is also, however, the root of the term by which Ephrem titles his own hymns—*madrāšâ*—and, as such, parallels the Hebrew "midrash." Moreover, in its noun form *dārûšê*, "scholar," the term will be used elsewhere in Syriac literature with entirely positive connotations.[184] Nevertheless, in the *HF draš* appears predominantly as a term that denotes the activity of "debating," an activity Ephrem persistently condemns, and *dārûšâ* refers exclusively to the ones who engage in it, and who, in Ephrem's hymns, seem to represent an identifiable unit. As best I can tell, the term has no positive valence in the *HF*. While Ephrem only allusively delineates the specific qualities that mark this "debating," *draš* appears most specifically to refer to inappropriate discourse about the Father's begetting of the Son. At the same time, it also seems to condemn a discourse that is generally marked by presumption, extreme wordiness, or the false belief that knowledge can be attained. Ephrem writes in 1:18:

> All who wish to extol and magnify God,
> [God], being majestic in his nature, magnifies the one who magnifies him.
> Refrain from debating (*drāšâ*), which cannot comprehend him, and acquire silence, which befits him.

Here, as elsewhere, *draš* is explicitly juxtaposed with silent doxology, and is identified as a means of discourse that cannot comprehend God. The term appears similarly throughout the *HF*.

D. *'qab* ("to discuss," "to dispute")

'qab has as its basic meaning "to tread upon," or "to follow," but in its extended forms can mean "to investigate, search for." In the *HF* it appears most frequently in two forms: first, in its noun form *'ûqābâ*, where it means "investigation," "debating," or "discussion," and second, in a negative participial form, *d-lâ met'qābâ*, where it means "incomprehensible," or "unsearchable." 2:2 provides one such example:

---

184. For example, John of Ephesus frequently uses it in a positive sense; see *Lives of the Eastern Saints*, ed. and trans. E. W. Brooks, *PO* 17–19 (Paris, 1923–1925).

Blessed is the one who has approached the knowledge of truth,
And has learned through it that God is unsearchable for
humanity.

These four terms form the predominant vocabulary for investigation and discussion that Ephrem employs throughout the *HF*. Their frequency lends the hymns a poetic and polemical consistency and, more than any other literary feature, unites these eighty-seven often disparate hymns. Moreover, while these four terms are the most recognizable, Ephrem has in fact a further nine terms that he uses similarly. I list them here, in order of frequency of occurrence and with their basic meanings in parentheses: *'etdrek* ("to understand, comprehend," but typically used as a negative adjective to denote the "incomprehensibility" of God),[185] *māš* (its basic meaning is "to touch," and while it frequently retains this more physical connotation, it does move toward an abstract sense of "to search out, explore"),[186] *hmas* ("to meditate upon, examine," "to rush toward, attack"),[187] *š'el* ("to ask, question," often occurring as *šû'ālâ*, "questioning," or in the plural, "questions"),[188] and *bqâ* ("to observe, examine; to

185. Though it can be applied to more mundane things, such as in 43:6, where it refers to the "shame" of a dead body, unknown because it is covered in burial. See 30:2; 33:8; 38:15; 39:7; 41:5 (here in reference to things that *can* be comprehended by the senses, e.g., color, taste); 42:6; 43:6, 10; 45:4; 47:4; 48:1, 4 (here in reference to "the truth" that *can* be comprehended "through the rays of the law"); 50:1, 2; 51:3, 4, 5; 52:1; 54:1, 4 (in 52:1, 54:1, and 54:4, Ephrem speaks positively of the human capacity to recognize things about Christ—that he is God, Lord, and the Father's caretaker over the earth); 54:11; 57:3; 62:8; 64:5; 65:9; 70:14; 73:2, 15; 76:12.

186. *māš* almost always occurs in conjunction with other terms for investigation. See 8:6 (where it forms a pun on *mûšê*, Moses); 26:4; 27:4; 29:4; 43:1, 3; 44:7; 47:4; 48:8; 50:1; 55:9; 58:13; 64:5, 8; 65:1; 70:5; 72:3; 86:9. It occurs by itself in 33:1 (with *d-lâ*, as "unsearchable") and 37:25. It is coupled with *gašš* (also carrying the physical sense of "to touch") in 57:4, 73:9, and 87:2.

187. Carries a connotation similar to *b'â* and *bṣâ*. See 28:11; 45:2; 46:1; 52:8; 58:10, 12; 61:1; 68:6; 79:1, 3. But it can also have a positive sense. See 32:2, 6; 47:8.

188. 1:3; 2:4, 10, 22; 9:4; 27:8; 28:6; 29:5; 30:3, 7; 35:1; 36:19; 37:5, 18, 23; 39:2, 4; 43:9, 10; 44:9; 46:9; 47:8 (with a potentially positive, or at least neutral, valence); 51:9; 54:12; 56:4; 56:12; 61:1, 8; 62:3; 65:12; 66:10; 68:18; 79:9; 87:2, 19.

test").[189] Ephrem also uses some other terms as near-synonyms of these verbs of investigation, although they carry slightly different meanings and appear infrequently: *ṣadd* ("to gaze at, look upon"),[190] and *sbak* ("to assail; to fix upon").[191]

E. Other Vocabulary

Alongside all of these terms denoting various forms of "investigation," Ephrem also makes repeated use of some other, related words. Most prominent among these is *mraḥ* ("to presume"), appearing in various forms, which can mean "to be bold," but in Ephrem carries the sense of "to be presumptuous." *Mraḥ* often accompanies the language of investigation as a helping verb (see, for example, 8:8, "who will presume to investigate?"), and is sometimes juxtaposed with *ḥsap*, with the meaning "to be audacious," and is frequently posited as the positive version of *mraḥ*.[192]

Phâ ("to wander off") appears throughout the *HF* as a concept that parallels, or derives from, investigation. The verb means "to wander," and from there, "to go astray." While in these hymns it comes to mean, more or less, "to err," it still carries a dynamic sense.[193] On occasion, *phâ* can also have a positive connotation.[194]

Three final terms appear, albeit less frequently, in connection with all of the above vocabulary, and denote the state of

189. *bqâ* tends to be neutral in its connotations (e.g., 3:6; 34:4; 44:1). But see 9:2; 29:5; 47:7.

190. See 26:5; 28:1; 42:2; 45:10; 51:2; 57:3; 65:12; 70:2, 4; 72:14; 73:10.

191. See 26:4; 42:12; 45:2.

192. *mraḥ* occurs over eighty times in the *HF*, and its meaning is very consistent. *ḥûṣāpâ* is much less common. With a negative valence, see 28:9, 16; 54:12. Den Biesen notes the sometimes positive connotations of *ḥsap*, though he overstates the case: "For Ephrem, *ḥaṣîpûtâ* ... and *marrāḥûtâ* ... are two completely different attitudes ..." (*Simple and Bold*, 123). The above citations show that such is not necessarily the case.

193. I have tried to bring out this dynamic sense by translating it as "to wander" more often than "to err" or "go astray." For the subtle range of meanings of *phâ*, see 1:9; 9:13, 14; 11:4, 13. *phâ* occurs in the *HF* nearly fifty times.

194. See 24:11, where it has the sense of "to stand in awe."

affairs that Ephrem perceives in the world. *ṭ'â* carries the basic sense of "to go astray," "to be unmindful of/forget," or "to err."[195] Finally, Ephrem uses *ḥeryānâ* ("schism, controversy") and, much less frequently, *ḥeryāyâ*, to denote the "controversy" or "schism" that has resulted from this "presumptuous investigation."[196]

This vocabulary provides the most lexical continuity throughout the *HF,* and shapes the theological and polemical vision Ephrem articulates in these hymns.

VI. A Note on Translation

Anyone who has tried to translate Ephrem's poetry into readable English knows the challenges facing the translator. In the present work I have tried to represent Ephrem's Syriac accurately, while still producing a readable English translation. Consistently, I have left out Syriac particles (such as *tûb,* "again, moreover"), especially when they detract from the sense of the English and Ephrem seems to be including them for primarily metrical reasons. Occasionally I have made more substantial changes, such as switching a passive construction to an active one. Otherwise, if I have pursued a translation that departs significantly from the literal sense of the Syriac, I have indicated this, along with a literal translation, in a footnote.

The *HF* come to us in four manuscripts, which, unsurprisingly, do not agree in every detail. Beck's critical edition is based upon ms A, which he almost always prints in the body of the text, even when mss B, C, and D clearly preserve better readings. Because my translation follows Beck's critical edition, A forms my base manuscript as well. Unlike Beck, however, I have willingly substituted readings from other manuscripts

195. *ṭ'â* occurs just under fifty times, and its meaning is relatively straightforward.

196. On *ḥeryānâ,* see 1:2; 2:6; 7:5; 23:5; 28:11, 12; 35:3, 7, 9; 36:10; 37:4, 16; 41:8, 10; 42:5, 10; 43:5, 9; 44:5; 46:6; 47:6; 47:12, 13; 48:3; 53:3, 10; 50:5; 51:4, 12; 52:2, 8, 14, 15; 54:9; 56:7; 58:5; 59:7, 8, 9; 61:5; 62:4, 6; 66:3, 12, 17; 67:12, 18; 68:1, 13; 70:15; 78:28, 29; 86:14; 87:17, 19. On *ḥeryāyâ,* see 52:12; 53:14; 86:21.

when they seemed to me preferable. I indicate such variants with { }. The majority of these variants are orthographical, and I have provided the Syriac (in transliteration) to indicate to the reader the relationship between the variants.[197] When the decision to choose one reading over another demands an interpretation of a more subjective nature, I have explained my choice in a lengthier note.

197. See the transliteration chart, p. xi.

THE HYMNS
ON FAITH

{The Hymns on}[1] Faith, spoken by
Blessed Mar[2] Ephrem

HYMN ONE

According to the melody, "All the things you have endured, O Lord, are a marvel."[3]

[1:1] In place of that all-vivifying sign,[4] which the Teacher-
   of-all has set {before us},[5]
This {presumptuous}[6] generation of ours has established
   a new faith.[7]
But the Knower-of-all {knows}[8] the cause of their rumblings.

   REFRAIN: *Glory to you from every mouth!*

1. B.
2. "Mar," literally "lord," is a common Syriac title, applied variously to saints, bishops, and generally venerable figures.
3. This meter, attached only to the first hymn, is 7+7 / 7+7 / 7+7.
4. While the ER took "sign" (*nîšâ*) as a reference to the "Regula Fidei," Beck defined it instead as "Scripture's message about the Son of God" ("die Gottessohnaussagen der Schrift") (*HF [G]*, 1, n.2). The term appears throughout the *HF*, including three more times in this stanza (1:3, and twice in 1:4). While its meaning is ambiguous in these passages, some other usages clarify it somewhat. In 67:1, it is explicitly connected to Scripture, and in 63:7, it suggests basic doctrinal content, namely, that the Father and Son are one. This is similar to the Greek notion of the *skopos* of Scripture, a term which *nîšâ* later comes to translate in Syriac.
5. B.
6. B.
7. Throughout the *HF*, Ephrem frequently juxtaposes "this" or "our generation" with past generations. See also *HF* 2:3; 5:19; 9:1, and 9:3.
8. B.

[1:2] If [their rumblings] result from pride, may our Lord
rebuke haughtiness.
If they result from [a desire for] schism, may our Lord
increase unity.
But if love is their cause, let him reveal his own, to his own!⁹
[1:3] O you who shot your arrows at the great mountain:¹⁰
do not think they reached it!
They barely left your side; they did not arrive at that target!¹¹
For the begetting¹² of the Son is exalted above the
questioning of humanity.
[1:4] A sign is placed before you—one of your own kind.¹³
Compare it to something nearby,
Since through the testimony of something nearby we come
to believe what is far-off.
Let your soul be for you a sign, for investigators have
abandoned it.¹⁴

9. Cf. Jn 1.11.
10. Syr., *ṭûra rabbâ* ("great mountain"), which could also be vocalized as
ṭawrâ rabbâ, in which case it would translate as "across a great space." While
Ephrem uses this phrase in *HF* 4:5, 6:1, and 11:3, *SF* 6:31 best suggests his
meaning: "The truth is revealed as something clear, but they seek it as something lost. / Look: they seek a great mountain through miniscule cracks!"
Ephrem's interest in the metaphor is thus based simply on a "big versus small"
distinction: God is something big—something obvious—yet these theological
investigators cannot see what looms large before their eyes, and are instead
fixated on various miniscule questions related to the surface. Beyond this,
however, mountains form a consistent site of biblical theophanies (e.g., Mt. Sinai, the Transfiguration) and feature prominently elsewhere in Ephrem's corpus (e.g., the depiction of Paradise as a mountain in *HPar*).
11. Syr., *nîsâ*. On this term, see note 4 attached to 1:1.
12. The root *y-l-d*, rendered here as "begetting" (*yaldâ*), can be vocalized in
two different ways. As a noun, *yaldâ* can mean "birth," or "begetting," or that
which is begotten, i.e., "child." As a participle, *yāldâ* (in the emphatic case) can
still refer to "begetting," but it can also mean "the One Who Begets," i.e., the
Father (though Ephrem typically uses *yālûdâ* for the latter).
13. Syr., *bar ṭûhāmāk*. Lit., "of your same kind."
14. The following eleven stanzas (1:5–1:15) will pursue a rhetorical investigation of the soul, which intends to demonstrate the impossibility of achieving
certainty about the soul's existence. The whole discussion functions as an argument *a minore ad maius*, with the soul being "less," and "the begetting of the
Son" being more. The implied rhetorical question, then, is "if the soul cannot

[1:5] Indeed, one professes that [the soul] exists, and another
that it does not exist.

One posits it as subject to death, another as transcending
death.[15]

One makes it from something, and another from nothing.

[1:6] He who has seen its greatness, has considered it[16]
part of the Great One.[17]

He who has seen its dissolution, has considered it a breath
of air.

There is one who considers it a blowing, and another who
calls it blood.[18]

[1:7] One, who has seen its heat, says that it is from fire.

Another, who has seen its relationship to wind,[19] posits that it
has come from the wind.[20]

One [makes it] a part of God, and another [makes it] a
puff of air.[21]

[1:8] There is one who posits it as from Being, and another
from many beings.[22]

One has made it from one thing, and one from seven
mixtures.[23]

---

be understood, how can the Son's begetting?" This question will be stated outright in 1:9, but then Ephrem will continue his discussion of the soul.

15. Literally, "One places it below death, and another above death."

16. Syr., 'abdeh (lit., "has made it," here and in lines 2 and 3).

17. Syr., rabbâ ("The Great One") could also be "a great one," or "a great
thing."

18. Cf. Gn 9.4 and Lv 17.11.

19. Syr., rûḥānûtâ ("wind"), lit., "its windliness," or "its spirituality."

20. Or, "spirit" (Syr., rûḥâ). Given the reference in 1:5 and 1:6 to air and
fire, "wind" seems the better translation.

21. Syr., mappûḥîtâ ("puff of air"), which is derived from the verb pāḥ—to
breathe. The latter is the verb used in Gn 2.7, where God breathes life into Adam's nostrils. Ephrem alludes to this twice more in the hymn (1:11–12), as well
as at CH 48:3, 17, and 18.

22. 'îtyê saggî'ê. On the term 'îtyâ, and its plural form, see Beck, Die Theologie, 7–13.

23. Cf. CH 53:4, where this teaching is attributed to Bardaisan. While not
referencing this particular passage, Possekel has argued that Ephrem is influenced by Stoic theories of the soul, which divide the soul into seven parts, with
an eighth resting above them (Evidence, 190–92). See also the Testaments of the

One has extolled and increased its nature; one has
  impoverished and diminished its substance.
[1:9] And if the soul wanders, [they say that] dreams cause
  it to wander.
Thus, the debaters wander around investigating [the soul],
  which they have abandoned.
[So] who can discuss that Child who cannot be discussed?
[1:10] Come and marvel at him who says, concerning the soul,
  "it does not exist."
For, the soul, {since it dwells within him},[24] has argued, by
  means of itself, against itself.[25]
It has rejected itself if it has affirmed, concerning itself, that
  it does not even exist.[26]
[1:11] The soul, which has never explored whether it exists or
  does not exist,
Cannot perceive itself. It does not understand that its mouth
  has blasphemed it,[27]
Nor can it investigate him by whom it was created.[28]
[1:12] Nevertheless, the soul is visible in the word, which
  is its mirror.
In this word, the soul is able to see itself,

Twelve Patriarchs, "Testament of Reuben" (TReu), in which humanity is made
up of three groupings of "seven spirits"—the first grouping is responsible for
the "deeds of youth" (TReu 2:2); the second accounts for "every human deed"
(TReu 2:3–4). With these are commingled seven "spirits of error" (TReu 3:2–
7). On top of these, finally, rests an eighth spirit, "sleep" (TReu 3:8) (in *The
Old Testament Pseudepigrapha, Volume 1: Apocalyptic Literature and Testaments,* ed.
James H. Charlesworth [New York: Doubleday, 1983], 782–83). I would like to
thank Matthew Thiessen for the latter reference.

24. BC. A, "since it dwells within itself."

25. Ephrem depends upon *napšâ*'s basic sense of "breath." Taking this literally, the breath (*napšâ*) that is evident when one says "the soul does not exist,"
ironically testifies to its existence. He will reference this idea more directly in
1:12.

26. These lines are terse, but Ephrem's meaning is clear: if the soul did not
exist, one would not be able to deny its existence. Thus, the very denial of its
existence depends upon that existence which is being denied. The terseness
of the lines, moreover, may be intentional, so as to suggest the impossibility of
arguing about things that are unknown.

27. That is, if it says that it does not exist.

28. Cf. Gn 2.7, and the following stanza.

While in that word its honor is greater than the dumb beasts.[29]

[1:13] Moreover, though the soul exists, it does not exist self-consciously.[30]

And how could it not exist: see how it is evident in its operation?

And though its existence comes from its Creator, it has perished on account of its freedom.[31]

[1:14] If, therefore, the soul has so thoroughly refused the truth about itself,[32]

And, having denied its very self, has not perceived its [own] greatness,

Then by what means can it confess how something truly exists?[33]

[1:15] And if, through the discussion of its substance,[34] the soul has slipped away,

What will you investigate through debating? What will you arrive at through investigation?

Since it is far-off, you have come to something that is hidden.[35]

---

29. "This word" refers to the spoken word, in which the soul/breath can "see itself." "That word" is an oblique reference to Gn 2.7, which Ephrem has already alluded to in 1:7 and 1:11. Commenting upon Gn 2.7 in his *CGen.* 2:4, Ephrem writes, "Even though the beasts, the cattle, and the birds were equal [to Adam] in their ability to procreate and in that they had life, God still gave honor to Adam in many ways: first, in that it was said, *God formed him with his own hands and breathed a soul (napšâ) into him.*"

30. Syr., *b-'îda'tâ*, lit., "with knowledge."

31. BC read "will" (*ṣebyānâ*) instead of "freedom" (*ḥîrûtâ*), though the two concepts are closely allied in Ephrem. For a discussion, see Nabil el-Khoury, "Willensfreiheit bei Ephraem der Syrer," *Ostkirchliche Studien* 25 (1976): 60–66.

32. Namely, that it exists (1:12), that it is from God (1:13), and that "it has perished on account of its freedom" (1:13).

33. Syr., *'a(y)k d-'îtaw(hy) šarrîrâ'ît*, which could also be rendered "how *he* truly exists," referring to God, or even the subject in which the soul dwells.

34. Syr., *qnômâh*, which can function either as a reflexive pronoun ("self"), or in reference to the substance of a thing.

35. Thus the argument that Ephrem began in 1:4 reaches its rhetorical point. In his relentless discussion of the soul, it has "slipped away." The soul, as he told us in 1:4, represents something "nearby," and through the evidence of something "nearby," we can arrive at an understanding of something "far-off." Importantly, his discussion of the soul has not taught us *about* the soul. Rather, in discussing the soul, he finds only variance of opinion, self-contradiction, and, ultimately, destruction of what is being discussed. Here, then, he applies

[1:16] If, moreover, our knowledge knows that it does not
    know itself,

How do you presume to meditate upon the birth of that
    Knower-of-all?

How does a thing-made,[36] which does not know itself,
    investigate its Maker?

[1:17] Great is the nature that has never been spoken by
    any mouths!

The mouth which wishes to speak about him who is
    unspeakable,

Makes him small, for it is insufficient to his greatness.[37]

[1:18] All who wish to extol and magnify God,

[God], being majestic in his nature, magnifies the one who
    magnifies him.

Refrain from debating, which cannot comprehend him, and
    acquire silence,[38] which befits him.

[1:19] Enable me, my Lord,[39] to use both of these discerningly:

May I not debate presumptuously; may I not be silent
    impudently.

May I learn beneficial speech; may I acquire discerning
    silence.[40]

    The End.[41]

---

this to his original subject, the "Son's begetting," and the impossibility of in-
quiring into it (1:3). Moreover, unlike the soul, about which some things are evident (e.g., through perceiving our own breath), the "far-off" thing is "hidden."

36. Syr., *'bādâ*. On my translation of this term, see Introduction, p. 34, n.
144.

37. If the masculine pronouns in these last two lines still refer to "nature"
(as opposed to him whose nature it is), then they should be translated, "The
mouth which wishes to speak about *that which* is unspeakable, / Makes it small,
for he is insufficient to its greatness." Either option is possible.

38. Here we have the first mention of "silence," a virtue which Ephrem will
extol through the *HF*.

39. This Syriac phrase—*hab lî mār(y)*—functions as an almost formulaic petition in the hymns. See, for example, *HF* 35:1; 41:10; 48:1. *hab* is derived from
the verb *y(h)ab*, from which the noun *mawhabtâ* ("gift") is also derived. This
notion of "gift" and "giving" is crucial to Ephrem's understanding of his own
poetry: it functions as a divine "gift," which must then be lent out to others
(i.e., an audience). On this notion, see, e.g., *HF* 5:20.

40. Literally, "speech of benefit," and "silence of discernment."

41. C omits (B is illegible).

HYMN TWO

According to the melody, {"God, whom you have loved ..."}[1]

[2:1] Blessed is the one who[2] has hung a clear mirror of truth,[3]
And has seen within it Your Birth, which is greater than all
tongues!

> REFRAIN: *Glory to you, voice of your*[4] *Father!*

[2:2] Blessed is the one who has approached the knowledge
of truth,
And has learned through it that God is unsearchable for
humanity.
[2:3] Blessed is the one, my Lord, who has become the salt
of truth in this generation,[5]

---

1. BC. A, "God in his mercies," which appears elsewhere in the *HF* (hymns 26–30 and 79) attached to a different meter. The meter of this hymn, which continues through *HF* 3, is 7+7 / 7+7. Technically speaking, hymns 2 and 3 represent *mêmrê* rather than *madrāšê* (see Introduction, p. 13).

2. The entirety of the following two hymns (with the exception of 3:12, 14, and 15) follow this introductory formula, "blessed is the one who" (*ṭûb l-d-*). The phrase features prominently in the Syriac Bible, introducing Psalm 1 as well as the Beatitudes in Matthew 5. Indeed, Ephrem seems to envision these hymns as standing in a mimetic relationship with the Psalms. In addition to their echoing of the Psalm's introduction, Ephrem references David in 2:9 as an ideal hymnist. By connecting these hymns to David's psalms, Ephrem subtly crafts himself and his hymns as standing within a Davidic lineage—a lineage outside of which his opponents clearly stand.

3. On Ephrem's use of mirror metaphors, see Edmund Beck, "Das Bild vom Spiegel bei Ephrem," *OCP* 19 (1953): 5–24, and S. Brock, *The Luminous Eye*, 74–77.

4. Literally, "his." Ephrem very commonly shifts between 2d and 3d person in these doxological phrases.

5. On "this generation," see p. 57, n.7.

And whose faith has not lost its taste among the tasteless who
investigate you.[6]

[2:4] Blessed, too, is the one who has set a wall of silence
around his ear,

And the inquiries of the wise who fight against you have not
penetrated it.

[2:5] Blessed is the one who has secretly sprouted spiritual
wings,

And whenever debate has arisen on earth, he has abandoned
it and ascended to heaven.

[2:6] Blessed is the one who sails on his faith,

And away from the storms of schism he flees to the silent
harbor.

[2:7] Blessed, too, is the one who has perceived that his
mouth's word is inadequate,

And its womb[7] cannot comprehend[8] that indescribable Child.

[2:8] Blessed is the one who has turned his tongue away from
a matter not permitted him;

Blessed is the one who has chastened himself with what was
commanded him.

[2:9] Blessed is the one whose lyre has played the songs David
played:

Revealed things, without debating, and hidden things, without
investigating.[9]

6. See Mt 5.13; Mk 9.49–50; Lk 14.34–35. Interestingly, the Matthean version follows immediately from the Beatitudes, which utilize this same "blessed is the one" formula.

7. That is, his mouth, the "womb" from which his word proceeds.

8. In its Peal form, *spaq* means, *inter alia*, "to grasp, comprehend," but in its Pael form can mean "to vomit." Ephrem probably intends to echo both meanings, especially given the physical description of the mouth as a womb. In this reading, the mouth's womb would "vomit forth" the word, suggesting the undesirability of trying to communicate what cannot be communicated.

9. "Lyre" (*kennārâ*) forms one of Ephrem's favorite metaphors for himself, and one that echoes throughout these hymns. See especially *HF* 21–23. For the biblical and cultural background of the metaphor, and a study of its use in Ephrem, see Andrew Palmer, "'A Lyre Without a Voice': The Poetics and the Politics of Ephrem the Syrian," *ARAM* 5 (1993): 371–99, and J. Wickes, *Out of Books, A World: The Scriptural Poetics of Ephrem's* Hymns on Faith (Ph.D. diss., University of Notre Dame, 2013), 167–76. F. Cassingena-Trévedy touches

[2:10] Blessed is the one who everyday has made a balance of truth,

And has weighed all his inquiries on it, so as not to inquire after unnecessary things.[10]

[2:11] Blessed is the one who has made[11] a straight measure, which is set

By that of the Prophets and Apostles—a measure which righteousness has made.

[2:12] Blessed is the one who weighed his investigation with the benefits of his hearers,

And found it was neither too light (lest it be insubstantial), nor too heavy (lest it engulf).[12]

---

on the metaphor within the broader context of Ephrem's self-presentation in "Les «confessions» poétiques d'Éphrem de Nisibe," *Le Muséon* 121:1–2 (2008): 24–31.

10. "Unnecessary things" refers not to extravagant possessions, but to overly speculative modes of questioning.

11. In the Syriac, "has made" is followed by *leh,* made up of *l-*, which can either be the preposition "to, for," or a direct object marker, and *-eh,* which is the third person masculine pronoun. The *leh* can be taken three different ways: (1) as a direct object marker which introduces a new object, it can be translated "has made *him,*" in which case it would probably refer to Christ (see *Rhythms,* 111); (2) self-reflexively, so that it would be translated "has made for himself" (see *HF [G],* 6); or (3) as a direct object marker which anticipates "a straight measure," and is thus otiose in translation (as I have taken it). Option two or three would change the interpretation of the passage in no way. Option one would introduce the notion of Christ, established by the Old and New Testaments, as the measure of one's speech. While this is a reasonable idea to find in Ephrem, there are two problems with it: (1) in the previous and following stanzas, Ephrem is addressing measurement in a more general way, so it seems out of place suddenly to introduce the concrete reference to "him"; (2) the final stich of this stanza defines the measure as one which "righteousness has made." It seems odd to speak of Christ being a measure made by righteousness.

12. Ephrem here indicates a positive role for investigation. He offers similar affirmations in *HF* 2:18, 7:5, 12:11, and 17:5. In all instances besides 17:5, the term he uses is *b'â.* As we noted in the Introduction, this term, while typically synonymous with *bṣâ* ("to investigate"), can carry this positive valence (see p. 48). His emphasis on the beneficial speech, moreover, reflects a concern evidenced throughout the hymns. While here its connection to his own hymnody is implicit, he makes it explicit at 21:1. At 26:8 it is applied to the images that God uses to communicate in Scripture.

[2:13] Blessed is the one who has not crossed the boundary
lightly;[13]
Blessed is the one whose deliberation has labored to arrive
at a resting-place.[14]
[2:14] Blessed is the one who labored to investigate what he
could find;
Blessed is the one unwearied by investigation of the
incomprehensible.
[2:15] Blessed is the one whose tongue has become a zither[15]
for you;
He has played on it songs to heal those who hear them.[16]
[2:16] Blessed is the one, my Lord, who has acquired the
truth that stays the weak,
And his firmness[17] has become like a staff for the one whose
mind is infirm.
[2:17] Blessed, too, is the one whose teaching has become
good leaven,
And with it he has offered a strong taste to the fool who is
unleavened.
[2:18] Blessed is the one who has polished his investigation
like a mirror

13. See *HF* 64:12, where trespassing a "boundary" is specifically connected
with using non-scriptural language.

14. Within the *HF*, "resting place" (*âwwānâ*) forms a key aspect of Ephrem's
understanding of the means by which one comes to know God. Knowledge ac-
quisition is considered as a path that one must travel with great patience, taking
frequent rest in specific places God has provided. See *HF* 65:1 where Ephrem
identifies this "resting place" as "the apostles," and couples it with "mile markers" identified as "the prophets." On the appearance of the metaphor throughout Ephrem's corpus, see Edmund Beck, "Das Bild vom Weg mit Meilensteinen
und Herbergen bei Ephraem," *Oriens Christianus* 65 (1981): 1–39.

15. Syr., *qîtārâ* ("zither") is a less common noun than *kennārâ* ("lyre"), but
functions in a similar manner. See p. 64, n. 9.

16. Given the connection of "lyre/zither" and David, coupled with the allusion to David in *HF* 2:9, this stanza is reminiscent of 1 Sm 16.14–23. There is,
however, no lexical overlap between the two.

17. Syr., *šrāreh*, another word which means "truth," (like *qûštâ*—"truth"—in
the previous line), but which can also be translated "firmness" or even "stabil-
ity." The third person possessive pronoun attached to truth (here translated
as "his") could also be taken as "its," referring to the truth of line 1. See also
note 33 attached to 7:9.

For those lacking in faith,[18] so that with it they might wipe
    clean their stains.[19]

[2:19] Blessed is the one whose word has become like the
    medicine of life[20]

And has enlivened wordy dead men, who have exalted
    themselves above the enlivener-of-all.

[2:20] Blessed is the one who became mute when your birth
    was discussed;[21]

Blessed is the one who became a trumpet when your birth
    was declared.[22]

[2:21] Blessed is the one who knows, Lord, that the force of
    investigating you is harsh;

Blessed is the one who knows that the taste of speaking your
    praise is sweet!

[2:22] Blessed is the one, my Lord, who has not let his mouth
    become a passage

For the foolish questions which have sprung up among paltry
    debaters.

[2:23] Blessed is the one, my Lord, whose tongue has become
    a well-tuned[23] instrument,

And with it he has spoken the truth which proceeds from the
    Prophets and the Apostles.

[2:24] Blessed is the one who has not tasted the bitterness of
    the wisdom of the Greeks;

Blessed is the one who has not relinquished the simplicity of
    the Apostles.[24]

18. See Mt 6.30; 16.8; Lk 12.28.

19. As in 2:12, "investigation" is here given a very positive interpretation.

20. "Medicine of life" is a Christological title for Ephrem, which refers predominantly to Christ's presence in the Eucharist. See S. P. Brock, *The Luminous Eye: The Spiritual World Vision of Saint Ephrem* (Kalamazoo, MI: Cistercian Publications, 1992), 99–103. Ephrem's application of this metaphor to the hymnic word suggests the ritual capabilities of speech: just as Christ gives life in the bread and wine, so he gives life in the beneficial word.

21. Cf. Lk 1.18–20 and *HF* 9:8–9.

22. Note the distinction between "discussing" (*met'aqqab*) and "declaring" (*metmallal*): silence is not a virtue privileged in the abstract, but is an appropriate response to a certain type of speech, i.e., "discussion."

23. Syr., *šapyâ*, lit., "luminous."

24. On Ephrem's condemnation of Greek things, see pp. 24–25, 31, and 41–42, as well as *HF* 47:11, 79:3, and 87:4.

HYMN THREE

According to the same melody.[1]

[3:1] Blessed is the one, my Lord, who has become worthy to
   call you, with great love,
"Beloved Son,"[2] just as God Your Begetter called you.

   REFRAIN: *Glory to you, O Son of God!*

[3:2] Blessed is the one, my Lord, who has kept his mouth
   from all inquiries,
And has called you "Son of God," as the Holy Spirit called you.

[3:3] Blessed is the one, {my Lord},[3] who has become worthy
   of believing simply:
He calls you "Son," as all the Apostles and the Prophets
   called you.[4]

[3:4] Blessed is the one, my Lord, who knows that Your
   Greatness is incomprehensible,
And quickly checks his tongue, so that it honors your birth
   with silence.

[3:5] Blessed is the one, Lord, who has acquired a clear[5] eye
   with which he can see
How the watchers[6] fear you, and how humanity forges ahead.

---

1. See note 1 attached to melody of hymn 2.

2. See Mt 3.17; Mk 1.11; Lk 9.35 (the scene of Christ's Baptism), and Mt
17.5; Mk 9.7; Lk 9.35 (the scene of Christ's Transfiguration). On the importance of the name "Son," see pp. 34–37.

3. B.

4. For "Apostles," see, e.g., Mt 14.33. For "Prophets," see, e.g., Ps 2.7.

5. BC, "hidden."

6. "Watchers" (*'îrê*) is one of Ephrem's most frequent angelic titles. The
term has a long history prior to him, beginning in Daniel (see 4:13, 17, and
23). On its usage in Syriac literature, see Robert Murray, "The Origin of Ar-

[3:6] Blessed is the one, Lord, who stretched out his mind and
  considered you—
Creatures do not comprehend you—and gave thanks that he
  was deemed worthy for you to dwell with him.
[3:7] Blessed is the one, Lord, who knows that you are God—
  the Son of God.
And he knows himself—whose son he is, that he is mortal—
  the son of a mortal.
[3:8] Blessed is the one who has discerned that your Begetter
  is Adonai.[7]
He has called to mind, too, his own birth—that he is a son of
  Adam, of dust.[8]
[3:9] Blessed is the one who has discerned that the watchers[9]
  praise you in silence,
And has immediately rebuked himself, for how hasty his
  tongue has been!
[3:10] Blessed is the one who has perceived that heaven above
  is quiet,
And earth below is troubled, and has quieted himself amidst
  the waves.
[3:11] Blessed is the one who has learned, Lord, that the
  Seraph cries holy and falls silent,
But {the scribes}[10] just investigate. Abandon the scribes and
  choose the Seraphim!
[3:12] And who would not marvel that though you sit upon
  the right hand,
Dust, which sits upon the dust upon a dung-hill, investigates
  you?[11]

---

amaic *'îr*, Angel," *Orientalia* 53 (1984): 303–17, and idem, "Some Themes and
Problems of Early Syriac Angelology," *OCA* 236 (1990): 143–53.

  7. Syr., *'adwny*.

  8. Syr., *'aprānâ* ("of dust"). This term (and the term *'aprâ*, from which it is
derived) comes ultimately from God's creation of Adam in Gn 2.7. Within the
HF, it becomes one of Ephrem's favorite metaphors for humanity, being derived
from Scripture and indicating so succinctly humanity's status *vis-à-vis* God.

  9. See note 6 attached to 3:5.

  10. Syr., *sāprê*, BC. A, *srāpê*, "seraphim." On Ephrem's depiction of the
scribes, see Shepardson, *Anti-Judaism*, ch. 4.

  11. Cf. 1 Sm 2.8; Ps 113.6–7. Note that this stanza, as well as 3:14 and 15,

[3:13] Blessed is the one who has recognized, Lord, that you are in the womb of Essence,[12]

And has recalled that he himself has fallen into the womb of the earth, his Begetter.

[3:14] Who will not marvel, Lord, that though you are the Creator of all created things,

Humanity seeks to investigate you, though it does not know itself—what it is.

[3:15] This is a wonder, Lord: you alone know your Father,[13]

But low-down dust, my Lord, is so arrogant as to investigate your Father along with you.

[3:16] Blessed is the one, Lord, who has become divine in his way of life[14]

So that whenever he has sanctified himself, he calls you God, Son of God.

The End.[15]

---

breaks the *ṭûbaw(hy) l-aynâ* formula. Andrew Palmer has argued on this basis that these stanzas arose as later glosses. See his "Interpolated Stanzas in Ephraim's Madroshe III–VII on Faith." *Oriens Christianus* 93 (2009): 1–27.

12. Syr., *'îtûtâ*. When speaking of God's "being," Ephrem typically uses two terms, both derived from the Syriac *'ît*, "to be": *'îtyâ*, which I translate as "Being," and *'îtûtâ*. Because the latter is an abstract noun, I translate it as "essence," or "existence," though Ephrem often uses it as a proper noun. Both of these nouns are connected in Ephrem's mind to the divine name revealed in Ex 3.14. On these terms, see Beck, *Die Theologie*, 5–13; Lange, *Portrayal*, 121–23, and Possekel, *Evidence*, 55–59.

13. Cf. Mt 11.27; Lk 10.22; Jn 10.15.

14. Syr., *dûbāraw(hy)* ("his way of life").

15. BC omit.

HYMN FOUR

According to the melody, "On the birth of the Firstborn . . ."[1]

[']² [4:1] A thousand thousands stand;
Ten thousand ten thousands hasten—
Thousands and ten thousands—
To the One they cannot investigate.
All of them in silence
Stand to serve.
No one shares his throne
Except the Child who is from him.
Investigation of him exists within silence.
Whenever the watchers³ go to investigate,
They arrive at silence and are kept back.

{REFRAIN: *Glory to your Father who sent you!*}⁴

[b] [4:2] The firstborn entered the womb
And the pure [woman] did not suffer.
He moved and went forth with pangs

---

1. The meter of these hymns consists in indeterminate variations of five-
and six-syllable lines, forming eleven-line stanzas. Thus, the meter of 4:1 is
6+6+5+6+5+6+6+7(?)+5. The meter of 4:2 is 5+5+5+5+5+5+5+5+6+6+6.
The meter of 4:3 is 5+6+5+6+5+5+5+6+6+6+6.

2. *HF* 4:1–3, 7, and 11 are repeated verbatim in the *HNat,* as hymns 21:20–
24. See also note 14 attached to 7:5. This hymn forms an acrostic on the Syriac alphabet, though inconsistently executed: stanzas 6–9 do not fit with the
acrostic, while stanzas 4, 5, 10, 11, and 12 are all *dālat* (the fourth letter of the
alphabet), and stanzas 13 and 14 are both *he* (fifth letter). The hymn then
ends on *ṭēt* (only the ninth of 22 letters), and hymn 5 resumes the acrostic (see
note 2 on hymn 5).

3. See n. 6 attached to 3:5.

4. BC.

And the fair [woman] felt it.
Glorified and hidden is his entrance,
Lowly and revealed his exit.
For he is God in his entrance,
And human in his exit.
It is a wonder and a bewildering thing to hear:
Fire[5] entered the womb,
Put on a body[6] and went forth.
[g] [4:3] That Chief of Messengers,
Gabriel, called him, "My Lord."[7]
He called him "my Lord" to teach
That he is his Lord, not his companion.
For Gabriel there is
Michael, a companion.
The Son is the Lord of things-made.
His nature is great, just like his name.
A thing-made is not able to investigate him,
For as great as it may be,
Greater is the one who made it.[8]

5. "Fire" functions in Ephrem as a metaphor for divinity, often affiliated with the Spirit (see *HF* 10:8 and 40:10). On this aspect of Ephrem's thought, see Brock, *The Luminous Eye*, 38–39.

6. "Putting on a body" forms one of Ephrem's most prominent metaphors for speaking of the Incarnation. See S. P. Brock, "Clothing Metaphors as a Means of Theological Expression in Syriac Tradition," in *Typus, Symbol, Allegorie bei den östlichen Vätern und ihren Parallelen im Mittelalter,* ed. by M. Schmidt (Regensburg: Pustet, 1982), 11–40.

7. Ephrem alludes to Lk 1.28. Unlike the Greek New Testament, where Gabriel simply exclaims "*The* Lord is with you" (ὁ κύριος μετὰ σοῦ), in P he says to Mary "*our* Lord is with you" (*māran 'ammek[y]*). Ephrem takes this as a literal reference to the child who is now within Mary's womb, and Gabriel's statement then reads as a confession of the child's lordship. By extension, the proclamation signals Gabriel's own recognition of the gap between himself and Mary's child.

8. Ephrem does not explicitly quote Prv 8.22, but given his awareness of the importance of that verse in the Christological controversies (as clearly evidenced by hymn 53), he surely has it in mind here. Moreover, in this stanza Ephrem poetically articulates an important aspect of his thought, namely, the divide between Creator and creatures, and the placing of Christ firmly on the side of the Creator. On this, see Ayres, *Nicaea and its Legacy,* 231–32; S. Brock, *The Luminous Eye,* 26–27.

[d] [4:4] It is astounding that the mind,
Whenever it readies itself,[9]
To crack open and look upon your splendor,
Your smallest glimmer emerges,
Scatters, and dispels it entirely.
Who shall gaze upon your birth?
For the dreadful rays—
All of them are crowded together in all of it.[10]
He is the sun whom the prophets proclaimed—
"Healing in his wing,"[11]
But pain in his investigation.[12]
[d] [4:5] Though with hands we touch you,
A subtle mind[13] is not
Able to touch or investigate you,
Even though you are a great mountain.[14]
Though with ears we hear you—
In thunder you are dreadful—
You are quiet, inaudible,
Silent, unheard.
Though one might see you with the eye—
Since your light has dawned—
Your appearance[15] is hidden from all.

9. Syr., *kanneš ḥyāreh,* lit., "gathered its sight."

10. On the expression "crowded together" (*sbîsîn*), see 4:10, 71:16, and 74:1.

11. Mal 4.2.

12. Note the symbolic development of this hymn, which demonstrates the overlap between natural and scriptural metaphors in Ephrem: from the beginning of the stanza, "sun" is the implied metaphor for the mystery of Christ's birth. The metaphor is initially only hinted at through the words "splendor," "gleam," and "dread rays." It is finally stated outright in the antepenultimate line, at which point the natural metaphor is explicitly connected to Scripture, namely, to Malachi's prophecy that "the sun of righteousness shall rise, with healing in its wings."

13. Syr., *med'â d-qaṭṭîn.* In the *CH* 22:4 Ephrem describes Aetians as "subtle," using the verbal form of the adjective—*qaṭṭîn*—which he uses here. On this term and its relationship to Aetius, see p. 24.

14. See n. 10 attached to 1:3.

15. Syr., *ḥzātâ,* which Ephrem uses again in 4:6 and 8. At *HF* 7:3, moreover, Christ is said to hide "his appearance" under a "veil of flesh." We might then say that *ḥzātâ*—appearance—refers to that aspect of Christ, which, following

[?]¹⁶ [4:6] Your appearance was not greater
Than only the weak,
Nor your investigation hidden [from only them].
Rather, the body's senses,
Because they desperately need
New senses, which are within—
Within thought—
Not even small things
Have they confined by means of investigation.
Instead, let us inquire about the watchers¹⁷
Who draw near to your gate.¹⁸
[?] [4.7] When the watchers stand
Before you with songs,
They do not know which
Side to look upon you.¹⁹
They sought you above, on high;
They saw you below, in the deep.
They searched for you within heaven;
They saw you in the abyss.²⁰
They looked for you alongside him who is worshiped;
They found you within creation.
They descended to your side and sang praise.
[?] [4:8] When they began to seek
Your appearance within creation,
They did not hastily arrive
At an understanding²¹ of your investigation.

4:4, utterly dispels the mind. We can certainly call this "divinity," but we should understand the term broadly, as denoting everything in Christ that is beyond human understanding.

16. 4:6–9 does not fit within the acrostic.

17. On watchers, see note 6 attached to 3:5.

18. Conceptually, 4:6 brings the reader back to 4:1, since what is described in 4:1, namely, the angels standing before God, is what is offered here as an antidote to failed inquiry. The following stanza, then, stands as something of a replay of 4:1.

19. See *HF* 81:2.

20. Cf. Gn 1.2 (P).

21. Syr., *la-mqām 'al b'ātāk*. On the translation of *qām 'al* as "to understand," see *LS*, under *qām*, 5c., 1331, col. 1.

Though they saw you in the deep,
They saw you above on high.
Though they saw you in the tomb,
They saw you inside the bridal chamber.[22]
Though they saw you dead,
They discovered you, the one who resurrects.[23]
They marveled, they wondered, they ceased.[24]
[?] [4:9] Your symbols, Lord, are everywhere,
Yet you are hidden from everywhere.
Though your symbol is on high,[25]
What you are cannot be perceived.[26]
Though your symbol is in the deep,
What it is cannot be understood.
Though your symbol is in the sea,
You are hidden from the sea.
Though your symbol is on dry land,
What you are is unknown.
Blessed is the hidden one who has appeared!
[d] [4:10] Even your smallest symbol
Is a font of symbols[27]—
And who can explain
Symbols which never wane?
When a human receives your likeness,[28]

22. On this metaphor, see Brock, *The Luminous Eye*, ch. 7.
23. Syr., *mnaḥḥmānâ*, a substantivized participle from *naḥḥem*, to resurrect.
24. That is, ceased investigating, or, generally, trying to understand the paradoxical mystery.
25. Syr., *b-rawmâ*, lit., "in the height."
26. Syr., *lâ rāgeš d-'a(n)t-û*, lit., "it does not perceive what you are." Beck takes "height," from the previous line, as the subject of "to perceive" (*rāgeš*), thus translating the clause, "[The height] does not perceive ..." (*HF [G]*, 11). See also Brock's translation in *The Luminous Eye*, 55, which follows Beck. I have taken this as an impersonal construction, which Ephrem utilizes again in lines 6 and 10 of this stanza.
27. Regarding the phrase "font of symbols" (*mabbû'â*), Ephrem expresses a similar idea in *HF* 81:1, though using a different term (*m'înâ*). And *m'înâ*, in turn, appears in the present stanza, in line 6.
28. Cf. Gn 1.26, where God says, "Let us make a human (*'nāš*) in our image (*b-ṣalman*), according to our likeness (*dmûtan*)." We have "your likeness" (*dmûtāk*) here, and "your image" (*ṣalmāk*) below, in line 9 of 4:10.

It becomes for him a fountain,
Letting flow every likeness:
Upon that we are able to gaze.[29]
Your image is in our heart.[30]
In your one venerable icon,[31]
A myriad of beauties are crowded together.[32]
[d] [4:11] You are a complete marvel,
On all the sides into which we search for you.[33]
You are near and far,
And who can arrive at you?
Investigation's reach
Is unable to come to your side.
Whenever it has reached out to come [to you],
It was cut off and fell short.
It stands beneath your mountain.[34]
Faith reaches [you],
And love, with prayer.[35]
[d] [4:12] It is easier for us to think
Than to speak a word.
Thinking—which is able
To stretch out everywhere—
Whenever it sets off
On your road, toward your investigation,
Its path disappears in front of it.
It becomes confused and stalls.
If thinking is so defeated,

29. That is, we can look at things revealed, but we cannot look at the source of their revelation.

30. BC "Thus, let us depict your image in our heart." On the "heart" in Ephrem, see *HF* 26:10.

31. Syr., *yûkānâ*, a calque on the Greek *eikōn*.

32. See n. 10 attached to 4:4.

33. See *HF* 81:2.

34. Literally, "is shorter than your mountain." "Your mountain" (*ṭûrāk*) follows 1:3 and 4:5. The phrase could also be rendered "it is shorter than your size" (*ṭawrāk*). See above, n. 10 attached to 1:3.

35. We have already seen in 2:18 a caveat to Ephrem's typical condemnations of investigation. These last two lines provide further evidence of such a stance.

How much more a word,
Whose path [lies] amidst confusion?
[h] [4:13] It is fitting for the mouth
To give praise, and then to be quiet.
And when it refuses to rush,
It takes refuge entirely in silence.
Therefore, one can understand
If one has not hurried to understand.
The one who is quiet has greater understanding
Than the hasty one who hurries.
The ignorant one, who has investigated,
Look: that weak one toils,
For the dreadful sea is treacherous.[36]
[h] [4:14] Lord, look: if a mouth
Has ceased from investigating you,
It has not [necessarily] done a good thing.
Whoever is able to investigate but has turned away,
His weakness has restrained him,
While his presumption has imprisoned him.
It was a good thing
When he decided to keep quiet.
Then silence became his vessel,
So that he did not perish in your sea,
And in your unceasing flood.[37]
[w] [4:15] If it is possible for us to investigate,
Come! Let us investigate the hidden one!
Come! Let us wander around and explore him
If he can be perceived!
You have been revealed, Lord, to the children,[38]

36. The "sea" (*yammâ*), because it is vast, full of mysterious life, and because it is from here that the pearl comes (see hymns 81–85), forms one of Ephrem's favorite symbols of the incomprehensibility of God. Ultimately, within Ephrem's use of the metaphor stands an *a fortiori* argument: if you cannot comprehend the sea, how can you comprehend God?

37. The sense of this stanza is difficult to understand. Following 4:13, Ephrem seems to be juxtaposing two ideas of silence, one born of virtue, and one born of weakness and presumption.

38. Cf. Mt 19.13–15; Lk 18.15–17; *HF* 7:7.

But hidden from the crafty.[39]
To the one who believes, you are found.
To the one who investigates, you are concealed.
Blessed is the one who is
Simple when it comes to your investigation
And clever when it comes to your promise.[40]
[z] [4:16] Investigation is too small, my Lord,
{To contain}[41] you within it.
{A power}[42] which reached every place
Would be able to investigate you—
To depict you on high,
And explore you in the deep.
But since it has not come to every place,
It cannot investigate you.
Blessed is the one who perceives
That in the womb which bore you,
All your investigation dwells.[43]

39. Cf. Mt 11.25.

40. "Promise" (*mûlkānâ*) is used in a very general sense in the *HF* (see, e.g., 5:17; 22:4). At 56:3, however, Ephrem refers to Isaac as "the son of the promise," and at 53:9 he refers to the "land of the promise." It thus seems likely that this pentateuchal resonance, albeit interpreted christologically, stands behind the more general usages, such as the one we have here.

41. Syr., *teḥbšāk*, BC. A, *teḥšbāk* ("to reckon").

42. Syr., *ḥaylâ*, BC. A, *šelyâ*, "quiet." Both readings make sense. I have gone with BC ("power") because it makes more sense, given that "quiet" is usually juxtaposed with "investigation." Here, however, it would offer a means of investigation.

43. Both Beck and the ER take the penultimate line as a reference to the Father's begetting of the Son (the ER even interpolates *yālûdâ*—"begetter"—to erase any ambiguity). The following stanza, 4:17, provides potential justification for this, in that it appears to be a hymn to the Father. Given, however, that the hymn thus far (especially in the first three stanzas) has offered a reflection on the ineffability of both the Father's begetting of the Son, as well as Mary's birth-giving, it seems likely that these final three stanzas continue that reflection, and that Ephrem intends to invoke the wombs of both the Father and of Mary. Note, for example, that the verb Ephrem uses here for "to dwell" (*šrâ*) is the verb he usually uses to refer to Christ's dwelling in Mary's womb (Brock, *The Luminous Eye*, 111–12), and that the concluding blessing of this stanza echoes Lk 11.27 (albeit with different vocabulary than either P or the Old Syriac versions preserve). Equally, it would be strange for Ephrem to refer to the Father's womb as something "confined."

[ḥ] [4:17] The Seraph, which flies and wheels,
Is too frail to investigate you.
Next to you, its wing is too weak
To reach the extent of your greatness.
Worlds reside in your womb—
How far we have wandered inside a confined [place]!
The Seraph, whose voice cries "holy,"
Honors your investigation with his silence.
Woe to him who has scorned [it]!
For, look: the Seraph before you
Covers its face with its wings.[44]
[ṭ] [4:18] The Cherubim carry
The power which carries the Ark.[45]
The [Cherub] lowers his eyes,[46]
As he hides
Beneath your chariot in awe.
[The Cherub] is afraid to look inside it.
They bear [it] but are not able to investigate [it].
Though near, they are far-off.
Blessed is the one who has learned
Your glory from them:
He sings praise then keeps dreadful silence.

44. See Is 6.2.
45. See, *inter alia,* Ex 25.18–22; 1 Sm 4.4 (where the Lord is identified as "enthroned on the cherubim").
46. BC maintain the verb in the plural, so as to preserve consistency with the opening and closing lines. But, then, these manuscripts keep the singular in lines 4–7. I have followed A, despite the awkward changes in number.

HYMN FIVE

According to the same melody.[1]

[y][2] [5:1] The watchers' knowledge
Investigates in a measured way.
Human knowledge
Wanders around without measure.
Your compassion has placed on your path
Resting-places and mile-markers[3]
So that confused investigators
May travel in an ordered way.
Blessed is the one who has {measured}[4]
His journey[5] alongside his knowledge,[6]
In order to come to a resting place.

> REFRAIN: *Glory to you, my Lord Christ!*

[y] [5:2] Human knowledge
Compared with the knowledge of the watchers

1. See note 1 attached to melody of hymn 4.
2. Hymn 5 continues the acrostic of hymn 4 (see note 2 attached to 4:1).
3. See note 14 attached to 2:13.
4. Syr., *mšaḥ*, BC. A, *meškaḥ,* "to be able; to find."
5. Syr., *ṭāwrâ*, literally means "extent; territory, boundary" (*LS*, 521, col. 1, sub. *ṭāwrâ*). In the context of this stanza, lines 9–11 function as a gloss on lines 3–8. Ephrem casts the human quest for knowledge as a path through an unknown landscape: if unaware of their inborn limitations, humans will fail to take proper notice of mile-markers (which indicate where they are on the path) and resting-places (which give them respite from the long journey). In this context, *ṭāwrâ* refers to the "extent" one has to travel, an extent which must take into account the practical limitations of human knowledge. A looser translation might render this "Blessed is the one who has measured / the distance he has to go alongside his knowledge ..."
6. C, "his walking."

80

Is like the dim twilight.
Even more, the knowledge of the watchers
Compared with the knowledge of the Spirit
Is like a tiny flash.
The Spirit said concerning the Son,
"Who shall declare his generation"?[7]
Presumption wishes
To hasten across the border.
The Spirit arrived and fell silent.
[k] [5:3] When the watchers {wish}[8]
To learn things about the Son,
They send out questions
To those more exalted than they.
And those noble ones
Are taught by the gesturing of the Spirit.[9]
The ranks of the watchers are just like
The questions of the watchers.
There are none among them who presume
To reach out toward something
Which is greater than it.[10]
[l] [5:4] Nature bears witness to this
In its ordering:
Rank passes on rank
All the way up to the crown.
So too Jethro's advice
Established ranks,
Step by step
Up to Moses.[11]
The lowly human ranks

7. Cf. Is 53.8, though where Ephrem has *šarbteh* ("his generation"), P has *dāreh* ("his age" or "generation").

8. Syr., *neṣbûn*, BC. A, *nebṣûn*, "to investigate."

9. Here we have a basic angelic hierarchy: first "watchers" (*'îrê*), then "noble ones" (*rawrbê*), leading up to the Spirit. The "gesturing of the Spirit" refers back to the Spirit's question in 5:2:8. See also note 6 attached to 3:5.

10. Literally, "which is greater than its size." The word for size—*mšûḥteh*—is the same translated as "measure" in *HF* 5:1.

11. Ex 18.13–27.

Trespass the ranks of watchers,
When they come to investigate the firstborn.
[l] [5:5] My Lord, it is not because you are envious[12]
That your works are smaller than you.
[Rather], a thing-made[13] cannot
Be equal to its Maker—
Dreadful blasphemy!
If it could be equal,[14]
Then the servant would be the companion of its master,
And the master a friend[15] to his servant.
Blessed is the one who {has perceived}[16]
That the Lord, in his love, bent down
And as a servant clothed himself with his servant.
[l] [5:6] As for the Maker, he cannot
Be compared to what he has made,
For not even the names
Of the two agree.
And more than the names,
The substances do not agree.
The Lord, in his love, wanted
To confer his names upon his works.
Priests and kings, by grace,
Put on your titles,[17]
And Moses and Joshua, your names.[18]

12. Literally, "because of your envy" (*men ḥsāmāk*).

13. "Thing-made" (*'bādâ*) and "servant" (*'abdâ*) both derive from the root *'-b-d*, "to make, do" (see p. 34, n. 144). In this line, I have translated it as "thing-made" because it is juxtaposed with *ābûdâ*, "maker." In lines 7 and 8, however, where it is juxtaposed with *mārâ*, "Lord," or "master," I have translated it as "servant."

14. Lines 5–6 could also be punctuated as follows: "It would be a dreadful blasphemy / If it could be equal."

15. While "companion" (*ḥabrâ*) and "friend" (*knātâ*) have informal connotations in English, for Ephrem the terms imply categorical similarity. To call servant and master "friends" or "companions" would place them both on the same side of the Creator-created distinction. On these terms, see especially *HF* 6:8–12.

16. BC.

17. Syr., *kûnāyê*. See n. 18 immediately below.

18. Syr., *šmāhê*. Ephrem here refers to "borrowed names" as "titles" and to

[m] [5:7] Merciful is the Lord,
Who has put on our names,
Even to the point of humbling himself
And being depicted as a mustard seed.[19]
He has given to us his names;
He has taken from us our names.
{His names have made us great.}[20]
Our names have made him small.
Blessed is the one who has spread
Your good name over his own name,[21]
And adorned his own names with your name.
[n] [5:8] Let nature be for us a crucible[22]

"true names" as "names." See pp. 36–37. In 5:6–7, Ephrem articulates the basic theory of names that emerges throughout these hymns. As Ephrem presents it, scriptural language can be divided into two categories: "borrowed," which belongs properly to humanity, but which God puts upon himself so that humans can comprehend him to some degree, and "true," which belongs properly to God, but which he puts upon humans so that they can share in his glory. See also *HF* 30 and 60–63. As for Moses and Joshua putting on the Lord's names: Joshua "puts on" Jesus's name, insofar as the names "Jesus" and "Joshua" are identical in Syriac (*yešû'*). Moses "puts on" the name of God in Ex 4.16, where he is told that he will be Aaron's God (*'allāheh*).

19. Ephrem's statement that the Lord "depicted himself as a mustard seed" is curious. The phrase "mustard seed" occurs three times in the Syriac versions of the New Testament, namely, in Mt 13.31, Mk 4.31, and Lk 13.19. In each of these passages, however, it is the "Kingdom of God" (Lk 13.19; Mk 4.31) or "Kingdom of heaven" (Mt 13.31; *CDia* 11:20) to which the "mustard seed" is likened. Beck (*HF [G]*, 15, n.8) thus rightly points out that the sense of 5:7 is actually closer to Jn 12.24, where Christ likens himself to a "grain of wheat," which "if it dies, bears much fruit" (*HF [G]*, 15, n.8). Metrically, the two phrases are identical in Syriac, and there is no textual evidence to suggest that Ephrem had a New Testament version that combined the synoptic and Johannine readings. Perhaps Ephrem is aware of both the synoptic and Johannine passages, and has simply conflated them in his hymn; or, he could be reading "Kingdom of heaven" as co-extensive with Christ.

20. BC.

21. Ephrem uses this same metaphor with a negative sense in *CH* 24:17: "The name 'wolves' they have spread over sheep, / and they have clothed doves with the name 'hawks.'"

22. This metaphor of the "crucible," or "furnace" (*kûrâ*) occurs frequently in Ephrem's writings, and he uses it to describe a number of different things. For example, in *CJ*, it refers generally to the time of the Roman-Persian battle

For the word of truth.[23]
Look: the sun has revealed
Everything to the whole eye.
Nothing which [the sun] has concealed even in part
Can [the eye] investigate.
[The sun] has revealed everything to [the eye],
But [the eye] is unable to investigate[24] [the sun].
Your concealed birth has revealed
A hundred times more than the sun.[25]
Who will gaze upon your brightness?[26]
[s] [5:9] Think, too, about
That hostile sea—
It is not something hidden far off.[27]
Look: though many sailors
Move within it,
They cannot comprehend its expanse.
Ten thousand also dwell within it—
Powers, natures, and messengers.[28]
Everything inside of it,

---

over Nisibis, and, more broadly, to the entire reign of Julian, in which true Christians could be separated from the false, as in a crucible (see *CJ* 1:13, 2:2:24, and 4:1). In the *HF*, it can be used with the sense of trial (36:17), or as a metaphor for the baptismal font (39:4), or even to describe a person in whom various views are tested (48:2).

23. That is, to test and determine what is true.

24. BC, "to see."

25. Beck renders this, "Your concealed birth is a hundred times more revealed than the sun" (*HF [G]*, 15). Ephrem, however, has emphasized the sun as something which makes visible, but is itself not visible (that is, it cannot be looked at). If we extend that metaphor, then the point is that Christ's hidden birth has revealed a hundred times more than the sun has, and just like the sun it cannot be directly looked upon.

26. BC, "strength."

27. On Ephrem's argument from "something near-by," cf. *HF* 1:4. On the metaphor of the "sea," see note 36 attached to 4:13.

28. "Messengers" (*mal'akê*) can also be translated "angels." Moreover, both "powers" (*haylê*) and "natures" (*kyānê*) can function as names of angels. "Sea," then, functions as a metaphoric double of the heavenly court—a lesser version, which is nevertheless unknowable. On angels, see notes 6 and 9 attached to 3:5 and 5:3 respectively.

Look, dives down and springs back up.
And none can investigate it.
['] [5:10] So too this common air
Is mingled with everything.
Our breath depends upon it,
Without breaking it up.[29]
It enters us and leaves,
As if it were not within us.
The hand grasps it,[30]
But what is under [the hand] remains untouched.
It flees without leaving.
It is both in [a thing] and not in [a thing].
It depicts, but cannot be depicted.
['] [5:11] Breath passes through bodies.
They are bound by it, even as they are free.
For, wherever they wish to turn,
They come and go inside of it.
Everything depends upon one breath.
It carries all without growing tired.
Inside its fullness [all] dwell,
And they dwell as in an empty [space].
Great is that which partly conceals!
Look: it is hidden, though not concealed
For it veils itself with itself.
[p] [5:12] The metaphors of air
He has made [to be] colors[31] for you.[32]
With them he depicts for you the likeness
Of the imageless Being,[33]
Who is both near to us and yet far-away.
And though he is within us, he is not [within us].

29. Lit., "without breaking its bond."
30. Lit., "falls upon it."
31. Syr., *sammānê,* which could also mean "medicine."
32. That is, Ephrem has used these air metaphors to paint a picture of how God can be both known and unknown. While he has crafted nature rhetorically, he ascribes this rhetoric to God. Thus, his rhetorical reading of nature represents merely an uncovering of the reality that is always present.
33. Lit., "without being depicted."

Though creation is in him,
It is not as though he is inside of it.
Though there is nothing that can
Veil him inside of itself,
He can conceal it with himself.
[ṣ] [5:13] We have depicted for our salvation[34]
The unsearchable Being.
Let us not go about speculating;
Let us head straight for silence.
If a blind man speculates about
Whether to touch a coal,
Its brightness will not help him,
But its strength will hurt him.
So too, the hidden Essence
Humbles its investigator[35]
But magnifies its worshiper.[36]
[q] [5:14] The Son is near to his Father
In glory, as in name.
Just as he is near in two,[37]
He is not far in the third:
Since the Father cannot be investigated,
The Son cannot be investigated.
Whoever wishes to investigate the Firstborn
Wishes to investigate the Father.
Disputing over the Child is a bridge,
Which, if someone crosses over,
He crosses over to investigate the Father.[38]
[r] [5:15] Think of someone who wants
To rush to investigate fruit:
Investigation hastens
To the root which begot [the fruit].

---

34. Syr., *ḥayyê*. On *ḥayyê* as "salvation," see *LS*, 444, sub. *ḥayyê*, n. 2.
35. B, "investigators."
36. B, "worshipers."
37. That is, "glory" and "name."
38. So the likeness of Father and Son is demonstrated by the fact that neither can be investigated, because investigation of the Son leads to investigation of the Father.

The Son is a treasure, in whom there is
Investigation as well as riches.
Your investigation is for the presumptuous;
Your treasure is for the merchant.[39]
Wonder at both of them:
Misery fills your investigation;
Good is hidden in your mercy.
[š] [5:16] The fruit dropped and came down to you:
Taste it with love.
Its sweetness will gladden you;
Let its investigation not harm you.
The medicine of life can
Also be medicine of death.
Take from him what he has brought,
And give to him what he will receive.[40]
Take from him and give to him.
Take the mercy he has brought.
Give to him works that he will receive.
[t] [5:17] Give thanks to the One who brought a blessing
And received from us prayer.
Since the Venerable one came down to us,
He has made worship ascend from us.
Since he gave divinity to us,
We have given humanity to him;
As he brought a promise[41] to us,
We have given faith to him—
That of Abraham his friend.

---

39. Within the *HF*, the language of "treasure" stands alongside several other economic terms (e.g., "gift," "loan," "credit," "interest," "debit"). This broad nexus of economic language enables Ephrem to conceptualize his hymnic speech as a loan from God, which he can both repay and gain interest on by "loaning" to his audience, i.e., delivering his hymn. *HF* 5:25–20 trace the outlines of this economic metaphor. See also 10:1 and 22; 16:2–5; and 25. Gary Anderson situates these economic metaphors within a broader Near Eastern context in *Sin: A History* (New Haven: Yale University Press, 2009), esp. ch. 9. See also notes 39 and 42, attached to 1:19 and 5:17 respectively.

40. On *nawbel* as "to receive," see *Thes. Syr.*, vol. 1, 1539, sub. *'awbel*.

41. See note 40 attached to 4:15.

Since we lent him alms,
Let us demand it back again.[42]
[t] [5:18] Give thanks to the hidden light
Through the ray which is from it.[43]
It is difficult for the eye of the soul
To see the secret light.
Through the splendor which is from it,
[The eye] can go near it.
He sent a ray from himself
To those sitting in darkness.[44]
He turned their eyes aside
From the beauty which withers
To the beauty of the One who sent him.
[t] [5:19] [There is] a marvel and a wonder in our
        generation:[45]
Wounds on our body,
Bruises on our soul,
Sores on our spirit.
For, instead of seeking
Which medicine is appropriate for us,
We have speculated among ourselves about our Healer,
So as to investigate his nature and his birth.
O how bitter our sorrow!
For with the healing which banishes our pain
We have harmed ourselves!
[t] [5:20] May your faith be
Rennet[46] in my thinking.

---

42. The verb "to lend" (*'awzep*) in line ten can imply, in addition to the loan itself, a degree of interest amassed on the loan. Ephrem draws out this implication in the final line of this stanza: the sense is not only to demand divine repayment of the human loan, but repayment with interest accrued. This sense of interest will then be made explicit in 5:20. On this passage, see also Anderson, *Sin*, 155–57. See also notes 39 attached to 1:19 and 5:15 respectively.

43. In 5:14, Ephrem articulated the idea that investigation of the Son passes directly to the Father. Here, it is thanksgiving which, directed at the Son, passes directly to the Hidden Father.

44. Is 9.2.

45. On "our generation," see note 7 attached to 1:1.

46. Syr., *mst'*, which could be vocalized *msâtâ* ("rennet"), or *mestâ* ("abun-

May it gather my dispersed mind
From discussing and wandering.
I will knock, Lord, at your door,[47]
That you might {drop down}[48] to me, as alms,
Your gift, which unexpectedly
Will come and enrich my poverty.
Though I owe ten thousand talents[49]
You make me a creditor,
So that I lend you what belongs to you.[50]

---

dance," etc.), BC. I have taken it as *msātâ* ("rennet") because it preserves the six-syllable meter, and makes more sense within the context: rennet is a congealing agent, and likewise faith "gathers." See also *HF* 25:20. A, *masa'tâ*, "scale."

47. Cf. Mt 7.7.
48. BC, *tešdê*. A, *tešrê*, "to reveal."
49. Mt 18.24.
50. See *HF* 1:19, 5:15, and 5:19.

HYMN SIX

According to the same melody.[1]

[']² [6:1] How can someone
Miss the truth?
For truth is a great mountain
Visible even to the blind.
Who does not perceive
That the Father has a Son?
He did not need to beget him,
For the one who begot him does not lack.
He was not begotten for [any other] reasons.[3]
It was the Father: in his love
He begot the glorious Son.[4]

1. See note 1 attached to melody of hymn 4.
2. Here begins another acrostic on the Syriac alphabet. It concludes with *yod*.
3. "Reasons" (*'ellātâ*) is the subject of "to beget." Literally, the line reads, "Reasons did not beget him." This follows from the previous point—that the Father did not beget the Son out of necessity—and anticipates the following— that the Father begot him solely on account of love. Thus, Ephrem's point is that the Father begot the Son for *no* reason other than love.
4. Ephrem here distinguishes between begetting out of necessity and begetting out of love. This distinction is common in the fourth century outside of Ephrem. See esp. the "Long-lined Creed," which emphasizes the freedom of the Father's begetting (Kelly, *Early Christian Creeds,* 3d ed. [New York: Continuum, 1972], 279–81). The "Long-lined Creed," typically interpreted as an anti-Nicene document, represents the official position of the church of Antioch in the 340s. Ephrem's position here corresponds to that document. At the same time, on the pro-Nicene side of things, Athanasius's *Against the Arians* 3:62–66 counters claims that the Father begot the Son out of necessity, but the immediate distinction he draws is not between necessity and love, but between necessity and being. As part of his argument, however, he frequently

REFRAIN: *Glory to the womb of your Father!*[5]

[b] [6:2] The eye is too weak to gaze upon
The great strength of the sun.
[The sun] allays its severity,
And eases its strength.
Its ray is dispersed,
It descends to the eye.
Except for the Child of the Hidden One,
No one has seen the Hidden One,[6]
For he is stronger[7] than his works.[8]
Through his Child he is seen—
The Being which is unseen.[9]
[b] [6:3] His stunning strength
Has been softened in the ray that came from him.
He did not become weak in any way;
He became sweet to us when he was softened for us.
We have compared him with a ray,
Though this is not his image,
Since there is nothing which can depict him with accuracy.[10]
With images let us depict him,
So that, according to our strength, we might learn him
Through his blessed benefits.
[b] [6:4] In the bread is eaten
The might which cannot be eaten.
In the wine, again, is drunk
The strength which cannot be drunk.[11]
With the oil we measure

---

does reference the place of love between Father and Son, especially in 66. I
would like to thank Brian Daley, SJ, for pointing this out to me.
    5. BC, "Glory to the Hidden One who has been revealed!"
    6. Cf. Jn 1.18.
    7. C, "more concealed."
    8. "Works" is *'abdaw(hy)*. The same noun occurs in Prv 8.22, "he created me
at the beginning of his creation, before all his *works*" (P). By echoing Prv 8:22,
Ephrem makes the point that the Son, because he has seen the "hidden one,"
stands on the side of the Father *vis-à-vis* the things he has made.
    9. Cf. Col 1.15.
    10. On the relationship between God and images, see esp. *HF* 31:11.
    11. Cf. *HF* 10:8.

The power which cannot be measured.[12]
And just as [food] {is softened}[13] in the mouth
During a meal, and [a person] eats it,
He has softened his appearance for the eyes.
He has softened his strength in words
So that the ear can hear him.
[b] [6:5] Of things conceived, you are most astonishing.
Of things begotten, you are most glorified.
Of the baptized, you are the most renowned.
Of saviors, you are the most envied.
In sacrifices, you are slain.
In a meal, you are eaten.
Within the Prophets, you are mingled.
Within the Apostles, you are mixed.
All of you, my Lord, in everything!
In the deep you are buried,
And on high you are worshiped!
[b] [6:6] In the beginning, things-made[14]
Were created by means of the Firstborn.[15]
For "God said,
'Let there be light,'" and it was created.[16]
To whom did he command,
When, look: there was nothing?
When he commanded the light,

---

12. The word here translated as *mšaḥ* can mean either "to measure" or "to anoint." *Mešḥâ*, "oil," is derived from this verb. The sense of the passage is this: "With oil we convey the power which cannot be conveyed [with oil]." Following the Eucharistic allusions in lines 1–4, Ephrem here refers to baptismal anointing. As has been shown, within the Syriac liturgical tradition these anointings, which preceded and followed the immersion in water, were emphasized over the immersion itself. On this, see Sebastian Brock, "The Transition to a Post-Baptismal Anointing in the Antiochene Rite," in *The Sacrifice of Praise: Studies in Honour of A. H. Couratin,* ed. Bryan D. Spinks, 215–25 (Rome, 1981), and Gabriele Winkler, "The Original Meaning of the Prebaptismal Anointing and Its Implications," *Worship* 52 (1978): 24–45. On oil in Ephrem, see especially *HVir* 4–7.

13. Syr., *'etrkak,* BC. A, *'etkrak,* "to be surrounded."

14. On "things-made," see n. 144 in the Introduction.

15. Gn 1.1.

16. Gn 1.3.

He did not command it, "Be!"
But he said, "Let there be!"
Indeed, the word is different—
"Be" from "Let there be." [17]
[g] [6:7] He revealed and explained the Firstborn
When he created Adam:
"Let us make a human being
In our image, according to our likeness."[18]
It would be blind to think
That he spoke [those words] to Adam.
[Rather,] he who gave him life through the wood [of the cross]
In the last millennium—the sixth—
Fashioned [Adam] in the beginning,
Also on the sixth day,
When [Adam] provoked anger through the wood [of the tree].
[d] [6:8] Or, if we think to claim[19]
That he commanded the watchers,
It would clearly be presumptuous,
For it would render a servant a partner
And companion with its Lord.
Were it fitting for a servant,
How much more fitting would it be for the Son—
Who ministers to the voice[20] of his Father—
To be able to complete,
With a voice, what is made,[21]
And creation with a word?

---

17. Ephrem is here distinguishing the Syriac imperative *hway* ("Be!") from the imperfect, *nehwê* ("Let there be," or "there will be"). Whereas in lines 3–4 and 11, Ephrem quotes the Genesis text verbatim, in line 9, where he distinguishes the imperative from the imperfect, he renders the biblical *nehwê* as an infinitive absolute (*nehwê mehwâ*), so as to distinguish it all the more from the imperative. On a theological level, this grammatical analysis enables him to posit creation as a mediated act.

18. Gn 1.26.

19. Lit., "Again, to think and to say ..."

20. BC pluralize "voice," which could thus be rendered "his words."

21. *ʿbādâ*, "what is made," reflects an alternate vocalization of the same noun (*ʿbdʾ*) translated in lines 4 and 6 as "servant" (*ʿabdâ*). Consequently, "what is made" could be "servant," and vice versa.

[h] [6:9] This is something to debate:
Why did God
Speak through words,[22]
And then a thing came to be?
Was his will too weak
To create silently?
Or, did the voice which spoke
Become embodied and [then] things came to be?
Both of these are defeated,
A third is victorious:
He commanded the Second.[23]
[w] [6:10] And should someone say
That God commanded a thing-made
To be created,
This [suggestion] is abrogated by Adam.[24]
For he did not say to him,
"Let us make a human being in our image."[25]
He neither spoke to [the human's] companion,[26]
Nor did he command what he had made.
It would not be fitting for a thing-made
To come into being through its equal.[27]
All of them were created by the Son.
[z] [6:11] A thing-made is too small to create
Creation, alongside its Creator.

22. C, "a word."

23. On the Son as "second," see *HF* 23:13 and 43:4.

24. Ephrem is mocking a subordinationist position. That is, if (a) the Son mediates in creation, but (b) he is himself a thing-made, it then follows that at some point the Father would have commanded the Son (a creature) to create himself—the Son would need to mediate his own creation. Not only is the position logically absurd, but as Ephrem will argue in lines 4–6, it would place Christ as an equivalent to Adam. In Ephrem's reading, Gn 1.26 can thus be taken as a refutation of the position: he did not command Adam to create himself, and thus he did not command the Son to create himself.

25. Gn 1.26.

26. That is, a created thing.

27. That is, if Christ is a "thing-made," and yet all agree that Christ functioned as a mediator at the time of creation, how would it be fitting for him—a creation—to bring other creatures into being? That all relevant fourth-century parties did agree that Christ was creator, see Anatolios, *Retrieving Nicaea,* 37.

There is not some other Being
Who could be like a partner to him.
"Thing-made" and "friend" have fallen short.[28]
The {only}[29] Child has risen up,
For he is not commanded like a thing-made,
And is not equal like a companion:[30]
His Child comprehends his voice.
Blessed is the Being who softened
The strength of his voice through his Child.
[ḥ] [6:12] Now look upon the Firstborn,
Who is different from {companions},[31]
And distinct from things-made.
He is higher and more humble:
He is raised above things-made,
And lowered beneath companions.
He is neither counted among things-made,
Nor reckoned alongside companions.
Above both of them he is exalted.
The Child is not a work,
And the Firstborn is not a companion.
[ṭ] [6:13] Fully revealed is the truth
To the one who wishes to see it:
The six days that were created
Bear witness to the six sides:
They proclaim the four corners,
And the height and the depth.[32]
He did not command works
To make themselves.[33]
By means of one another, [works] were created:

28. That is, Ephrem has proved that neither of these are possibilities for divine mediation at creation.

29. BC. A lacks "only," and thus its sixth line is two syllables short.

30. That is, "equal" to other things that have come into being.

31. Syr., ḥabrê, BC. A, "his companion" (ḥabreh).

32. Cf. CH 3:6.

33. Obviously, Ephrem is reading Genesis's six days of creation as an allegorical representation of the fullness of the world. It is not clear to me, however, how this then affirms that God did not command works to create themselves.

The Father commanded with a voice,
The Son brought the work to completion.
[ṭ] [6:14] It is clear that if
He commanded the earth, "let it bring forth,"[34]
It was fitting, in terms of a command,
That he speak with her who was of the earth
As he spoke to Eve:
"You will bear with pains."[35]
[But] instead of saying, "it shall bring forth,"[36]
He said, regarding [the earth], "He caused to grow."[37]
His Son sowed and planted.
In the one Tree of Life,
The planter depicted his[38] likeness.[39]
[y] [6:15] He knew to show
How he spoke with the waters,
As he knew to show
How he spoke with Cain.
While he said, "Let [the waters] bring forth swarms,"[40]
He could have said, "Bring forth swarms."[41]
The saying which is for them[42]

---

34. Gn 1.11.   35. Gn 3.16.
36. Gn 3.18.   37. Gn 2.9.
38. That is, Christ's.

39. Ephrem is reading the first and second creation accounts together (Gn 1.1–2.3 and Gn 2.3–3.24) so as to show Christ's direct role in the planting of the Tree of Life. So, in the case of Gn 1.11 (alluded to in line 2) and 3.16 (alluded to in line 6), Genesis depicts earthly things playing an active role in their own propagation (in 1.11, the earth "puts forth vegetation," and in 3.16, Eve "brings forth children"). In both of these verses, the earthly/human forms the active subject of the verbs used. In Gn 2.8 and 9, however, there is a different grammatical arrangement: in these verses, it is the Lord God who is the active subject: he "caused to grow" (Gn 2.9, and line 8 above). Ephrem thus reads this christologically: while the earth and Eve have an active role in various aspects of creation, it is Christ himself ("the Lord God") who plants "the tree of life, and the tree of the knowledge of good and evil" (Gn 3.9; lines 9–11).

40. Gn 1.20.

41. That is, he could have created the waters in an unmediated fashion, but he chose to do it through a mediator.

42. That is, for created things.

Is different from [the one] for the other.[43]
The beautiful Child he told
To create beautiful fish
And fair birds.[44]
[y] [6:16] The Knower-of-all made sure
To reveal clearly his Firstborn
Through the making of Adam.
He saw that, more than all things-made,
The son of Adam would turn aside.
He revealed his Son openly,
So that whoever denied the Firstborn
Would slay his father Adam,
Who by means of the Firstborn was created.
Though he was not with him, he created him.
And when he had sinned and gone astray, he called
    out to him.[45]
[y] [6:17] O Jesus, glorious name!
Hidden bridge for crossing
From death to life!
To you I have arrived and stood—
By a *yod*—your letter—I am kept back.[46]
Be a bridge for my word,

43. That is, for the Son.

44. As far as I can tell, the allusion to Cain does not depend upon any spe-
cifics of Gn 4.1–17. Rather, Ephrem's inclusion of Cain in this passage seems
to be simply a rhetorical way of distinguishing creatures from the Creator (Father and Son). The way God speaks to creatures—whether it be the water or
Cain—is fundamentally different from the way he speaks to the Son.

45. Gn 3.9.

46. *Yod* (y) is the first letter of the name Jesus in Syriac, and this stanza
begins with a *yod*. As the final stanza in an incomplete acrostic, this line reveals it to be an intentionally abandoned acrostic. Ephrem's cessation on the
letter *yod* thus represents his unwillingness to go beyond Christ in his investigation of the divine hiddenness. Or rather, it represents the indispensability
of Christ in approaching the Father. On this, see A. Palmer, "Restoring the
ABC in Ephraim's Cycles on *Faith* and *Paradise*," *The Journal of Eastern Christian
Studies* 55 (2003): 147–94, and idem, "Words, Silences, and the Silent Word:
Acrostics and Empty Columns in Saint Ephrem's *Hymns on Faith*," *Parole de
l'Orient* 20 (1995): 129–200.

So that it might cross to your truth.
Let your love serve as a bridge for your servant—
In you I will cross to your Father.
I will cross over and say, "Blessed is he
Who has softened his strength through his Child!"

The End.[47]

47. BC omit.

HYMN SEVEN

According to the same melody.[1]

[']² [7:1] Who has strayed from himself,
Ignorant of his own thought,
So that he declares[3] the nature of the Firstborn?
Who can investigate
The Lord of natures,
In whose hand natures exist?
The one who exists in him
Cannot [even] investigate his own nature.[4]
Thus, by his very self he is rebuked.
For, not comprehending himself,
How can he comprehend his Lord?

> REFRAIN: *Glory to your concealed Child!*

[p] [7:2] A simple sign is before us—
It is great, clear, and near.
The one who wishes to toss it aside,
Slips and falls.
And if no one can toss aside
The sign which is near,
Who can toss aside
The hidden {sign}[5] which is far-off?
We cannot understand his humanity:

1. See note 1 attached to melody of hymn 4.
2. The first five stanzas of this hymn form an acrostic on Ephrem's name, after which any acrostic features disappear.
3. Cf. Is 53.8 and *HF* 5:2.
4. For a similar argument, see *HF* 1:4–17.
5. "Sign," BC.

Who could understand
His hidden divinity?[6]
[r] [7:3] He bent down and covered his appearance
Behind a veil of flesh.[7]
With a shard of his light
All the Jordan was illumined.[8]
When he shone even a little on the mountain,
They {trembled}[9] and swayed and were terrified[10]—
Those that the Apostle reckoned
The three pillars.[11]
According to the measure of their power,
He offered them a glimpse
Of his hidden glory.
[î] [7:4] The sea saw him[12] and shook.
Its waves crashing,
It lowered its back and carried him[13]—
Better than a foal it bore him.

---

6. 7:2 extends and rephrases *HF* 1:4. Whereas, however, in 1:4 the human soul is the sign that is "near," here the sign—the thing near—is Christ's humanity. In the remainder of hymn 7, Ephrem will weave together New Testament scenes in which various characters and natural phenomena respond to the humanity of Christ with awe and wonder. As a whole, these stanzas trace out the argument *a minore ad maius* which Ephrem articulates here: if, as these New Testament scenes attest, humans cannot comprehend the revealed flesh of Christ, how will they comprehend his humanity?

7. This covering "with a veil" foreshadows *HF* 8:1–6, in which Ephrem reflects upon the veil of the transfigured Moses (Ex 34.29–35).

8. Mt 3.13–17; Mk 1.9–11; Lk 3.21–22. In the biblical account, the Jordan is not illumined. This reflects, instead, Ephrem's notion of the "robe of glory," which Christ deposits in the Jordan at the time of his baptism. On this theme, see S. Brock, "Clothing Metaphors as a Means of Theological Expression in Syriac Tradition," in *Typus, Symbol, Allegorie bei den östlichen Vätern und ihren Parallelen im Mittelalter,* edited by M. Schmidt, 11–40 (Regensburg: Pustet, 1982). Poetically, it also anticipates the allusion to the Transfiguration, which occurs in the next line.

9. Syr., *ratt[w],* BC. A, *rtaḥ[w],* "they grew hot" or (metaphorically), "they were deeply moved."

10. Mt 17.6 and parallels.

11. Cf. Gal 2.9.

12. Cf. Ps 114.4, which will be echoed again in *HF* 8:13 and 9:1.

13. Mt 14.22–36; Mk 6.45–52; Jn 6.16–21.

When he was sitting in the boat,
The shipmates supposed he was human.
When he descended and subdued the sea,
Those on board were astonished by him.
They did not investigate him at all,
They simply marveled at him:
They glorified and stood silent in awe.
[m] [7:5][14] And the Magi, too, sought him.[15]
And finding him {in a manger},[16]
Instead of investigation, worship
They offered him silently.[17]
Instead of useless schisms,
They gave him offerings.
You, too, seek the Firstborn.
And when you have found him on high,
Instead of convoluted discussion,
Open your treasures before him,
And offer to him your works.
[7:6] Come and marvel at those[18]
Who saw the King humbled
And neither discussed nor investigated[19]—
None of them debated.
Pure faith
Shone there in silence.[20]
The Magi, when he[21] was humbled,

14. This hymn is quoted verbatim in *HNat* 21:25. See also note 2 attached
to *HF* 4.

15. Mt 2.1–12. Here Ephrem uses the verb *b'â* (typically "to investigate," but
here translated "to search") with a positive valence. See n. 12 attached to 2:12.

16. Syr., *b-'ûryâ*, BC. A, *b-'ûrḥâ*, "on the road."

17. Mt 2.1–12.

18. Lit., "at the humans."

19. The word here translated as "to investigate"—*b'â(w)*—is the same word
which in the previous stanza Ephrem uses in a positive sense: "The Magi …
sought him."

20. Ephrem suggests a juxtaposition between "faith" and "investigation."
The latter evidences the absence of the former. Ephrem will develop this connection in 7:7, and will articulate it most clearly in *HF* 9:10 (see notes 32–33
attached there).

21. That is, Christ.

Did not presume to investigate.
Who will presume to investigate
Now that he has ascended and sits
At the right hand on high?
[7:7] Neither did the thief debate.
He believed without investigating.
The son of the left hand did debate—
His debating cut off his hope.[22]
The scribes debated and fell,[23]
Along with Herod, who questioned him.[24]
Satan tested him:
He wished to know who he was.[25]
To none of these who disputed
Did the Messiah give himself,
As he gave [himself] to the children.[26]
[7:8] The star stood above him,[27]
Declaring without controversy:
"He is the light of the peoples,"[28]
For they have seen truth in him.
The Spirit, in the form of a dove,[29]
Stood over him when he was baptized.
She, without questioning, shows
That he baptizes with fire.[30]
A voice called out clearly,
"This is my Son and my beloved."[31]
That voice checks investigation.
[7:9] They refused these signs
Which prevented investigation
And gave respite to the soul,
Which believes without labor.
The Pharisees questioned,

---

22. Lk 23.39–43.
23. BC, "The scribes who debated fell."
24. Lk 23.7–12.
25. This is most likely a reference to Mt 4.1–11 / Mk 1.12–13.
26. Cf. Mt 19.13–15; Lk 18.15–17.   27. Mt 2.9.
28. Is 42.6; 49.6.   29. Mt 3.16; Mk 1.10; Lk 3.22.
30. Mt 3.11; Lk 3.16.   31. Mt 3.17; Mk 1.11; Lk 3.22.

"Who is this? Whose Son is he?"[32]
Insofar as they investigated the truth,
They fell from the truth.[33]
Insofar as they investigated the truth,
They destroyed it, through investigation of it:
Everything is supported by faith.[34]
[7:10] The centurion became great
{When}[35] he marveled at him as God.[36]
With faith he honored him,
And did not let him enter.
He honored his entrance,
But you honor investigation of him.
Since in our day we cannot impede
His revealed entrance,[37]
Impede and honor his investigation,
So that, before the watchers on high,

---

32. Cf. Lk 5.21; Mt 22.42.

33. I have translated two different terms as "truth": in line 7, Ephrem uses *šrārâ*, and in lines 8 and 9, he uses *qûštâ*. These two terms are used together elsewhere in the *HF* and, as here, do not seem to carry any difference in meaning (see *HF* 2:16, where I translate *šrārâ* as "firmness," and 13:9; 7:9; 8:4; 22:2; 26:3; and 27:3).

34. B and C switch lines 8 and 9.

35. Syr., *d-*, B.

36. Mt 8.5–13. There are two possible readings of these first two lines, both of which present problems. The problem with the rendering I have given above is that it makes the centurion the subject of "to marvel" (*thar*), whereas in the scriptural account it is Jesus who marvels at the centurion (Mt 8.10). This difficulty can be overcome, however, if we assume that Ephrem is playfully twisting the scriptural account, especially given that lines 3 and 4 preserve the same structure of centurion (subject) / Jesus (object). The lines, however, could also be rendered, "The centurion became so great / that God marveled at him." Making Jesus (here called "God") the subject of "to marvel" and the centurion the object would accurately represent the scriptural scene. The problem here, however, is that, in all the other instances where Ephrem calls Christ "God" (*'allāhâ*), it is qualified in some way (e.g., 3:7, "Son of God"; 4:2, coupled with "man"; in 6:6, and throughout hymn 6, it is ambiguous whether it refers to Father or Son, or both, etc.). This line would represent the only occurrence in which the word "God" refers to Christ, and stands as a grammatical subject without ambiguity and without qualification.

37. That is, because Christ is no longer on earth in the body.

He will praise your faith.
[7:11] Weigh them together—
The centurion who believed,
And Judas Thomas[38]
Who wished to touch and investigate.[39]
His Lord praised the former.
His teacher rebuked the latter.
If he is to be blamed who presumed
To investigate and [only] then believed,
Then shame awaits the one
Who wishes first
To investigate. How will he come to believe?[40]

38. On the identification of Thomas as "Judas Thomas" in Syriac literature, see Drijvers, "The Acts of Thomas," 324.

39. Jn 20.24–29.

40. Syr., *'aykan nhaymen*. B and C change *'aykan*—"how"—to *hāydên*, "then."
The sentence then reads: "... who wishes first / to investigate, and then believes." This reading, however, simply repeats the sense of lines 7 and 8, i.e.,
that someone who first investigates and *then* believes is to be shamed. Ephrem,
however, is clearly constructing an *a fortiori* argument, which moves from both
Thomas (the stronger) to Ephrem's own audience (the weaker), and from *then*
(when Christ was physically available) to *now* (when he is physically absent; cf.
7:10:7–9). Thus, by asking, with A, "*How* will you investigate?" Ephrem con-
trasts the time of Thomas with the time of his audience, and the stature of
Thomas with the stature of his audience: unlike Thomas, they cannot investigate because of the Lord's physical absence, and because they are far less
than Thomas.

HYMN EIGHT

According to the same melody.[1]

[8:1] O the splendor of Moses
Upon which no one could look![2]
The spectators were unable
To look upon a mortal:
Who will presume to look upon
The awesome Life-giver of all?
If the splendor of a servant
Possessed this strength,
Who will gaze upon his Lord?
Mount Sinai, when it saw him,
Smoked and burned before him![3]

REFRAIN: *Glory to the mercy which sent you!*

[8:2] The circumcised[4] were unable
To look upon the glory of Moses.
A veil stood[5]
Between his splendor and the People.
Instead of a veil which has worn out,[6]
The brilliance of living fire

---

1. See note 1 attached to melody of hymn 4.
2. Ex 34.29–35; 2 Cor 3.7–18. Ephrem does not explicitly quote 2 Cor 3 in this hymn, though his rhetorical reading of Moses's transfiguration parallels 2 Cor 3 in many ways.
3. Ex 19.18.
4. Syr., *gzîrê*. B, *zîzâ*, "strong."
5. Lit., "ministered."
6. Note the similar idea in 2 Cor 3.13, though there it is Moses's splendor that has faded.

Non emp

Encircles the chariot,
So that the Cherubim need not fear.[7]
But for you, quiet and silence:
Let it be for you a curtain,
So that you do not glare at his splendor.
[8:3] No one approached the area[8]
Behind the revealed veil
To investigate the splendor of the servant,
Who dwelt inside of it.
Whenever Moses went to look [inside the tent],
All the tribes trembled.[9]
How much more awesome is investigation
Inside of which your story is hidden?
If you should look [only] at the watchers,
Heaven and the highest heaven[10]
Would be terrified before you!
[8:4] By Moses's veil,
Your shining truth was hidden.
By his stutter was hidden
Your clear[11] explanation.[12]
Under two coverings
Were hidden your truth and your speech.
You have drawn aside the veil
And fixed[13] the stammering.
You have been revealed entirely.
Look: your truth[14] is spoken by the mouth
And your reality[15] is revealed to the eyes.
[8:5] The veil of his face
And the stammering of his mouth:

7. Cf. Ezek 1.4 and 13; 1 Chr 28.18; Sir 49.8.
8. Lit., "womb / of ..."
9. Ex 33.10.
10. Dt 10.14; 1 Kgs 8.27; Neh 9.6.
11. Syr., *mlîlâ;* lit., "rational," "speech-endowed."
12. Gn 4.10.
13. Lit., "straightened out" (*pšaṭṭāh*). C, "explained" (*pšaqtāh*).
14. Syr., *qûštâ*. See note 33 attached to 7:9.
15. *šrārāk*.

Both coverings
Covered the blind People.[16]
[But] to the just ones you were revealed—
Those who desired to see your day.[17]
But the deniers[18] of our day
Are blinded by a veil.
They stammer; they cannot see.
They are blind to your beauty
And silenced[19] by the interpretation of you.[20]
[8:6] He has depicted parables
Through Moses for fools.
Two coverings
Were spread over the crucifiers.
Truth has dawned clearly:
Let us not grope in darkness!
Let there be no investigation among us—
It is another veil.
Beauty has gone forth openly.
Do not be like {that}[21]
Which is like its father in everything!
[8:7] The priest entered
The holy of holies in silence,
Only once per year;[22]

16. Cf. 2 Cor 3.13–15.

17. Cf. *HNat* 1:20; Jn 8.56.

18. Syr., *kāpûrê*, refers here to subordinationists (who are connected with Moses's ancient audience), but can also refer to Jews and pagans (e.g., in *CJ* 1:4).

19. Lit., "muzzled."

20. In Ephrem's reading, Moses's veil represents the obscure truth—the truth without interpretation. Once the interpretation is revealed, the "deniers" (ancient and modern) are rendered silent (lit., "muzzled"). The veil over Moses has thus morphed into a veil over the people. The one whom the "just ones" wanted to see (line 5, 8.5) is now visible, but the deniers (the "investigators" of Ephrem's own day) cannot see, because this veil now covers them. In the final line, however, the veil becomes a muzzle, rendering these Jews/investigators speechless: they cannot articulate the correct interpretation, but it is also this interpretation which has rendered them incapable of speech.

21. Syr., *meddem*, BC. A, *'ādām*, "Adam."

22. Cf. Heb 9.7 and Lv 16.34.

He entered with fear.
If that dwelling place
Was entirely distinguished,
Who will presume to investigate
The power which dwelt inside of it?
Let us render honor
To the investigation of the Firstborn,
For he is the Lord of truth.[23]
[8:8] Two hundred and fifty priests
With censers were burned up,[24]
For they wished to seize
The priesthood of Aaron,
And those of the house of Korah
Wished to become priests.
If the priesthood of Aaron was this dreadful,
How much more dreadful is the Lord of priests,
Who ministers[25] with his own blood?[26]
Who will presume to investigate him?
[8:9] There was great terror when, unexpectedly,
The sons of Aaron were burned up.
A strange fire
They dared to bring in, and they were burned up.[27]
Who then will escape

23. C, "the holy."

24. Nm 16. Ephrem identifies these figures as "priests" (*kāhnê*), even
though in P they are simply identified as *rîšê da-knûštâ*, "leaders of the synagogue." The misidentification is probably ironic, insofar as the story involves
these figures' attempt to usurp the Aaronic priesthood. It is also likely that
this line contains a covert polemic against certain bishops of Ephrem's own
time. (As is clear from, e.g., *CNis* 13–14, 18–19, and 21, *kāhnâ*—priest—functioned as a title for a bishop in Ephrem's time.) Elsewhere, in *HF* 53:2 and
87:23, Ephrem clearly criticizes the bishops of his own day. In the immediate
context, *HF* 8:8–11 all rewrite scenes of ritual transgressions from the Old Testament involving "priests." These biblical scenes, then, become literary figures
of the investigation of Ephrem's own opponents. By weaving together all these
biblical scenes of priests, Ephrem most likely intends to allude covertly to the
situation in which he and his audience find themselves.

25. Syr., *d-kahhen*, "who performs the priestly service."

26. Cf. Heb 9.12.

27. Lv 10.1; Nm 3.4 and 26.61.

The great fire
Which has entered into the Church—
Strange investigation!
In the Church there is
Investigation which discusses revealed things.
There is no investigation of hidden things.[28]
[8:10] Uzzah, the chief priest,
When he tried to steady [the Ark], was thrown down.[29]
What he was commanded, he did not do.
What he was not commanded, he did.
Concerning the Ark, they commanded him
To carry it upon his shoulders.[30]
He stretched out his hands to steady
The power which steadies all.[31]
He thought that the Ark
Was about to fall.
When he steadied it, it killed him.
[8:11] Do not honor what is holy
In a way not commanded you.
Uzzah did show honor,
But his honor was a disgrace.[32]
Do not, desiring truth,
Investigate[33] and disgrace the Firstborn.
Do not think that the faith,
Which steadies those cast down,
Is about to fall.[34]

28. Lines 8–11 could also be rendered, "Strange investigation / There is
in the Church. / Investigation is for discussing revealed things. / It is not for
investigation of hidden things." Either way, these lines suggest a redeemable
sort of investigation—investigation of what is revealed. For a similar idea, see
HF 2:12, 18, and 4:11.

29. 2 Sm 6.6–8. The verb *'estaḥḥap* ("was thrown down") also carries the
sense of "overturned." Thus, Uzzah unwittingly adopts the very characteristics
which led him to steady the Ark in the first place.

30. Cf. Nm 7.9; 1 Chr 15.2.

31. Cf. *HF* 4:18.

32. 2 Sm 6.6–8.

33. Syr., *tebṣê*. B, *teṣbê*, "wish to disgrace …"

34. Note that 8:10 and 11 apply identical language to the Ark and to

Do not steady the faith like Uzzah,
Lest it destroy you in anger.
[8:12] The disgraceful tyrants
Honored the Ark
As they tested its power.[35]
With offerings, they venerated it.[36]
Dagon was cast down before it;
It cut off his limbs.
How much more should we honor the Gospel,
Before which the Evil One has been cast down,
Severed by its power?
Let us meet it with offerings,
For it has healed our wounds.[37]
[8:13] The Jordan, too, saw
The Ark and was divided.[38]
Though it had run forward,
It fled backwards.
It flowed unnaturally,
For it saw the Lord of natures.
If the Ark was so dreadful,
Which had [only] tablets inside,
How much more dreadful is investigation?
Who will draw near to it?
For the Lord of the tablets is hidden inside it.
[8:14] Daniel saw

---

faith. Whereas elsewhere in these hymns, Ephrem's typology has worked on a spectrum of less to more—from "Ark" to "the Lord who resides in the Ark"— here the figuration is one of equivalence: the Ark equals the faith. "Faith" thus represents that within which the Lord resides.

35. That is, the Philistines. The following stanza draws on 1 Sm 5 and 6.

36. "Testing its power" presumably refers to the episode in 1 Sm 5, as do the following lines on "Dagon." "Venerated it with offerings," on the other hand, refers to 1 Sm 6.

37. Ephrem appears to refer to the physical Gospel book, given the connection he makes to the story in 1 Sm 5–6. While it is not clear what sort of offerings he has in mind, the last four lines suggest a talismanic or apotropaic use of the book.

38. The episode is recorded in Jos 3.13–17, but also commemorated in Ps 114.3, along with the crossing of the Red Sea. Ephrem patterns this line on the Psalm verse, though removes the allusion to the Red Sea. See also 7.4 and 9.1.

The wondrous beasts.[39]
He saw, too, the Ancient
Of Days, sitting in glory.[40]
He approached the beasts
To ask and learn.
The glory of the Exalted One he did not
Approach to see.[41]
Fools abandon creatures
And hasten to the Maker,
To investigate who he is.
[8:15] Daniel saw
One of the watchers[42] and was terrified.[43]
He did not approach in order to investigate.
He was not fit to hear his voice;
Daniel could not
Even hear [the messenger's] voice.[44]

---

39. Dn 7.3.
40. Dn 7.9.
41. Instead of "to see," ms B has "for investigation." Either way, Ephrem is here drawing upon Dn 7.15–18. There, following his vision, Daniel "approached one of those who stood there and asked him the truth concerning all this." In reply, Daniel is told what the four beasts represent, but nothing about the Ancient of Days. This silence seems to be the inspiration for Ephrem's comment that Daniel "did not / approach to see" "the glory of the Exalted One."
42. On "watchers," see note 6 attached to 3:5.
43. Dn 8.17–18.
44. Literally, these three lines read: "He was not fit to hear his voice. Daniel was not able / to hear his voice" (*qāleh d-nešma' lâ sāpeq / dānî'êl lâ 'etmṣî / 'âp lâ qāleh l-mešma'*). At Dn 8.15–16, following his vision, Daniel sees "one having the appearance of a man," and hears a voice (apparently God's) say, "Gabriel, make this man understand the vision." Line 4, then, presumably refers to this voice, and Ephrem assumes that Daniel was unfit to hear it (and thus Gabriel had to deliver the message). Gabriel then approaches Daniel, but when he begins to speak, Daniel falls into a deep sleep. He reawakens and hears the message, but at its conclusion, Daniel tells us that he "was overcome and lay sick for some days" (Dn 8.27). This, then, is presumably the second voice, which Daniel cannot hear. A second option would be to translate the second line, with the double negative, as "He was not able / *not* to hear his voice." This could then refer to the fact that Daniel passes out when Gabriel first begins to speak, but is then awoken and made to listen to the words. Nevertheless, this latter option is unlikely, given that the Syriac double negative, especially with

The one who serves he did not see:[45]
Who will look upon the one who is served?
The sea which saw his sign[46]
Grew afraid, fled and shook—
It was rent in two.
[8:16] Daniel, when he asked
About the words, he heard
"They are sealed and hidden."[47]
Temporal hidden things
One ought not investigate,
[So] who will presume to investigate
The treasury within which
All knowledge dwells?
The Firstborn is the treasure of his Father.[48]
All thought depends upon him;
Who is fit to investigate him?

   The End.[49]

'āp lâ prior to the noun that is negated (as we have here), simply adds emphasis to the negative. See Nöldeke, *Compendious Syriac Grammar,* §330.

45. Dn 8.17, where, upon seeing Gabriel, Daniel falls on his face.

46. See 7:4, 8:13, and 9:1.

47. Dn 12.8–9. Ephrem reverses the word order of P, but uses the same vocabulary.

48. Apparently, "treasury" (*bêt gazzâ*) is the Father, and "treasure" (*gazzâ*) is the Son. By the same token, the Son is presumably the "all knowledge" which dwells in the "treasury."

49. C omits. (B is illegible.)

HYMN NINE

According to the same melody.[1]

[9:1] Investigation was upright,
But it has changed in our generation.[2]
Call out and investigate who the Child is,
Do not investigate "how."[3]
The Jordan fled and turned back,[4]
To honor the Ark.
You search and enter in,
So that you dishonor Greatness.
The upright[5] turned backwards
So they would not look upon Noah,
So they would rebuke the rash.[6]

1. See note 1 attached to melody of hymn 4.
2. On "our generation," see *HF* 1:1, and attached note 7.
3. Ephrem consistently forbids these questions of "how" (often coupled with "why," "where," etc.), with respect to divine things. See *HF* 21:4; 23:15; 27:3; 30:2-4; 33:3, 6, 8, 15; 36:19; 40:11; 41:4, 6; 43:5, 10; 44:7; 47:4; 50:1, 4; 55:10; 57:4; 59:4; 64:2; 65:12; 72:14. There are, however, permissible "how" questions, i.e., those that relate to revealed things. See *HF* 17:6; 25:4; 34:3; 48:1; 55:2.
4. See *HF* 7:4; 8:13; and 9:1.
5. "Upright" (*taqnê*), derives from the verb *tqen*, which has the basic sense of "to stand, be established," or "to stand upright." From there, as a noun form (*taqnâ*), it takes on the moral valence of "just, upright." Here, Ephrem is interested in both senses of the word: *taqnê* describes the physical appearance of Noah's two sons as they walk backwards into their father's presence, but also the moral "uprightness" which their lack of presumption demonstrates.
6. Gn 9.20-25.

REFRAIN: {*Glory to you, my Lord, and to your Father, O venerable Son who has saved us!*}[7]

[9:2] They walked backwards
To hide what was revealed.
You turn to investigation
To reveal what is hidden.
At that time, they hid what was revealed;
Now, we explore what is hidden.
The chaste spread out a garment
And hid [him], so as not to look.
An investigator, were he able,
Would strip off all the glory of the Son[8]
To observe {all of him}.[9]
[9:3] {Try}[10] this on yourself:
Everything easy becomes difficult
When you turn its nature around,
And upset its order.[11]
Walking is easy,
But difficult if you turn backwards.
All investigation has become difficult,
For they have pursued it crookedly.
Presumption has turned faith
Backwards in our generation,[12]
To ask questions turned backwards.[13]

---

7. C. B lacks the whole first stanza, along with the refrain. A lacks only the refrain.

8. BC, "Firstborn."

9. Syr., *b-kulleh*, BC. A, *b-qāleh*, "his voice."

10. Syr., *nassāh*, BC. A, *naskāh*, "to pour," but, by extension, "to instill." The sense here would presumably be "instill this within yourself."

11. Lit., "uprightness" (*taqnûteh*). On this term, see note 5 attached to 9:1.

12. See *HF* 1:1 and the references there.

13. Note the development of the logic of this hymn. In 9:1 and 2, Ephrem focused on two narratives (Ps 114/Jos 3 and Gn 9), which depict "backwardness" in varying ways. Most recently, in 9:2, Ephrem has focused on Noah's two sons, whom he lauds for their decision to walk backwards. Here in 9:3, Ephrem continues this theme of walking backwards, but projects it into the natural world. Moreover, he eliminates the positive valence of walking backwards, and instead focuses on its difficulty, due to its "unnatural" character. As such, it

[9:4] God came
To Job in judgment.
He asked him of revealed things
And with his questioning silenced him.[14]
If Job was unable
To speak of revealed things,[15]
Who will presume to demand
The hidden things of the Firstborn?
Do not presume, O weak one!
Job, famous for [enduring] castigations,
Was overcome by questions.[16]
[9:5] For, on the side
That was his, he triumphed.
But on the side that was not
His, he was conquered.
In the struggle,[17] he triumphed,
For we can conquer what is ours.
In discussing, he was conquered,
For it is not ours to investigate.
The Evil One makes trouble
When he keeps us quiet about what is ours,
And occupies us with what is not.
[9:6] He asked Ezekiel
Whether dry bones could rise up.[18]
And though the prophet knew
That the dead would be resurrected,

becomes an image of investigation—difficult and contrary to the nature of
things. Thus, in two stanzas Ephrem has shifted from Scripture to the world,
and has shifted the meaning of "backwards" from positive to negative.

14. Jb 38–41.

15. This interpretation of the Job passage reveals a facet of Ephrem's understanding of "revealed things," that is, natural phenomena. Though these
things are "revealed," however, and thus permissible for investigation, the example of Job demonstrates that they are still incomprehensible.

16. "Questions" (*šû'ālâ*), is derived from the root *š'el* (see Introduction,
pp. 50–51). In various forms, this root will echo through stanzas 6, 7, 8, and 10
of the present hymn.

17. Ephrem uses the Greek loan, *'aggûnâ*.

18. Ezek 37.3.

He did not presume to say what he knew.[19]
He gathered all his knowledge,
And offered it to the Knower-of-all.
Who will presume to investigate
A question which is concealed from all,
And manifest to one alone?
[9:7] Zechariah also asked
About the meaning[20] of revealed things,
But the angel wanted
To test whether he would falter.[21]
He seized him with this [question]: "Do you not
Know these things?"[22]
He was not ashamed to confess,
{In order to shame}[23] the proud.
The prophet did not rely on
His own knowledge,
As the presumptuous of our day.[24]
[9:8] But Zechariah the priest
Asked in order to investigate.[25]

19. Ezek 37.3 gives no indication that Ezekiel knew that the bones could come back to life. Ephrem assumes that he *did* know, but refused to say so out of humility. He thus becomes an exemplum of holy reticence.

20. Syr., *rāzâ*. Whereas *rāzâ* can denote a revealed thing which discloses some hidden meaning, here it clearly refers to the "true" meaning, or reference, of the Temple objects depicted in Zechariah. On this term and its importance in Ephrem, see T. Bou Mansour, *La pensée symbolique de saint Ephrem le Syrien* (Kaslik: Université Saint-Esprit, 1988), 26–35, and Brock, *The Luminous Eye*, 53–59.

21. Zec 4.

22. Zec 4.5. Though Ephrem here uses the particle *lam*, indicating quotation, he actually cites a compacted form of the biblical text. *HF* 9:7:5–6 reads, *d-lâ lam/yāda' a(n)t hālên*, whereas the P of Zec 4.5 reads *lâ yāda' mānâ ('e)nnôn hālên*.

23. Syr., *'a(y)k d-nnakep*, BC. A, *'aykan d-nākep*, "how he *had* shamed." BC take Zechariah as an exemplum aimed directly at Ephrem's own audience. In A's reading, it is not clear exactly who "the proud" would be.

24. See note 7 attached to 1:1.

25. Lk 1.18–20. See also *HF* 21:2–4. Ephrem now shifts to the namesake of the former Zechariah, the father of John the Baptist. On the idea of "priests" and investigation, see note 24 attached to 8:8.

The angel took away his speech,
To frighten that investigator.
If the high priest was punished
Because he discussed and investigated[26] in order to learn
[About] the birth and conception
Of the preacher and thing-made,[27]
[There is] shaking, fear, and terror
If someone presumes to investigate
The begetting of the Lord of all.
[9:9] Zechariah, because he discussed,
His mouth was muzzled with silence.[28]
He then honored with silence
What he had discussed.
How much more should we honor with silence
The begetting of the Firstborn?
He who discusses the Child
Of his womb is to be blamed.
Let him be afraid, who approaches[29]
Essence, to investigate
Its Beloved in its womb!
[9:10] Zechariah uncovered[30]
The truth about himself with his question.
Likewise, everyone who
Asks in any way,
Shows by his question[31]
That he had not previously believed.
His investigation uncovers

26. Syr., *bṣâ*, AB. C, *ṣbâ*, "to wish."

27. Syr., *'bādâ*, which could also be *'abdâ*, "servant." There the reference is to John the Baptist.

28. Literally, "they muzzled his mouth with silence." Cf. 8:5.

29. Syr., *qāreb*, A. BC, *bā'ê* ("investigates").

30. *šrâ* ("uncovered") has a wide range of meanings, many of which would fit here. I have used "uncovered" to suggest Ephrem's understanding of questioning as revealing the absence of faith (see, e.g., *HF* 56:8). The word, however, can also mean "to violate," "to destroy," "to abolish," and Ephrem could feasibly have any of those senses in mind.

31. Lit., "his question shows."

What belief he has believed.[32]
Through the question of his mouth,
Zechariah testified that he destroyed
The faith of his heart.[33]
[9:11] Snakes bit
The People in the desert.
[Moses] set up another snake
So they could look upon it, and live.[34]
The vision gave the People life,
Faith, the peoples.[35]
Behold, a symbol of the Firstborn:
Investigation of him did not heal.
Only his vision healed.[36]
With faith, look upon
The Lord of the mysteries that give you life.
[9:12] And also the sprinkled[37] blood,
Poured upon the gates;[38]
The manna and the quail;[39]
The stone[40] and the rock;[41]
The pillar[42] and the staff[43]—

---

32. That is, it uncovers the reality of his belief, namely, that it is non-existent.

33. This stanza expresses as well as any the idea that, at its basis, investigation emerges from a lack of faith (see also *HF* 7:7–8).

34. Nm 21:4–9.

35. Throughout his hymns, Ephrem distinguishes between God's chosen people (*'ammâ*) and the "gentiles" or "peoples" (*'ammê*) to whom God's covenant has now been extended. On this idea in early Syriac thought, see Murray, *Symbols,* 41–68, and Robin A. Darling, "The 'Church from the Nations' in the Exegesis of Ephrem," *OCA* 229 (1987): 111–21.

36. Syr., *assyat,* AB. C, *aḥyat* ("gave life").

37. "Sprinkled" (*rassîsâ*) is largely redundant in English. It also appears in *CNis* 29:19, and both here and there it appears to function as a non-semantic qualifier of "blood." It does appear in connection with blood in P (see the variant at Ex 12.7), but is used there in its verbal—not adjectival—form. Beck suggests that Ephrem adds it strictly for metrical purposes, and leaves it out of his translation (see *HF [G],* 32, n. 9).

38. Ex 12.7–28, esp. 7 and 22.   39. Ex 16.4–36.
40. Ex 17.6.   41. 1 Cor 10.4.
42. Ex 13.21.   43. Ex 14.16.

These things were symbols of the Firstborn.
Though the People denied,
They did not investigate the glorious symbol.
Do not, O peoples, investigate
The Firstborn—the treasure of the symbol,[44]
Lest the blind rejoice.
[9:13] Though you [were] united,
You have become entirely divided,
For you have come to investigate
The nature that cannot be investigated.
The blind thought
That our truth was false.
If it were false,
It would be small enough to investigate.
Look: it is far bigger.[45]
The blind do not perceive
That they have been wandering around in his Greatness.
[9:14] If he were an angel,
Or merely human,[46]
Investigation of him would be easy,
Since it would be known that he was a thing-made.
Investigation, which has come opposite him,
Stands in place of him.
It proclaims that he is great.[47]

---

44. Here the term "treasure" (*gazzâ*) indicates the reality to which the symbol points—the antitype of all these types. We have already mentioned, in connection with Ephrem's economic metaphors, the role that "treasure" plays (see note 39 attached to 5:15). Ephrem also uses the metaphor of the "treasure" to indicate the place from which divine things come: here and at 81:10 he speaks of a "treasure" of symbols, but also "benefits" (22:8), "teachings" (38:4), "revelations" (47:7), "springs" (of water) (64:7), and "mercy" (67:19, 72:14).

45. Syr., *me'šan 'āšen*. While *šan* carries the sense of "to be strong," or "to be superior," I have nevertheless used "far bigger" to bring out the disjunctive character of the infinitive absolute, juxtaposed with "small" of the previous line.

46. Lit., "a weak human."

47. Lines 5–7 are difficult to understand as a whole. If we take lines 5 and 6 as a complete unit, they make sense as an expression of the idolatry of investigation. But line 7 appears syntactically related, and it is there that the meaning becomes more obscure. The verb "it proclaims" (*sāhdâ*) is a feminine active participle, and "investigation" is the only available feminine subject. Is

Therefore, let him not be investigated,
Since he is proclaimed as God.
For, look: people have wandered around inside him,
And [yet] have not found his limit.
[9:15] And if every standard of measurement[48]
Came down to the sea,
[All] would be vanquished and overcome.
They would not be sufficient for all of it.[49]
They are contained within it,
They do not contain it.
Because they are conquered, it does not mean
That the sea does not exist.
But, because it exists,
Fools presume to go down
To measure its abundance.[50]
[9:16] The one who is able to investigate
Set limits upon it.[51]
A knowledge that can
Limit the Knower-of-all
Is greater than he, for it can
Measure all of him.
Whoever has investigated the Father and the Son
Is greater than both.
God forbid that
The Father and the Son would be investigated
And dust and ash would be exalted.

> *The End.*[52]

Ephrem thus saying that investigation proclaims the greatness of God simply because it fails to understand him? This coheres with lines 1–4 and 10–11. Thus, the sense is probably as follows: "Investigation, *by* standing in place of him (and failing to give an account of him), demonstrates that he is greater."

48. Lit., "measure."
49. BC, "its measure."
50. On the metaphor of the "sea," see note 36 attached to 4:13.
51. "It" refers back to the sea.
52. BC omit.

HYMN TEN

According to the melody, "Messenger, leader ..."[1]

[10:1] [2] You dictated, my Lord, "Open your mouth
   and I will fill it."[3]
Look: the mouth of your servant is opened to you, together
   with his mind.
Fill it, Lord, from your gift
So that I might sing your song, according to your will! [4]

   {REFRAIN: *Make me worthy to approach your gift with awe.*}[5]

[10:2] Your story has steps of every size, for every person.
To the lowest step I approach, though I presume.
Your begetting is sealed within silence:
Whose mouth will presume to rush toward it?
[10:3] Though your nature is one, its interpretations are many.
[There are] narratives exalted, intermediate, and lowly.[6]

---

1. This melody continues through hymn 25. The meter is 5+6 / 7+4
/ 4+4 / 4+5.
2. This hymn has been translated into English twice previously. See S.
Brock, *A Hymn on the Eucharist* (*Hymns on Faith, no.10*) (Lancaster, 1986), and
R. Murray, "A Hymn of St Ephrem to Christ on the Incarnation, the Holy
Spirit, and the Sacraments," *Eastern Churches Review* 3:2 (1970): 142–50. On
Ephrem's self-presentation in this hymn, see Jeffrey Wickes, "The Poetics of
Self-Presentation in Ephrem's *Hymns on Faith* 10," in *Syriac Encounters: Papers
presented at the Sixth North American Syriac Symposium, 2011* (Leuven: Peeters,
forthcoming).
3. Ps 81.11.
4. See note 39 attached to 5:15.
5. BCD.
6. On this three-tiered arrangement, see also *HF* 12:15, 8; 21:1; 22:3. Cf.
also Origen, *On First Principles* 4:2:4.

On the lowly side, like scraps
Deem me worthy to gather the crumbs of your wisdom.[7]
[10:4] Your {exalted}[8] narrative is concealed beside your
    Begetter.
Look: the watchers marvel at your mediating riches.[9]
A small drop of your explanations for the earthly, my Lord,
Is a flood of interpretations.[10]
[10:5] For if John, that great one, called out,
"I am unworthy of the straps of your sandals, my Lord,"[11]
Then, like the sinful woman, I will take refuge
In the shadow of your garment, dwelling inside of it.[12]
[10:6] And like her who was afraid and then took heart
    when she was healed,
Heal my fearful trepidation, and let me be heartened by you.
From the side of your garment I will be passed down
To your body, that I might declare it[13] in accordance with
    my strength.
[10:7] Your garment, my Lord, is a font of medicine.
In your revealed clothing dwelt your hidden strength.
A tiny bit of saliva from your mouth, too,
Is the great {wonder}[14] of the light within the mud.[15]
[10:8] In your bread is hidden the Spirit which cannot be
    eaten.
In your wine dwells the fire that cannot be drunk.[16]
Spirit in your bread, fire in your wine:
It is a distinct wonder that our lips have received!

---

7. Mt 15.21–28.

8. Syr., *'ellāyâ*, BCD, which preserves the meter. A, *galyâ*, "exalted."

9. That is, the riches which come from the hidden God, but are made available to humans.

10. On the sea metaphor (implied here), see n. 36 attached to 4:13.

11. Lk 3.16; Jn 1.27. While Ephrem indicates that this is a quotation through the use of the particle *lam*, he drops one word (*'ešrê*, included in both Luke and John) from the biblical account to accommodate his meter.

12. Lk 8.43–48 and 7.37.

13. BCD, "declare you." Ephrem is possibly echoing Is 53.8. See also *HF* 5:2.

14. Syr., *tehrâ*, BCD. A, *nûhra*, "light."

15. Jn 9.6.

16. Cf. *HF* 6:4.

[10:9] When the Lord came down to earth among mortals,
He made them a new creation,[17] like the watchers,
Within which both fire and spirit mingle,
Since fire and spirit exist secretly.
[10:10] The Seraph did not touch the coal with his fingers.
It touched only the mouth of Isaiah.[18]
[The Seraph] did not hold it, and [Isaiah] did not eat it.
But to us our Lord has given both.
[10:11] Abraham offered bodily food[19]
To the spiritual watchers, and they ate.[20] A new marvel
Of our great Lord: for bodily ones
Fire and spirit to eat and drink!
[10:12] Fire descended and consumed sinners in anger.[21]
The fire of compassion has come down and dwelt within
    the bread.
Instead of the fire which consumed humanity,
The fire inside the bread you have consumed and lived.
[10:13] Fire came down and consumed the sacrifices of
    Elijah.[22]
The fire of mercy has become for us a living sacrifice.[23]
Fire consumed the offering:
Your fire, O our Lord, we have eaten in your offering.[24]
[10:14] "Who holds the wind in the palm of his hand?"[25]
    Come see,
O Solomon, the thing which the Lord of your father[26]
    has done:

---

17. Cf. 2 Cor 5.17; Gal 6.15.   18. Is 6.7.

19. Lit., "food of bodily ones."   20. Gn 18.1–8.

21. There are a few references Ephrem could have in mind here: see Gn 19.24 (which follows the scene he mentioned in the previous stanza); 2 Kgs 1.10 (which, like the following stanza, treats an episode involving Elijah); Nm 16 (which Ephrem references in 8:8 and 28:16).

22. 1 Kgs 18.38.

23. Lit., "sacrifice of life." Cf. Rom 12.1.

24. Syr., *qurbānâ*, which is the Syriac term for the Eucharistic liturgy.

25. Prv 30.4. Ephrem reverses the word order of Prv 30.4. P has *w-mānaw 'āḥed rûḥâ b-ḥûpānaw(hy)*. Ephrem has rendered it *rûḥâ b-ḥûpānaw(hy) lam mānaw 'āḥed*.

26. A playful reference to Ps 110.1.

Fire and Spirit, contrary to nature,
Mingle and flow into the palms of his disciples!
[10:15] "Who has bound the waters in a veil?"[27] he asked.
Look: a font in a veil—the bosom of Mary!
From the cup of life, a drop of life,
We, your handmaids, have received in a veil.[28]
[10:16] See the hidden power behind[29] the veil {of the sanctuary},[30]
A power which the mind has never contained:
His love bent down, descended, and hovered[31]
Over the veil of the altar of reconciliation![32]
[10:17] Behold the fire and the Spirit in the womb which bore you.
Behold the fire and the Spirit in the river in which you were baptized.[33]
Fire and Spirit are in our baptism.
Fire and the Holy Spirit are in the bread and the cup.
[10:18] Your bread has slain the greedy one, who made us his bread.
Your cup destroys death, which, lo, had swallowed us up.
We have eaten you, my Lord, and we have drunk you,
Not to nullify you, but to receive life in you.
[10:19] The strap of your sandal is a terror to the discerning.[34]
The hem of your garment is awful to those who understand.[35]
Our foolish generation, through discussing you,
Look: it is mad, for it has become drunk on your must.[36]
[10:20] There is a marvel in your footsteps,[37] which walked upon the water.

27. Prv 30.4. Ephrem quotes P verbatim.
28. Ephrem apparently refers to a practice of women receiving Communion veiled.
29. Lit., "in."
30. Syr., *d-bêt qûdšâ*, BCD. A, *d-rûḥ qûdšâ*, "of the Holy Spirit."
31. On divine hovering, see note 13 attached to 38:12.
32. See *HF* 12:7, where Ephrem refers to a "cup of reconciliation."
33. BC read: "*he* was baptized" (*'mad*).
34. See 10:5.   35. Ibid.
36. "Must" is the juice from freshly crushed grapes.
37. Ephrem is punning on the word "footsteps": the latter is *'eqbātâ*, which

The great sea you subjugated beneath your feet.[38]

Yet, {your head}[39] was subjugated to a little river,

When it bent down and was baptized in it.

[10:21] The river was like John, who {baptized}[40] in it:

Both together were depicted in smallness.

To the small river and the weak servant

The Lord of both was subjugated.

[10:22] Look, Lord, my lap[41] has become full of the crumbs
    of your crust.[42]

There is no place left in my garment.

As I worship, withhold your gift,

And as a deposit keep it in your treasury, that you may return
    it to us again.[43]

---

is derived from the same root as '*ûqābâ*, "discussion," which Ephrem referenced two lines earlier (10:19:3).

38. Mt 14.22–33; Mk 6.45–52; Jn 6.16–21. See also *HF* 7:4.

39. Syr., *rîšāk*, BCD. A, "he" (*hû*).

40. Syr., '*a'med*, BCD. A, '*mad*, "was baptized."

41. Syr., plural.

42. BCD, "your blessings" (*bûrkātāk*).

43. See note 39 attached to 5:15.

HYMN ELEVEN

According to the same melody.[1]

[']² [11:1] Lord, I do not understand, and therefore I do
{not}³ presume.
Even if I do presume, as I ascend, I do not arrive.
Whoever has presumed mocks himself,
Not you—you who are exalted above all.

> REFRAIN: *Glory to you from all the upright who believe in you!*[4]

[b] [11:2] With its breath, your nature rebukes us, terrifying
us.
Your height, so high and exalted, condemns us.
Your mercy, too, look: it shames us—
How low it has brought down its head to wrongdoers!
[g] [11:3] Let us demonstrate clearly: whoever has presumed,
[Is like one] who sees a great mountain from afar:
His eye reproaches his mind,[5]
For investigation of [the mountain] is immeasurably far-off.
[d] [11:4] He whose course admonishes him, his seeing
reproaches him.

---

1. See note 1 attached to melody of hymn 10.
2. Here begins an acrostic on the Syriac alphabet. It is executed perfectly,
with the exception of 11:8, which breaks with the acrostic entirely. Because the
stanza it accompanies addresses the strange "voice of the wild animals," the
break in the acrostic may signify the incomprehensibility of human speech.
For another theory, see A. Palmer, "Restoring the ABC in Ephraim's Cycles on
Faith and *Paradise*," p. 151, and "Words, Silences, and the Silent Word: Acrostics and Empty Columns in Saint Ephraem's *Hymns on Faith*," p. 140.
3. BCD.
4. BD, "Glory to that revealed one, hidden in you!"
5. That is, for thinking it can understand what it cannot clearly see.

His course rebukes his tongue—how it wanders
Inside that Greatness, in whose womb
Is placed the earth as in the palm of a hand![6]
[h] [11:5] Look: the ear cannot hear a great lightning bolt[7]
Nor can it hear the quietest silence.
How will it hear the great sound[8] and silence of the Father,
Whose silence speaks?
[w] [11:6] "The heavens declare the glory of God."[9]
Behold the silence, all of which {sings},[10] with all tongues,
To all tongues—this firmament that, lo,[11] declares[12]
The glory of its Maker.
[z] [11:7] A person cannot understand all languages.
And even if he could understand the language of the
      Spirit's watchers,[13]
Would he then be so exalted as to understand the silence

---

6. Cf. Prv 30.4 and *HF* 10:14. In spite of its terse language, the meaning
of this stanza is fairly clear: Ephrem carries over from 11:3 the metaphor of
a person looking upon a mountain from far away, thinking he can accurately describe the topography of that mountain. The "course" here is the path
that lies between the person and the mountain. "Seeing" refers to the visual
evidence, which indicates how far-off the mountain is. His "course" and his
"seeing" rebuke his mind (from 11:3) and his tongue, which incorrectly claim
knowledge of the mountain's topography. At 11:3:3–4, this metaphor is seamlessly applied to human knowledge of God, following Ephrem's standard argument *a minore ad maius:* if one cannot acquire knowledge of a distant mountain, how can she claim knowledge of God?

7. Presumably Ephrem has in mind lightning which is far-off, so that it can
be seen but not heard.

8. Syr., *qālâ rabbâ,* ABD. C, *qālâ da-brâ,* "voice of the Son." I have kept "great
sound" because of its parallelism with line 1 ("great lightning bolt" [*paq'â rabbâ*] and "great sound" [*qālâ rabbâ*]), and because Ephrem refers to the Father's
qālâ ("sound," but more often "voice") far more frequently in these hymns
than he does to Christ's voice (see 6:8–9, 11, 13; 7:8; 46:4; 51:7; 65:13). See esp.
11:8, where it is the Father's silence which speaks with the Son. On Christ's
voice, however, see 63:3–4; 80:10.

9. Ps 19.1, quoted verbatim from P.

10. Syr., *l'ez,* BCD. A, *l'es,* "to chew, dine."

11. Syr., *hâ,* BCD. A, *beh,* "in which," a reading that would demand "declares" be taken as passive, "in which is declared the glory."

12. B adds "every day" (*kulyôm b-yôm*).

13. On "watchers," see note 6 attached to 3:5.

Spoken between the Father and his Son?

[?][14] [11:8] Our language is different from[15] the voice of the
wild animals.

The language of the watchers is different from every language.

[Yet], the silence with which the Father speaks with his Beloved

Is strange [even] to the watchers.

[ṭ] [11:9] It is good that[16] as he clothed himself in all forms for
our seeing,

He has also clothed himself in all voices for our persuasion.

One alone can see his nature;

One alone can hear his silence.

[y] [11:10] The Child who is from him comprehends him.

Whoever is a stranger to his nature is a stranger to discussion
of him.

He has gone far astray,

For there is no road that leads to what is hidden.

[k] [11:11] Though the Creator has tread a path to creation,

That the offering of prayers may come to his gate,

There is no road for investigation,[17]

Upon which someone could travel to the gate of Essence.[18]

[l] [11:12] To the one who goes carrying an offering of prayer,

The {road itself}[19] is shown to him, and he follows it.

And that gate, when it sees him,

Opens itself before his offering.

[m] [11:13] But whoever goes toward Greatness discussing,

The roads are concealed, the gates are closed.

There is waste and desolation. The chaos

---

14. See note 2 attached to 11:1, acrostic.

15. Syr., *nûkrāy ... men;* lit., "stranger than" (as I take it here in line 4), or
"alien to."

16. Or, "he is good who ..."

17. BC add "my son" (*ber[y]*) as an address.

18. Whereas we have seen elsewhere in these hymns the juxtaposition of
faith and investigation (see *HF* 9:10), note here the juxtaposition of prayer
and investigation.

19. Syr., *šbîlâ napšeh,* BCD. A, *leh l-napšeh,* "it manifests itself to him," or
"to his soul" (*napšâ* can function either as the noun "soul" or as a reflexive
pronoun).

Is real,[20] and the presumptuous one wanders astray.
[n] [11:14] We know that Satan has brought this[21]
To the one who thinks he can comprehend your divinity.
His nature is frustrated,[22] because he has wandered off in you:
He cannot even recognize himself.
[s] [11:15] He is a fool who thinks he can conquer death,
Since he cannot know death or its substance.
Understanding[23] has not come to
The one whose nature has gone astray in your nature.
['] [11:16] Whoever has destroyed what is his without finding
    what is yours is to be blamed.
The one who thinks he understands and has investigated you
    mocks himself.
It is not you he harms by means of your knowledge.
All [knowledge] is in you, and what is outside of it[24] is his.[25]
[p] [11:17] My mouth has not understood you, yet I rejoice that
    I have not understood,
For if I understood, it would be a blasphemy in two ways:[26]
Human nature would be greater than that of God,
And this is difficult.[27]
[ṣ] [11:18] Your feast thirsts {without limit}[28] for those invited.[29]
Your banquet rejoices in the guests and their garments.[30]
Your bridal chamber longs for the virgins[31]
Whose lamps are rich in oil.[32]

---

20. Syr., ḥattîtâ. D, taḥtāyâ, "earthly."
21. That is, the controversies within which Ephrem is writing.
22. Lit., "his nature is reproached." The idea here, however, is that his nature is shown to be less than what he thinks it is.
23. That is, an understanding of death.
24. B, "outside of you."   25. B, "is yours."
26. Lit., "on both sides."
27. Thus the two blasphemies are an overestimation of a human nature, and an underestimation of divine.
28. Syr., d-lâ sakkâ, "without limit," BCD. A, d-lâ zākê, "who have not conquered."
29. Cf. Jn 2.1; HF 14:1.
30. Mt 22.1–14; Lk 14.15–24.
31. BCD reads "virgins" as feminine (btûlātâ), thus "virgin women."
32. Mt 25.1–13.

[q] [11:19] Many are called who desire your gate.[33]
But since your gate is so narrow,[34] few are those
Who strip off and cast away everything
And find and enter through [that gate] which hates
   possessions.[35]
[r] [11:20] Your crucible rejoices in us, who are perfected
   through trial.
Let us be firm amidst trial.
As his seal is depicted in our word and our mind,
Lord, let the seal of your truth be stamped [upon us].
[š] [11:21] Your long road is short for us in its compassion.
Out of love, it becomes smaller[36] for the one who is weak,
And longer[37] for the one who is quick,
To increase his reward. Glory to your wisdom![38]
[t] [11:22] The throne of your glory and the seat of your justice
{Rejoice in the victorious},[39] who shames the enemy.
Your compassion stays the weak,
And Gehenna is cooled by your dew.[40]

   The End.[41]

33. Mt 20.16.
34. Mt 7.13.
35. Cf. Mt 19.21.
36. Lit., "it shortens its length."
37. Lit., "it lengthens its extent."
38. The malleability of the means by which God is known is an idea attested in Ephrem in a variety of forms. Within the *HF*, Ephrem speaks of Scripture's malleability (e.g., 22:4), and of the malleability of his own words (e.g., 21:1). In the *HPar* 2:2, it is the door to paradise which waxes and wanes depending upon the person who enters.
39. Syr., *ḥādyâ b-zakkāyâ*, BCD. A, *ḥādê zakkāyâ*, "the victorious one rejoices."
40. Cf. Lk 16.24; *HPar* 10:15.
41. BCD omit.

HYMN TWELVE

According to the same melody.[1]

[12:1] Your salt of truth has seasoned our thought.
You give fruits to be tasted by the one who eats them.[2]
Understanding, taste, and thought
You mingle and give to the childlike ear.[3]

> REFRAIN: *Glory to you, and with you, to the Father, your*
> *Begetter!*[4]

[12:2] Look: your furnace is set up. Each one of us brings
Metal[5] and teaching, which it seals and teaches.
If someone is clothed in falsehood, your furnace spreads over
   him
The image and form of truth.
[12:3] Your scale is lifted up. Let us weigh our thought in you.[6]
Against[7] your will, let us weigh all our wills.
If our will weighs much less than your will,
Balance it with your compassion.
[12:4] The two sides[8] of your scale are grace and justice.

---

1. See note 1 attached to hymn 10.
2. Cf. *SF* 2:17, 29.
3. Cf. Mt 19.13–15; Lk 18.15–17; *HF* 7:7.
4. BD, "Glory to your gift, toward which you must turn all."
5. *LS* defines *nepqâ* ("metal") as "mine, quarry," or "mining products," i.e., things that are mined. Here, Ephrem is playing on the double meaning of *kûrâ* as both "furnace" (as translated in line one), but also "baptismal font" (for which, see 39:4). Here, "metal" simply stands as a metaphor for that which is shaped by the baptismal font.
6. BCD, "in it."
7. Literally, "in comparison with."
8. Lit., "scales."

How and when they are balanced, you know.
Though imbalanced, they become balanced,
Because they are not divided against the one Lord of all.
[12:5] Your scale is pleased with the small who weigh little,
As well as those in the middle: they weigh the same in the
     balance.
With a perfect balance [weigh] the perfect.
With a merciful balance [weigh] investigators.[9]
[12:6] Look: the womb of your kingdom looks upon the
     luminous.
Your paradise, too, my Lord, looks upon the pure.
The table of your kingdom waits for your twelve
To dine at it.
[12:7] In {your}[10] rain, all grows. By your dew, all {is
     moistened}.[11]
Your teaching is hidden dew for the hidden earth.
Gather, Lord, your fruit like a harvester,
     And offer to your Father a cup[12] of reconciliation.[13]
[12:8] You are the branch of the vine from Egypt,[14]
Which the boar from the forest ravaged.[15]
How has a shoot sprouted and gone out of it, and brought
A blessed cluster, and the cup of the medicine of life?[16]
[12:9] From the house of the circumcised and the place of the
     tares,
A bowl full of new bread has gone out to us.
From the bitter ones, a sweet fruit;
From the murderers, the Healer who has healed all.
[12:10] Through the sweet root,[17] the Son of David was passed
     down.

9. On this three-tiered schema, see note 6 attached to 10:3.
10. BCD.
11. Syr., *metraggê*, "is moistened," BCD. A, *metga'ê*, "bubbles up."
12. BD, "offering."
13. See *HF* 10:16, where Ephrem refers to an "altar of reconciliation."
14. Ps 80.8.
15. Ps 80.13 (P, 14).
16. On the significance of the cluster, see Murray, *Symbols*, 118–20.
17. D, "upon the sweet head."

Out of the parched earth, the font of life[18] has rushed toward
  us.

How can we refuse that font

That mercy has poured upon parched lands?

[12:11] Your key manifests itself to the one who seeks[19] it.

Your treasure rejoices in the thief who captures it.[20]

You rejoiced in her who, from your side,

Secretly took the medicine for her wound.[21]

[12:12] Your leaven, my Lord, longs for the dough of sinners,[22]

To change and draw them to repentance.

Your light clarifies the way of truth—

It clears it of stumbling blocks completely.

[12:13] Your money, my Lord, loves the needy one who does
  business with it.

Your coin loves to bring ten [more] to the wretched.

Your talent is pleased to bring ten [more] to the slothful.[23]

Glory to the One who enriches all!

[12:14] Your armament,[24] my Lord, rejoices in the debtor[25] who
  conquers [his debt].

Your vineyard rejoices in the unemployed who, along with the
  hardworking,

18. BCD, "mercy."

19. Syr., *b'â*. On the positive use of this term, see note 12 attached to 2:12.

20. Mt. 6.19; 13.44; Lk 23.39–43.

21. Mt 9.20–26; Mk 5.25–34; Lk 8.43–48; *HF* 10:5; 10:19.

22. Mt 13.33; Lk 13.21.

23. Mt 25.14–30; Lk 19.13–27. Ephrem is blatantly (and presumably intentionally) misreading the Gospel narrative. The term "slothful" (*ḥbannānâ*) is
taken directly from Mt 25.26, where it refers to the slave who gained no interest on his single talent, and was thus chastised, losing even the single talent he possessed. Ephrem uses this term, but otherwise casts this character
as the "good and trustworthy slave" (Mt 25.21), who gains ten total talents.
This misreading mirrors Ephrem's presentation of the relationship between
God and humanity: God exists infinitely beyond humanity, but out of love tra-
verses that distance to reveal himself to humanity. By misreading the Gospel
narrative, Ephrem can recast that narrative as an image of God's boundless
benevolence, giving fully even to the one who deserves none. On economic
metaphors more generally, see note 39 attached to 5:15.

24. "Armament" (*zînâ*) glosses the economic terms of 12:13: it is through
the giving of alms that the debtor conquers his debt.

25. B, "penitent."

Seeks a wage with open mouth and uncovered face.[26]
{Glory to the one who repays all!}[27]
[12:15] Your yoke, my Lord, loves to subjugate the rebellious.[28]
Your staff, my Lord, takes joy in scattering the gathered wolves.
May your yoke gather the wandering sheep into the sheepfold.
Glory to the one who shepherds all!
[12:16] Your harbor looks for our ship to arrive.
Your Spirit lovingly guides it with the rudder of your mercy.
[Your Spirit] arrives, O Lord, and shuts the mouth of the
    greedy sea.
Glory to your succor!
[12:17] Lo, your rock beholds the building whose foundations
    are placed upon it.
All those looking [upon it] give glory.
May their tower not be a disgrace, my Lord![29] May it be
    completed in you!
Glory to the One who completes all!
[12:18] Lo, your seed beholds the tilled lands.
Among the smallest, your seed will come up thirtyfold.
Among the middle ones, it will come up sixtyfold.
Among the perfect, it will come up a hundredfold.[30]
[12:19] Your mirror is clear, and entirely turned towards you.
Your beauty entices the hateful, so that they are scoured by it,
Since the one who is dirty cannot be united with you,
Unless he cleanses himself of stains.
[12:20] Your hyssop looks to pardon us with its compassion,
And with the sprinkling of your compassion, Lord, we are
    cleansed.[31]
The Lord takes no delight in our hatred,
But since he is very just, he adorns [us] with his beauty.[32]

26. Mt 20.1–16. On the idiom of "face," see also *HF* 14:9 and 16:13.
27. C.
28. Mt 22.1.
29. Cf. Gn 11.1–9.
30. Mt 13.8. On this three-tiered schema, see note 6 attached to 10:3.
31. Cf Ps 51.9 (P).
32. BCD, "he is adorned by our beauty."

HYMN THIRTEEN

According to the same melody.[1]

[13:1] I will guard my faith from the deception that now
    springs up,
Which, though confessing the Father, denies his Only-
    Begotten.[2]
And while the debaters approach all the heights,
I will guard my faith on the way of truth.

> REFRAIN: *Thanks to the Father and to the Son and
> to his Holy Spirit!*

[13:2] I have offered [my faith] to the Father, and he has
    inscribed on it his fatherhood.
I have offered it to the Son and he has mingled it with his
    Essence.[3]
The Holy Spirit, too, has sanctified it,
And depicted on it the all-sanctifying symbol.[4]
[13:3] Every faith not inscribed has gone astray.
Let us prepare ourselves for suffering, should it come.
Our spirit will suffer, our soul will separate, and our
    body will burn.
But who will conquer us?

---

1. On this melody, see note 1 attached to hymn 10.
2. Ephrem here offers the most succinct statement of the polemical aim of
these hymns.
3. Syr., *'îtûtêh*. BC, *îlîdûteh* ("sonship").
4. Ephrem uses this same language in a baptismal and Eucharistic context
in *HF* 40:10. Here, it seems likely that the "all-sanctifying symbol" refers to the
pre-baptismal anointing, which was such a central part of the Syriac rite at
this time. See note 12 attached to 6:4.

[13:4] It is written: "Neither height nor depth
Nor sword can cut off our faith."[5]
Who could cut off the impervious rays
Of the sun of truth?
[13:5] Our baptism depends upon three names.
Our faith is illumined by three symbols.
Three names our Lord handed down to the twelve,[6]
In which we take refuge.
[13:6] The soul not inscribed[7] is like a wandering sheep.
And the one who is inscribed with one name [only] is
    also rejected.[8]
So too, the one whose inscription is stolen has gone astray.
Blessed is the one who has inscribed us for himself.
[13:7] Faith's teaching is a treasure.
The voice [is] a key; the tongue, like a treasurer.
Never has faith been quiet,
For it establishes and distributes truth to hearers.[9]
[13:8] A trumpet and faith are strangers to silence.
Never has a trumpet whispered in a closed room,
Neither has faith acted with stealth.
Truth has whispered in the hidden and secret [place].
[13:9] Who has seen a tree produce only one fruit,

5. Cf. Rom 8.35 and 39.
6. Mt 28.19.
7. I.e., with the trinitarian baptismal seal.
8. *Apostolic Constitutions* 8.47.50 and the 7th canon of the Council of Constantinople both condemn single-immersion baptism. The Council of Constantinople identifies this as a specifically Eunomian practice (Abp. Peter L'Huillier, *The Church of the Ancient Councils: The Disciplinary Work of the First Four Ecumenical Councils* [Crestwood, NY: St. Vladimir's Seminary Press, 1996], 131), and Rowan Williams has argued convincingly that *Constitutions* 8.47.50 has the same target in mind ("Baptism and the Arian Controversy," 166, and 172–77). It is possible that Ephrem here references such practices, though elsewhere Ephrem's baptismal rhetoric seems to depend upon shared baptismal practices (e.g., see 22:7 and 59:1).
9. In *HF* 13:7–10, Ephrem depicts faith as necessarily public and vocal. In this view, unlike truth (see *HF* 13:8) or prayer (*HF* 16:13; 20:1), both of which can exist in silence, faith must be manifest vocally, or else it dies (*HF* 20:2). See also *HF* 16:12–13; 18:1; and 20:1.

And that fruit stay on it forever alone?
The faith of the single one
Upon truth[10] is suspended, for truth[11] is one.[12]
[13:10] May my tongue be neither silent nor reserved
    concerning my faith.
From my lips to you, Lord, it ascends as an offering.
Look: from branches prolix and silent,
My tongue has plucked you.

10. Syr., *qûštâ*.

11. Syr., *šrārâ*. On *qûštâ* and *šrārâ*, see note 33 attached to 7:9.

12. Beck erroneously divides these lines as follows, *haymānûta-w d-'îḥîdāyâ b-qûštâ tlê bāh / šrārâ gîr ḥad-û*, which scans as 4+8 / 5. Instead, the break should go after *îḥîdāyâ*, thus scanning as 4+4 / 4+5. Further, C omits the *b-* before *qûštâ*, as a result of which the line reads, "The faith of the single one, / Truth hangs upon it, for truth is one." The question, then, is whether faith is suspended upon truth (AB), or truth upon faith (C)? Metrically, semantically, and contextually, either is possible. See also *HF* 80:7 for similar metaphor, but with a different arrangement.

HYMN FOURTEEN

According to the same melody.[1]

[z][2] [14:1] I have invited you, Lord, to a feast of hymns!
The wine—a discourse of praise—has run out in our feast![3]
The one whose vessels are full of good wine is invited![4]
May your song fill my mouth!

> REFRAIN: *Glory to you from all who perceive your truth!*[5]

[ḥ] [14:2] Wine in vessels is similar—of the same kind.
But this is speech-endowed wine, which begets praise.
This wine has begotten praise
Among drinkers who have seen a marvel!
[ṭ] [14:3] It was indeed right that at someone else's feast,[6]
You filled six vessels with good wine.[7]
In this feast, instead of vessels,
Lord, fill a myriad of ears with delight!
[y] [14:4] Jesus was invited to the feast of others.
Look: your pure and fair feast has gladdened your guests![8]
For behold, those you invited, Lord, need
Your songs: let your lyre speak!
[k] [14:5] Your bride is your soul, and your body is your
  bridal chamber.[9]

---

1. On this melody, see note 1 attached to hymn 10.
2. This acrostic begins mid-alphabet, continues until *nun,* and then is absent for the final two stanzas of hymn 14.
3. Jn 2.3.   4. Jn 2.10.
5. BD, "Glory to you who has poured your gift upon your servant!"
6. Lit., "a feast which was not yours."
7. Jn 2.6–8.
8. On *'ālmayk* as "guests," see *LS,* 1105, col.1, sub. *'ālmâ,* num.3c.
9. BCD read, "Your bride is *the* soul, and *the* body is your bridal cham-

Your invited guests are the senses, with the thoughts.
And if one body has become your banquet,
Your feast is the Church, being complete.
[l] [14:6] The Holy One wedded the synagogue on Mount
   Sinai.
Its body gleamed in white garments,[10] but its heart was dark.
It slept with the calf, and the Exalted One despised it,
And broke the tablets—the book of its covenant.[11]
[m] [14:7] Who has ever seen [such a] calamity in the midst
   of a shameful deed?
The bride, as she defiled her bridal chamber, raised her
   voice.[12]
She had dwelt in Egypt, where she learned of
Joseph's pursuer,[13] who cried out though she had sinned.[14]
[n] [14:8] The light of the pillar—fire and cloud—
Drew its rays within itself,[15]
Like the sun that was darkened
On the day [the bride] called out to the king, claiming
   another crime.[16]
[14:9] How, Lord, shall my lyre keep your song quiet?
And how has my tongue taught about iniquity?
Your love has given confidence to the shamed,[17]
Yet my will is iniquitous!
[14:10] It is right for humans to give thanks to your divinity.
It is right for those exalted to worship your humanity.
The exalted marvel at how small you have become.
The earthly marvel at how exalted you have become.

---

ber." Thus, whereas A takes this as a statement of the relationship between the divine Christ and his human body, B takes it as a statement about his relationship to, and indwelling of, a given human being. Either reading is possible. If we read it with A, then the final line reflects the Church as the feast gathered around the divine-human Christ. If we read it with BCD, then the Church reflects the assembly of bodies inhabited by Christ.

10. Ex 19.14.   11. Ex 32, esp. v. 19.
12. Ex 32.17–18.   13. Syr., *mārteh,* lit., "mistress."
14. Gn 39.15.   15. Nm 9.15–23; 14.14.
16. Mt 27.45.

17. Lit., "given openness of face to the shame-faced." For this idiom, see also *HF* 12:14 and 16:13.

HYMN FIFTEEN

According to the same melody.[1]

[15:1] A human being heeds what concerns humanity,
A mortal meditates on what has been commanded,[2]
And a sinner
Seeks medicine fit for his wound.

> REFRAIN: *Glory to your birth, hidden from all in investigation of it!*[3]

[15:2] The one who is discerning honors divinity[4] with silence.
The one who has knowledge marvels at Greatness[5] quietly.
The sage, with a strong voice,
Proclaims to children the glory of the kingdom.[6]
[15:3] Let not our soul forget itself[7] and muse upon our God.
Let us mark our mind and measure our thought.
Let us know our knowledge—how
Small and scorned it is which investigates the Knower-of-all.
[15:4] Tell me: how have you depicted in your mind
That birth so far from your discussion?
Do you suppose only a tiny hill
Lies between you and investigation of him?[8]
[15:5] Silence yourself.[9] Let your tongue not presume.

---

1. On this melody, see note 1 attached to hymn 10.
2. That is, that all humans die.
3. B, "Receive, O merciful one, the offering for your reconciliation."
4. B add "your."   5. Ibid.
6. Ibid.   7. BC, "Let us not forget our soul."
8. On "mountain" as a metaphor for God (implicit here), see *HF* 1:3; 4:5; 6:1; 11:3.
9. Lit., "seal your mouth with silence."

140

Know what you are—created, made, fashioned.[10]
The chasm is immeasurably great
Between you and the Son when it comes to investigation.
[15:6] Difficult things are not for one who is weak.
Hard things are not for one who is lacking.
Whoever is earthly should not exalt himself,
So that his mouth runs to challenge its Fashioner.[11]
[15:7] Whoever merely talks about[12] an injured limb
Needs healing, lest he injure the whole body.
Because it has become wounded,[13] the Healer of all our pains
Will excise and cast it from the flock.[14]
[15:8] Anyone who investigates is a companion to the lost.
Whoever investigates is a neighbor of the one who has strayed.
Never has one lost sought
And found himself. So too the debaters.
[15:9] Let each limb[15] be strengthened by Christ.
Let its tongue not be divided against its root.
For the Vine-dresser will tear it out
If he senses that his fruit is bitter.
[15:10] Let not the eye of our thought be blinded by
      investigation.
Because our mind has grown dim, it cannot
Investigate with a luminous eye
The Father, Son, nor even the Holy Spirit.
[15:11] Let no one unsheathe his tongue instead of his sword,
Nor let the mind be a bow for words,
Nor let our evil debating become
A serpent flinging poison at its hearers.

---

10. Lit., "son of a fashioned thing." On the root *gbal* ("to fashion"), see Gn 2.7.

11. B, "its maker."

12. Syr., *m'aqqeb.*

13. I am reading the subject of "has been wounded" as "it," continuing the metaphor of the limb and the body. It could also be "he."

14. Thus, Ephrem applies the analogy of amputation to the community: Christ the physician amputates the tainted limb for the health of the rest of the body.

15. Lit., "the one who is a limb."

HYMN SIXTEEN

According to the same melody.[1]

[16:1] Lord, how shall your servant cease from your hymn?
How shall my tongue abstain from thanking you?
How shall I dam the sweet flood,
When you have broken through my mind, thirsty for you?

> REFRAIN: *Blessed is the birth, in which we have perceived truth!*[2]

[16:2] With what is yours, I sing glory to you from your gift!
In you, Lord, I become rich, you I magnify!
In you, I become great, and yet I deprive you your due, O Magnifier-of-all!
Blessed is the One who sent you to us![3]
[16:3] Your treasure is sweet, and we[4] are your guard.[5]
Let my deposit become great in your treasure—something like a seed.
You demand this [deposit] because of your kindness,[6]
So that you can return a small thing to me multiplied!
[16:4] Look: many are our debts. Who will presume to borrow more?
Look: in your mercy, fear is lifted from those who owe more than they can repay.

---

1. On this melody, see note 1 attached to hymn 10.
2. B, "Make me worthy to send up glory to you without disputation!"
3. On the application of economic metaphors to Ephrem's own poetic project, see note 39 attached to 5:15.
4. Syr., *'naḥnan.* BC, "mercy" (*ḥnān*).
5. Lit., "your treasure keeper."
6. Lit., "This is demanded because of your kindness."

They have taken, cheated and held [some] back,
And have come to the gate of your treasure. Give to us and
  increase us!
[16:5] Whether I wish to be audacious, or am ashamed to
  presume,
Either is acceptable to you, Lord.[7]
The audacity of our love is sweet to you,
Just as you find it sweet[8] that we steal from your treasury.
[16:6] To you, Lord, I offer my faith as an offering.
I offer it bare, without adornment.[9]
May it be enriched, Lord, by what is yours alone,
And I by it. By myself, I am in need.
[16:7] A merchant offers to the king a pearl.
He takes it bare[10] and with it magnifies [the king],
So that the king, with his crown, will magnify the pearl.
Lord, how much greater will my faith become in you?
[16:8] If a vinedresser offers a peeled[11] fruit,
The master of the vineyard takes joy in it and clothes him.
If a vinedresser, because of a simple fruit, receives clothing,
May your mercy clothe me!
[16:9] The one whose faith is great is not small.
Though in me, faith has been small, in you, Lord, it will
  become great.
If you enrich a grain of wheat in the dirt,

---

7. Ephrem distinguishes between the positive activity of *'aḥṣep* ("to be audacious") and *mraḥ* ("to presume"). On this distinction, see note attached to
mraḥ in Introduction, p. 51, n. 192.

8. Lit., "it is sweet to you."

9. "Adornment" (*dûbārê*) is a difficult term to translate. In later Syriac literature, it will represent the monastic "way of life" (see the *incipit* to John of
Ephesus, *Lives of the Eastern Saints, PO,* vol. 17, p. 2). In Ephrem, it also has
the sense of "right conduct" or "appropriate way of life" (see, e.g., *HF* 80:7),
but here it most immediately modifies *'arṭellā'ît,* "bare" or "naked" (a concept
developed further in the following two hymns). The idea is that Ephrem offers
his faith without the virtuous decoration that comes from a righteous way of
life.

10. That is, unadorned (see *HF* 16:6:2).

11. Syr., *šlîḥâ,* lit., "stripped." Ephrem thus makes a pun: the worker offers
a peeled fruit, and, as a result, receives clothing (i.e., receives the wages which
buy clothing).

You will also enrich my faith with your treasure.

[16:10] He is therefore enough for [wheat] and for faith,

Though we, like cheaters, have not given it[12] what belongs to it.

Do not strip it of what belongs to it!

Though [faith] has not been great in us, Lord, do not become
  small in us!

[16:11] If we see a house of idle debaters—woe![13]

We are lazy workers, who have grown weary and fallen asleep.

But we are vigilant investigators

And debaters who do not labor at all!

[16:12] In this time,[14] many have slept on faith,[15]

And have placed it fearfully under a veil of silence.

Thus, faith is awake in the heart,

But its proclamation sleeps in the mouth.[16]

[16:13] [Faith] is not prayer, which is served by silence.

Faith is symbolized in a face uncovered.[17]

Whoever hides his faith,

It would better to cover his face.

---

12. I.e., "faith."

13. Cf. Mt 24.42–23.13. An alternate translation of this line: "Woe, if we
have seen [faith] among the idle debaters" (*HF [G]*, 51). Lines 1 and 2, however, echo Mt 24.42–25.13, and Ephrem seems to be picking up the language of
"house" from those verses.

14. On Ephrem's sense of distinct times, see note 7 attached to 1:1.

15. Syr., *dmek(w)*. BC, *d-kām(w)*, "to be reserved about [faith]."

16. On faith as necessarily public and vocal, see note 9 attached to 13:7.
The coupling of this theme here with the idea that many are silent about faith
raises questions about the context of this particular hymn. If later reports
about Valens's persecution of Nicene Christians in Edessa are accurate (see
Introduction, pp. 26–27), that may be the best context for these lines.

17. Cf. 2 Cor 3.18. On this metaphor, see also *HF* 12:14 and 14:9.

HYMN SEVENTEEN

According to the same melody.[1]

[17:1] The one who seeks the truth with envy,
Even if he happens upon it, cannot know it,
Since jealousy has stirred up his mind.
He does not understand [the truth] but attacks it.

> REFRAIN: *Glory to your greatness, within which*
> *investigators wander!*

[17:2] The mind[2] has raged and revolted without thought.
It troubles the earth, and, lo, even attacks heaven,
Not recognizing a companion
Or a thing-made as distinct from its Lord.[3]
[17:3] Who does not weep, seeing that his own[4]
Have given up the struggle with outsiders?[5]
Like strangers, look:
They assault one another with debating.
[17:4] Who does not blame the one who, not understanding
The things hidden from him within himself,
Lo, exalts himself above the Creator,
Without even approaching creatures.
[17:5] God, seeing that he was ever unsearchable,

1. On this melody, see note 1 attached to hymn 10.
2. Syr., *re'yānâ*. B, *ḥeryānâ,* "controversy."
3. Cf. *HF* 6:8–12.
4. Lit., "sons of his side."
5. On "insiders" and "outsiders," see Sidney Griffith, "Setting Right the Church of Syria," 102–7. According to Griffith, "insiders" (both in the *HF* and in the *CH*) refer to subordinationist Christians, whereas "outsiders" refers to Marcionites, Manichaeans, and the followers of Bar Dayṣān.

Put on a body which could be searched,
That we would cease from searching out his divinity,
And revive ourselves with questions of his humanity.[6]
[17:6] We are permitted to ask how divinity
Came down and kept silent nine months in a womb.
Thirty years, too, he was on the earth,
That slowly we might acquire it through habit.[7]
[17:7] He left the highest and became a companion to
    the lowest.
He left those found and sought the lost.
He left the crafty and chose the simple.
Through them he spread his Gospel to every one.
[17:8] The chariot of the four living [creatures] he left and
    came down,
And made the cross a vehicle to the four corners.[8]
He left the Seraphim and the Cherubim,
And came down to endure the mocking of the crucifiers.
[17:9] You are the Son of life and the son of a mortal.
You are the Son of our Creator, Lord, for in you everything
    is established.
But you are also the son of Joseph—
That carpenter who learned from you.
[17:10] Through you, without instruction, the Maker
    established [the world].
With your finger, the Creator put together all his creatures.
Through you, even Joseph put together
His carpentry, for he saw that you were his master.
[17:11] Son of the Creator, son of the carpenter!

6. Here and in the following stanzas Ephrem indicates the sort of things humans can discuss, all of which relate to Christ's human body. The verb he uses for "discuss" is *'qab*. On similarly positive affirmations, see n. 12 attached to 2:12.

7. The "it" of the last sentence could refer to the earth (from line 3) or divinity (from line 1). I assume it refers to the earth, echoing Mt 5.5. Another option would be to take the verb as third-person masculine singular, in which case the sentence would read, "That slowly he [i.e., Christ] might acquire [the earth] through habit." It is difficult, however, to understand what the latter reading would mean.

8. Ezek 1, esp. v. 5. See also *HF* 5:18.

Since when he created, he created everything in the symbol
    of the cross,
Even the house of Joseph the carpenter
Now meditates on the cross every day.[9]

9. Ephrem intends the phrase "house of Joseph" to refer to the Jews of his
own day. This closing stanza anticipates the theme of the following hymn, in
which Ephrem will cull symbols of the cross from creation. His aim is to argue
for the cruciform nature of reality and to suggest that, through one's use of
created materials, one is inevitably drawn to contemplate the Creator.

HYMN EIGHTEEN

According to the same melody.[1]

[18:1] A baby bird, when it is not yet mature,[2]
Cannot crack its shell because of its weakness.
Faith under silence,
Is also lacking. Perfect it, Perfecter-of-all!

REFRAIN: *Make me worthy to glorify your birth with silence!*[3]

[18:2] The genus of bird is passed on in three stages:
From the womb to the egg, and from it, to the nest [where] it
    chirps.
And when it has matured and has flown in the air,
It stretches out its wings in the symbol of the cross.
[18:3] So too faith is perfected in a threefold manner:
Since the Apostles believed in the Father, and the Son,
    and the Spirit,
The proclamation has flown to the four corners
Through the power[4] of the cross.
[18:4] The three names are disseminated threefold,
In the spirit, the soul, and the body, symbolically.
Our trinity,[5] perfected by the Three,
Has ruled over {the borders}.[6]

---

1. On this melody, see note 1 attached to hymn 10.
2. I.e., still in the shell.
3. A refrain which seems to contradict the content of the stanza which it immediately follows.
4. B, "through the symbol."
5. That is, the human trinity of spirit, soul, and body.
6. Syr., *sawpê*, B. AC, *saypâ*, "sword."

[18:5] When the spirit suffers, it is entirely inscribed by the
   Father.
When the soul suffers, it is entirely mingled with the Son.
When the body confesses and is [then] burned,
It shares entirely in the Holy Spirit.
[18:6] If a bird withdraws its wings and refuses
The simple[7] shape of the cross, the air too
Refuses her, and will not bear her,
Unless her wings have confessed the cross.
[18:7] When a ship stretches out the rudder in the shape
   of the cross,
And, together with the beams, makes a womb for the wind—
Whenever it has spread out the cross,
Then the way for its journey is spread out.
[18:8] And if the ship belongs to a Jew,
He is unwittingly rebuked by the action,
For, in his ship, with his hands,
He extends and stretches out the shape of the cross.
[18:9] The sea submits to the deniers through the cross.
If the crucifier does not raise the raised wood[8]—
Linen hung upon it like a body—
His course will be hindered.
[18:10] O pure womb[9]—symbol of the body of our Savior—
Filled by the wind,[10] without limiting or confining it.
Through the wind that dwells in a linen [sail],
Bodies live, in which dwell the soul.
[18:11] And the earth would not have {submitted}[11] to the
   crucifier
Without the fair symbol of the luminous Cross:

7. Or, "stretched out" (*pšîṭtâ*).
8. In Syriac, this sentence reads *d-'elâ zâqep zâqûpâ qaysâ zqîpâ*. The word
"crucifier" and the two occurrences of "to raise," are all derived from the verb
zqap. "Raised wood" could thus also be translated "crucified wood."
9. While Ephrem ultimately means to invoke the wombs of the Father and
Mary, the more immediate referent is the "womb," or recess, of a ship's sail.
10. Syr., *rûḥâ*, which also means "Spirit." Throughout the remainder of this
stanza, Ephrem clearly intends to evoke both meanings.
11. Syr., *metramyâ*, B. AC, *mettrîmâ*, "exalted."

That sign of the cross connects the wagon to [the horse],
Softens [the earth], and scatters its seeds within it.
[18:12] And his shirt would not have fit him[12] without the
    shape.
He stretched out his arms and put it on, like the cross.
This clothing is his mirror,
And on it is inscribed the sign that he denied.
[18:13] The lamb—when the crucifier buys and slaughters it—
He hangs it upon wood, Lord, to depict your murder.
And when he buries wheat in the earth,
A seed of life proclaims your resurrection.
[18:14] Behold your symbol in his flock, protected by your
    staff.
And in his vineyard, the cluster, full of the symbol of your
    blood.
And on his tree, fruit hangs:
A symbol of your cross[13] and of the fruit of your body.
[18:15] Look: in the denier's house, your proclamation
    calls out.
For in a clear symbol [the rooster] flaps his wings there.[14]
Look: it proclaims the resurrection of the dead to
The one living entombed, for his sleep is [like] his death.[15]
[18:16] And when in her nest, with her wing, in a holy manner,
[The hen's] womb conceives through {the heat}[16] of her wing's
    incubation,[17]
She bears a child without partner.
Look: in his house there is a mirror of Mary.

12. Syr., *leh reḥmat,* lit., "loved him."
13. Lit., "your wood."
14. Ephrem is connecting two things in this stanza: the flapping of the
rooster's wings, which proclaims the cross, and, implicitly, the rooster's morn-
ing call, which proclaims the resurrection of the dead.
15. That is, his sleep offers an image of the impermanence of death.
16. Syr., *ratḥâ,* B. AC, *rûḥâ* ("spirit/wind").
17. Ephrem is apparently referring to the production of an unfertilized
egg.

HYMN NINETEEN

According to the same melody.[1]

[19:1] Glory befits the teacher who has taught truth.
Praise is for the Lord who became a brother to his servants.[2]
Splendor befits the One older than all,[3]
Who became a servant and tended to the guests.[4]

> REFRAIN: *Glory to you and through you to that Good One,*[5]
> *your Sender!*

[19:2] Who is worthy of your garment—the clothing of your
humanity?
Who is worthy of your body—the clothing of your divinity?
Lord, you had two [sets of] clothes:
A garment and a body—the bread, the bread of life.[6]
[19:3] Who does not wonder at the clothing of your
transformation?[7]
Look: the body hid your brightness—the awesome nature.
The garments hid the weak nature.
The bread hid the fire that dwelt in it.
[19:4] Never have mortal minds touched him.

---

1. On this melody, see note 1 attached to hymn 10.
2. Cf. Jn 15.15.
3. Cf. Jn 8.58.
4. Syr., *smîkâ*, lit., "those reclining." Cf. Jn 13.12.
5. B, "your Father."
6. Thus, Christ's "two garments" (his body, and his clothing) stand as images for interpreting the Eucharist: the bread is like his clothing, and the life of the bread (the sanctified bread) is like his body.
7. Syr., *šûḥlāpâ*, a term which refers specifically to Christ's taking on of a human body. See *HF (G)*, 56, n. 5.

151

Who has a hand of fire and a finger of spirit
To explore him in the presence of his hiddenness?
Even our mind is like a body!
[19:5] Revealed[8] knowledge has not understood
That Luminous One who is inside and outside of all.
His is the knowledge within our knowledge.[9]
He is the life of the soul which dwells within us.
[19:6] Who does not wonder that though all are in him,
None have ever touched him, though they are in him,
In the way that a body has never touched
The soul within him with its own hand.
[19:7] Who will not give thanks to that one more hidden
    than all,[10]
Who revealed himself more than all![11]
When he put on a body, bodies touched him,
Yet minds never explored him.
[19:8] Great it is[12] that the small have hemmed in that
    Greatness,
So that it becomes smaller than their form, so that it
    becomes like them.[13]
Though difficult it is for them to imitate him,
It is easy for that [Greatness] to become like them.
[19:9] A hunter set a trap for a bird.
Since he could not go up to it, he called it to himself.
You, [Lord,] are the hunter. You came down to us,
Who were too weak to go up and live with you!
[19:10] This is an aberration: [while] someone weak covers
His soft body by putting on dense armor,
You, Lord, put upon your nature
An infirm body, to be able to suffer in it.
[19:11] Various drugs have issued from you to the needy,
Though all are one in power, undivided.

8. B, "knowledge of the exalted ones."
9. Lit., "He is the knowledge of our knowledge."
10. Lit., "that hidden one more hidden than all."
11. Lit., "He came to a revealed revelation more revealed than all."
12. Or, "Great is he …"
13. Cf. Phil 2.1–10.

He has increased for the sick and spread out for the needy.
He has diminished and become one truth[14] for the true.[15]
[19:12] Your love has brought together [various] means
   because of our need,
For you to give each a path from your treasure.[16]
With easy paths, Lord, you incited
Our necessity to approach your treasury.[17]

14. *qûštâ*.
15. *šarrîrê*. On *qûštâ* and *šarrîrê*, see note 33 attached to 7:9.
16. For the idea of God making a path that descends from him, see *HF* 11:11.
17. B, "your gate" (*tarʿāk*).

HYMN TWENTY

According to the same melody.[1]

[20:1] To you, Lord, I offer my faith out loud.
Prayer and petition can
Be conceived in the mind,
And born in silence voicelessly. [2]

> REFRAIN: *Blessed is your birth, which your Father alone
> knows!*[3]

[20:2] If the womb keeps back a fetus, both die.[4]
O our Lord, let my word not keep back my faith,
For the former would perish, and the latter would wither:
Both would perish, one after the other.
[20:3] A tree that keeps back its blossom dries up.
The pangs accompanying the wind[5] beget the tender blossom.
If a tender blossom can spring from a wooden womb,
May my faith also thrive!
[20:4] The seed in its tenderness cleaves the earth's surface,[6]
And the blade of wheat is seen—full of symbols!
The faith whose womb is full of good fruits
Becomes a blade of song![7]

1. On this melody, see note 1 attached to hymn 10.
2. On the vocal nature of faith, expressed in the following stanzas, see note 9 attached to 13:7.
3. B, "Blessed is your birth, which has provided discernment to the simple!"
4. I.e., mother and child.   5. Lit., "the pangs of the wind."
6. Lit., "the veil of the earth."
7. The metaphor seems to work as follows: faith represents the earth in its entirety. "Womb" is the hidden earth—the dirt that the seed must break through, while "good fruits" refers to the seeds that are buried in the earth. The hymns themselves, then, become the visible manifestation of faith.

[20:5] The fish's conception and birth happen in the sea.
If [someone] {dives deep down},[8] [the fish] flees from his side.
In the luminous silence within your mind,
Let prayer gather itself without wandering.[9]
[20:6] A virgin in an inner room is [like] a refined petition.
And if,[10] wandering off, it crosses the gate of the mouth,
Truth is its bridal chamber and love its crown.
Quiet and silence are the assistants[11] [standing] at its gate.
[20:7] The one betrothed to the king's son cannot go and act
    shamelessly.
Faith is the bride of the exalted one,[12] [carried] in the
    market place.[13]
[Faith] is carried on the back of the voice,
From the side of the {mouth}[14] to the bridal chamber of the
    ear.
[20:8] Indeed, it is written that many have believed in our
    Lord,
But out of fear their voice has denied faith.
Though the heart {within}[15] confesses,
He has numbered the silent among the deniers.[16]
[20:9] Jonah prayed a prayer silently.
The preacher was quiet in the fish's belly.
{Within}[17] the mute [fish], his prayer crawled,[18]
But the Exalted One heard: to him silence is shouting.[19]

8. Syr., *'āmed w-'āmeq*, B. AC, *'āmeq w-'āmar* ("goes deep and dwells").

9. This hymn articulates two related but distinct metaphors. In lines 1 and 2, the sea functions as a metaphor for divinity, represented by the hiddenness of the fish's conception and birth, and the failure of the diver to comprehend. But in lines 3 and 4, the metaphor shifts: the "sea" becomes a metaphor for the silent place within a human, where one should dwell, content not to understand.

10. That is, the petition (like a virgin).

11. Syr., *mhaymnê*, lit., "faithful."

12. B, "revealed one."   13. I.e., on a royal conveyance.

14. "Mouth," B. (A is illegible.)   15. B.

16. See note 16 attached to 16:12.   17. Syr., *gaw*, B. A, *gêr*, "indeed."

18. Syr., *reḥšat*. B, *leḥšat*, "whispered."

19. Jon 2.1–10. Given that all the stanzas thus far have focused on the public nature of faith, the inclusion of Jonah here is curious. It may well be the case that Ephrem expects his hearers to connect this episode to Jonah's broader narrative: while his silent prayer proved successful, he only found

[20:10] In one body, [there is] both prayer and faith,
The hidden and revealed for the hidden and revealed:
Hidden prayer for the hidden ear;
Faith for the revealed ear.
[20:11] Our prayer, like taste, has been hidden in our body.
But the scent of our faith grows strong and [then] goes out.
The scent announces the taste,
For the one who has acquired a crucible [for testing] scents.
[20:12] Truth and love are wings undivided.
Truth cannot fly without love.
Love cannot soar without truth.
Their yoke is one of unity.
[20:13] Sight and the movement of the eyes are one thing.
And though there is a difference,[20] the nostrils are not divided.
Nor can a quick blink
Steal one eye from the other.[21]
[20:14] Feet have never been divided on two roads,
[But] the heart that walks on two roads as one is divided.
On two paths—of darkness and light—
[The heart], through its freedom, has walked in opposition.
[20:15] His feet and his eyes slay the one who is divided.[22]
O heart—wearied bull, equally divided:
It has divided itself between two yokes—
The just yoke and the yoke of wickedness.[23]
[20:16] He has enslaved his will to an accursed farmer.
He draws a harsh yoke, and ploughs a wasteland.
Instead of grain, he sows thorns,
As the goad of sin drives him on.
[20:17] Inner prayer cleanses troubled thoughts.
Faith cleanses external senses.
One person who is indeed divided,
Let him be gathered, Lord, and become one before you!

---

himself inside the fish because he failed to proclaim initially as God had commanded him.

20. B, "Though this is clear...."
21. That is, both eyes reflexively blink at the same time.
22. That is, the feet and the eyes of the one divided.
23. Cf. 1 Cor 6.14–16.

HYMN TWENTY-ONE

According to the same melody.[1]

[21:1] Sing, Lord, on my lyre, every helpful thing:[2]
With strong[3] words,[4] let us sing for perfection,
With pure [words], for the virgins,[5]
And with simple [words], let us sing for the simple.[6]

REFRAIN: *To the Father, sing praise, and to his Son a song!*[7]

[21:2] Come hear about Zechariah, who spoke back to
   Gabriel.[8]
Old man, study and investigate: where is your speech?
Likewise, they become quiet and silent,
All who presume to debate with truth!
[21:3] If Gabriel, though a thing-made, became this powerful
When his word was not believed by the Levite,
How strong must the Son of the Just One be,
Since {you have not believed him}[9]—that he is the Son, as he
   says?
[21:4] O Zechariah—barren one whose word became barren
Because his tongue was divided. [He asked] how he would
   beget[10]

1. On this melody, see note 1 attached to hymn 10.
2. Hymns 21–23 offer a trilogy of hymns drawing upon the metaphor of
the lyre. On this metaphor, see note 9 attached to 2:9. For another series of
hymns on the lyre, see *HVir* 27–30.
3. Syr., *ḥlīmān*. D, *ḥāleyn*, "sweet."   4. Syr., *mellê*. BD, *mennê*, "strings."
5. B, "virginity."
6. On this three-tiered system, see *HF* 10:3; 12:5, 18; 21:1; 22:3.
7. B, "thanksgiving."   8. Lk 1.18.
9. D. A, "since he did not believe him."
10. Lk 1.18.

157

When his refuter was there, my son,

Inside the Ark: a staff {that had budded}![11]

[21:5] If an equal grew irritated with his equal[12] and cast

A muzzle of silence [on him], since he was in doubt about
    John,

Then the mouth that disgraces the Only-Begotten

Deserves the muzzle of Sennacherib.[13]

[21:6] Let the clarity of Abraham be a mirror for you,

[Showing] that discussion is a foul mark upon faith.

{Insofar as}[14] he believed, he was justified.[15]

Wherever he discussed, his seed was subjugated.[16]

[21:7] Like "the partridge who calls out to one it did not bear,"

Or the bird whose voice deceives whoever trusts it,

Do not let their voices lead you astray—

[Voices] that confess the Son, though [say], "He is not the
    Begotten."

[21:8] There is a bird that alters its call:

Like[17] the fowl that changes its call and hunts its friends,

There is a deceitful one who changes his words

Among his hearers for his [own] profit.

[21:9] But you, O lyre, do not deceive your hearers!

Do not sing to humans with two faces!

Both secretly and openly

---

11. BD. A, "a staff was budding." On the budding staff, see Nm 17.2–12; Heb 7.4; *HNat* 1:17.

12. Syr., *kentâ*. Gabriel and Zechariah are equals in that both are created beings.

13. 2 Kgs 19; Is 37.37. See also *CNis* 35:7.

14. BD. A, "how."

15. Gn 15.6.

16. Cf. Gn 15.8–16. In Gn 15.8, following Abraham's expression of faith, he asks "how am I to know that I will possess" the land? In response, God asks for a ritual sacrifice. After the latter is performed, Abraham falls asleep and, while sleeping, the Lord warns him that his seed will be subjugated and oppressed in a foreign land. Ephrem thus connects Abraham's question to the impending subjugation of his seed. For a parallel in Rabbinic sources, see *Midrash Tanḥuma Qedoshim* 7:13, in *Midrash Tanḥuma (S. Buber Recension), Vol. II: Exodus and Leviticus,* trans. John T. Townsend (Hoboken, NJ: Ktav Publishing House, Inc., 1997), 312.

17. BD, "there is."

May your voice establish the taste of your truth!
[21:10] And Moses, in a symbol, prepared trumpets.[18]
In the camp, only two {trumpets}[19] sounded.
See the fulfillment of the symbol in the Church:
Two Testaments blew and sounded forth![20]
[21:11] And David's lyre sang three times:
With strings[21] exalted, it sang your divinity;
With [strings] in the middle, it sang your humanity.
With weak [strings] it sang about your death![22]
[21:12] And your Church: may it be a lyre for your song!
Reconcile the tuneless[23] strings divided within it.
Let us sing with the Lord of peace
On this lyre of peace, truth in unity!

18. Nm 10.1–10.

19. B (missing in A).

20. Ephrem here likely intends a polemic against Marcion, a figure in second-century Rome who taught the existence of two gods: the god of the Old Testament, who created the world in all its fallenness, and the God of Jesus Christ, who came to free us from this creator god. On the basis of this theology, he rejected the Old Testament, and forged a New Testament canon which lacked any references to the Old Testament. Much of Ephrem's *CH* and *PR* deal with Marcionite issues, which suggests that his ideas were alive and flourishing in fourth-century Northern Mesopotamia. Ephrem mentions him by name in *HF* 86:17–19. On Ephrem's response to Marcionism see Han J. W. Drijvers, "Marcionism in Syria: Principles, Problems, Polemics," *The Second Century: A Journal of Early Christian Studies* 6:3 (1987–88): 153–72, reprinted in idem, *History and Religion in Late Antique Syria* (Aldershot: Variorum, 1994).

21. Syr., *mennê*. D, *mellê*, words.

22. See also *HF* 10:3; 12:5, 18; 21:1, 11; 22:3.

23. Lit., "angry."

HYMN TWENTY-TWO

According to the same melody.[1]

[22:1] Give thanks to the Lord of all, who formed and
    fashioned for himself
Two lyres—of the Prophets and of the Apostles.
But one finger {has played}[2] both:
Different voices, two testaments.

> REFRAIN: *Glory to your hidden birth from your Begetter!*

[22:2] And whenever a lyre changes sounds,
The lyre and its player stay the same.
And the lyres of truth,[3] my son,
Change sounds, while the truth[4] is one.
[22:3] And a single flute can produce different [sounds]:
For healthy ears, it plays healthy sounds.
For childlike ears, simple sounds.
For sick ears, gentle sounds.[5]
[22:4] These horns of truth
Have established perfect sounds for the perfect.
And for the one who is like a child, they construct
Even promises of milk and honey.[6]
[22:5] What lyre, trumpet, or horn
Plays simply one sound and then stops?
With different sounds it is able to provide help.
Therefore the voices of truth have increased.
[22:6] Jesus is used to being reviled by fools.

---

1. On this melody, see note attached to hymn 10.
2. B. A, "has sounded."   3. Syr., *šrārâ*.
4. Syr., *qûštâ*. On *šrārâ* and *qûštâ*, see note 33 attached to 7:9.
5. See also *HF* 10:3; 12:5, 18; 21:1, 11; 22:3.
6. See, *inter alia*, Ex 3.8.

Father and Son in their names, my son, are true.
It shames the Son [to say] his name is false.
It shames the Father [to say] his name is not true.[7]
[22:7] Jesus endures the mocking of strangers.
Look: he bears great shame from [his] worshipers.
Great is the disgrace to the Three,
If someone is baptized with borrowed names.[8]
[22:8] How do you consider your songs to be glorification?[9]
How will your loss become like gain?
How will your controversy,
O presumptuous one, become a treasure of benefits?
[22:9] He knows his Father as a fruit its tree.[10]
He also knows his fruit as a root.[11]
Look: both of their knowledge
Is hidden and secret in both of them.
[22:10] This knowledge of the Begotten and his Begetter
Sits within a treasure whose gate is sealed with great silence.
Its veil is awesome stillness
And its guard is the powerful Cherub.
[22:11] My son, whose is the mouth that will debate or speak
At the gate of that treasury—hidden and quiet?
The watchers above, whenever they gazed upon it,
Sealed their mouths with the silence of discernment.
[22:12] He who knows not the splendor of that place,
Babbles like a drunk—both he and his hearers.
But if, my son, he {shakes}[12] off his arrogance,
Having been drunk on it, he becomes silent and sings praise.[13]

---

7. On Ephrem's understanding of divine names, see pp. 36–37.

8. On Ephrem's references to various baptismal practices, see note 8 attached to 13:6.

9. Ephrem seems to refer here to rival hymnists. On this, albeit dealing with the *CH,* see S. Griffith, "Ephraem, Bar Dayṣān and the Clash of *Madrāshê* in Aram: Readings in Ephraem's *Hymni contra Haereses,*" *The Harp* 21 (2006): 447–72.

10. These tree metaphors form one of Ephrem's primary means of speaking about the relationship between the Father and the Son. See also *HF* 30:5 and *SF* 2:1–25.

11. That is, the Father knows the Son as his source.

12. B. The form used by A—*metnṣep*—is not attested in the lexica.

13. Cf. Ps 78.65.

HYMN TWENTY-THREE

According to the same melody.[1]

[23:1] Speak, lyre, you whose enemy is silence,
But speak something that can be spoken,
Since every unlawful thing,
If spoken, is blasphemy to the Just One.

> REFRAIN: *The earth sings glory to you, for in you it has been redeemed!*

[23:2] Whoever dares to investigate becomes like the deniers.
The presumptuous one, too, stands at the steps of death,
Since, by debating, he has stripped off his faith,
To go down and investigate the sea of hidden things.[2]
[23:3] Child, do not be alarmed at these things I have said
   to you.
Compare them separately:
One denies his divinity,[3]
And the other investigates in order to diminish God.
[23:4] The Lord of all is greater than all, like his title:
Let us see in the name "the Lord of all" that he is greater
   than all.
Whose knowledge is so great
That he can explore and measure the abyss of wisdom?
[23:5] Lyre, cleanse yourself from controversy!
Let haughtiness not sound its own will within you,
Nor let arrogance chant within you

---

1. On this melody, see note 1 attached to hymn 10.
2. On the metaphor of the sea, see note 36 attached to 4:13.
3. I.e., the "deniers" (23:2).

With its songs, for it is utter ruin.

[23:6] Therefore, fix the strings that have become tangled
through debating.

Collect the songs that have wandered off in discussions.

Stand, my son, before divinity,

And then sing praise to God.

[23:7] For you, lyre, are living and speech-endowed!

Your strings and your words have freedom!

O lyre, which by itself,

According to its will, sings to its God!

[23:8] Stand[4] up straight and sing—no controversy!

Cleanse the rust from your songs and sing for us—nothing
hidden!

Be a disciple of all revealed things,

And, without fear, speak of beautiful things.

[23:9] Therefore, measure [your] words, blameless voices.

Measure and sing songs undisputed,[5]

That your song, my son, may be a delight

To the servants of your Lord, and your Lord repay you!

[23:10] Therefore, do not sing damage[6] to humanity!

Do not divide united brothers through discussion.

Do not place a sword[7]—that is, investigation—

Among the simple, who have believed simply.

[23:11] Therefore, do not sing to God in a backwards way[8]

Instead of [singing] praise, lest you stray and sing wickedness.

Sing like David to the Son of David:

Call him "Lord" and "Son," like David.[9]

[23:12] Do not shame the Father and the Son with one
another.

Do not sing to the Father the dishonor of his Son,

---

4. BD add "yourself" (Syr., *napšāk*).

5. BD, "blameless." By "undisputed," I take Ephrem to mean that the songs
are neither the product of disputation, nor treat topics that lead to disputation.

6. This term (*ḥûsrānâ*) can also have the sense of "expense," an economic
resonance that would cohere with the last line of 23:9.

7. On "sword," see *HF* 53:2.   8. Cf. *HF* 9:1–3.

9. Ps 110.1; Ps 2.7.

Lest you also sing to the Son

The dishonor of his Father, [by saying] "He is not the
    Begetter."

[23:13] That the Father is first, this is uncontroversial.

That the Son is second, this is undoubted.

The name of the Spirit is third,

So why do you destroy the order of the names?

[23:14] "Teach and baptize in the three names:

In the name of the Father, of the Son, and {of}[10] the Holy
    Spirit."[11]

The name of the Son cannot go before

The name of the Father, lest there be confusion.

[23:15] How and why: this stays within silence.[12]

Inside and outside that silence, speak glory.

Let your tongue not become

A bridge of voices trespassing all words.

[23:16] Send up to him glory—a tithe of your songs!

Offer to him a sheaf of words from your thought!

Send up first an alleluia

From the songs your tongue has gathered![13]

---

10. BD.

11. Cf. Mt 28.19, which Ephrem quotes quite liberally, though he uses *lam*
to signify it is a quotation.

12. That is, how and why the Son is begotten. On Ephrem's refusal to discuss questions of "how" with respect to God's begetting, see note 3 attached
to 9:1.

13. Ephrem is conceptualizing hymnody through the metaphor of harvest
offerings: hymnody must begin with an "alleluia," which parallels the ten per-
cent commanded in Dt 12.17.

HYMN TWENTY-FOUR

According to the same melody.[1]

[24:1] With the armor of a condemned fighter,[2] our Lord
    prevailed.[3]
He put on a body from Adam and from David,
That with that body evil had condemned,
In it, he would be abased, to overcome disgrace.

> REFRAIN: *To you, my Lord, a song from the peoples*[4] *that have
> believed in you!*

[24:2] Even your childhood is too great for the talkative:
Who will open his mouth against the One who nourishes all—
Who, at the meager table
Of Joseph and Mary, has grown up?
[24:3] From a great womb—rich and all-enriching—
In the meager womb of Mary you were nurtured.
You had a mortal father on earth,
While you yourself were living and giving life to all.
[24:4] He mounted a despised foal, and hid his victory in
    its lowliness.[5]

---

1. On this melody, see note 1 attached to hymn 10.
2. Syr., *'atlîṭâ*, a calque on the Greek ἀθλητής (i.e., "athlete").
3. Cf *HPar* 4:2–4.
4. On "peoples," see note 35 attached to 9:11.
5. Mt. 21.1–9; Mk 11.1–10; Lk 19.28–38; Jn 12.12–18. Stanzas 4–7 offer in-sight into Ephrem's subtle exegetical thinking. Ephrem begins, in 24:4, with an allusion to Christ's entry into Jerusalem on a donkey. This scene spurs a question in his mind: if Christ is truly the Son of God, why did he not enter Jerusalem on a nobler animal, i.e., a horse? This brings Ephrem to David—a noble warrior who rode horses, but was nevertheless conquered by a "tender

Riders of horses and chariots are subdued, conquered.
David conquered valiant battle lines,
But a tender wife humbled his strength.[6]
[24:5] An ass spoke, and recognized that it was an ass.
Its master, too, it recognized as its master.[7]
Who is so learned that he cannot distinguish
A thing-made[8] from its maker?
[24:6] And if Nabal was punished for his brash speech[9]—
An insolent man who opened his mouth savagely,
For he made David the great king
Small, and named him one of the servants[10]—
[24:7] What fool, then, would be like Nabal?[11]
Flee, my brothers, from his tongue and from his death!
For it was not the son of Jesse that his mouth disgraced,
But the Son of David!
[24:8] The cross is the seal and mold of created things.[12]
By its length and breadth—by its shape—everything is sealed.
The cross that bears every bird on two wings,

---

wife" (24:4:4). This equine terminology then leads Ephrem to the narrative of
Balaam, whom he uses to shame those who call Christ a "thing-made" in 24:5.
In 24:6, however, he returns to the narrative of David and the "soft wife" introduced in 24:4, by explicitly alluding to David's conflict with Nabal. Finally,
by rephrasing, in 24:7:8, a question which Nabal asks in 1 Sm 25.10, Ephrem
brings this exegetical rabbit trail back to its original point: the divine Sonship
of Christ.

6. Ephrem's allusion could be to Bathsheba (2 Sm 11.2–5), or to Abigail
(1 Sm 25). Given the allusion in 24:6–7 to Nabal, Abigail's husband, Abigail
seems more likely.

7. Nm 22, esp. v. 30.

8. Syr., *'bādâ 'bîdâ*, lit., "a thing-made made."

9. Syr., *'al d-'awrek leššānāk*, lit., "because he stretched out his tongue." See
1 Sm 25.

10. Lines 2–4 of this stanza could also be rendered as follows: "… [Na-
bal], an insolent man, who opened his mouth savagely, / That one, David the
great king / made small, and named him among the servants." I have, however, chosen my translation on the basis of what appears to be an allusion to 1
Sm 25.10, in which Nabal characterizes David as a "servant" (*'abdâ*) who has
broken from his master.

11. Lit., "Who is the fool, then, who would be like Nabal?"

12. On the cruciform shape of creation, see *HF* 18:2, 6–16.

Through its strength all stands.

[24:9] The Lord inclined and came down. To the servant he
  became a servant.[13]

He was like a companion, like an equal; he washed feet.[14]

My friends, let us investigate these things,

If we are able, in accordance with grace.

[24:10] The Lord of heaven came down to earth and lived.

He became a stranger, an inhabitant, and a sojourner,

To bring us up to dwell

In his kingdom—in an eternal dwelling.

[24.11] With all mouths let us praise the Lord of all tongues.

As much as we have wandered, so much more should we praise
  that Son of life,

Who, because he raised up a body in his love,

The crucifiers assaulted and the investigators went mad.[15]

13. Cf. Phil 2.7.

14. Jn 13.1–17.

15. Here Ephrem explicitly connects "crucificiers" and "investigators" in a
dual movement against Christ. On this aspect of Ephrem's thought, see Shepardson, *Anti-Judaism*, esp. ch. 4.

HYMN TWENTY-FIVE

According to the same melody.[1]

[25:1] Who has given me a little breath of the Spirit?
It is not for prophecy—this would be a request for death—
But that I might be able to proclaim the glory
Of him who is greater than all, with my poor tongue.

> REFRAIN: *Enable me not to presume to discuss your birth!*

[25:2] Without the very gift of that Greatness,
Mouths could not distribute from its treasures.
Yet, with its key they are opened—
Its treasure, before its treasure-keepers.
[25:3] Glory to the gift of speech in the mouth of orators,
Though it does not hinder their freedom through its
    discourse!
The mouth possesses both at once:
By itself it can attack him, by itself it can magnify him!
[25:4] Without the gift of the word, the mouth could not
Tell about the Word—how [it exists] or how great it is.
With the word, a person can even
Speak as his own advocate.
[25:5] And the eye can see the light by means of [the light].[2]
Through [the light's] rays, it can see its beauties.
So too heavenly lightning:
One can see through the shining from him.
[25:6] Without a guide sent from the light,
The eye cannot go to the light.

---

1. On this melody, see note 1 attached to melody of hymn 10.
2. B, "And the eye cannot see light by itself, / But through the rays ..."

So too with fire in the darkness:
It illuminates and draws the pupils to itself.
[25:7] Inscribed in creation is the type of the Son of the
    Creator:
In light, fire, and water, along with the rest,[3]
Through which and with which he can
Draw humanity into the type of Greatness.
[25:8] With the sea's gift, the swimmer dares
To swim in its depths, for the strength of the water carries him.
There are floods mingled there,
Along with whirlpools, waves, and vortexes.
[25:9] And when the sea's back[4] is ready and prepared
For the craft that can ride upon it,
Look: it[5] dives into its depths, like
Knowledge into the narratives of Greatness.
[25:10] And though a seed from us [produces] fruits on its own,
Laziness does not teach us [about] his gift.
Through prosperity, he signifies his prosperity to us,
That we might plunder the riches his mercy brought us.[6]
[25:11] And the rain that his gift likewise scatters upon all:
It does not teach laziness to farming.
His labor increases the harvest
And his riches increase delights.
[25:12] May your gift quickly lift me up, Lord, to your height.
In you I can become great, therefore I will come to you.
If a person, through and by means of created things,
Can come to you, I, Lord, will come to you.
[25:13] May the example of Zacchaeus, who grew up,[7]
    instruct me:[8]
In you his shortness grew tall and he rose up to come to you.

3. That is, the whole range of natural symbols which Ephrem has been
interpreting theologically.
4. That is, the surface of the sea.
5. I.e., a boat.
6. Ephrem's point here is that the lesson we are to draw from a fruit's easy
growth is not that growth requires no effort, but that God bestows bounty
upon humanity.
7. Syr.,'eštawšeṭ, literally, "to stretch out, to advance."
8. Lk 19.2–10.

{A word from you}⁹ brought him
To its¹⁰ side, though he had been far from you.
[25:14] A fig tree with no fruits brought forth a wondrous
    fruit;
Something insipid, with no taste, brought forth taste.
An insipid fig tree, by means of its sickly
Fruits has seasoned the insipid.¹¹
[25:15] It is a marvel that the fig tree was deprived of its
    natural fruit
And bore another fruit, not of its nature.
While there was no food from one perspective,
The hungry ate it in the portions that he divided.¹²
[25:16] May your gift call even to me, as to Zacchaeus.
Not because I have divided [my] riches {like him, Lord},¹³
But because I have hastened—even me—
{To return}¹⁴ your money with interest!¹⁵
[25:17] And consider this: when he gave his money to the
    merchants,
He showed us that without his abundance there is no
    commerce,
Just as without
His gift, there is no true praise.
[25:18] Run, my brothers, and collect all the images with us!
Look at how many there are for our mouth to depict!

---

9. Syr., *hî ba(r)t qālê d-mennāk ṣîdēh*, B. A misspells *ba(r)t* as *brît*.

10. I.e., the word's side.

11. In the Lukan narrative, Zacchaeus climbs a sycamore tree to see Christ. The Syriac term for "sycamore tree" is *tîtâ pakkîhtâ*, lit., "tasteless fig tree." While never using the term, Ephrem clearly alludes to it in this passage, rendering the "sycamore tree"—a fig tree without figs—an image of Zacchaeus. Ephrem will continue the pun into 25:15, though he probably also has Mt 21.18–19 in mind.

12. See Lk 19.8, where Zacchaeus promises to divide his portions among the poor.

13. B. Absent in A.

14. B. Absent in A.

15. Ephrem alludes vaguely to the parable of the talents, from Mt 25.14–30 / Lk 19.11–27, and then makes the allusion more obvious in the following stanza.

Come delight in our discoveries!
It is right that we should take delight in you!
[25:19] Dough is unable, without the gift
Of {leaven},[16] to share its tastes.
Through the gift from you, it can be
Drawn together, all of it {with}[17] all of it.[18]
[25:20] Neither can un-curdled milk congeal
Without the hidden power of rennet.
Through its gift, it makes
Soft milk firm.[19]
[25:21] Bestow upon my softness your noble things!
Lord, in you my lowliness is raised to your greatness.
In you, my wretched self is stretched out
To your height: there I will worship you!

The end of the sixteen hymns in one melody.[20]

---

16. Syr., *ḥmîrâ*, B. A, *ḥamrâ*, "wine."

17. Syr., *'am*, B. A, *lwātan*, "to us," which makes less sense semantically, and upsets the meter.

18. I.e., all the dough with all the leaven.

19. Lit., "it brings / the softness of milk to firmness." Ephrem is referring to cheese-making.

20. Omitted in B.

HYMN TWENTY-SIX

According to the melody, "God in his mercy ..."[1]

[']² [26:1] God is hidden by his Firstborn,
Wondrous Maker not laboring.
He needed no instruction,
Nor did he grow weak alongside creation.
With a gesture of his gentle and humble will,
He created all and ordered all from nothing.
And just as he created without labor,
Without anxiety he sustains all.

> REFRAIN: *Glory to you, hidden from all in your*[3] *investigation.*

[b] [26:2] In the beginning he created, though his thought
Was with him without beginning.
His thought was not like a human's,
Thus newly moved, like something born of flesh.
His movement was not new, nor his thought recent.
His creation was subject to time, start, and beginning,
Yet his foreknowledge

---

1. In A, *HF* 2 and 3 are also called by this same melody, though they display a different meter (see note 1 attached to melody of hymn 2). This melody and meter is also attached to *HF* 26–30, and 79, and consists in eight-line stanzas, broken into the following metrical pattern: 5+3 / 5+3 / 5+3 / 5+4 / 5+5 / 5+5 / 3 +3 / 6+3. Very often, Ephrem adds an extra syllable to these lines. In the critical edition of the Syriac text, Beck erroneously scans 26:2, 3, 11, 12; 27:3, 8; and 79:9. I have corrected these stanzas and provide the correct Syriac lines in the notes to these hymns.

2. Here begins an acrostic on the Syriac alphabet. It repeats several letters and concludes with *yod*.

3. Lit., "his" or "its."

Is more exalted than times and beginnings.[4]

[g] [26:3] The natures of the Seraphim are concealed from us,

For us to investigate how "six wings" are fastened,

What the wings are, and of what they are made,

And how the Spirit needs to fly by means of the wings.[5]

Is this then a parable? Is it then true?

If it is true, it is very difficult [to understand].

If it is a type or a title,[6] it is very hard [to understand].[7]

[g] [26:4] Limitlessly concealed is the Hidden One.

His investigation is too deep for the weak,

His inquiry too exalted for mortals.

Who will go up to his height or explore his depth?

Whoever has rushed up to his height has slipped and fallen
    badly.

Whoever has rushed down to his depths has sunken deep
    and drowned.

The death of the one who has investigated him is bitter.

The one who dives down to explore him sinks.

[g] [26:5] Clearly the sun teaches, my brothers,

That damage comes to the one who looks upon Greatness.

Its nature is more powerful than all mouths

And all of it is stranger than all tongues.

The senses do not grasp how to depict it.

Their reach is not able to attain it.

But the Books of the Prophets

Have lifted understanding and depicted him in names.

{d}[8] [26:6] {Those} reasons thus demanded that

He speak with them weakly.

---

4. The Syriac text of the final three lines should be scanned *brîteh tẖêt zab-na-y w-rîšeh w-šûrāyâ / w-'îda'tâ mqaddmtâ / men zabnê w-šûrāyê 'elāyê-(h)y.*

5. Is 6.2.

6. Syr., *kûnāyâ.* On the significance of this term, see pp. 36–37.

7. That is, if Isaiah is representing reality, it is difficult to understand what these creatures are. If he is speaking figuratively, it is difficult to explain what the figures represent. The final three lines of this stanza should be scanned: *matlā-(h)w kay hānâ šrārâ-(h)w kay hānâ / 'en qûštā-(h)w ṭāb 'āseq / w-'ên ṭupsâ w-kûnāyâ ṭāb 'āṭel.*

8. B. The initial *d-* of the acrostic is absent from A, which begins with '.

If he had begun to speak
According to the marvel and wonder of his divinity
[It would have] led the ear astray, and offended innocence.[9]
Since the simple have perished and the perfect are wanting,
He has used all images,
That, according to his power, and insofar as able, a person
   might understand.
[d] [26:7] It is a great error for a person to think
That Essence is like a creature,
Where there is a mouth, ears, and eyes:
This is a feeble construct.
To give it a body is dangerous. To construct it is dreadful.
To confine it is wickedness. To limit it is evil.
Yet, though he is above all these things,
He bent down beneath them in his mercy.
[d] [26:8] The images useful for humanity
Have come from the treasury of the Lord of all.
According to time and situation, he has distributed an image
   to help.
In the time of anger, the time of delight;
In the time of fear, in the time of quiet.
Though he is the same in his substance,
In his law,[10] toward us, he changes.
[d] [26:9] Look: Moses, when he taught the People
With our images, he spoke about its greatness.
[Yet] he abolished them when he said,
"You did not see an image inside the fire."[11]
The Hidden One put on no image on Mount Sinai,
Lest the People depict him with paint.
He acquired an image and a face
In Moses, to depict himself in his heart.
[w] [26:10] And just as he helped without showing
A face or an image on Mount Sinai,
So that he would not provide an excuse for paganism,
Which depicts him for humans mistakenly,

9. Lit., "An error for the ear, offense to innocence."
10. Syr., *nāmûsâ*.
11. Cf. Dt 4.12.

He helped also when he put on the likeness of a face,
To show us his beauty, and make his comeliness known.
When he did not show himself, he prevented error.
When he did show [himself], he made help increase.
[w] [26:11] When the seventy elders looked and thought
They had seen the limit of Greatness,
Moses repudiated the whole illusion.
He asked to see him, so he could inform and teach them,
For the elders did not see what they thought they saw.[12]
And though Moses indeed saw,
He knew he had not seen.
The discerning one was aware that his Lord had put on
    borrowed images.[13]
[z] [26:12] He whose appearance is greater than all became
    smaller
Than the dust that he who establishes all formed.[14]
For as he bent down and fashioned it through grace,
He was humbled, and manifested himself in smallness.
And if, even though in our images, Moses saw him and was
    afraid,
How can anyone stand before the precise
Strength of his Essence,
Which the Son alone comprehends?[15]
[ḥ] [26:13] Consider: he is and is not.
When the True One put on an image,

---

12. Ephrem is drawing upon three scenes: (1) Ex 24.9–11, in which Moses
and the elders see "the God of Israel"; (2) Ex 24.15–18, in which Moses ascends Mt. Sinai alone, and enters the cloud; (3) Ex 33.18–23, in which Moses
asks to see a vision of the Lord, and the Lord allows it partially. Implicit in
this as well is that in Ex 24.9–11, the divine appearance (at least its feet) is described, whereas in the other two references, there is no physical description.
For Ephrem, then, since Moses is undoubtedly "higher" than the 70 elders, his
vision-scenes demonstrate that the vision experienced by the 70 elders was an
illusion.

13. The Syriac of lines 6–8 should be scanned as follows: *w-kad ṭāb ḥzâ mûšê
yādaʿ d-lâ ḥzâ-(h)wâ / lâ tʾāteh l-pārûšâ / d-demwātâ šʾilātâ lbeš māreh.*

14. Cf. Gn 2.7.

15. Lines 6–8 should be scanned as follows: *ʾaykan mṣâ-(h)wâ kay la-mqām
qdām ʿûzâ / ḥattîtâ d-ʾîtûteh / hāy da-brâ-(h)w balḥûd sappeq leh.*

Fullness was found within it,
And that brightness covered our form,[16]
For the image could not contain Greatness.
The image was not divinity.
A veil made for
Greatness an aid for the childlike.
[ṭ] [26:14] The tastes of his words are different
When he corrects fools' ears.
The images of his face are marvelous,
For his beauty kindles the eyes of the children.
And being entirely constant, he did not grow small and
 then big:
He was small without being small, and big to make
 [others] big.
He grows to speak with every person,
And contracts and grows small to speak with one person.
[y] [26:15] To fools, his knowledge seems
To belong to him as [ours] to us.
But he himself exists without necessity,
While he is seen by us according to [our] necessity.
They do not see that he devised practices[17] for that People
To seize them, for they had wandered into the sacrifices of
 paganism.[18]
Because he captured them with a sacrifice,
Fools think he has demanded a burnt offering.

16. Beck translates this as "brightness was covered by our form" (*HF [G]*, 74). The latter is difficult to justify grammatically (one would expect *b-* before "our form"), and the line makes sense as is: though he put on an image—something to cover his brightness (i.e., divinity)—it was in fact too weak to mask his divinity.

17. Syr., *ṣen'ātâ*, which has the connotation of sneakiness, or even deceit. The idea here is that Jewish ritual practices were provided because of the Jews' habitual tendency toward paganism. On this theme in Ephrem, see Shepardson, *Anti-Judaism*, esp. ch. 3.

18. Cf. Gn 32.

HYMN TWENTY-SEVEN

According to the same melody.[1]

[27:1] God, who exists essentially,
His nature, like his name, is glorified.
And if that Being is different from all in name,
The narrative of that Being is concealed from all.
How things-made are tormented when they investigate him,
For there is nothing in him similar to creatures!
How minds gaze,
Seeing themselves instead of him!

> REFRAIN: *Glory to you—the Son, the Messiah—and to your*
> *Father!*

[27:2] Look: natures think they see him
Whom they have never been able to see,
For they have seen through themselves and, lo, have gone
      astray,
Thinking that God is like them.
If they had seen him through him, it would be good to think
      they saw.
Instead of him, they have seen themselves and thought, lo,
      they had seen him.
Woe to the fool who explores himself
And thinks he can name[2] the Hidden One.
[27:3] It is impossible to depict in our heart
The "how" of the nature that exists.[3]

---

1. On this melody, see note 1 attached to hymn 26.
2. B, "explore."
3. On questions of "how" in relation to divinity, see note 3 attached to 9:1.

To what would we liken it without going astray?
What we would find would be truly certain to us.
If we think that we have seen him in an image,
Greatly we have erred and caused error; greatly we have
    wandered, and caused wandering.
The fruit that is from him
Alone knows him truly.[4]
[27:4] Woe to the blind assembly of investigators!
They stand inside the light, but go around looking for it.
They have touched gold and likened it to light.
They have handled jewels, thinking light was within.
They have touched everything and handled everything,
And look: fools think that they have handled the light.
Each one, as he thinks,
Has captured and depicted the light in his mind.
[27:5] They do not think of how they have
One sense like the light,[5]
[While] the other senses are concealed,
And all are foreign to the light.
[The light's] color is not perceived, its scent not smelled.
Its brightness is inaudible, and its light cannot be touched.
Only seeing is similar:
It understands it, as a child its parent.[6]
[27:6] The light dwells in the mouth unperceived.
Shining, it dwells in the ear without suffering.
It dwells in the hand, yet how has [the hand] not felt it?
The nostril has not inhaled what rises up to it.
And the mind and the heart—king, commander—
And assembly of the thoughts—and the soul, their dwelling,
Have failed to understand the light,
Yet investigate the Lord of the light.
[27:7] See the dishonor, disgrace, shame,
And reproach of them all in one thing:

---

4. This stanza should be rescanned as follows: line 6 and 7 should be combined to comprise a single 5+5 line, and line eight should be broken up into two lines: *pîrâ gêr d(a?)-menneh / hû balḥûd yāda' leh ba-šrārâ*.

5. I.e., sight.

6. Or, "the Child its Begetter."

{None}[7] of them can see
That tiny glimmer before them.
Look: it has rubbed itself on them, spread its color on them,
And its rising has anointed them. And though they are well
    clothed in it,
It is far-off in the distance,
And the weak have perceived it only by report.
[27:8] Look: the blind with their questioning are like
Some haughty blind man who held a bow
And shot arrows into flames,
Not perceiving how his arrows were ruined.
The arrows which he shot arrogantly
Became ash upon the fire, and dust in the wind.
And if he himself had gone into [the fire],
He would have been destroyed there, along with his arrows.[8]

7. B. A adds in margin.
8. In Beck's scansion lines five (with total five syllables) and seven (total twelve syllables) do not fit the meter of this hymn. I have not been able to scan this stanza in a way which makes it fit within the hymn's meter.

HYMN TWENTY-EIGHT

According to the same melody.[1]

[28:1] If watchers, lightning, and rays,
Earthquakes, storms, and floods[2]—
The equals of creatures—are dreadful
When they bring force against our weakness;
Yet if the ministers who serve him
Likewise fear Adam,[3] who is [also] ministered to,
Who will presume to look upon
That force in whose power all exists?

REFRAIN: *Blessed is the Child who cannot be discussed!*

[28:2] Another force, medicine,
Causes harm when undiluted.
Wine, too, can weary with its vitality,
And spices with the strength of their scent.
Sleep and food, too, are loathsome when disordered.
And if weak things unmixed are difficult to bear,
How much more difficult, unordered,
For someone to investigate the Consuming Fire?[4]
[28:3] The Good One, therefore, who has arranged for us
Weights, scales, and measures,
So we can approach created things through order,
To accept their aid in measure:

1. On this melody, see note 1 attached to hymn 26.
2. On "watchers," and the relationship between cosmological phenomena and angelic forces, see note 6 attached to 3:5.
3. Or, "man" (Syr., *'ādām*).
4. Cf. Dt 4.24; 9.3.

180

The One greater than all surely has not given himself for
    them to approach
Him with measure, yet without order![5]
How would he order all
And not order his investigation for investigators?
[28:4] Look: his boundaries extend over all,
And his rules[6] spread over all.[7]
Force governs nature,[8]
The mind and the will, freedom.
Natures are bound. Things unbridled must be guarded.
The law[9] is a wall guarding freedom.
Who can complain
About the law[10] and the freedom it orders for us?
[28:5] Look: the sun marks a boundary with its course
And the moon orders through its waxing.
He bounds earth and heaven.
He bounds the firmament through the waters above it.[11]
[The world] is not confused. Rather, we are stirred-up.

---

5. The grammar of lines 5 and 6 is difficult. Ephrem is presenting a rhetorical question as the apodosis of lines 1–4. As I have taken it, he is drawing a slight distinction between the "measures" (*mšûḥtâ*) through which God is reached, and the way we proceed through these measures (i.e., orderly or disorderly). Another way to represent these lines, although more difficult to justify grammatically, would be to take the negative accompanying "give" alongside "measure," and read "measure" and "order" in parallel. In that case, the sentence would read: "Has the one greater than all given himself without measure? / That they would approach him, yet without order?"

6. Syr., *ṭûkāsaw(hy)*, from the same word (*ṭaksâ*) translated as "order" in 28:3.

7. As Ephrem makes clear in *HF* 46:1–2, there are boundaries embedded in Scripture and the world, beyond which humans cannot pass. "Rules" likely refers to the "measures" (referenced in 28:3) which humans *can* pass through, provided they do so in the correct order. Either way, Ephrem conceives of reality as manifesting a divine ordering. If humans respect this divine ordering, it can become revelatory of God.

8. The word for "force" (*qṭîrâ*) can also be translated "necessity." The sense is that "nature" is limited, and cannot be transcended.

9. Syr., *nāmûsâ* (a calque on the Greek *nomos*). Here and in line 8 "law" appears to refer to the laws of nature.

10. B, "about nature."

11. Cf. Gn 1.6–7.

If even the waves are bound by the sand,
Look upon the presumptuous one,
Who exalts himself above the Lord of all.
[28:6] Look now, my brothers, at him alone.
May his ordering teach the bold one:
His conception was bound within the womb,
And his birth in the belly of the earth.
Look: he bound conception. Look: he bound birth.
Look: he bound death, the tomb, resurrection.
Look: by these he has become bound,
The presumptuous one, who does not bound his questions.
[28:7] Look: let us further rebuke his confusion,
For his will is troubled by its freedom.
His nature is ordered through grace,
So that nature will become known through freedom.
If someone wished to harm his limbs,
He would hate those doing harm, and love [his] limbs,
[For] the arrangement of his joints is protected.[12]
Unbound and upset is the ordering of his life.[13]
[28:8] Look: the Cherub bounds Paradise,[14]
And dreadful force Mount Sinai:
"Whoever draws near will be stoned without mercy."[15]
Through revealed things, he warns of hidden things.
And whereas a full day marked the mountain's boundary,[16]
The Exalted One eternally marks the boundary of his
    hiddenness.
At that time, [there was] death for the one who presumed.
Now, Gehenna for the one who investigates.

12. I.e., by nature. According to Ephrem's argument, the person would have no choice but to value their own limbs over against the person trying to hurt them.

13. Ephrem's point here is that the natural world (of which humans are a part) has certain innate limitations, which all humans are bound to accept, yet when humans turn to God to investigate him, they act as if no such limitations exist.

14. Gn 3.24.

15. Cf. Ex 19.12. Though Ephrem indicates a quotation through the use of *lam*, this line diverges quite significantly from P of the Exodus passage.

16. Cf. Ex 19.13.

[28:9] Look: the leprosy which rebuked the chatterboxes
Rebukes the audacity of the investigators!
For if Miriam, because she spoke against the humble one,
Her lips wove for her a garment of leprosy[17]—
Her love for the infant in the waters overflowed.
On dry ground, she flooded the heart of Pharaoh's daughter,
So that child who floated,
From what he earned nourished even his mother.[18]
[28:10] Look: wonder, marvel, and terror:
If Miriam, who spoke against the mortal
Who was indebted to her in the water—
She was even older than Moses,
And the Just One, who commanded that they should honor
    elders,[19]
Pitilessly disgraced that elder prophetess!—
Who will claim innocence when he investigates
That Only-Begotten, who exacts vengeance on the talkative?
[28:11] So if the Exalted, for a servant, punished
His sister—the prophetess who attacked him—
Who will examine the Child of that Greatness,
The Son of whose womb is a consuming fire,[20]
By whom lightning and tongues are ignited?
The investigation of the presumptuous is like stubble beside
    him,

17. Nm 12.3–15.
18. Ex 2.3–9. Ephrem here weaves together two scenes from the life of Moses. The first, from Nm 12, recounts an episode in which Miriam and Aaron criticize Moses for marrying a foreign woman, as a result of which Miriam is struck with leprosy. This is balanced with the scene from Ex 2, in which Miriam (identified in vv. 4–8 only as "his sister") cares for the infant Moses, and secures their mother as his midwife. Ephrem juxtaposes these two scenes to make his rhetorical point more strongly: if such an inimitable character as Miriam received leprosy for speaking out of turn, how much more so investigators? Syntactically, too, 28:9 and 10 are quite dense. In 28:9:3–4, Ephrem posits a rhetorical question. Instead of providing an apodosis, however, he shifts to the scene from Numbers, only returning to the initial rhetorical question in 28:10.
19. Lv 19.32.
20. Dt 4.24; 9.3.

And debate and schism
Like chaff and brambles swallowed up.
[28:12] So too Gehazi, who mocked and was mocked:[21]
He deceived the heart of his master, and was exposed.[22]
The presumptuous have deceived humanity,
For they baptize in three names.
But, appeal to the word of three judges:[23]
Look: three witnesses who have undone every controversy!
Who, then, will be divided
Against the holy witnesses of his baptism?
[28:13] If he avenges [his] house when it has been disgraced,
Who will investigate and disgrace[24] the Lord of all?
Do not touch what belongs to him, lest you perish.
When Uzziah offered a censer, he was struck.[25]
And since he was not ashamed to reach[26] for the glory of the
    holy [place],
He was ashamed all his days, for he had to hide his leprosy.
And since he shamed the Temple,
He had to confine himself inside his house as one unclean.
[28:14] Look: both are depicted for those who understand
In a clear[27] mirror of thought:
One image of will they put on,
And one seal of anger, out of freedom.
Both wished to become priests of God.[28]
With their revealed offering, their hidden heart was depicted,
Since, because of their offering,
Their hidden [intentions] were laid bare.
[28:15] The Temple, sanctifying all:
From it went forth leprosy, defiling all.
Teaching,[29] straightening all,

---

21. 2 Kgs 5.20–27.

22. Ibid.

23. Dt 19.15. Here the "three judges" are the Father, Son, and Spirit.

24. B, "diminish" (nez'ar).   25. 2 Chr 26.16–21.

26. B, "to profane" (d-'anšûṭ).   27. B, "hidden."

28. That is both Uzziah (2 Chr 26.16–21), and Korah (Nm 16). The latter
will not be mentioned explicitly until 28:16.

29. Ephrem uses the single word yûlpānâ, though clearly he means "right
teaching."

Has brought us debate, troubling all.
Rain, helper of all, harms us with its excess.
The sun, adorning all, blinds us with its strength.
Even bread, giving life to all,
Destroys the one who eats it greedily.
[28:16] His arrangement rebukes[30] the audacious:
With fire he marked the boundary of the Temple,
And the two hundred who presumed [to try] to become
     priests,
Against them fire—beloved of the holy [place]—burned.
It consumed the sons of Aaron,
Who brought in strange fire like a harlot.[31]
The holy [fire] was aroused, and true knowledge
Has become aroused by abominable investigation.

30. B, "orders."
31. Lv 10.1–2; Nm 26.61; 1 Chr 24.2.

HYMN TWENTY-NINE

According to the same melody.[1]

[']² [29:1] God, in his mercy, called
Mortals gods, by grace.[3]
He who is God—
Whom they limit, like some human, through debate:
The Cherubim carry him who has put on your body.
The Seraphim gleam before him. {The watchers fall silent
    before him}.[4]
But you, debased,
Debase the birth of the honorable one.

    REFRAIN: *Blessed is he, hidden in the womb of his Begetter!*

[p] [29:2] The weak body which he came down and put on,
His names and his actions are like it.
And just as it was necessary for him to be hungry,
It was necessary for him to pray.
And just as all his hunger was of the body.
All his want was of the body.
Do not die because of the names
That Life put on to make all live.
[r] [29:3] The Great One has put on
Needy names out of love for you, because of the body.
To which of them will you appeal?

---

    1. On this melody, see note 1 attached to hymn 26.
    2. This hymn forms an acrostic on Ephrem's name, albeit broken at one point (28:4), and concluding with a repeated *mim*.
    3. Ps 82.6.
    4. B.

He is true, honorable, and glorified.
True is the name of the Father. We believe the name of the
    Son.
Beloved the One who forgives, feared the One who judges.
Because he is human, he is limited.
Because his nature is God, he is without limit.
[?] [29:4] A little lump of earth presumed to come down
To explore the sea—how it came to be.
It debated about the springs, to know
Whence they came up and to where they went.
But that low-down thing, look: it could not investigate itself,
Nor from which place that hand
Which fashioned it had brought it up
And established for it limits[5] which it has despised.
[m] [29:5] Who has seen chaff presume to examine
The wind's[6] force with questions?
The presumptuous die through debating about him
Whose breath revives the dead.
Cedars are uprooted, forests rolled aside.
Straw comes to investigate the nature of the Holy Spirit,[7]
And by a breath that blows it,
Hastens to the furnace door.
[m] [29:6] The Lord and Father who judges no one,
Perhaps judges the investigators.
Why do you investigate that Child
By whose hand you have come to be and were created?
Clay cannot investigate the potter.
[It is] a lifeless vessel he made for [some] use.
The Maker who made you
Rational and knowledgeable, you deny him.

---

5. Lit., "measures" (*mšûḥtâ*).
6. Ephrem plays on the ambiguity of *rûḥâ,* which can be translated "wind"
or "spirit."
7. Or "holy wind."

HYMN THIRTY

According to the same melody.[1]

[30:1] God is Lord of everything.
He is not confined within things, alongside what he has made.
He does not give himself to measuring or weighing,
Touching, color, or measurement.
He is not confined in a place, for he is not stretched out like
The winds and the lightning, that something might confine
   him.
Knowledge is his essence,
Yet all knowledge is foreign to the investigation of it.

> REFRAIN: *Blessed is the Hidden One, hidden from all in his
>   investigation!*

[30:2] This is the straying of the rebellious,
For a thing-made cannot comprehend its maker.
The natures of watchers are fire and spirit.
The natures of bodies are dust and water.[2]
Who can sense the nature of the Lord of all—
A nature that natures cannot interpret?
There are three [questions], and they are defeated:
How, where, and how much?[3]
[30:3] So let us interpret these three things:
"How much?" is asked,
"How much is its measurement and weight,
And the height and length of what exists?"

---

1. On this melody, see note 1 attached to hymn 26.
2. On this passage, see Possekel, *Evidence,* 81.
3. On such questions, see note 3 attached to 9:1.

188

Again, "what is its color,
And is it hard or soft, hot or cold?"
And let the location be explained—
Whether he dwells in a location or a place.[4]
[30:4] Everything that is made, created, or established,
Possesses, along with those like them,
Weight and measurement,
Touch and color, extent and location.
In these three things—three mysteries—
All is confined, all is established, except the Three.
Creatures have these:
How, how much, and where.
[30:5] The Glorious One was humbled in all images,
And put on hunger to the point of abasement.
The tree bent down as far as needed.
Its fruit came down to every [level of] abasement.
The tree, through images, clothed itself in abasement.
Its fruit came down and put on suffering in reality.[5]
He said and did {everything}[6] that he taught,
To be a mirror for his hearers.
[30:6] Just as he taught with words, so he demonstrated
His teaching through his own actions.
He positioned his cheek just as he taught,
And received spitting, though he did not teach it.
They forced him to go, and he went without calling out.
So too he put his knowledge under cover, to instruct
The puffed up and proud,
So that crazy [things] would be held back by his story.
[30:7] Blessed is the fruit which is like its root.

4. The three questions are thus "how" (lines 2–4), "what" (lines 5–6), and "where" (lines 7–8).

5. Here, in one of Ephrem's favorite metaphors for describing the relationship between the Father and the Son, the Father is depicted as a tree that can bend down, but not quite as far as humanity. The fruit, however, which hangs from the tree branch, reaches all the way down. This passage also implies that Old Testament images reflect the condescension of the Father (the "tree"), juxtaposed with the Son (the "fruit") who takes on these images in reality.

6. Syr., kûl, B. A, 'al d-, "on account of [what] ..."

Abasement he put on in temptations.

Floods and waves of his wisdom

He veiled and covered, when he was questioned.[7]

The Books which we scorn he recited to the serpent.

He restrained him and his debating and his questioning.[8]

Our Lord recited from Moses.

The rash, look: they recite from error.

[30:8] Since the serpent[9] is crafty and a debater,

He clothed his disciples in his skin.

Strip off and cast away his skin, lest you perish,

Corrupted by his company, he who corrupts all.

The new and the white have put on in their newness

A decaying will. Since he disguised himself in their garments,

They have been corrupted and stripped themselves.

Put on leaves foreign to decay![10]

[30:9] Though the debater is crafty and subtle,[11]

The backtalk of the guileless casts him down.

Do not clothe yourself in the debating of that thing-made.

Do not let your freedom be his companion.

That evil slave[12] has oppressed his companions,

Depicting in them his image, sealing them with his defect.

For if they have put on his images,

They are unable to rebuke his crimes.[13]

---

7. See *HF* 77–79, and their interpretation of Mt 24.36.

8. Mt 4.3–10.

9. In the previous stanza, Ephrem used for serpent the term *tannînâ*, perhaps because of its similarity to the verb *tnâ*, to recite. Here he uses *ḥawyâ*, the term which appears in Gn 3. Typologically, this stanza subtly connects Christ's wilderness temptation to the temptation of Adam and Eve in the garden. Equally, Ephrem constructs Satan in language identical to that with which he casts his opponents. Their "debating," then, becomes a replaying of famous biblical temptation scenes—first in the Garden of Eden, and then in the Wilderness.

10. Ephrem casts these neophytes as finding themselves in the same situation as Adam and Eve, just after eating the forbidden fruit, but prior to their encounter with the Lord and expulsion from Paradise (see Gn 3.7).

11. The term here translated as "subtle" (*qaṭṭînâ*) is the same Ephrem uses in *CH* 22:4 to describe Aetians.

12. Or, "thing-made."

13. B, "his foulness." Ephrem shifts from plural to singular in the ultimate

[30:10] So when you have seen the Knower-of-all
Having made himself small through this unknowing,
It was your love[14] that made him small unknowingly.[15]
If he became small to keep you from becoming small,
It is low for you to go mad investigating the Investigator-of-all.
And if you are weakened by wine, thrashing about—
If this feeble [thing] has conquered you—
Then how much will that Child set you reeling?

---

line, but I have retained the plural for the sake of readability. Literally, the
final line reads, "... no one is able to rebuke his crimes."

14. That is, presumably, "his love *for* you."

15. Syr., *d-lâ yâda'*. B, *d-lâ nedda'*, "so that he would not know."

HYMN THIRTY-ONE

According to the melody: "Take comfort in the promises ..."[1]

[31:1] Let us give thanks to him who has put on the names of
    body parts:
He has named for himself ears, to teach that he hears us.
He has designated for himself eyes, to show that he sees us.
He has only put on the names of things:
Though in his essence he has neither anger nor regret,
He has put on their names for our weakness.[2]

> REFRAIN: *Blessed is he who has appeared to our humanity in
> all images!*

[31:2] Let us understand: if he had not put on the names
Of these very things, he would have been unable to speak
With our humanity. With {what is ours},[3] he drew near to us.
He put on our names, to put on us
His way of life. He borrowed and put on our form,
And like a father with children, he spoke with our
    childishness.
[31:3] This image of ours he put on and yet did not put [it] on,

---

1. This melody is used for hymns 31 and 39–48. Its meter is 5+5 / 5+5 / 5+
5 / 5+2 / 5+5 / 5+5, although we also find occasional 6- or 7-syllable lines. On
this hymn, see also Brock, *Hymns on Paradise*, 60–63, and Sebastian P. Brock
and George A. Kiraz, *Ephrem the Syrian, Select Poems: Vocalized Syriac Text with
English Translation, Introduction and Notes* (Provo, UT: Brigham Young University Press, 2006), 18–27.

2. This hymn represents one of Ephrem's most sustained reflections on
biblical language. While elsewhere in the *HF*, Ephrem will present Scripture
as utilizing both "true" and "borrowed" names (see note 18 attached to 5:6),
here he reflects solely on the latter category.

3. B. A, "with what is his."

Stripped it off and yet did not strip it off—putting it on,
  stripping it off.
He put it on as an aid, and stripped it off in exchange [for
  another].
Stripping off and putting on every image,
He taught that none were the image of his essence.
Though hidden is his essence, he depicted himself through
  revealed things.
[31:4] In one place he was like an old man—the ancient of
  days.[4]
He was like a warrior, too—strong and brave.[5]
He became an old man for judgment, and became strong for
  war.
In one place he was sluggish,[6] in another place
He ran so that he became weary.[7] In one place he slept,[8]
In another he was in need.[9] In every way, he worked to acquire
  us.
[31:5] This is the Good One: though with force he could
Have adorned [us] without laboring, he labored in every way,
To make our will beautiful, that we might depict our beauty,
Gathered together with the paints of our freedom.
If he were to adorn us, we would be like an image
That someone else depicted, decorating it with his paints.
[31:6] The one who teaches speech to a bird
Hides behind a mirror to teach it.
Whenever [the bird] has turned to the place of the speaking,
She finds her [own] image before her eyes,
And speaks with it, believing it to be her companion.
He has fixed his image[10] before you, for you to learn his speech
  through it.
[31:7] That bird is like a person,
But though similar, they are also like strangers.

4. Dn 7.9.
5. Ex 15.3.
6. Ephrem's reference here is not clear.
7. Cf. Is 1.14; Jn 4.6.   8. Cf. Ps 78.65.
9. Cf. Mt 25.35–36.
10. I.e., his human image, behind which his humanity hides.

[The trainer] taught [the bird] through a ruse, speaking with
    it by himself.
The Essence, exalted above all in all,
Bent down his height lovingly and acquired our habit.
He labored in every way to turn all to himself.
[31:8] His image is that of an old man,[11] or of a warrior.[12]
It is written that he slept,[13] yet that he does not slumber.[14]
It is written that he grew weary,[15] yet that he does not grow
    weary.[16]
Through [the image] he binds, he looses, and he helps, to
    teach us.
He contracted[17] himself and stood above a pavement of
    sapphire.[18]
He expanded and filled heaven, everything resting in the palm
    of his hand.[19]
[31:9] He manifested himself in one place, yet is manifest in
    every place.
We thought, look: he is in that place, while he was filling all.
He became small to fit us,[20] and great to enrich us.
He was small, then great, to make us great.
If he had been small and not become great, he would be small
    and dishonored by us,
Seeming weak. For that reason, he became small, and then
    great.
[31:10] Let us marvel: when he became small, he made our
    smallness big.

11. Dn 7.9. See *HF* 31:4.   12. Ex 15.3.
13. Mt 8.24; Mk 4.38; Lk 8.23.   14. Ps 120.4.
15. Is 1.14; Jn 4.6.   16. Is 40.28.

17. Syr., *etqpes.* Interestingly, in the Aphel form this verb can mean "to pave
a floor with mosaic" (*LS,* 1394, sub. *qps,* #2). Given the reference that follows,
Ephrem may well intend to evoke that sense.

18. Ex 24.10. See also *HF* 26:11.

19. Cf. Is 40.12 and 45.12. In this stanza, esp. lines 2–3, Ephrem makes
New Testament descriptions of Christ and Old Testament descriptions of God
predicates of the single subject "he," thus subtly positing Christ as the subject
of all biblical theophanies.

20. Syr., *nspq,* which I have taken as Aphel, "to make fit." It could also be
rendered as the Pael, "to be enough for us."

Had he not changed into something great, he would have
  made our mind small,
Thinking he was weak, [our mind] small because of what it
  thought.
We are insufficient for the greatness of Being—
[Insufficient] even for his smallness. He becomes great, and
  we wander astray.
He becomes small, and we languish. In every way, he has
  worked with us.
[31:11] He wishes to teach us two things: that he is and that he
  is not.
In his love he made the face, so his works could look upon
  him.
Yet, so we would not be hurt, and think, "He is that way,"
He changed from image to image, teaching us
That he has no image. And though he did not come from
The human form, he came to it in his transformation.

HYMN THIRTY-TWO

According to the melody: "He is the long-suffering . . ."[1]

['][2] [32:1] Turn to me your teaching, for I have sought to avert
   myself,
But I see that I have harmed myself: my soul gains nothing
Except through converse with you. Glory to the study of you!

   REFRAIN: *Praises to your Sender!*

[b] [32:2] Every time I meditated upon you, I acquired a
   treasure from you.
Every time I thought of you, a spring gushed from you,
And I drew as much as I could. Glory to your font!
[g] [32:3] Lord, your font is concealed[3] from whoever thirsts
   not for you.
Your treasury is empty to whoever hates you.
Love is the keeper of your heavenly treasure.
[d] [32:4] When I forsake your company, your beauty entices
   me.
When I follow your greatness, your glory unnerves me.
Whether coming or going, I am conquered all the same.
[d] [32:5] When I sensed you, I was afraid. When I declared
   your greatness, I was great.
Though you have not increased, the one who has declared
   your greatness
Has become great in you. Glory to your greatness!

---

1. This melody extends through *HF* 32–33. Its meter is 5+5 / 5+5 / 5+5.
2. Here begins an acrostic on the Syriac alphabet. It repeats several letters
and concludes with *ḥ*.
3. D, "vanishes."

[h] [32:6] I thought and then uttered you. I did not limit you.
I grew weak and silent. I did not destroy you.[4]
In you I have wandered yet then grown quiet. Glory to your
hiddenness![5]
[w] [32:7] Though grieving because powerless, I was silent
because I did not understand
That no one can limit you, for you limit all.
Yet, were you limited, I would grieve.
[w] [32:8] You did not increase your glory for us,
To make [us] recognize that you are great. Your nature is
great,
And for humans you have made your glory as small as can be.
[w] [32:9] Before you created Adam, you were great, alone.
Humans made you small, so you bent down to their side,
And put on their types, so they would become great through
your humility.
[w] [32:10] And if the likeness made you small—the human
image
Which you borrowed and put on—how much smaller did the
body make you,
Which out of love you put on—in truth, not in likeness.[6]
[z] [32:11] You became small when you created, coming down
From greatness to lowliness, since creation could not
Be cultivated by you except in smallness.

4. D, "I did not magnify you."
5. Ephrem applies to himself the verbs *hemset* ("I thought," but which can
also have the sense of "to rush at," or "attack") and *phît* ("I have wandered"),
which he typically uses to characterize the errant speech of his opponents.
Here he admits the potential danger of his own poetic speech, but checks it in
two ways: his speech does not limit God (line 1), and, if he does wander off, he
dutifully falls silent (line 3). By presenting himself in this way, Ephrem presents himself an exemplum of righteous poetic speech.
6. Ephrem juxtaposes the creation scene at Gn 1.27, and Christ's Incarnation. Interestingly, this stanza suggests that the "image and likeness" of
Gn 1.27 is not something which belonged to God properly, but which belonged properly to humanity, God only taking it on so as to become comprehensible to humanity (see also *HF* 32:12). Here, too, Ephrem reflects a clear
sense of "type" ("image"—*dûmyâ*) and "antitype" ("truth"—*qûštâ*): the type is
the image God took on in the original creation, the antitype the body he took
on in the incarnation.

[z] [32:12] He who is Creator put on smallness first
And then was able to create. If he had not become small
He would not have been able to make great. Glory to your will!

[z] [32:13] You became smaller than you are and bigger than
    you are:
You became smaller when you lowered yourself beneath
    greatness,
And bigger when you mercifully created creatures.

[z] [32:14] Outwardly you became small, outwardly you
    became big—
Not in substance. Your glory grew small then big.
Your nature stayed the same, exalted above these changes.

[z] [32:15] My smallness has uttered you, desiring your
    greatness
To fall beneath words, and be subject to voices,
To increase the mouth and the ear.

[ḥ] [32:16] The Father and the Son are one, for their nature is
    one.
They are not absorbed into one another. They are mingled
    with one another.
They are distinct, one with another. Glory to your mingling!

HYMN THIRTY-THREE

According to the same melody.[1]

[33:1] John's truth—when he beheld you and depicted you—
[Was] that you are Word and God unsearchable, so that
Everyone would depict you in his mind through that type.[2]

> REFRAIN: *Glory to your hiddenness!*

[33:2] Let no one depict something foreign to you.
The pattern that the Spirit sketched for us through John
Is impressed upon our heart, mind, and thought.
[33:3] His nature is hidden and revealed, though ultimately hidden.
It is revealed in that it exists, but hidden as to how it exists.
Let us abandon what he has abandoned, and what he has allowed us to grasp, let us grasp.
[33:4] If it is difficult for artists to depict the wind[3]
For us with paints, whose tongue can depict
The Child whom mouths cannot depict with their voices?
[33:5] And though they can depict the body, they cannot depict the soul.
Though they can depict the mouth, they cannot depict the voice:
Such things will never submit to a picture.

---

1. See note 1 attached to melody of hymn 32.
2. Jn 1.1. Lines two and three could also be translated: "[You are] Word and God. The 'how' is unsearchable. / Thus everyone must depict you in his mind through that type." This translation is harder to justify grammatically, but semantically it does reflect Ephrem's thought (see, e.g., *HF* 33:3).
3. Syr., *rûḥ,* which can also be translated "spirit."

[33:6] The Books that depict the Son do not depict for us
"where."

Proclaiming the Father, they do not proclaim[4] "how,"

For such things are not subject to discussion.[5]

[33:7] And if a demon cannot be depicted with paints,

Who can depict the Holy Spirit with discussions?

[Even] an unclean spirit is hidden to its interpreters!

[33:8] As the soul is hidden from artists,

Divinity is a hundred times more hidden

From minds which cannot grasp "how."[6]

[33:9] And just as paints cannot depict the voice,

Thoughts cannot comprehend the Son,

For the sign at which they aim is subtler than the mind.

[33:10] Who among painters has gazed upon that brightness

Which covered Moses?[7] They would be unable to depict it—

Whether painters of walls, or painters of garments.

[33:11] Nor could the heavenly colors

Of that brightness be perfectly understood

By the eye or the mind, for it is foreign to both of them.

[33:12] But if the face of an old man—a mortal—

Over which a bit of heavenly color has been spread,

Has shamed the paints and dazzled the artists,

[33:13] Who shall depict the nature of Essence?

It is altogether unseen. Concerning it, it is written: whoever
has seen it

Has not seen it, but the form it has assumed.[8]

[33:14] Look: none of the mind's rational paints

Are akin to the Son. With them he depicts an image

Of himself for the hearer, to know "how" he is.

[33:15] And if that wind[9] that blows tangibly

They cannot depict, who will depict the Child

Revealed to the Father alone, and concealed, more hidden
than all?

---

4. Syr., *makrzîn*. C, *makrîn*, "withhold."
5. On God's "how," see note 3 attached to 9:1.
6. Ibid.
7. Ex 34.29–35; 2 Cor 3.7–18.
8. Cf. Jn 1.18.
9. Or, "spirit."

HYMN THIRTY-FOUR

According to the melody: "O my disciple, {who has persuaded you?}"[1]

[34:1] Before Adam sinned,
All creatures were pure.
And while they were pure,
He adorned them with their names.[2]
When that human sinned in his will,
The Creator rejected [creatures] because of [Adam's] sins.
He declared some of them unclean, so that through them
He could teach and bring [Adam] to {purity}.[3]

> REFRAIN: *Blessed is he who, through an animal, taught*
> *[Adam] that he would become like them!*

[34:2] As it is written, he became like
Both wild and domestic animals.[4]
Through them [God] depicted [Adam's] foulness,
So that he could see himself—how foul he had become—
That when he saw his foulness, he would despise it;
That when he saw his great wound, he would be ashamed.
And when he saw what he had become like,
He would weep and seek the splendor he had wasted.
[34:3] One mirror can
Serve many as a single thing,
But there are many things in which Adam

---

1. B. This melody occupies hymns 34 and 35 (though see note 1 attached to melody of hymn 35). Its meter is 7+7+7+7+10+10+7+7.
2. Gn 2.19–20.
3. Syr., *dakyûtâ*. A, *dakyātâ*, "pure things."
4. Ps 49.13, 21 (P).

Can see the multitude of his wounds.
He has taken our mind and extended it to the animals,
So we could see ourselves in them—how we are.
O wise Maker,
Who with [animals] revealed our self to us!
[34:4] The mind could
See itself if it were well.
Without a mirror, a body cannot
Observe its face.
Since the mind had become like the body,
And could not see its substance by itself,
The mirror of animals
He established so it could see itself.
[34:5] With {animals}[5] a person reproves and reproaches
      himself—
That he not become ravenous like a wolf,
Nor kill like a savage beast.
He will not acquire the snake's hissing,
Nor the scorpion's silence.
Neither like him will he strike his friend in secret,
Nor like the dog will he rage against his maker,
Nor "be like a horse or a mule, without understanding."[6]
[34:6] A fox he called Herod,
Who profaned his hole at every moment.[7]
He scorned the law with immodesty,
And in his impurity killed the Nazirite.
He married a woman who was like him,
And a girl was brought up, sealed by both.
As a joke—a debased feast—
They killed the glorious prophet.[8]

> {*The End*}[9]

---

5. Syr., *ḥaywātâ*. A misspells as *ḥawwātâ*.
6. Ps 32.9. Ephrem marks this final clause with the particle *lam,* signifying quotation.
7. Lk 13.32.
8. Mt 14.1–14; Mk 6.21–29.
9. B.

HYMN THIRTY-FIVE

According to the same melody.[1]

[35:1] Nature is like the book,[2]
And insiders are like those outside:[3]
Their transgression lies in their questions,
Their ruin in their arguments.
Those outside look upon nature and are injured.
Those inside read[4] the book and become troubled.
Grant, O our Lord, that I will be able
To persuade both, according to your will.[5]

> REFRAIN: *Blessed is he who does not keep even the lazy from*
> *trading {his}[6] money![7]*

[35:2] "In the beginning" is like "in the beginning,"[8]
And John is like Moses.

1. While the mss identify hymn 35 as possessing the same melody as 34, there is a slight difference between the two: in mss A and C of 35, stanzas 2–10 each conclude with two or four extra seven-syllable lines. Much like the refrains that follow the first stanza in a given hymn, these lines offer short benedictions or petitions. Given that they break the meter in which the hymn is written, they probably derive from after Ephrem's time. For that reason, and because they are similar to the hymns' refrains, I have set them apart from the text of the stanzas to which they are attached.
2. I.e., Scripture.
3. I.e., those inside or outside the Church. On these categories, see note 5 attached to 17:3.
4. B, "look upon."
5. In this hymn, Ephrem reads John as a symbol of Scripture, and Moses as a symbol of Nature. See also *HPar* 5:2, where Ephrem presents Scripture and nature as two "witnesses" to the single Creator.
6. B.   7. Cf. Mt 25.14–30.
8. Gn 1.1; Jn 1.1.

In the beginning their writings reproached
The scribes[9] who debated in an evil way.[10]
One proclaimed the God who has come to suffer,[11]
And Moses, nature, which has come into pain.[12]
So that hearers not lose strength,
In the beginning, their writings described their beauties.[13]
     Blessed is the luminous who with luminous things
      Has opened for us the mouth of the luminous fonts![14]
[35:3] From the words written
About the humbling of the Creator's Son,
Debaters have come to believe that he is a creature,
And have stirred up the spring.[15]
Upon stirring up investigation through their controversies,
They have turned and given to drink from the waters their feet
    stirred up.

9. Syr., *spārê*. This could also be vocalized *seprê*, "scribes," as it is in line 3.

10. As Shepardson has pointed out, part of Ephrem's anti-subordinationist rhetoric involves conflating his opponents with the biblical Scribes and Pharisees (*Anti-Judaism*, ch. 4), so that what his opponents are doing in debating the divinity of Christ amounts to a replaying of the biblical mistrust and ultimately crucifixion of Christ. Here, Ephrem brings Moses into the picture, so that he and John are engaged in a unified effort against "the scribes," the latter representing anyone who debates "evilly." At the same time, Ephrem's hymns, insofar as they offer a refutation of the "scribes" of his own day, replay Moses's and John's earlier literary endeavors.

11. That is, John's Gospel.

12. That is, Genesis.

13. That is, the beauty of God and the world.

14. See note attached to melody.

15. Ephrem has two scriptural referents in mind here: Prv 8.22 and Ezek 34.18. Ephrem will echo Ezek 34.18 through the next six stanzas of this hymn, finally quoting it directly in 35:9. The 34th chapter of Ezek, from which the text is taken, offers a condemnation of the "shepherds of Israel," who have failed in their pastoral duties, insofar as they have taken care of themselves, while ignoring their sheep. Within such a context, Ezek 34.18 accuses these shepherds of drinking clear water, but, having drunk, dirtying the rest, so that their flock must drink dirty water. If we follow this echo, then the "debaters" of *HF* 35 resonates as a cryptic reference to pastors or bishops of whom Ephrem is aware, who are espousing subordinationist readings of the biblical text. Just as the "shepherds" of Ezekiel give their flock unclean water, so these "debaters" filthy the text of Scripture, and render it to their congregation in such an impure state.

And though the teaching is clear,
They have drunk the dregs off [the top] of its clarity.
     Have mercy, Lord, on our will,
      Which first stirred up and then drank.[16]
[35:4] O font of wonder,[17]
Clear yet sullied on either side:
It is completely clear to the clear,
Who, by its clear drink, are purified.
It is sullied for the sullied, because they are sullied.
Like something sweet, yet bitter to the sick,
Truth is sullied among the schismatics,
Like a sweet thing among the sick.
     O our Lord, heal our sickness,
      So we will hear your story well![18]
[35:5] Those outside look upon nature—
All of it sullied because of Adam.
In it [there are] debts, born out of freedom,
And awful punishments, born out of justice.
Fools think nature despised and confused,
While those inside slander our Lord's humanity:
They have seen his smallness and have become troubled.
The evil one mocks both sides.
     O our Lord, rebuke the deceitful one,
      Who scorns us like Samson![19]
[35:6] Though they have sullied [the water's] flow through debating,
They think that it itself is sullied—both it and its source.
Let us ascend to the fountains' head!

16. See note attached to melody.

17. The term "font" (*mbû'â*) occurs throughout the *HF* in reference to the Eucharist (see, e.g., 10:7). On a more basic level, we can understand "font" as a Christological title, referencing Christ in his capacity as giver (of teaching, life, etc.), or, even more basically, as source from which symbols flow. See *HF* 12:10; 32:2–3. Equally, given the more obvious resonances of "font," "water," etc., it is hard to overlook the baptismal echoes. In this hymn, however, the language pertains ultimately to Scripture, which has been "sullied" through subordinationist interpretation.

18. See note attached to melody.

19. Jgs 13–16. On this refrain, see note attached to melody.

Taste the abundance out of their mouths!
Without Adam, nature was clear of its debts,
And Christ, without a body, [clear] of needs.
Because of Adam, nature has diminished.
Because of the body, Christ has become small.

> Blessed are you, Lord of nature,
> Who grew small and then big: I will proclaim you.[20]

[35:7] John tasted that
Font before [other] drinkers.
Tasting, he marveled, cried out and proclaimed:
"He who is with God is God!"[21]
Moses, who inscribed nature long ago,
Wrote, "God saw all, and it was good."[22]
Nature is pure and the book is pure.
Those sullied, [however], drink in controversy.

> O our Lord, rebuke the controversy
> That sullies clear fonts![23]

[35:8] Is it not enough for you, debaters,
To sully the clear fonts?
Our sin sullied nature,
And our controversy has upset the book.
The clear flock, which came to drink,
Is now sullied, since we have given [it] our sullied melodies[24] to
    drink.
[The flock] came to nature and we destroyed it.
It came to the book and we sullied it.

> Lord, cleanse the rivers that the sullying
> Debaters have sullied![25]

[35:9] Ezekiel foresaw
This all-disturbing debate,
And this all-sullying controversy,
When he rebuked the shepherds:
"My sheep have grazed the pasture your heels have trampled.

---

20. See note attached to melody.   21. Jn 1.1.
22. Gn 1.31.   23. See note attached to melody.
24. The Syriac *qālê* could also be "voices."
25. See note attached to melody.

They have turned and drunk the waters your feet have
    sullied!"[26]
Look at [his] words! Look at [these] acts!
The proud have sullied creation!
        Let us give thanks: before the debaters,
        The fonts were cleansed by the apostles!
        Lord, cleanse, the drink the shepherds
            Have sullied in your pasture![27]
[35:10] O our Lord, establish my simplicity
Among the wise, who have become very foolish.[28]
If they knew your greatness,
They would not be so bold in discussing you.
If they considered nature alongside the book,
They would learn from both the Lord of both.
Nature demonstrates through revealed things,
And the book through simple things.
        Blessed is he who gives life to the body at one time
            And life to souls at another!
        Through a clear shepherd,[29] give me to drink
            From the clear river of Books![30]

    {*The End*}[31]

---

26. Ezek 34.19. On Ephrem's use of this passage, see note 15 attached to
35:3 above. Ephrem here replaces the word "feet" (*reglaykôn*), which appears
in Ezek 34.19, with "heels" (*'eqbayhôn*). The latter puns on the word *'ûqābâ*,
"discussion," which recurs throughout these hymns (though not here).

27. See note attached to melody.

28. Cf. 1 Cor 1.27 and 3.19.

29. On this term *'allānâ* ("shepherd"), see p. 12.

30. See note attached to melody.

31. B.

HYMN THIRTY-SIX

According to the melody, "O free one ..."[1]

[36:1] The Son came down to care for things-made.
Their diseases had stuck around, lingering.
[Their] doctors had come quickly,
But then labored and grown weary. They healed a little,
But left much over.

> REFRAIN: *Blessed is the One who sent you!*

[36:2] Because they could not see him,
He took clothing from a lamb.
The flock came close to him,
And did not reject him, for the flock's scent
Rose from his garments.
[36:3] But the wolves, crafty,
Came to fear him when he had changed [clothes].
They tore his garments and revealed his glory.
And though it was not what they intended, his brightness
    shone
From beneath the veil.[2]

---

1. Syr., *'â bar ḥîrê*. B, *'â bar ḥayyê*, "O living one ..." This melody occupies hymns 36–38. Beck (*HF [S]*, XI–XII) divides these hymns into stanzas of four lines, with a meter of 8/8/8/11 (though he divides 36:1 and 2 as 8/8/11/8). It seems to me the lines more consistently divide into five-line stanzas, with a melody of 4+4/4+4/4+4/4+4/4, which is what I have represented here. There is, however, variation in the meter of some lines (36:3–6, for example, begin with a line of 3+4).

2. In this mythic retelling of the Passion, the "veil" represents Christ's flesh. When the latter was torn in the Crucifixion, Christ's divinity—hidden behind the veil—was made manifest, in the Resurrection.

[36:4] The pastors³ of our day, having seen
Him so disgraced because of his sheep,
Like those drunk with the taste of wine,
Think that he is the chief of pastors
And shepherds.⁴
[36:5] The laborers who crucified him sensed
That he was the heir and master of the vineyard.⁵
The shepherds thought him a companion
Of the sheep, because he lovingly became
The Passover lamb.
[36:6] It makes you want to cry:⁶
With their names, things-made have slandered
The Son of the Maker, by whom we are made. ⁷
They have returned [their] pay, for he had magnified them
With his names.⁸
[36:7] Woe to the fashioned one, who with words changed
His Fashioner in an unnatural way.
The color of wool is also changed!
Do not {call}⁹ the Son
By the name "creature."
[36:8] He has set you apart from the animals,
So do not reckon him alongside the animals.
There is freedom in your slavery.
Do not place your yoke upon the lordship
Of the One who frees all.

3. Syr., *'allānâ*. On this term, see Introduction, p. 12. Here it has a clearly negative connotation.

4. That is, they anthropomorphize him. This statement likely intends to echo the Arian identification of Christ as "first among creatures." These references to subordinationist readings of Christ continue in the following stanzas.

5. Mt 20.1–16.

6. Lit., "tears burst from the eyes."

7. Instead of "the son," BC read "of the Son," thus rendering lines one and two as "Tears burst from the eyes / of the Son …"

8. That is, Christ gave humans his names (e.g., priest, king, etc.) as a reward. Yet, in applying human names to him (i.e., "creature"), they have nullified the linguistic gift he bestowed upon them.

9. Syr., *tkannûnāy(hy) la-šmeh,* C. A, *tebṣûnāy(hy) la-šmeh,* "investigate the name of …"

[36:9] Tell us: of what have you been accused?
Perhaps your grief is like [his]?
Who could comprehend how great [your own sufferings] are?
Are they like the things
He has suffered on your account?
[36:10] What have you endured for him?
If you have not honored [him], you cannot claim disgrace.
With what fire have you been burned for him,
That the smoke that rises up to him
Is [only] your controversy?
[36:11] Being's zeal, look: it zealously engulfs you,
For one cannot be divided into three.[10]
Leave his name alone, and declare his nature,[11]
For nature provides eyes
For investigation.[12]
[36:12] It belongs to the nature of a rock to be divided,
And there are other natures like it.[13]
But the nature of light is indivisible.
This experiment involving natures can be [like]
Eyes for us.
[36:13] They are similar in their names,[14]
But far different in their natures.
Do not declare for us the common name,[15]
In which things divisible and indivisible
Are equal.
[36:14] Look: each and every thing
Is named as a single thing:
Each body, each substance,

---

10. That is, Being's nature is one, not three.

11. Here, "his nature" refers not to the divine nature, but to the natural world that he has made. The following stanzas make this clear.

12. That is, as the following stanzas will show, certain natural phenomena (such as light) bear out the truth that "one is not divided into three."

13. On the use of "nature" to mean "created thing," see Beck, *Die Theologie*, 13–18.

14. I.e., rock (*kîpâ*) and light (*nuhrâ*), which, though not similar morphologically, both represent created things.

15. I.e., "created," the name that they both share.

Each one, along with everything that can be
Counted.[16]
[36:15] If because you have called him "one,
Indivisible," you have gone far astray,[17]
[See that] water's nature is one and
Divisible, yet changed
By fruits and seeds.[18]
[36:16] There is no way to understand him
Without testing his nature.[19]
That [his nature] is one has not enabled us
To comprehend the interpretation of his being,
Concealed from all.
[36:17] There are two distinct crucibles—
Faith and testing.
Either someone truly has faith,
Or a test can teach him
How he is.
[36:18] Faith does not need
The sons of truth to discuss [it].
For us there is a path: to follow
All tests with examinations
Beyond the presumptuous.
[36:19] Take and throw him[20] into the waves,[21]
So that all questions will vanish.
Demand [from him] his experience of Essence—
How it is, where it is, and
Whence it has come.
[36:20] [Ask] whether the Child can be explained by
     something,

16. On this passage, see Possekel, *Evidence*, 77.

17. That is, because you cannot accept that he is God by nature, yet has
become man.

18. Apparently Ephrem understands water to change into the substance of
the things it makes to grow.

19. That is, discerning basic principles about his nature through observation of the natural world.

20. That is, the presumptuous.

21. That is, the waves of divinity. On "waves" and "sea" as a metaphor for
divinity, see note 36 attached to 4:13.

Or creatures by nothing.
Plow the earth's thorns, again and again,
And see that it has given you a word of truth,
Though unwittingly.

The End.[22]

---

22. C omits.

HYMN THIRTY-SEVEN

{*According to the same melody.*}[1]

[37:1] Isaiah indicated,
That he had placed a bridle of error
Upon the jaws of humans[2]—
A lowly sign that made
Humanity into a dumb beast.

> REFRAIN: *Blessed is he whose truth has rooted out error!*

[37:2] Once we had become like the animals,
God came down and became like us,
So we could turn and become like him.
O Blessed One, whose mercy has called us[3]
From here to there!
[37:3] Because humanity would not heed
His glory,[4] he angered and denied [God].
Israel grew fat, kicking in rebellion,[5]
And overturned and scattered that goodness.
O great mourning!
[37:4] Satan has crafted savages
Out of the wise and learned.
Instead of a yoke that evens out the divided parts,
He has divided them with a yoke of schism
Through their disputations.
[37:5] Between steep and difficult places
He makes them run among stumbling blocks:

---

1. BC. On this melody, see note 1 attached to melody of hymn 36.
2. Is 30.28.   3. BC, "has called me."
4. Ps 49.13 (P).   5. Cf. Dt 32.15.

On one side, a desolate mountain,[6]
And on the other side, questions
Misshapen[7] and dreadful.
[37:6] In a place full of pits,[8]
With ten thousand eyes invited,
They run around scornfully.
Who will hasten, in the presence of {his friend},[9]
To accept death?
[37:7] With the bridle of your compassion, Lord,
Order and turn back our confusion.
Since you are all eye,[10] be a path for us,
So, from steep and difficult places, we may go
To a clear place.
[37:8] For our humanity, Lord, needs
Help, because of our debts.
Our knowledge, too, Lord, needs
Order, because of drifting
And hidden wandering.
[37:9] As the eagle lowers his wings for his children,[11]
Lower the wings of your mercy for me, Lord.
And instead of air—the wing's earth—
By the Holy Spirit[12] lift our wing
To our treasure!
[37:10] Lord, guard our belief
From unbelief,
And our knowledge from ignorance.
The names are acquired: do not be deceived
By their names![13]
[37:11] The peoples have worshiped one who is not God,
But we have a true God.
The Evil One has envied us and sown among us a lie,
That {the last would be without God

---

6. BC, "mountain of debts."

7. Ephrem puns on the word *šqîpâ*, which can mean either "misshapen" or "crag."

8. Lit., "with a full pit," which could also mean "deep pit."

9. BC. A, "his death."   10. Cf. Ezek 1.18.

11. Cf. Dt 32.11.   12. Or, "wind."

13. On names, see pp. 36–37, and note 18 attached to 5:6.

Just like the first.}[14]

[37:12] From nature alone
He made idols, through craftsmen.
From the Book alone,
{Through}[15] investigators, he made gods
Among the deniers.[16]

[37:13] To a craftsman he[17] has given [his] teaching.
With a finger he carved a dumb idol,
And with a finger and a reed-pen he wrote a lie.
He wanted [his] finger to be like the finger
That wrote the tablets.[18]

[37:14] As he [made one] name like [another] name,
Calling idols "gods,"
He wanted every group to imitate [the other],[19]
So none could discern truth
From falsehood.

[37:15] One worships water,
And {he has inundated}[20] another, who worships fire.

---

14. Syr., *'ḥrāyê 'a(y)k qadmāyê*, C. That is, that the "peoples" of Ephrem's own day, who now worship the true God, would return to their former worship of false gods. AB, *qadmāyê a(y)k 'ḥrāyê*, "the first … just like the last."

15. BC. A, "among."

16. "Deniers" is here a reference to subordinationists. The idea is that by positing Christ as created, Arians inevitably end up worshiping a created being. Beck (*HF [G]*, 101, n.7) notes a parallel with Athanasius's *Life of Antony* 69:5 (see Athanasius of Alexandria, *The Life of Antony: The Coptic Life and the Greek Life,* trans. Tim Vivian and Apostolos N. Athanassakis [Kalamazoo, MI: Cistercian Publications, 2003]).

17. The Evil One.

18. I.e., that God gave to Moses. On writing with a reed-pen, see also *HF* 87:13. In Ephrem's view, his opponents, working under satanic inspiration, aim to write a new law, attesting to a new God.

19. Syr., *nmarrê*. B has *nm'*, which is not a word. Though without any textual support, Beck suggests *ndammê*, which would render the sentence "He wished each side to be alike." I have kept *nmarrê*, because it makes sense, assuming that Ephrem's omission of the direct object simply exhibits poetic elision.

20. Syr., *'abreh*, BC. A, *'abdeh* ("he has made"). The latter would render lines 1–2 as follows: "One worships water. / He has made another, who worships fire." Both readings make sense. I have gone with BC because it keeps the worshiper as the subject, and because it parallels the sarcastic comparison made between moon and sun worshipers in lines 3–5.

There is also one [group] who venerates the moon,
[But] the one who worships the great sun
Hastens to cover them.
[37:16] In the symbols of these factions
See our own current divisions.[21]
Our arrogance is like their pride,
And our battling, which we must overcome,
Is like their controversy.
[37:17] Quiet [your] mouths, silence [your] tongues.
Let a stupor fall upon [your] lips,
A wonder inhabit [your] souls.
The senses and the limbs will quake
At the Son's story.
[37:18] The tongue is a drawn sword.
Let the word be returned to your sheath!
Investigation has sharpened your mouth's speech.
The Son's silence dulls the edge
Of your questioning.
[37:19] Lips like bows
Should be neither opened nor stuck out.
The vehement face of the Holy Spirit
Like a whirlwind shoots arrows back
To their masters.
[37:20] He is an iron wall—
Like the one the prophet saw symbolically.[22]
If one shoots arrow-like words at [a wall],
Failing to knock it down, [the words] return and become fixed
In those that spoke them.
[37:21] Look at the potter's wheel,
And see a wheel of transformations:[23]
The movement of one makes the clay greater,
While the other makes the Son smaller,
Without him becoming smaller.

21. Ephrem admits to being uninterested in these groups *per se,* using them instead as pedagogical symbols for the concerns of his own audience.

22. Am 7.7–8 (P). C, "spiritually."

23. Syr., *šûḥlāpê,* by which Ephrem refers to Christ's movement from heaven to earth. C, *ḥûšābê,* "thoughts."

[37:22] Do not fight with your potter,
Though he has made you a vessel that speaks.
A potter's vessels are silent,
But the vessels that the Good One has made greater
Argue with him.
[37:23] Let there be no doubt: the smallest bit
Of his disputation is a foreboding mountain.[24]
Two words which question him:
They are heaven and earth to you,
And how you have wandered!
[37:24] No one has crossed your border, Lord.
No one has overcome your great height.
The nature of Being and the womb of the Father:
These are the Son's walls,
Which cannot be breached.
[37:25] As no nature
Can enter and explore what is inside fire[25]—
All stand outside of it,
And it has no wall, not even an outer wall, yet every one
Is illumined [by it]—
[37:26] Whoever presumes to investigate the womb
Of the Essence more powerful than all,
[As] rivers are stopped by the sea,
All presumptuous ones [are stopped] through debating
The birth of the Son!

> {*The End.*}[26]

---

24. On the metaphor of the mountain, see note 10 attached to 1:3.
25. Lit., "fire's womb" (*'ûbeh*).
26. B.

HYMN THIRTY-EIGHT

According to the same melody.[1]

[38:1] Lord, your love incites us,
And encourages us, even as it reproves us.
It shakes to awaken, impedes to order.
It neglects and then teaches [us] to live in all things
As the Knower-of-all.

> REFRAIN: *To you, a song, O Teacher of all!*

[38:2] [This] game[2] draws [us] out of silence,
Lest we become mute like the animals.
It also checks hateful speech,
Lest we become like the demons, chatty
With their curses.
[38:3] Debating has sometimes made a profit.
When silence has suffered loss, [debating] has flourished,
Its teaching growing rich on the deceived.
Instead of the deniers, it has come
To fight the faithful.
[38:4] He has filled his treasuries with instruction,
And his coffers with interpretations,
Laboring to teach the one who strayed.[3]
He destroyed the principle and the interest
That presumed to investigate.[4]
[38:5] The evil one's pursuer has abandoned him

1. See note 1 attached to melody of hymn 36.
2. Syr., *šeʿyâ*, referring to the back and forth movement described in 38:1.
C, *šelyâ*, "the quiet."
3. Cf. Lk 15.3–7.
4. Thus far in the *HF*, Ephrem has used these economic metaphors to

218

And began to pursue those of his own side.[5]
His enemy[6] has blinded the one struggling,[7]
And has cast his own self down,
Defeated by his very self.[8]
[38:6] Enable us, our Lord, to recognize
Our own side, and the children of our side.
Lord, let the right hand not battle
Itself, when its battle
Is with the left hand.
[38:7] Let us not hate the evil ones, our Lord,
Since you yourself hate [only] the one evil one.
Deceit—hidden sickness—
You excise with the word of truth. You cast it away
To bring them to life.
[38:8] Your scale has weighed and distributed both silence
And speech, in imitation of you.
Likewise, does nature teach, my brothers,
That with only one half of a scale[9]
Something can be weighed?[10]
[38:9] Let us use both silence and speech:

---

articulate the virtuous lending that passes between God and his faithful poet:
God lends poetic speech to Ephrem, he then lends it to his audience, and
thereby stores up interest in the heavenly treasury, from which he can draw
again at a later date (see note 39 attached to 5:15). In stanzas 38:4 and 5, however, Ephrem turns the metaphor upside down: now it is the debaters who are
attempting to loan from the treasury of divine teachings, but by investigating,
rather than praising. As a result, God shuts down the initial gift, along with
any profit it has acquired. Ephrem will further draw this out in the final stanza
of this hymn, 38:20, as well as in 52:6.

5. That is, through debating Christians have become divided, and, rather
than pursuing the evil one as a single entity, have begun to fight with one
another.

6. I.e., the evil one's enemy, who is now persecuting "those of his own side."

7. Syr., *atlîṭâ* (i.e., "athlete").

8. Here Ephrem depicts debating as a single entity warring against, and
eventually defeating, itself.

9. Lit., "With one partner-less plate." C, "with one stone."

10. Literally, this is a straightforward negative sentence: "Likewise, nature
does *not* teach ..." I have changed it to a rhetorical question to make it more
coherent, since lines 1–2 offer a positive statement, which then connect to a
negative statement with "likewise not" (*'âp-lâ*).

Let our speech be like the day,
And our silence like the night,
Since both the ear and the tongue
Desire rest.

[38:10] These things can be compared:
True teaching [is like] the visible light,
Silence and quiet are like the night,
And like sleep and rest is
Great joy.

[38:11] Let there be laborers for the word of truth:
Come and labor for it as in a field!
Let us sow love and reap peace.[11]
Let us bring a bushel of reconciliation
To the Lord of peace! [12]

[38:12] Look at the breath of the Holy Spirit:
It cleanses through its hovering.[13]
Straw disperses and chaff scatters.
Wheat is gathered into the granary of life
Without the tares.[14]

[38:13] Blessed is the Good One who has given us speech!
Blessed is the Just One who has increased silence!
He has given us sides about which we can debate,
And, as the Teacher-of-all, he has impeded others,
About which we must be silent!

---

11. "Peace" (*šaynâ*) also carries the sense of "cultivated land."

12. Ibid.

13. Here and at *HF* 51:7, in his use of the word "hovering" (*rûḥâpâ*), Ephrem appears to echo the movement of the *rûḥ* ("wind" or "spirit") in Gn 1.2 (where we find the participial form *mraḥḥep*, derived from the same root *r-ḥ-p*). This suggests that Ephrem is using the language of Gn 1.2 to speak theologically about the movement of the Holy Spirit, or, as in 51:8 and 77:20, the movement of the Trinity as a whole. What is interesting, however, is that in his *CGen.* 1:7, Ephrem explicitly denies the affiliation of the *rûḥ* of Gn 1.1 with the Holy Spirit (see Lukas Van Rompay, "L'informateur Syrien de Basile de Césarée. A propos de Genèse 1,2," *OCP* 58 [1992]: 245–51). Assuming a single Ephremic authorship for both the *CGen.* and the *HF,* this suggests that Ephrem either changed his position at some point, or that he was simply willing to read verses differently in different literary contexts.

14. Mt 13.24–30.

[38:14] He has not given us the whole earth
To walk upon, but a measure [of it].
Nor the sea to cross,
Nor the sun for the eye to rule
Over all of it.
[38:15] And how is it that the mind
Could wish to rule entirely over
That incomprehensible Greatness?
Does it think it smaller
Than creation?
[38:16] And if the things given us,
Are not given us fully,
How shall we investigate the hidden birth,
Which is every day marked off, brothers,
As Mount Sinai?[15]
[38:17] Adam wanted to inherit splendor,
Yet he gained the earth.[16]
Uzziah wanted to add to himself the priesthood,
But [instead] despicable leprosy
Was added to him.[17]
[38:18] Who will attack the hidden things,
Whose borders are marked by quiet and silence,
Whose walls are fire and judgment,
And whose barriers are lamentation, weeping,
And gnashing of teeth?
[38:19] Who will break through these bitter walls
To enter and accept awful woe?
He who shattered the partitions, barriers, and walls [did it] for
    [our] gain,
But we, brothers,
For loss!
[38:20] I thank you, Lord, for protecting me

---

15. That is, it is marked every day, whereas Mt. Sinai was marked for only
one day (Ex 19.12). See also *HF* 28:8.

16. Gn 3.

17. 2 Chr 26. See *HF* 28:13. On Adam and Uzziah together, see *HPar* 3:14.

From hidden things and their vain pursuit.
While the orators empty their treasure,
I have repaid my debts from things revealed.
Glory to you![18]

> {*The End.*}[19]

---

18. On the economic interpretation of oration, see note 4 attached to 38:4.
19. B.

HYMN THIRTY-NINE

According to the melody, "Take comfort in the promises ..."[1]

[39:1] My son, when the pagans and crucifiers mock
Our Lord because he is human, affirm that he is God
Whose glory is inscrutable. And instead of the debaters
Who discuss his glorious birth,
He loves the martyrs, who, with the blood of their necks
Have proclaimed his birth—that he is the Son of God!

> REFRAIN: *Glory to the single Child and, through him, his*
> *Begetter!*

[39:2] Understand how our arguing has covered up
All those in error, so that not one waves
His arm in the marketplace, grunting with questions.
If those in the Church were unified,
The ray from all the children of light would also be unified:
It would destroy error through the power of unity.
[39:3] Those with knowledge perceive that among
The erring there have sometimes been schisms.
Yet never because of them or their schisms
Has the world suffered, or raged, or grieved.
But kings have heard and become aware of our investigation,
[As well as] people and creatures—ten thousand all together.
[39:4] Our teaching has been mocked, and they[2] have
    expected it not to stand
On its own in a contest. They thought the furnace[3]

---

1. On this melody, see note 1 attached to hymn 31.
2. That is, all those observing these controversies (mentioned in 39:3).
3. Here referring to the baptismal font.

Would rebuke its victory, for they saw the debaters
Troubled by questions. They have divided it,[4]
And strayed from that Greatness whose depth cannot be
    explored,
Into which they were baptized. The scribes have wandered
    away in their debating.
[39:5] That which is spoken and can be interpreted
And explained, so that it can be discussed, debated, and
    declared,
Belongs to the mouth, and interpreting is related to it.
But what cannot be
Debated or declared is marked off by silence.[5]
Not even our mind[6] is like its hiddenness.
[39:6] [They say:] "There is no way for him to beget."[7]
The [issue of] the way[8] outdoes you, for when you discuss it,
It is not only the begetting that it is too difficult and too hard
    for you,
But that you do not even believe he exists.[9]
Let it not be asked, then, whether there is a way
For him to beget: he is the Lord of all ways.
[39:7] Divinity is not puzzling from one perspective [only].
It is difficult from every perspective. Who can comprehend
Seeds, or a drop [of rain], or the grass of every generation?
He is an utter wonder in all of them.
If the movement[10] of our own birth is incomprehensible to us,
Who could comprehend the Birth from his womb?

    {*The End.*}[11]

---

4. That is, the baptismal font.
5. Lit., "silence is its border."
6. I.e., the hidden counterpart to our visible mouth.
7. Ephrem marks this as a quotation with the particle *lam*.
8. That is, the way he would beget.
    9. Ephrem's argument is this: if you believed the Lord exists *as* Lord, you would believe that he transcends qualifications such as "cannot beget." If he is a being on whom you can set limitations, you have undermined him as God.
    10. Syr., *zaw'â*. B, *'ûzâ*, "force."
    11. B.

HYMN FORTY

According to the same melody.[1]

[40:1] The sun is our lamp, and no one understands it.
As much as [this is the case] for a human being, how much
    more for God!
The sun's shining is no younger than [the sun itself],
And there is no time when it was not.[2]
[Though] its light is second and its heat is third,
They are neither less than it, nor are they the same as it.[3]

> REFRAIN: *Glory to your Sender, from all who believe
> in you!*

[40:2] Look at the sun on high, which appears to be one.
But bend down and look and see its shining—a second.
Test, touch, and examine its heat—a third.
They are like one another, and not alike.
The second is mingled with [the first], though very different
    from it.
And the third is mixed—distinct, yet mingled and mixed.
[40:3] Fire and sun are single natures.
Three things are mingled within them threefold—
Substance, heat, and, third, light—
And they dwell in accord with another.

---

1. See note 1 attached to melody of hymn 31.

2. On this line, and its possible echo of the famous Arian formula, see pp.
33–34.

3. On the Trinitarian imagery in this hymn, see E. Beck, *Ephräms Trinitätslehre im Bild von Sonne/Feuer, Licht und Wärme. CSCO Subsidia,* vol. 425 (Louvain, 1981), 24–70.

Mixed without being confused, and mingled without being
  bound [by one another],[4]
They are gathered together unforced, and free, yet without
  wandering.
[40:4] The {tyrants}[5] are clearly silenced,
For look: one is three and three is one.
They are mingled, yet not fastened [to one another]. They
  are divided, yet not cut.
This marvel silences us entirely.
A human, too, is established in a threefold way,
And will rise in the resurrection, being perfectly complete.
[40:5] The sun, though it is one—a single nature—
There are three mingled in it, distinct, yet undivided.
Each one is entirely complete, [yet] all [three] are completed
  in one.
Its splendor[6] is one, yet not one.
That nature is marvelous, for it has given birth uniquely,
And then drawn together, and spread out threefold.
[40:6] And if someone presumes to think that fire
Is not three, who will err with him,
Cleaving to his foolishness, and following his stupidity?
Who will deny the three that are seen,
Which, though equal, are distinct? One is glorious and
  dreadful,
Another hidden and powerful, and [yet] another bright and
  gentle.
[40:7] The first one gathers all of itself to itself.
After it is another, which proceeds according to its will,
And the third is poured out[7] abundantly.
A power rules inside the fire,
Though they neither command nor are commanded by one
  another.[8]

---

4. That is, their mingling does not limit their freedom.
5. Syr., *ṭrûnê*, BC. A, *ṭûrānê*, "tyrannical acts."
6. Syr., *tešbûḥtâ*, BC. A misspells as *tšbḥt'*.
7. Syr., *meštpa'*. BC, *meštlaḥ*, "sent."
8. A, *ḥad men ḥad*. B, *b-šûlṭānâ*, "by power," or "authority."

They are completed by [one another], with love {and}[9] order.

[40:8] Three names are visible within the fire,
Yet each one stands alone on its [own] authority,
And each appears {distinctly}[10] in its action,
Unique strengths mingled together.
Fire marvelously, heat distinctly,
And light gloriously dwell together with one accord.

[40:9] If fire's nature is such a marvel
(It begets, yet suffers no loss; it spreads evenly,[11] without
    growing cold;
Though its heat is distinct, it is not cut off from it;
Though it passes through everything, it does not privilege [any
    thing];
It spreads throughout bread and is mingled inside water,
And dwells in everything and everything dwells in it),

[40:10] [It bears] the mystery of the Spirit—the type of the
    Holy Spirit:
[The Holy Spirit] is mixed with water for absolution,
And mingled in bread for an offering.[12]
And though they are so like one another,
[Fire] is still far different, for it cannot depict
The Trinitarian mysteries, which can never be depicted.

[40:11] And if the investigation of this fire inundates us—
How can it be one? How can it be three?
How can those things that dwell within it be three?
How can its heat be divided and not cut off?—
A nature that we have received lovingly, in a threefold
    manner,
Yet have not, along with it, possessed divisive debating,

9. BC. A, "love *of* order."

10. Syr., *prîšâ'ît,* BC. A, *pešîṭâ'ît,* "simply."

11. Syr., *šāwê.* It is difficult to make this verb fit, and the meaning I have supplied stretches its semantic range. Beck (*HF [G],* 109) leaves the word out of his
translation, though suggests in a note a possible correction to *ṭāwê,* "to bake."
While this makes sense morphologically, it makes less sense semantically than
one would think: the verb should describe an action which gives off heat (and
thus *should* result in coldness). "Baking" does not fit.

12. Syr., *qûrbānâ.* On this term, see note 24 attached to 10:13.

[40:12] How much more should we receive simply
These Three, with love that does not dispute?
Their nature does not come after us, to become like us,
For they are like each other in every way,
[While] the natures of creatures are distinct and dissimilar.
How much more distinct than all is the nature above all?

    {*The End.*}[13]

  13. B.

HYMN FORTY-ONE

According to the same melody.[1]

[41:1] Who has ever seen a raven mating,[2]
Or a virgin[3] bee consummating a marriage?
The virgin bee gives birth virginally,
And the worm brings forth alone.
A cloud, too, bears lightning gloriously,
And a sprout is manifest within a rock miraculously.

    REFRAIN: *Glory to your unique birth from your Father!*

[41:2] A pool of water produces creeping things by the sun
And refutes the deniers.[4] As he begot in purity,
So in the beginning [the waters] produced creeping things
    with splendor.
Who will not marvel at all these things?
Moles are buried in the earth without suffocating,
Like fish in the sea and babies in the womb.
[41:3] How is iron drawn
From itself to a rock? Another thing that can be
    discovered
Is a nature that never burns inside fire.
There are ten thousand more of [such] discoveries—

---

1. See note 1 attached to melody of hymn 31.

2. Cf. *CH* 8:1:5. In the latter, Ephrem is refuting the notion that seasons of mating are ordered by the stars, and writes, "The stars have not made ravens chaste in their [habits of] mating."

3. Syr., *btûlâ*. BC, *memtûm*, "ever," which Beck suggests we read (*HF [S]*, 133, n. 1). While "virgin" is somewhat redundant, it makes sense within the passage, and I have thus kept it.

4. Cf. Gn 1.20.

Of rocks, plants and the power of medicine.
Who could limit or discern their natures?
[41:4] [These] individually begotten things, which have come
    to be without mating,
Their natures are more perplexing than that of the
    investigators,
And debating about them more difficult than [the natures of]
    inquirers.
They demonstrate the righteousness of the Child who is Lord
    of all.
"Where" should not be sought out, "how" not debated,
"Why" not mentioned, and "when" not investigated.[5]
[41:5] Though scent, color, and taste are truly
Rarefied and subtle, and cannot be felt by the hand,
They can be understood through the senses, their close allies:
One [sense] smells and another tastes.
What sense, though, is like that Greatness?
Through what similar thing could we approach to discuss it?
[41:6] That which is unlike us, or our race:
Who can seek it out? Who can investigate it?
It pleased him to reveal his nature—how it is.[6]
It pleased him to make himself small, and bend down
To show himself to us, mingle his Son with us,
Mix his Spirit with us, and show his love for us.
[41:7] When that donkey unexpectedly spoke,
Balaam saw the miracle, but completely failed to marvel.[7]
Yet as the donkey's mouth was rational,
[Balaam] forgot about himself and was persuaded by his
    donkey.[8]

    5. On these questions, see note 3 attached to 9:1.
    6. As the following lines make clear, there are certain aspects of the Lord's nature of which we can ask "how," namely, those related to his revelation of himself in the Incarnation. See also note 3 attached to 9:1.
    7. Nm 22.28–30. I have used "to fail completely" to convey the verbs 'arpî, "to neglect," and šbaq, "to abandon." Ephrem is alluding specifically to Nm 22.29, where Balaam initially responds to the miracle of the talking donkey by simply rebuking it.
    8. Nm 22.30. The term for donkey in line 1 was 'attānâ. In this line, A switches this to a synonymous term, ḥmārâ, while B retains attānâ.

The scribes forsook the marvel [of] the blind [whose eyes]
    were opened,
And stirred up an investigation into the Sabbath and the
    clay.[9]
[41:8] If you are capable of learning, these things are for
    your aid.
If you are {quarrelsome},[10] they reprimand you.
If you are presumptuous, they reproach you whole.
Examine and see your lowly body.
Be shamed by its intestines, all of which are filthy.
Let its defects be for you a bridle, [to restrain] your debating.
[41:9] Whenever the Evil One swarms us with his thinking,
If he is a stranger, somehow he becomes an ally,
His movements and his extensions becoming like our mind
And our understanding, which is exalted.
But if the Evil One, our enemy, is mindless,
How does he, by means of our mind, {corrupt}[11] and cause us
    to wander?
[41:10] The nature of the Lord of natures is hidden from all.
Let me not depict your nature as a creature!
And if it is depicted, [may it be] done in a way that sets the
    presumptuous wandering.
The Gospel is your wondrous mirror.
In it three are seen without controversy,
For in them the apostles went forth to baptize without
    controversy.[12]
[41:11] O our Lord, may investigation of you not nullify my
    baptism.
There is one who has {nullified}[13] his baptism through
    disputing.
And if he has become a disciple again, made new,
It is right for him to be baptized again.

---

9. Jn 9.1–41.
10. Syr., ḥeryāyâ, BC. A, ḥrîpâ, "bitter."
11. Syr., mšargel, BC. A, mašreg, "to dazzle."
12. Mt 28.19.
13. Syr., sarqeh, BC. A, sadqeh, "to split."

If he was baptized, he has blasphemed. If he was not baptized,
   know
That, because he found nothing new, he has remained.[14]

     {*The End.*}[15]

    14. The meaning of "remained" is unclear. It seems unlikely that Ephrem
means the person has remained "unbaptized," because this would make no
sense with "because he has found nothing new" (as if finding something new
would have rendered him baptized). Beck (*HF [G]*, 112, n. 10) suggests that
the person has remained "in the catechumenate." This makes more sense: because he has found no new teaching to lead him away, he should be allowed to
remain in the catechumenate.
    15. B.

HYMN FORTY-TWO

According to the same melody.[1]

[42:1] Who can contain, in some sort of stream,
The waves of hidden things, and traverse [them] in thought?
Honey, for our sickness, is like a bitter thing.[2]
How much more severe is that glorious strength?
Who has acquired senses sound enough to comprehend
The strength of that power whose birth cannot be
    discussed?

> REFRAIN: *Blessed is the One who, through creation,*[3] *sent*
> *your discussion wandering!*

[42:2] The Spirit's sight is not like [the sight of] our eyes,
And its color is strange for our eye to gaze upon.
Who, through his debating, has become like the Hidden
    One,
Who is stranger than everything, in every way?
Whose mouth has become a flame,
And has tasted that flame never tasted?
[42:3] Learn from that fire whose strength cannot be
    tasted,
Though its power can be tasted through the taste of cooked
    food,
Thus becoming beneficial and entirely profitable.
So it is with the concealed Essence:
Mix and receive its power in beneficial stories,

---

1. See note 1 attached to melody of hymn 31.
2. Cf. *HF* 35:4:6.
3. Syr., *ba-brîtâ*. B, *b-karyâtâ*, "small things."

For the investigation of the Strong One[4] is too difficult on its
 own.

[42:4] In a jar, the sun passes into water
And produces hot fire inside the cold.
He has miraculously produced a Child who is like him.
The Child has arisen from him, not being severed from him.
Just as light is not cut off, nor water severed,
That pure Child has shone forth brightly.

[42:5] Gold is single. A blossom is triple.
A stone is single. Fire is triple:
Flame, heat, and light are mingled in it.
The natures of created things are not offered
Through [only] one metaphor. Therefore, without controversy
Receive these Three as they have been proclaimed.

[42:6] [These things] do not exist as a work of our will.
Nature, as it exists, exists in a threefold way,
And the "why" cannot be comprehended: it is [simply] found
 that it is so,
For it exists as it exists without discussion.
Who has criticized fire for existing in three?
No one judges it, for everyone accepts it.[5]

[42:7] Transitory fire has been established for you as a miracle:
How is it conceived within the sun, yet hidden within it?
How is it concealed in the womb from which its rays [come]?
The pangs that have produced it are unsearchable.
The miracle of that marvelous birth has silenced you
And hemmed in your thought, which has passed beyond your
 mind.

[42:8] A fruit that you have never tasted, [to know] how it is,
Even if you touch it with your hand, and smell it, and see it,
Because you have never tasted it or tried it,

4. Syr., *da-'zîzâ*, "of the strong one." BC changes *da-* to *wa-*, which renders
the sentence as follows: "For the investigation of it is too difficult and too
strong on its own."

5. In the following stanzas, Ephrem extends his argument against investigating the "how" of divinity to the natural world. Implied in all of this is an
argument from the less to the greater: if the "how" of nature cannot be investigated, how can the "how" of divinity be investigated? Ephrem will articulate
the latter point in 42:12:6.

You will trust another who has tried it.
Since that hidden Being is stronger than you,
Believe that fruit, in which his power is tasted.
[42:9] Take a grain of wheat. Bind it, investigate it,
    and show us
How[6] the stalk is hidden, and the spike and the root,
Each perfected inside of it in a threefold manner.
Which is younger, older, or [came] first?
Though there is a beginning, it is difficult to comprehend,
For their beginning is hidden in them alone.
[42:10] Because that symbol falls short,[7] and cannot be
Reaped or cleaned, to come to any use,
It is as if the image has been defeated through controversy.[8]
But look upon it well:
The stalk is symbolically the body, and the fruit symbolically
    the mind.
Symbolically, the spike is the soul. This is a glorious similitude.
[42:11] Look: every parable inscribed and constructed,
If it could depict everything perfectly,
Would be no longer an image, but the thing itself.[9]
Shadows must pass.
With a temporary net[10] and a summer grain,[11]
[Our Lord] depicted the kingdom and our salvation
    to help us.
[42:12] These parabolic examples[12] are weak and inadequate,

---

6. Syr., *'aykan*. BC, *'aykâ*, "where."

7. That is, because the symbol of the wheat is only an analogue, and does not perfectly represent the thing it symbolizes.

8. Ephrem's point will become somewhat clearer in 42:11: the mere fact that a "symbol" or "parable" does not form a perfect analogue to the reality it depicts does not render parables entirely meaningless.

9. The word Ephrem uses here is *ḥattîtâ*. Literally, this would translate, "but an accurate [thing]." I think Ephrem intends something stronger than this, however, given that the parables are "accurate" in their own way. My sense is that he does not mean to convey a quest for a more accurate parable, but for some manner of representing the thing itself.

10. Mt 13.47–50.

11. Mt 13.24–30.

12. Syr., *ḥāwrê d-pellâtâ*. BC, *ḥāwrê w-pellâtâ*, "examples and parables."

And the reach {of}[13] images is frail, and cannot not {arrive}[14]
At that humble height. The [images] arise to rebuke
One self-exalted and pompous,
For if he cannot reach images,
How can he turn to assail the height of Greatness?
[42:13] Clouds are higher than fog,
Heaven [is higher] than both, and the highest heaven [higher]
    yet again.
Higher and lower! Created mountains
Are higher than things made of dust, down below.[15]
So too images: how they grow bigger to us!
We suppose[16] they are near when they are very far away.

    {*The End*}[17]

13. Syr. *d-*, B. A, *w*, "and."

14. Syr., *māṭeyn*, C. AB, *mṭappî*, "to attach to, embrace."

15. The Syriac for "mountains" is *ṭûrê*, which could also be *ṭawrê*, "extent" (see note 10 attached to 1:3). If vocalized as *ṭawrê*, these two lines would read, "The extents of created things are higher and lower— / higher than things made of dust down below." I have kept "mountains" to further Ephrem's juxta-position of "high" and "low."

16. Lit., "it is supposed."

17. B.

HYMN FORTY-THREE

According to the same melody.[1]

[43:1] Rebuke the presumptuous with a tiny egg!
A picture is hidden in three ways inside the yolk:
Where are the head, the feet, and the wings?
Ask these three things, to make it clear to you.
And if, through discussion, [someone] is suffocated inside the
   egg,
The one who has presumed to explore the Great Sea—how he
   has drowned!

> REFRAIN: *Blessed is the one who has thwarted our thought with*
>   *simple things!*[2]

[43:2] Look: wheat is naked, though a robe covers it.
We buried it naked, but then saw it glorified:
A corpse, stilled, yet it has crept up in the dust.
It is a wonder that it is concealed alone,
Its shame is unknown, but then it is consumed in glory,
And the whole thing is crowned with a garland.
[43:3] When wheat is buried in the grass,
It baffles investigators, and astonishes onlookers,
For they do not know where to explore or seek it.
It is revealed and apparent, and yet it is not [so].
It has rebuked investigators. See it calling out silently:
"Stand in awe of revealed things, you who are shameless
   among hidden things!"
[43:4] A treasure is hidden in that revealed plant:

---

1. See note 1 attached to melody of hymn 31.
2. B, "Praise to you from all, O Lord of everything!"

There three are hidden and there they are unsearchable.
Three are one, and though one, they are three.
Who has depicted the inside of a plant?
Where is its root, and, second, its fruit,
And, third, its leaf? They are mingled together.
[43:5] Do not let the Church of truth become
A house of controversies, and a divisive faction!
He has depicted and manifested himself—how he is—
For he can make himself known to us,
Even as the investigation of how he is, is revealed to him
    alone.[3]
Through his words, he has established his taste for the one
    who stands firm.
[43:6] Therefore, whoever investigates him hinders himself by
    him.
He disputes what he does not know and investigates what he
    will not find.
He loses what is in him, and finds what is not in him.
Thus he is only able to know him
If he does not seek to know how he is.
So if you have believed him, you have comprehended him.
[43:7] Choose for yourself one of the two, so you can be
    examined:
If he is true, confess and do not investigate.
If he has caused you to wander, what has brought you back?
In either of these, you should affirm him:
If he caused you to err, it would be wrong for you to rebuke
    him.[4]
How much more, then, should you believe[5] that he has written
    and given you truth?
[43:8] And if he had led us astray—God forbid!—
Who could know that he had led us astray?
Who would reveal to us what he had hidden?
His path is abundantly clear.

3. Here Ephrem refers to both permissible and impermissible questions of
"how." On this, see note 3 attached to 9:1.
    4. I.e., because, following line 3, he has "brought you back."
    5. Lit., "should it be believed."

His road, [open] before children, has been twisted by
  debaters.

His truth gathers us, but error inundates us.

[43:9] Children see and begin to wander off, for three paths
  lie open.[6]

The higher is tiresome and the lower is hard.

Choose for yourself the middle, and walk straight upon it.

Proclaim the Father and the Son without debating.

And though two roads quarrel with questions,

Stay clear on your road, without controversy.

[43:10] May you never investigate or presume to lower

To [the level of] these weak images

The Father and the Son and the glorious Spirit.

Nature, which never comprehends

How and what he is: flee from it silently,[7]

Since whoever searches into him is burned by his questions.

  {*The End.*}[8]

  6. The word for "to be opened" is derived from the same root (*d-r-š*) as
"debating" (*drāšâ*).

  7. That is, recognizing your own ability to understand Nature, flee from
thus trying to understand God.

  8. B.

HYMN FORTY-FOUR

According to the same melody.[1]

[44:1] His names teach you how and what you should call him.
One has taught you that he is, another that he is Creator.
He has shown you that he is Good, and he has explained to
   you that he is Just.
He is also named and called Father.
The Books have become a crucible. Why does the fool quarrel?
Test in his crucibles[2] his names and his forms.

    REFRAIN: *Praises to you from all who believe your titles!*[3]

[44:2] He has names perfect and accurate,
And he has names borrowed and transient.[4]
He has quickly put them on and quickly taken them off.
He has regretted, forgotten, and remembered.
And as you have affirmed that he is both just and good,
Affirm that he is Begetter, and believe that he is Creator.
[44:3] Be mindful of his perfect and holy names.
If you deny one of them, they all fly off and away.[5]
They are bound one {to one another},[6] and they bear
   everything.
Like the pillars of the earth—
Water, fire, and air—if one did not exist,

---

1. See note 1 attached to melody of hymn 31.
2. That is, Scripture and nature.
3. B, "... from all who give thanks without discussion."
4. On these names, see pp. 36–37.
5. See also *HF* 52:2.
6. Syr., *ḥad b-ḥad*, C. AB, *ḥad ḥad* "they are *each* ..."

Creation would fall.[7]
[44:4] The Jews recite the names of God,
But find no life in the multitude of titles.
Since they have rejected one name,[8] they are rejected by
many names.
The names which that People stripped off and cast away,
Into them the peoples are baptized. And who would remove
The names that have forged a chasm between us and the
People?[9]
[44:5] The People were expelled for one reason alone,
And the one who abrogates it will rebuild Jerusalem.
For the Jews were not uprooted because they debated,
But because they did not believe through the Son.
Seek the reason that Jerusalem was uprooted,
And see that the Church is supported by it without
controversy.
[44:6] Be reproved, presumptuous ones! Investigators, be
stopped!
See that no one can comprehend nature.
See that four things are buried in water.[10]
Also within it is a solitary nature,
And [a nature] that is two, and one that is three—
A threefold nature that has shown forth in three ways.
[44:7] Who can comprehend the Lord of natures—
To search into his divinity and seek out his fatherhood?
To explore his greatness and speak of how he is?
Look: he is completely hidden from all.
Even if he would wish to explain himself to us,
There is nothing in creation to interpret him.
[44:8] Since he has bent down to you to show you his Son,

7. Lit., "Then it would happen that creation would fall." On Ephrem's conception of the elements, see Possekel, *Evidence*, 80–112, esp. 99–103.

8. Presumably any name suggesting God as begetter (and thus Ephrem
connects his anti-Jewish and his anti-Arian polemic).

9. Note that Ephrem's rhetoric assumes that both he and his opponents
desire a strong Christian-Jewish distinction.

10. Ephrem's thought is not clear to me: is he envisioning the four elements each being present in water?

Bow down, fool, and thank him for making you worthy of all
   this.

Believe in and confess him, but do not dispute with him.

Do not bring him to court, for debating.

The nature of his Being is unspeakable.

Its gate is sealed in quiet, silencing words.

[44:9] The People have quarreled with him, questioning him:

"Who is he, and whose son?"[11] "How has he come?" and "Is he
   coming?"[12]

They thought it too difficult for a virgin to give birth,

And [so] the elders and scribes blasphemed him.

They have begotten themselves a messiah who does not exist—

A fabrication [born] of thought, and the mind's magic.

[44:10] Rebuke your thinking. Do not adulterously conceive
   for us[13]

A non-existent messiah, denying the One who does exist.

Take care not to construct an idol with your debating.

Take care not to depict in your mind

Something divined by your thinking, and begotten by your
   thought.

Let the true Child be depicted in your thought!

[44:11] Investigation belongs to an adulterous one, and
   inquiry to a harlot.

She has committed adultery in disputing and conceived and
   borne for us

A fabricated messiah and a constructed child,

To be like those who err in all things.

The Jews expect a fabrication of their mind.

The children of error labor for a prophecy [born] of their
   wisdom.

[44:12] The Evil One abandoned those outside, and set those
   inside wandering,[14]

---

11. Cf. Mt 22.42.

12. Cf. Mt 17.10, although there it is the disciples speaking, and in reference to Elijah.

13. C, "for yourself."

14. On Ephrem's division of "insiders" and "outsiders," see note 5 attached
to 17:3.

For he saw that investigation far exceeded the whirlpool.[15]
Instead of the abyss, investigation has consumed the denier.
If [only] you would weary of it, so that you would leave it!
This is his intention, to draw you to himself,
For he has cut off the hope of the one who lingers there.

{*The End.*}[16]

15. The Syriac term *ṣmārtâ*, "whirlpool," occurs only here in the *HF*. Clearly, it parallels *hāwtâ*, "abyss," in the following line. Together, the two seem to function as metaphors for the area outside the Church.

16. B.

HYMN FORTY-FIVE

According to the same melody.[1]

[45:1][2] The eye and the mind teach us about one another:
If something small falls into your eye,
It will bother and irritate it. It is the same with the mind.
Let the book and the light grant you wisdom.
The light pleases the eye, and truth the mind.
Choose light for your eye, and the Books for your mind.

> REFRAIN: *Praise to your hiddenness, O Child of the
> High One!*

[45:2] How the eye hates what falls into it!
The Evil One has cast meditation into our thought.
A crumb is difficult for the eye, but how much more difficult
[is meditation] for the soul?
Meditation always ruins everything.
The finger does not help the eye by poking at it,[3]
Nor investigation the mind by attacking it.
[45:3] His fatherhood is easier [to understand] than his
essence.
Another being cannot come from some [other] place,

---

1. On this melody, see note 1 attached to hymn 31.
2. This hymn has been translated twice previously. See R. Murray, "The Theory of Symbolism in St Ephrem's Theology." *Parole de l'Orient* 6/7 (1975–76): 19–20, and A. Palmer, "A Single Human Being Divided in Himself: Ephraim the Syrian, the Man in the Middle," *Hugoye* 1:2 (1998), at http://syrcom.cua.edu/Hugoye/Vol1No2/HV1N2Palmer.html.
3. Syr., *tehmûs bāh*. This is derived from the same root as "meditation" (*hemsâ*), but the verb, *hmas*, can also mean "to attack," from which (following the metaphor), I have derived "to poke at."

But [a father] can beget a son like himself. [4]

One thing from another thing is easy [to understand],

But what is difficult [to understand] is that Being who has
   come from nothing,

Yet bears everything, and dwells in everything. [5]

[45:4] If he dwelt in a place, [6] he would be small in spite of his
   greatness,

For there would be something greater than he, found dwelling
   in [another] place. [7]

He [would] be limited, and he who is unlimited

Would be unable to reach that [other] space. [8]

And as it would be impossible for him to fill it completely,

Neither could he possess its fullness in his mind.

[45:5] Yet even if, in his knowledge, he could reach the one
   from that place,

He would still be unable to reach it in essence.

His knowledge would [thus] be greater than his essence,

And he would be found composed of two [parts]. [9]

But look: he who is one is unlike both of them. [10]

But look: his smallness is the opposite of his greatness. [11]

[45:6] Along with that, he would not know whether there were
   in that place

Beings {unlimited—worlds} [12] and created things. [13]

4. "Father" and "son" could also be definite nouns.

5. While in the initial lines of this stanza, it sounds as if Ephrem is critiqu-
ing the language of "being" over against the language of "fatherhood" (and
"sonship"), the final two lines make clear that he is not positing one as to be
preferred over the other, but simply pointing to the incomprehensibility of the
language of being.

6. I.e., if he were spatially confined.

7. On this passage, and Ephrem's conception of space, see Possekel, *Evidence*, 127–54, esp. 131.

8. I.e., the one in which the greater thing would be dwelling.

9. I.e., knowledge and being.

10. Either the two theoretical beings, occupying these "spaces," or the two
parts—knowledge and being—which would make up this theoretical being.

11. That is, rather than his greatness existing in proportion to his smallness (following the hypothetical situation proposed in 45:4:1), his smallness
and greatness exist side by side, paradoxically.

12. BC. A mistakenly anticipates the following line (*saklâ b-pāhyâ*).

13. Beck takes the subject of "to know" as *man*. It seems to me that we can

Fools have thus fallen into blasphemous wandering,
And thus say at this time
That one [exists] by itself, and the Father by himself,
Complete and perfect, comprehending him totally.[14]
[45:7] For if he dwelt in a place, he would be small in his
   greatness.
And if he could not beget, his fatherhood would be empty.
And if he could not create, he would be weak in his Being.
Look: he is entirely perfect in every way,
For he has begotten without suffering,[15] and created without
   labor.
He does not dwell in a place, and he is rich without
   treasure.[16]
[45:8] There is no place that surrounds or confines him,
And no discussion that can investigate or comprehend him.
Great is his essence, as is his fatherhood.
Place fails, defeated along with the mind.
And as there is no place that comprehends his essence,
What mind can investigate his fatherhood?
[45:9] Though this is true, it is difficult for [humans] to
   discuss:
How did he create something when there was nothing?
There is no pattern to investigate, even if one were able,
And there is no way for a word
To allay your mind, by saying, "Look: it happened this way."
Believing, you have subjugated the height of discussion.
[45:10] Though your mind cannot gaze at his difficulty,
His action has sought another way,
So that, from another side, you can assuage yourself and be
   nourished:

---

stick with the hypothetical scenario, and read lines 1 and 2 as Ephrem continuing his depiction of all the ways this spatially defined God would be limited to the space in which he dwelt.

14. I.e., this hypothetical space would comprehend Father entirely. See
also *CH* 16:11: "If the place in which [beings] dwelt, / were a greater place
than his Being, / [that place] would limit him."

15. That is, when he begets he does not lose any of himself.

16. On this passage, see Possekel, *Evidence*, 131.

"All is explained by the Lord of all!"
Put on the argument by which the investigation of creation
Is silenced, and cease from the investigation of [his] begetting.

{*The End.*}[17]

17. B.

HYMN FORTY-SIX

According to the same melody.[1]

[46:1] Be careful, presumptuous ones, not to muse on and on.
A fish will jump up, but will not cross the river's border.
In our disputing, we have crossed the border that gives us life.
The breath of the Gospel carries us.
He has given water to the fish and the Books to the discerning.
Inside of them there is life, but outside is death.[2]

> REFRAIN: *Glory to the Father, who has declared that his Son*
> *is his Begotten!*

[46:2] Whoever presumes to enter, my son, where there is
no air,
Dies, because there is no breath there to give him life.
Let us learn that entering hidden things is not allowed.
That threefold breath carries us,
And if you go outside of it disputing,
The breath of error will fly up and kill you.
[46:3] A fool, angered, [asks], "Why does the Father have
a Son?
And if the True One begets, the ruler has impugned
himself."

1. On this melody, see note 1 attached to hymn 31.
2. This stanza gives the impression that Ephrem sees exegesis as standing at the heart of these fourth-century controversies. While the polemic here is general, it is interesting that it could be aimed as much at the Nicene *homoousios* as at, for example, the Eunomian "Unbegotten" (though 46:3 will suggest that Ephrem has Eunomius in mind). For Ephrem, the broader point is that, when speaking about God, one must use language found within Scripture. On this, see pp. 37–39.

Is your eye evil because he has truly begotten?[3]
You have become envious of the one who is without envy.
Leave all of these [things] and find out what his will is:
The Father wills that you believe that his Son is from him.[4]
[46:4] If he so wished it, the truth about him would
    correspond to his name.
And if he did not wish, it would be opposite his name—
The name "Father" would be borrowed, and the name "Son"
    would be borrowed.
His name and the true name of his Son are trustworthy.
Give thanks and do not fear, for his voice will comfort you.
His voice is like a pledge, which sounds forth regarding his
    Son.[5]
[46:5] Tamar, because her action was difficult [to undertake],
That faithful woman took witnesses to her innocence,
And received his pledge, to go and debate with him.
The silent things then went forth and acquitted her.
Learn, therefore, along with Judah, who was defeated by
    his pledges,
That if someone accuses you, [you have] his Books inside you.[6]
[46:6] No one else spoke, so that you should be in doubt.
Moses and Elijah were totally silent,
And the one who baptized him was as one who did not
    know him.
[John] surrendered that place so that his Father[7] could
    affirm him.

3. Mt 20.15.

4. On this passage, and its rendering in ER, see Introduction, p. 28.

5. Whereas elsewhere (for example, *HF* 31) Ephrem emphasizes the metaphoric nature of language, here he suggests a correspondence between the linguistic sign and the meaning it conveys: the words "Father" and "Son" convey their meaning truthfully. Within the context of the *HF*, his meaning is relatively clear: the terms "Father" and "Son" signify that the Father begets, and the Son is begotten. The final line of this stanza situates Ephrem's understanding of language within Scripture: ultimately, believers must accept the name "Son" because God himself uttered it at the Baptism (Mt 3.17 and parallels) and Transfiguration (Mt 17.1–9 and parallels).

6. Gn 38. The sentiment expressed here—that "the books" can serve as legal witnesses—will be echoed again in *HF* 53:8.

7. I.e., Christ's own Father.

If [someone] accuses you, repeat [the Father's] words to him.
Heaven was rent asunder, and he called out, rending
    controversy.
[46:7] If he abrogated [the voice] (for, look: humans
He called "sons"),[8] then [the voice] would have abrogated
    the one who spoke it.
For he showed that the nature of a human being is dust,
And he showed the nature of angels.
Concerning his Son, he called out "Son," and his Spirit,
    "Holy Spirit."[9]
He clearly set down these things that we have confused.[10]
[46:8] He knew that if he called mortals "sons,"[11]
Their body would refute them, for their nature is created.
Likewise, he knew[12] that watchers are our companions,[13]
[But] because their nature is more exalted than ours,
They were never called "sons of God,"
So they would not upset their name on account of their
    nature.[14]

8. Ps 82.6.

9. In reference to the name "Son" Ephrem clearly has the New Testament baptismal and transfiguration scenes in mind. With "Holy Spirit" it is more difficult to isolate a biblical scene that Ephrem has in mind. See, however, Mt 1.18, 3.11, and 28.19.

10. To reconstruct Ephrem's argument: he is arguing against those who refuse the name "Father" or "Begetter" as a primary name of God. Citing the scene of Christ's baptism as evidence for the name "Father" (on the basis of his calling Christ "Son"), Ephrem then imagines a rebuttal: on the basis of Ps 82.6 one could say that God calls all humans "sons," so why should we imagine that to be a special name? Ephrem's response then (in lines 3 and 4) is to point out that God also demonstrates the fallible nature of humans. So, in lines 1 and 2, his logic is this: if Ps 82.6 abrogates Mt 3.17, then God's voice renders God himself inconsistent, because God clearly places Christ in a different category from that of humanity.

11. Thus potentially implying that mortals are divine.

12. BC, "we know."

13. That is, that they are created. On "watchers," see note 6 attached to 3:5.

14. That is, with humans there is no possibility of them mistaking themselves for gods: their bodies clearly indicate otherwise. With angels, however, the temptation would be too great. For this reason, God called humans "gods," but not angels. Taken together with 46:7, this further demonstrates the particular meaning of "Son" in relation to Christ: it is a name he shares

[46:9] Go and call upon Adam, without question: he is dust.
Call even Gabriel, who is spiritual.
[But] he has sealed the Three in silence.
If someone asks you, there is written for you
An explanation of the highest, and the nature of the lowest.[15]
But he has not dictated for you [something with which] to
    investigate the Three.
[46:10] Fool, compel yourself to go after him with abandon.
In everything he has said to you, think not on whether it is
    fitting,
For you cannot understand it.
If you have believed in him till now, it is a small thing.
As often as you have believed in him well, worship still more,
    for he has bent down
The truth of his words to an ear of dust.
[46:11] It is a marvel that God bent down to dust,
Adorned it with life, magnified it with freedom,
And handed his Son over in place of it, to show it his love.
And instead of marveling at how great he is
(If one had before now marveled silently, it would be a small
    thing),
He[16] has gone right up to the honored one with the mockery
    of his disputations.
[46:12] They are called gods,[17] but he is the God of All.
They are called fathers, but he is the true one.
They are titled spiritual,[18] but there is [one] living Spirit.
Sons and fathers, which they are called,
Are borrowed names, which they have learned by grace.
The Father of Truth is one, and he has a Son of truth.[19]

　　　{*The End.*}[20]

---

with humans (not with angels), but which clearly has different significance
when applied to him.

　　15. I.e., angels and humans.　　　　16. I.e., the debater.

　　17. Ps 82.6.　　　　　　　　　　　18. BC, "spirits."

　　19. On the distinction between "true" and "borrowed" names, see Introduction, pp. 36–37.

　　20. B.

HYMN FORTY-SEVEN

According to the same melody.[1]

[47:1] These things are easy for those who know [them], but
    difficult for the simple:
The work of craftsmen, and the fine linen of the wise;
Weaving[2] and crafting, sculpture and ornament;
Treatises and calculations, weights and measures,
Which humans have discovered through wisdom,
Measuring the earth and weighing the waters.

> REFRAIN: *Glory to your knowledge, which has made humans*
>   *wise!*[3]

[47:2] If the simple cannot investigate the wise,
Who pass right by them with [just] a bit of teaching,
How much further is the wisdom of the wise behind
The Creator of all in his wisdom?
How mad they are!—who hope to discuss and investigate
The nature of the Creator, the Son of the Maker!
[47:3] Let us marvel: with these small and insignificant
Natures, which cannot comprehend, through the symbols
    within them,
The beauty of the Faithful One, or the Child of the
    True One,[4]

1. On this melody, see note 1 attached to hymn 31.
2. Lit., "weaver's beams."
3. B, "Glory to your knowledge, both hidden and revealed."
4. "Natures" (*kyānê*) here could refer either to the natural metaphors Ephrem has used throughout the hymns (see, e.g., *HF* 42), or to all created things, and their inability to understand God. For "nature" as "created thing," see note 13 attached to 36:12.

He has set investigators wandering in every way.
If they cannot reach creatures through disputation,
How they will be left behind by him who is beyond all!
[47:4] This lingering in brief moments of revealed things,
Has shown that the reaches of our thought cannot arrive at
The Son, whom no one comprehends or can explore his
    origin,
Since his Father is hidden from all, completely.
As far as someone may extend his mind and his thought,
His "where" is unsearchable and his "how" incomprehensible.
[47:5] Marvel therefore at created things and worship the
    Creator.
Do not quarrel and search into that nature more exalted
    than all,
For vain is the glory that motivates your disputation.
You are a nature—frail and weak.
Go—leave!—and see the dishonor in your struggle:
Your enemy mocks you. With him, you [mock] yourself!
[47:6] Know that pride motivates your controversy.
The prophets and righteous ones did not investigate these
    things.
Perhaps the apostles, who did not dispute, were too simple?
Moses will rebuke you, for he was educated,
Yet stripped away and cast off himself Egyptian wisdom,
And composed the truth simply, with revealed things.[5]
[47:7] Daniel was educated, too, and learned in Babylon
Wisdom you cannot glean.
The assembly of the wise, which entered a trial,[6]
[Daniel] covered them all with all wisdom.
Knowing that the treasury of revelations was locked,
Prayer gave him the key of explanations.[7]
[47:8] He was the most reflective of the just ones,
Yet when he heard that the word was sealed in secrecy,

5. On Moses's education, see Kugel, *Traditions of the Bible,* 509.

6. Syr., *bûqāyâ.* This is most likely an allusion to Dn 2.5 and 9, in which Nebuchadnezzar insists that the Chaldeans must reveal to him both his dream and its interpretation.

7. Dn 2.17–49.

He sealed his mouth with silence, and limited his question.[8]
Because the children of his people had been defeated,[9]
He asked [God] discerningly. And since he knew that he was
    [only] human,
He asked about what was human, and glorified Greatness.[10]
[47:9] The presumptuous one, therefore, has forgotten his
    nature—that he is human.
He has abandoned what is human and discussed Essence.
And if he has forgotten his nature, whose nature will he
    investigate?
He has forgotten his size, overreaching himself.
If he would shake off his wine[11] and recognize that he is
    mortal,
He would become quiet and heed the size of mortals.
[47:10] Look at Daniel: though he was a prophet,
He asked the watcher in order to learn simple things.[12]
Fools have urged one another to teach about hidden things.
Moses—also a glorious prophet—
Fearfully asked for the name of YHWH,[13]
But we have disputed about his hiddenness jokingly.
[47:11] The apostle was subtler[14] than the presumptuous ones
When he entered the city—the mother of the Greeks[15]—
And spoke to them of their own [gods], to reveal what he
    knew.
And when he had justified himself and disarmed them,
He established the truth for them. [Yet], they spit up the
    medicine of life,

---

8. Dn 12.8–9.

9. Dn 1.1–2.

10. In these latter two lines, Ephrem is probably alluding to Dn 2.20–23, in which, rather than directly asking God for an answer to the king's dream, he glorifies God, and acknowledges him as the possessor of all knowledge.

11. Ps 78.65.

12. Dn 7.16. See also *HF* 8:14–16.

13. Ex 3.14. Transcribed in A as *'lhyh,* and in BC as *'hyh.*

14. Syr., *qaṭṭîn,* "subtle," which is the same quality Ephrem ascribes to Aetians in *CH* 22:4.

15. I.e., Athens, following Acts 17.16–34. On Ephrem's distrust of things Greek, see note 24 attached to 2:24.

For they had been sick a long time with the illness of debating.
[47:12] Sit at a contest and watch the spectators:
In that open[16] place there goes before them
A crown, [but] they cannot see the obvious things[17] on it
When they quarrel, fight, and clamor.
If you have examined them—how they disregard even revealed
    things—
How much more [can you see that] fools are inundated in a
    sea of hidden things!
[47:13] Go[18] find a crowd totally quiet and agreeable,
And introduce investigation and controversy there.
Sit and observe that those who are firm change,[19]
And the quiet ones, who become troubled, then trouble
    [others].
One is pressed in there, yet all clamor together.
This is investigation, whose smoke will blind the multitudes.

     {The End.}[20]

---

16. Or "revealed" (*glîtâ*).   17. Or, "revealed things" (*galyāteh*).
18. B adds "sit."   19. Or, "are expelled."
20. B.

HYMN FORTY-EIGHT

According to the same melody.[1]

[48:1] Enable me to open my senses to your Beloved,
Who alone can declare you.
Whoever has not learned you[2] from him[3]—how you are—
Has strayed afar, thinking he has found you.
The threefold names are depicted among the faithful.
They are always beyond debating, always past understanding.

REFRAIN: *Enable our assembly to praise you without division!*

[48:2] If we could meet our own needs in everything,
The Lord of everything would leave us be.
If we could be a crucible for [testing] disputations,
No one would stray in his speech.
But our soul is like a hand, which cannot
Write letters without learning [them].
[48:3] Look: many, while grazing, have wandered off.
This has taught, without controversy, that we are not
A crucible [to test] everything, so that we can know, by
    ourselves,
That he is one, he whose proclamations have educated us.
Our creatureliness is like the eye: it is blind by itself,
And cannot distinguish colors without light.[4]

---

1. On this melody, see note 1 attached to hymn 31.
2. B, "him."
3. B, "you."
4. According to Possekel, Ephrem evinces a dual theory of optics, in which light comes from the eye, but is also aided by light outside of itself. See Possekel, *Evidence*, 205–10; 222–29.

[48:4] He has shone light upon us, and dictated writings for
us.
His light is for revealed things, and his book is for hidden
things.
In the beginning, [he taught] with revealed things. Now [he
teaches] with laws.[5]
His light and his law [are] without envy.
Through its shining, a lamp calls out to onlookers:
The truth is understood through the rays of the law.
[48:5] In everything, nature is eager to learn.
Every person, according to his ability, learns in proportion to
his labor,
And whoever does not learn is considered ignorant.
Compare one to the other,[6] and be persuaded
That whoever does not submit himself to the Teacher-of-all,
Is rightly considered to have strayed in his freedom.
[48:6] It is difficult to blame someone foolish and ignorant
For conceiving [God] without knowledge and forming [him]
without understanding.
But one can blame him for not having learned.
In the former [case] he escapes [judgment], while in the latter
he is judged.
Therefore, at the point when he thought he had escaped,
He was found not to have escaped, for they condemned him
solely for his [ignorance].[7]
[48:7] Ease off. Give the fish some time to wear itself out:
Its struggle is to your advantage; its labor is counterproductive.
It will bring you a crown [of victory] through its effort, not
even realizing it.
Mock the one who is presumptuous and deceived:
He is self-defeating, for whenever he thinks he is pulling away,
He is pulled back into the net, through his own will.

5. In the *CGen.*, prol. 2–3, Ephrem posits that, in the early days of the
world, Israelites had a natural grasp of monotheistic principles. During their
time in Egypt, however, they fell into idolatry. It was for this reason that Moses
penned Genesis.
6. I.e., the learned and the ignorant.
7. That is, he was condemned for not having tried to rectify his ignorance.

[48:8] Unable to explore the sea in which it dwells,
It desires to climb the air and investigate the height.
Though it cannot live outside its own place,
The fish's splashing has seduced it.
Leaping, it grows so arrogant that it goes up to touch the air,
Until its breath is scattered, and it is sent back to the water.
[48:9] Because it is born of water, it thinks everything
Dwells in water. Its river teaches it
That investigating places hidden from it[8] is foreign to it.
[Its dwelling] is no stranger than our dwelling,
And our investigation no stranger: it[9] cannot
Arrive at heavenly things, and investigate their natures.
[48:10] In the symbol of the Gihon,[10] the Gospel has rushed to
    give [us] drink.
His propagation is inscribed in the Euphrates, for it has
    increased its teaching.
In the Pishon is depicted his type, and the cessation of
    disputing about him.
You have cleansed us[11] like the Tigris[12] with [your][13] word.
Let us bathe ourselves and ascend with him to meet him in
    Paradise.
And let the fish not pass beyond the border of life.

> {*The End.*}[14]

---

8. Syr., *ma'mrâ d-qayṭûnê*, which is a calque on the Greek *koitôn*. Literally, it refers to an intimate room, which would be inaccessible to most people. Here, it refers to the world external to the sea, which the fish cannot access.

9. I.e., our investigation.

10. Gn 2.13. In his references to the four rivers that follow, Ephrem traces out an etymological interpretation for each of the names: he connects *Gîḥôn* to *gāḥ*, "to flow"; *prāt* ("Euphrates") to *prāyâ*, "propagation"; *pîšôn* to *pāwšâ*, "cessation"; and *deqlat* ("Tigris") to *deqlat*, "you have cleansed." Ephrem is by no means the only ancient exegete to perform an etymological analysis of the four rivers of Paradise. On Philo's reading of the rivers, see Lester L. Grabbe, *Etymology in Early Jewish Interpretation: The Hebrew Names in Philo* (Atlanta, GA: Scholars Press, 1988), 24–26.

11. Syr., *deqaltan*.

12. Syr., *deqlat*.

13. Lit., "his."

14. B.

HYMN FORTY-NINE

To the melody: "Bardaisan's herd ..."[1]

[']² [49:1] How glorious was Noah, who by comparison outweighed
All the children of his generation![3] When they were weighed with justice,
They were found wanting in the scale. One soul righted the scale
With the weapons of modesty.[4] They sank down in the flood,
Weighing too little in the balance. But chastity and honor
Were lifted up in the Ark.[5] Glory to the One who delighted in it![6]

>   REFRAIN: *Praises to your lordship!*

[p] [49:2] Noah stretched his ministry between two sides,

---

1. This melody includes hymns 49–65. Hymns 49–52 have a meter of 5+5 / 5+5 / 5+5 / 5+5 / 5+5 / 5+5. Hymns 53–65 subtract a 5-syllable hemistich from the last line.

2. *HF* 49–65 form a continuous acrostic on the name of Ephrem. At 50:2, however, the acrostic freezes on "m" (the final letter of Ephrem's name) and remains there through 65:13.

3. Gn 6.

4. Syr., *nakpûtâ*, which can mean "chastity" or even, more generally, "holiness," but here suggests Noah's deferential obedience to God's command. On Rabbinic notions of Noah's relative righteousness, see Kugel, *Traditions*, 187.

5. This stanza provides an excellent example of the pictorial quality of Ephrem's language: beginning with the image of a scale, he portrays Noah's righteousness as outweighing those of his other generation. Yet, he flips the image on its head when he joins it with the image of the Ark: now those who were "too light" sink down in the flood, while Noah is lifted up in the Ark.

6. Or, "in him."

And indicated two types. He sealed [the generation] that was
    passing,
And began this present one. Between two generations,
He tended to two symbols, for he dismissed the former
And invited the latter. He buried the old generation
And let the infant grow. Glory to the One who chose him!
[p] [49:3] The boat of the Lord of all flew through the flood.
It went out from the East, and arrived at the West.
It floated to the South, and marked the North.
Its watery flight became prophetic on dry land:
It proclaimed that his Birth[7] bears fruit on all sides,
And spreads to all regions. Glory to its Savior!
[r] [49:4] In its course it made the sign of its protector—
The cross of its sailor, and the wood of its navigator,
Who came and built for us a Church in the midst of the
    waters.[8]
In the name of the Trinity, he delivered [the Ark's] inhabitants:
Instead of the dove, the Spirit made its anointing,
And [drew] the image of his salvation.[9] Glory to its Savior!
[r] [49:5] In [his] Torah,[10] his symbols, and in [his] Ark, his
    type
Bear witness to one another: just as the insides
Of the Ark were emptied out,[11] so the types
In the Books have been emptied out.[12] Through his coming,
    the symbol
Of the Law has been completed,[13] and the types of the Ark
Have been fulfilled in the churches. Glory to your coming!

---

7. That is, Christ's.

8. A reference to Baptism.

9. Reading the motion of the dove in Gn 8.8–11 as cruciform, and of the
Genesis narrative as a type of baptism.

10. Ephrem uses two terms for "Torah" in this passage: here he uses *'ūrāy-
tâ*, an older Aramaic term, but in line 5 he uses *nāmûsâ*, a calque on the Greek
nomos. Both terms appear as synonyms in this stanza.

11. That is, when its inhabitants exited it.

12. That is, they have been interpreted in the Church.

13. Ephrem does not refer here to a specific symbol which represents the
Law. Rather, through Christ's coming, the Law has been revealed *as* symbolic
(as well as temporary).

[r] [49:6] Look: my mind has wandered, for it has fallen into
the terrible
Flood of our Savior![14] Blessed is Noah: though
His ship—his Ark—sailed through the flood,
He himself was calm.[15] Lord, may my faith become
A ship for my weakness. Look: fools are drowning
In the depth of your disputation![16] Praises to your Child!

{*The End.*}[17]

14. Cf. *HVir* 7:15.

15. Syr., *knîšâ-[h]wāt*, lit., "was gathered."

16. In *HVir* 7:15, Ephrem depicts himself as laboring wearily as he is buffet-
ed by waves of the Lord's symbols. Here, it is the disputants who are drowning,
but in a sea of disputation. In *HVir* 7:15, he acknowledges his state of peril, and
asks the Lord to save him "like Simon" (a reference to Mt 14.28–33). While
the two stanzas use different vocabulary (here the disputants "are drowning,"
ṭāb'în, while there Ephrem says the waves "press upon me," '*amlûn[y]*), the similar depictions of Ephrem himself and the disputants he rails against suggest a
similarity between the two. Ephrem recognizes the potentially presumptuous
qualities inherent in his poetic project. What differentiates his *madrāšê* from
the works of his opponents is his professed dependence upon the mercy of the
Lord.

17. B.

HYMN FIFTY

{2. *According to the same melody.*}[1]

[y] [50:1][2] The Child who was with the Father before all [else],
And transcends all time (for all times were created by him),
Is before numbers, spaces, and times.
"How" is unsearchable, "when" incomprehensible,
"Why" not to be debated, "how much" immeasurable,
And "where" cannot be explored. Glory to his Begetter![3]
[m] [50:2] Whose mouth would not grow quiet next to the
    Child
Whose glory mouths cannot utter?
Who would not rebuke himself, considering
That if the Child were comprehended, they would diminish his
    Begetter,
And if the fruit were investigated, they would limit its root,
Since one is mingled with another? Glory to your Father with
    you!
[m] [50:3] Who would not hesitate to hold within the tiny
Recess of his thought measureless investigation—
Unmeasured inquiry—into the Child and his Begetter?
Investigation into creatures by our mind is fine.

---

1. B. As indicated by the number "2," B provides individual numbers for
each of the 16 hymns that fall under this melody. In AC, however, hymns 49
and 50 are divided only by a single punctuation mark. On the acrostic of the
two hymns, see note 2 attached to 49:1.

2. The text of hymns 50–52 is taken from C, because the text of hymns
50–52 is missing from A and at points illegible in B. Thus C provides the main
manuscript for these hymns.

3. Hymn 50 is unique in that the manuscripts provide no refrain, but each
stanza ends with a doxology in the meter of the hymn.

There is no investigation into the Creator who completed
   [creation],
For the Great One is beyond every nature. Glory to his
   Greatness!
[m] [50:4] Who would not cease from investigating that Child,
And marvel at his Begetter? He is the Son: that is easy for us.
"How" is difficult for us. Perceiving [him] is simple for us.
Investigating [him] is hard for us, for inquiry into his essence
Is hidden from every nature. To the Father and to him[4] let us
   send up
Glory, silently. Thanks to his Sender![5]
[m] [50:5] Who will not bless the Good One who has given
   himself
To the dust, to perceive him? He gave speech
And reason to one made of dirt. He sent his Son to clothe
   himself [in the dirt]
And raise it up in glory. The Evil One envied how
He magnified humanity,[6] and [so] flung it down into
   disputation
And the depth of controversies. Praise his goodness!
[m] [50:6] O our Lord, keep from us the Evil One, who is
   irrationally evil.
He envied Adam and he envied his sons.
He deceived [Adam], pleasing him with the word that
   destroyed him.[7]
He mocks every generation, [but] our generation he has
   especially despised.
He has made us proud and scorned us. He has intoxicated us
   and insulted us.
He has divided us and derided us. Glory to the One who
   killed him!
[m] [50:7] Who would not be ashamed at his soul's
   foolishness,

----

4. That is, the Son.
5. B, "... praises, through the Holy Spirit. Thanks to his Father!"
6. Lit. *bar nāšâ*, "man."
7. Cf. Gn 3.1–6. In Ephrem's *CGen.* 2:23, he speaks of Adam and Eve being
pleased at the prospect of divinity which the Serpent offered them.

Which has not perceived the Evil One's company, even as he
    dwelt within it?
He is invisible to its eye, cannot be touched by its hand,
Nor can he be tasted, for it would recognize him as bitter.
He cannot be smelled, for it would perceive that he stinks,
For he resides entirely in blood.[8] Blessed is he who has brought
    him to nothing!
[m] [50:8] Therefore, the soul does not perceive the demon,
For, if [the demon] dwelt within it, it could neither reach nor
    touch it.
And if he rested outside of it, his company could not reach it.
So whether he were beside it or within it,
The soul would not perceive [him]. Let us mourn, for we have
    presumed
About the Son of our Creator.[9] Praise to you from all!

    {*The End*}[10]

---

8. Ephrem may have in mind ritual sacrifices. See *CNis* 47:103, where he
references unclean spirits dwelling in drink-offerings.

9. That is, if the soul cannot perceive a demon, how can it perceive the
truth of the Son?

10. B.

HYMN FIFTY-ONE

{3},[1] *According to the same melody*

[m] [51:1] Who can repay [you] for lowering your greatness
To every smallness, and {inclining}[2] your magnificence
To the limits of humility? You have brought your life
To the steps [that lead] to mortality. Your wealth has come
    down and dwelt
In all poverty, and you have submitted your lordship
To a yoke of servitude.[3] Glory to your goodness!
[m] [51:2] O our Lord, who could gaze upon your hiddenness,
Which has come to revelation? Your secrecy has become
Manifest and known, your hiddenness has become visible
In limitless revelation, and your dreadfulness has fallen
Into the hand of rulers.[4] These things have happened to you,
    Lord,
Because you have become a human being. Glory to your
    Sender!
[m] [51:3] Who would not fear? Though your manifestation is
    so apparent,
As is your human birth, your birth is [yet] incomprehensible,

1. B. See note 1 attached to hymn 50.
2. B.
3. Syr., *'abdûtâ*, which derives from the same root (*'-b-d*) as *'bādâ*, "thing-made." The latter is the term, derived from Prv 8.22, used to justify a subordinationist interpretation of Christ. As Ephrem will make clear in 53:11, he interprets Prv 8.22 as referring to the Lord's condescension. Thus *'abdûtâ* echoes these debates.
4. Lit., "those who hold," and, by extension, "those who hold *power*," i.e., "rulers" (see *LS,* 27, col. 1, sub. *'āḥûdâ*). I am taking it as an allusion to imperial involvement in religious affairs.

For it has caused debaters to wander. Look: one proclaims[5]
That you took only the body, and another teaches[6]
That [it was] the body as well as the soul. Still others,
    straying, think
The body[7] is heavenly.[8] Glory to your birth!

[m] [51:4] Lord, silence us! For if your revelation
Has caused the wise to wander, because they could not
    comprehend
Your birth from Mary, while the scribes, with controversy,
Have split your birth....[9] If they could not understand
Your humanity—a human [birth]—who could comprehend
Your divine birth? Praises to your Begetter!

[m] [51:5] Whatever is permitted, Lord, let us sing with our
    lyre!
Lord, let us not speak anything not under our authority,
For it is a weak lyre, and its melodies cannot
Debate your birth. Neither by the noble
And spiritual lyres of the heavenly watchers
Can your birth be comprehended. Glory to your
    hiddenness!

[m] [51:6] O our Lord, may my tongue be a reed [pen] for
    your praise,
And a finger for your goodness to inscribe and write
A beneficial treatise. Lord, a reed cannot
Write without one holding it, according to its own will.

---

5. B, "teaches."   6. B, "proclaims."

7. Syr., *gûšmâ*.

8. While Ephrem may just be offering a generic list of errant Christological options, the suggestion that there is debate about whether Christ took a body and a soul echoes the controversies surrounding Apollinaris. See Young, *From Nicaea to Chalcedon*, 245–53.

9. I am following Beck (*HF [G]*, 135, n. 2) in taking "the wise" as a reference back to the speculations alluded to in 51:3:4–6, and "scribes" as fore-shadowing the turn to the "divine birth" in the final line of this stanza. The "scribes" thus represent (here as elsewhere throughout the HF) Ephrem's main opponents, subordinationists. As for what Ephrem intends by saying the scribes have "split" the birth, it could refer to a division between the reality of the birth and the reality as they present it, or it could simply indicate the confusion they have wrought.

Let my tongue not slip, to speak, outside of you,
That which provides no help. Praises to your teaching!
[m] [51:7] It is presumptuous to call you by a name foreign
To the one your Father called you. For he called you only
    "my Son"
At the Jordan River.[10] And where you yourself were baptized,[11]
The threefold symbols baptized your humanity:
The Father with his voice, the Son with his power,
And the Spirit with her hovering. Praises to your hovering![12]
[m] [51:8] Who can deny the three names
Whose hovering first ministered at the Jordan?
Truly, in the names into which your body was baptized,
Look: bodies have been baptized. And though the names
Of the Lord of all are many, we clearly baptize in the Father,
    and the Son,
And the Holy Spirit. Praises to your greatness!
[m] [51:9] Who would not marvel at a painter, who, when
    he paints,
Even if only a lowly horse, though he could well add
A head or body parts,[13] he shrinks from adding [them]?
Foolish scribes! With questions, they have diminished
The Child who cannot be diminished. And though he is like
    the One,
They have made him like many. Praises to the Son of our
    King!
[m] [51:10] Who has seen in the air a straight path,
Something like the path of a bird,[14]
And a man walking [on it], as if borne by the wind?[15]

10. Mt 3.17.

11. The "you" has now switched to refer to Ephrem's own audience.

12. On the Spirit's "hovering," and its connection to Gn 1.2, see note 13 attached to 38:12. Here again it is associated with the Spirit, though in the next stanza it will be associated with the "three names" of the Trinity. Even there, however, the reference to a trinitarian hovering above water suggests a connection to Gn 1.2.

13. That is, the painter could depict the horse in any way he wishes, but chooses to depict it realistically.

14. Lit., "similar to the path, the path of a bird."

15. Lit., "as on the back of the wind."

A net[16] is stretched out, and a path is made for walking,
And he is warned not to depart from it at all,
For death is outside of it.[17] Praises for your warning!
[m] [51:11] O our Lord, allow me to walk with that fear,
Afraid to transgress the boundary of my faith.
Your truth is clear and straight. To the faithful it is clear,
But to the crooked it is difficult. The straight have stood
    straight up and gone out.
Scribes have turned aside and fallen into the depth of debate,
But our Lord will rescue them. Praises to the One who finds
    all!
[m] [51:12] From the names, the ability to interpret[18]
Has dawned and gone forth to us. The names "thing-made"
And "Son of his Lord" bear witness: the name "thing-made"
Teaches that he is not "Son," while the name "Son" proclaims
That he is not among equals.[19] Their names proclaim
Them without controversy. Praises to your Greatness!
[m] [51:13] Thus let us say to the presumptuous one
Who teaches a new thing: "My faith is complete,
And my pearl is perfect! Your polishing is unacceptable.
[My pearl] takes no delight in your crucible, for [its] beauty
    comes from itself.
If it were embellished, it would be rejected by the crown
Of the Heavenly King." Praises to your Kingdom!

{*The End.*}[20]

16. Syr., *nešbâ*, which could also be vocalized *nšābâ*, "blowing," in which case it would refer to the wind, mentioned in the previous line.

17. I assume that the image Ephrem has in mind is either of a tight-rope-walker, or some sort of rope-bridge.

18. Syr., *ḥayleh d-pûšāqâ*, lit., "the power of interpretation."

19. That is, he is not an equal to created things. See also *HF* 6:8–11. Ephrem here sketches a grammatical approach to Christology which he will draw out more clearly in *HF* 53. According to Ephrem, the names "Son" and "thing-made" are mutually exclusive. Thus, one must determine which is the true name, in light of which the other should be interpreted. So, if "Son" is truly Christ's name, then "thing-made" must refer to him in a different way. At 53:11, he will take "thing-made" in reference to the Lord's humanity.

20. B.

HYMN FIFTY-TWO

{4},[1] *According to the same melody*[2]

[m] [52:1] From God, let us learn God—
How, through his names, he is understood to be "God,"
"Just," and "good." Thus his name "Father"
Shows that he is Begetter, while the name "fatherhood"
Testifies to his Son. And though he is Father of one,
In his love he is the [Father] of many. Praises to his[3] goodness!
[m] [52:2] The Lord is true, and, look, his works exist.
He is the king of his possessions, and because he is Creator,
Look: his creation exists. And since he is the Father of truth,
He has a Son of truth. If his name "Father"
Is borrowed—God forbid it!—then all similar names
Are destroyed through controversy.[4] Praises to the True One!
[m] [52:3] Who could speak against the Father of truth?
"He cannot beget! Only in appearance has he put on
That name 'fatherhood.'" Though he is indeed the truth,
And his taste is preserved in his salt, fools have grown tasteless.
Who could abolish the name in which stand
Our baptism and our forgiveness? Praises to your forgiveness!
[m] [52:4] Say: a human being's work is outside of him,
And his voice is within him. Say: God
Makes, but not by himself, for his Word is his Child.[5]

1. B. See note 1 attached to hymn 50.
2. See note 1 attached to hymn 49.
3. B, "your."
4. See also *HF* 44:3, where Ephrem argues similarly that God's "perfect and holy name" acts as an anchor for the rest of his names.
5. This could also be translated: "... as for God, a thing-made is not from him, for his Word is his Child." This translation would emphasize that the one

269

It is not a spoken word, [but] a word that can
Declare everything. Ours is a word that
Cannot not declare him. [6] Praises to your hiddenness!
[m] [52:5] Why is your speech troubled, unprofitable scribe?
If the Father acknowledges his Son without aversion,
And if the Son acknowledges his Father without fear,
Go away and weep, child! They are equal, of one accord,
And we are divided. Heaven is full of peace,
Yet there is a dagger in the churches.[7] Praises to your
    peacemaking!
[m] [52:6] How could your debating harm God?
For if he announces, without shame, that he has begotten,
And, without fear, that he has brought forth, who are you—
    vile!—
To wish to collect from the Collector-of-all?[8]
Go, flee, and collect yourself from your enemy,
Who has murdered you with your [own] tongue. Praises to his
    Murderer!
[m] [52:7] The fool has thrown himself down, stirring up the
    two clear
And holy seas, [9] which are never [permanently] stirred up.
Those stirred up with waves settle [again] and become clear.
Those clouded with floods become beautiful and pure.[10]
But if someone investigates them, they cast him away, rejected:

---

who has come from God is not a "thing-made." As I have translated it above,
however, it emphasizes the role of the Word/Child in creation.

    6. On this verb "declare" (*ešta'î*), cf. Is 53.8 and *HF* 5:2.

    7. Cf. *HF* 53:2.

    8. The term Ephrem uses here—*tābû'â* ("collector")—has clearly economic
overtones. While most of Ephrem's economic metaphors emphasize the merciful interaction between God and his poet, here, as in *HF* 38:4–5, Ephrem
uses the metaphor against his opponents, satirizing them as one trying to collect money from someone to whom money is owed.

    9. That is, the two testaments (cf. *HF* 52:10).

    10. There is some ambiguity with lines 3–4. Ephrem provides no subject,
but uses "stirred up" and "clouded" as masculine plural substantives. Grammatically speaking, the subject could either be "seas," carried over from lines
1–2, or the substantives could refer to people, i.e., "Those stirred up," and
"Those clouded." I have chosen the former option because it makes more semantic sense following line 2.

He dies through his disputing. Praises to your righteousness!
[m] [52:8] Who would not silence investigation into hidden
    things—
A plague, which the apostle has called "gangrene"?[11]
Schismatic investigation pours out harm:
For the fool who muses upon it, pain, all of a sudden,
Comes to be mixed with it. What is sweet in its beginning
Is bitter in its end. Praises to the One who has extinguished it!
[m] [52:9] Who would want your weak eyes
Gazing upon things bright, concealed, and strong,
[Things] whose splendor watchers cannot look upon?[12]
Moses was content to look through a tiny crack.[13]
Since he did not look to investigate, the splendor rushed to
    meet him.
It blinds the investigators. Praises to your magnificence!
[m] [52:10] Who would not believe that the two Testaments
Everywhere indicate Father, Son, and Spirit,
And do not call [the Son] by the name "created" or
    "fashioned"?
The names of creatures are not there connected [to him].
As he wished, so he wrote. And because he is God,
We should believe him. Praises to his lordship!
[m] [52:11] Who would not submit himself to his teachers,
To learn as they taught him? And even if he thought he had
    surpassed
The measure of his teachers, who among the wise
Would [claim to] be like the One who gives wisdom to all?
    Who among saviors
Is like the One who frees all? Who in revelations
Can be compared to the Holy Spirit?[14] Praises to your
    teaching!
[m] [52:12] What remain of the arguments of the party of the
    contentious,
Since truth has seized all their arguments?

11. 2 Tm. 2.17.
12. On watchers, see note 6 attached to 3:5.
13. Cf. Ex 33.18–23.
14. For a similar list of comparisons, see *HF* 6:5.

One of the three is applicable to the presumptuous:
Concede that he is a denier, concede that he is a fraud,
Or declare him ignorant. The [side] of the investigators has
    perished,
While that of the faithful stands. Praises to your victory!
[m] [52:13] What then is left for this gossiping party?
Speaking as they do, even a liar
Can overcome them! For it was either [because of] weakness
That he could not beget, but he hid his weakness,
And made us think that he had begotten, or he was capable
    and did beget.
In both cases, the crown of victory [goes to] our side.
[m] [52:14] Why would we introduce some other thing into
    that
Truth he dictated to us? The names that we have added,
These, brothers, have become an excuse for the
    presumptuous—
For all hated additions. You have increased disputes,
And increased controversies. You have recited the things
    written
And silenced troublesome things.[15] Praises to your clarity!
[m] [52:15] O our Lord, make peace in my days in your
    churches.
Mingle and unite, Lord, the schismatic factions.
Reconcile and shepherd, too, the quarreling parties.

From all the churches, may there come one Church of truth.
May her righteous children be gathered within her womb,
Giving thanks for your grace. Praises to {your reconciliation}![16]

{*The End.*}[17]

15. On the historical context of this passage, see pp. 37–39. Lines 4b–6a
are difficult to interpret. Each begins with a second-person perfect verb, but
the accusations of 4b and 5a are clearly negative, while those of 5b and 6a
appear entirely positive. One possible interpretation is that Ephrem directed
the negative accusations at one party within his audience, and the positive at
another. Another possibility is that lines 5a and 6b are directed to the Lord
(the obvious addressee of the final hemistich), with an intended allusion to
Lk 4.17–21.

16. Syr., *tar'ûtâk*, B. A misspells as *tar'îtāk*, "your mind."

17. B.

HYMN FIFTY-THREE

{5},[1] *According to the same melody*[2]

[m] [53:1] Who would not marvel at the Just One, who
    did not neglect
To write of exalted things, or inscribe lowly things?
He writes of created things, and includes everything,
Even the staff[3] and the story of the mandrakes
About which simple women spoke.[4] He dictated through
    the Holy Spirit,
And it was placed in the Ark.

    REFRAIN: *Praise to your teaching!*[5]

[m] [53:2] Who would not fear? There is scandal
    throughout the land,
Bickering in the inhabited earth, and debate in the
    market-place.
There are schisms among congregations, and in the churches,
Destruction and dagger. Women fall upon women,
Men upon their friends, and priests upon kings.[6]
The whole world clamors!
[m] [53:3] Who would not weep at how often the earth

---

1. See note 1 attached to hymn 50.
2. On this melody, see note 1 attached to melody of hymn 49.
3. Beck, *HF (G)*, 141, n. 1, suggests Gn 30.37, but see Nm 17.2–10.
4. Gn 30.14–16.
5. B, "your justice."
6. Beck, *Die Theologie,* 62, takes this as an allusion to the ecclesio-politics connected with the fourth-century theological controversies, possibly to Valens's persecution of Nicene Christians in Edessa. On this, see Introduction, pp. 26–28.

Has quaked, and then settled again, while the quakes and the
    controversies
Of the churches have not grown silent? Waves and storms
Quiet down over the sea, but fools and debaters
Are stirred up on dry land. It is a blessing for sailors,
But woe to the scribes!
[m] [53:4] Is our war good because it provokes mercy?
God forbid! And if Satan
Mocks and derides us, [saying], "Why has the Good One
Not fashioned a path, writing simply
And openly, 'creature,'"[7] then [bring] two or three
So as to increase the witnesses.[8]
[m] [53:5] Because he is the God of truth, who is not misled,
He will not mislead anyone, for he is good and just.
For how often has he chastened us with his teaching,
And prepared, with true things, an unswerving path?
Yet, he has brought a curse upon "the one who misleads
A blind person on the road."[9]
[m] [53:6] Because he dictated distinct words[10] for us[11]—
They are like drugs, which agree even as they disagree,
Since, in the hope of {healing},[12] all of them
Are combined. The one who does not know
Their strength, kills with them. The one who knows
Their strength achieves victory with them.[13]
[m] [53:7] From this example of medicine,
Approach the Books. There are those who are completely
Ignorant of herbs, and there are those who are complete
Strangers to the readings. The words quarrel with themselves
In the mouth of the foolish scribes. The Books are filled with
    peace.

7. Prv 8.22.
8. Ephrem here echoes Dt 19.15, which he will then quote outright in 53:8.
9. Dt 27.18.
10. Syr., *qālê d-pûršānâ*, which also carries the sense of "words requiring discernment."
11. Line 2 begins a gloss on these "distinct words." Ephrem will resume his main thought in the next stanza.
12. Syr., *ḥûlmānâ*, BC. A misspells as *ḥûmānâ*.
13. For the likening of doctors and exegetes, see also *HF* 53:12.

The scribes [are filled with] conflict.

[m] [53:8] What is left to do, then, except this:
Let us appeal to witnesses—something the Just One,
Who is accused, commanded: "By the mouth of three"[14]
The judgment is decreed. Let us summon the great
Judge of justice, and let us summon the two sides—
Witnesses to their case.

[m] [53:9] Because you have been enlightened, turn away
    from words
Which proclaim the smallness of our Lord, as well as his
    greatness.
For one hears in them his humanity, and another
Hears his divinity. Let us put aside interpretations,
And seek clearly and openly the names
"Son" and "creature."[15]

[m] [53:10] They can say to us, like most excellent scribes,
Conversant with the law, and practiced in the things of the
    Prophets:
"See how Solomon encourages controversy?
For he perceives and calls him 'creature' and 'thing-made.'"[16]
Thus Solomon becomes a great refuge
For all their sophisms.

[m] [53:11] From my simplicity, hear succinctly:
All of this smallness which is in the Books,
Is fulfilled in the humanity of our Savior.
But if you are able, pass beyond his humanity
And come to his divinity, and you will find that above all
These things he is exalted.

[m] [53:12] Come and fly to his side on the feathers of the
    mind,
And the wings of thought. Polish and cleanse
The eyes of your mind. Ascend and look upon the Son.
Look upon him and look upon his Father, and see [the Son]
    entirely

14. Dt 19.15–16 (P).

15. On this passage, and the hermeneutic this and the following stanza imply, see pp. 29–30.

16. Prv 8.22.

Like his Begetter. For the Father is hidden from all
And the Son is concealed from all.
[m] [53:13] Count, therefore, how many times he is called
    "Son" and "Begotten,"
And then add up how often he is called "creature."
And once the words have been compiled, the names which
    predominate
Persuade those who are discerning of the accurate name.
The [true] name is repeated every time instead of the title[17]—
Two, three, and more [times].
[m] [53:14] We have counted and found that in one parable[18]
    alone,
Solomon calls out "creature." We have made a calculation, and
    have not [even] finished.
For the Father is in all marvels, the prophets in all mouths,
The apostles in all words, and the demons in all scourging.
As one, they have proclaimed him "Son." Who would not
    believe
And rebuke the quarrelsome?

    {*The End.*}[19]

17. On the distinction between "names" (*šmāhê*) and "titles" (*kûnāyê*), see
pp. 36–37.
18. Syr., *matlâ,* which is the Syriac name of the biblical book Proverbs.
19. B.

HYMN FIFTY-FOUR

{6},[1] *According to the same melody*[2]

[m] [54:1] When the Son of the heavenly King came down to
    the Earth,
The People who had known [him] not, knew [him] by their
    voice,[3]
For the Father bore witness to the Son,[4] and the Son called out
    to the Father.[5]
And in [the Son's] abasement, it was understood that he was
    Lord,
Who was glorified above all, for the sea became his vessel,[6]
And the air his chariot.[7]

    REFRAIN: *Praises to your Sender!*

[m] [54:2] In the way he was ministered to, he taught whose
    Son he was:
At the time of his abasement, the watchers came down and
    ministered
To the Son of their glorious Lord.[8] And just as if [it were] a
    maidservant,
He commanded creation.[9] The world, like a servant,
He led with a gesture, like his Begetter,

1. B. See note 1 attached to 50:1.
2. See note 1 attached to hymn 49.
3. I.e., the voices of the Father and the Son.
4. At Christ's Baptism and Transfiguration (Mt 3.17 and 17.5).
5. Cf. Lk 23.34, Jn 17, and *HF* 63:2.
6. Mt 14.22–36; Mk 6.45–52; Jn 6.16–21.
7. Acts 1.9.   8. Mt 4.11.
9. Mt 8.26; Mk 4.39; Lk 8.24.

277

Whose silence leads all.

[m] [54:3] Because he is the Lord, he has exalted the children
    of his house.

Fools had made themselves crazy, falling down defiled.

But he came down and lifted them up from their defilement.

Error strayed when it saw our dirt on his clothes.[10]

Knowledge alone knew that he had approached defilement

To cleanse it.

[m] [54:4] From his care, let it be understood that he is the
    son of the king,

Since, as a good heir, he took pains over his father's house.

He saw the servant who was lying down, and stood him in
    health.[11]

He saw the handmaid who was cast down, and rebuked her
    fever.[12]

He saw the bread that was running out, and filled the children
    of his house.[13]

They gave thanks to the One who sent him.

[m] [54:5] Who would not love the Lover of humanity,

Since he is mingled and mixed with them?[14] His handmaid
    became his servant.[15]

They invited him and he did not look down upon it. He went
    to a [wedding] feast,

And gladdened it with his greatness. He set down his gift—

Wine in vessels, for the treasure of his kingdom[16]

Walked along with him.

10. I.e., and thus assumed it to be a reflection of his nature.

11. Possibly Mt 9.1–8, but more likely Jn 5.1–18.

12. Mt 8.14–17; Mk 1.29–34; Lk 4.38–41.

13. Mt 14.15–21; Mk 6.30–44; Lk 9.10–17; Jn 6.15–21.

14. These terms "mingled" (*mzîg*) and "mixed" (*ḥlîṭ*) are characteristics of Ephrem's Christological language, but they also have mundane meanings attached to the preparation of wine. Thus Ephrem is taking a wine metaphor, according to which it would have been diluted before being served, and using it to speak about Christ's relationship to humanity, but doing so in the context of an allusion to the Wedding at Cana (Jn 2).

15. "Handmaid" here refers to creation itself (following 54:2:3–4), and this line anticipates the allusion to the Wedding at Cana in the following lines.

16. "Treasure of his kingdom" (*gazzâ d-malkûteh*) must be a metaphor for Christ's divinity.

[m] [54:6] Who would not be afraid and purify his body?
Upon entering the house of his Father—that great Temple—
He chastised them with cords.[17] And since they had cut off
their hope
By profaning the Temple, he gave to Jerusalem
A certificate of divorce: he took the vineyard
From [those] laborers.[18]

[m] [54:7] Who would not be afraid? Who would not love
Him who extolled his merchants, and multiplied the talents
they received?[19]
He punished that wicked and vicious slave,
Who abused the sons of his house and ravaged his
companions[20]—
The accursed—who, once he was wounded, cried through the
mouth of his demons,
"What do we have to do with you, Jesus?"[21]

[m] [54:8] It is written that the good Lord repented[22] and
grew weary,[23]
For he had put on our weakness. Then, he put on us
The names of his greatness. Fools saw what belonged to us
And thought it belonged to him—that which was from us.
They are shown to be guilty, without even realizing it.
     Therefore, what belongs to him,
Let us believe that it belongs to us!

[m] [54:9] Whenever his own true hearers
Surround him lovingly, they do not judge his words.
[But] those divided lie in wait for his utterances deceptively.
Their putrid[24] controversy is like some prosecutor
Of justice itself, which labors through discourse

----

17. The allusion to "cords" (*ḥablê*) suggests Ephrem is drawing upon the
Johannine version of this episode (Jn 2.13–16).

18. Mt 21.33–46; Mk 12.1–12; Lk 20.9–19.

19. Mt 25.14–30; Lk 19.12–27.

20. Mt 18.23–35.

21. Ephrem is reading Mt 18.23–35, alongside the possession scene of Mk 5.7
and Lk 8.28, so that Matthew's "wicked slave" becomes a type of the "Evil One."

22. See, *inter alia*, Gn 6.6; Nm 23.19; 1 Sm 15.11, 29, 35; 2 Sm 24.16.

23. Cf. Jn 4.6 and Is 1.14.

24. B, "foolish."

To conquer what is right.

[m] [54:10] Our Lord spoke: the luminous rejoiced,
The gloomy were afraid, the innocent heard and affirmed,
While the crafty heard and debated: "How can this one
Give his body to us?"[25] Their debating has deprived them
Of the medicine of life. Let it not deprive us also—
Our debating—so that we do not believe.

[m] [54:11] It is not fitting to examine God's words
In a crucible. Look at the disciples
And look at the deniers: the chaste believe,
While those mad debate. They thought he was not
Fifty years old![26]—he whose age[27]
Can never be comprehended.

[m] [54:12] With brief [words], therefore, let us say: all
Discussion belongs to the left hand—that of the thief
Who was crucified on the left hand.[28] He disputed,
To teach by his question the presumption[29] of the
    investigators.
Woe to you![30] Hope is cut off: even when he was nailed and
    crucified,
He disputed his Lord.[31]

[m] [54:13] But who would not marvel at the thief
Who was crucified on the right hand? Hanging, he saw and
    believed
That he was the Son of God.[32] As for us, who believe
That he ascended in glory and sits at the right hand:
The cross convinced the thief, but not even the Cherubim
Who bore him will persuade us![33]

> {*The End.*}[34]

---

25. Jn 6.52.   26. Jn 8.57.
27. Syr., *methâ*, which is more literally rendered "extent" or "reach."
28. Lk 23.39.
29. Syr., *ḥûṣpâ*. On the valence of this term within Ephrem, see note 192
on page 51.
30. The "you" here is directed toward the robber.
31. Ephrem switches to the third person ("he disputed his Lord").
32. Lk 23.40–41.
33. Acts 1.9–10. On the Cherubim, see Ex 25.18–22; 1 Sm 4.4; and *HF* 4:18.
34. B.

HYMN FIFTY-FIVE

{7},[1] *According to the same melody*[2]

[m] [55:1] Who, my son, would compare natures that are
    different from
One another in their offspring, to the nature of the
    Creator of all,
Who is foreign to them? For if explaining
The begetting of fire is difficult, though visible to the eye,
How hidden from us is the fruit of our Maker,
And the Child of our Creator?

> REFRAIN: *Praises to your hiddenness!*

[m] [55:2] Whoever would expound upon him who gives
    existence to all,
Should first expound upon every nature.
Let us leave his greatness and speak of his chariot.
Let us depict how it is, explaining how
Its wheels live, and whether there is
A word [to explain] his living creatures.[3]
[m] [55:3] Who has seen a chariot made for
Air instead of earth, and wind[4] instead of the road?[5]

1. See note 1 attached to 50:1.
2. See note 1 attached to melody of hymn 49.
3. Ezek 1.4–28. This passage is interesting because it shifts the discourse from an abstract discussion of the nature of God, to a concrete discussion of a scriptural text, albeit a difficult one. Underpinning this shift is Ephrem's understanding of Scripture as a revelation of the hidden God. Interpreting Scripture enables readers to access God in his revelation, though not to pass, through Scripture, to his hidden nature.
4. Or, "spirit" (Syr., *rûḥâ*).
5. There is wordplay evident in the Syriac: *ʾāʿar ḥlāp ʾarʿâ w-rûḥâ ḥlāp ʾûrḥâ.* Thanks to Blake Hartung for drawing my attention to this.

It leads itself,[6] and does not turn,[7]

For on the four sides it has four heads.

There is a question about the throne—whether its face and its countenance

Look in [only] one direction.[8]

[m] [55:4] Because the son of Buzi[9] saw the likeness

Of a man upon the throne,[10] and because that chariot

Does not turn, the throne therefore

[Must] have changed itself to face all sides.

And if the throne is a marvel, who can comprehend

The watcher who sits upon on it?[11]

[m] [55:5] Speak, and show us the nature of exalted things.

Michael's picture and Gabriel's image

Are of fire and spirit. How does fire see?

How does spirit breathe? Are [the angels] short, or tall?

What is their color, and their sense of touch?

[Tell us] if you have explored it!

[m] [55:6] Who {has gone out}[12] and investigated outside of the world,

To come and speak to us? And if [the world] is limitless,

Thus extended on and on, measure it with your mind,

So that it will dazzle you with its measurements. There is One who measures all,

Who is himself immeasurable. He contains everything,

Though nothing contains him.

[m] [55:7] What exists essentially is a nature that

6. Syr., *hāy dābrâ yāteh*. This could also be translated "[the spirit] leads it," echoing Ezek 1.20.

7. Ezek 1.9.

8. This last line is obscure. It is not clear whether the pronouns attached to "face" and "countenance" refer to the throne or to Ezekiel. I have taken it as the former, but it could also refer to Ezekiel's response to the scene, described in 1:28. In that case it would be translated, "for his face and his countenance / looked in only one direction" (i.e., at the ground).

9. That is, Ezekiel (see Ezek 1.3).

10. Ezek 1.26.

11. On "watchers," see note 6 attached to 3:5. As this makes clear, Ephrem interprets the one sitting upon the throne as an angel.

12. Syr., *npaq*, BC. A, *spaq*, "to comprehend" or "be able."

Never willed to give itself existence—and this is to its glory.[13]
The One [nature][14] did not [come to be] through the hands {of
the Lord, in whose hands all are}[15]—
And this is to its praise.[16] That will,
Above which none is exalted, is exalted by itself alone—
And this is for its crowning.
[m] [55:8] Although this is unspeakable,
It needed to be spoken—not that a hidden thing
Which can never be uttered or spoken, should be spoken.
It is investigation I wished to rebuke. For if something far from
him
Cannot give itself existence, how far from us
Must be the investigation of his essence?[17]
[m] [55:9] My beloved, who can touch or contain
Something that does not exist? In the same way, it is very
difficult
To investigate him who does exist. See how [a person] is
limited[18]
In investigating, my son, a thing that does not exist?
This demonstrates what does exist, because its discussion[19]
Is utterly unsearchable.
[m] [55:10] Through this alone, let us learn how error befalls
us

13. Ephrem's precise meaning is somewhat obscure. The question is whether the "nature" (*kyānâ*) "which exists within Being" (*meddem da-b-'îtûtâ-[h]w*)
refers to the Son, the divine nature, or the nature of created things. Beck's
translation (*HF [G]*, 148) implies the latter. While this interpretation makes
sense (i.e., created things have come into being not through any volition of
their own, and this is "for their glory," insofar as they accept the reality of it),
3–6 all seem to refer to the divine nature. This, then, suggests we should read
the whole stanza in reference to the divine nature.
14. Beck glosses this with "Being" (*HF [G]*, 148).
15. BC. Missing in A.
16. This could mean either that the Son was not created by the Lord, or
the divine being itself was not created by the Lord. Ephrem use of "the One"
(*ḥdâ*) suggests the latter.
17. Ephrem's syntax is terse here, but his meaning is clear: how can something that cannot create investigate the Creator's Being?
18. Syr., *mtaḥḥam.* C misspells as *mḥattam,* "sealed."
19. I.e., the discussion of what does not exist.

As often as we [try to] gaze upon that first Being.
When nothing [else] existed, he was found existing,
And there is no explanation as to how—that is another error,
However much we might move toward him. And just as he has
    begotten eternally,
He is eternally incomprehensible.
[m] [55:11] Through him, let us speak about him: just as one
    must
Confess his essence—[we are] compelled, without argument,
For he is greater than every argument—so one must
Magnify his fatherhood, without debating or discussing,
For he is greater than all debating. To investigate his
    fatherhood
You must seek his essence.
[m] [55:12] Who would not honor both with silence,[20]
Since they are concealed from all, yet mingled as one:
Whether being debated together,[21] or being justified together,
While his fatherhood is good, his essence is awesome.
Like hands, they help one another,
For their crown is one.
[55:13] Who with words—his speech capable—
Has spoken through any mouths to the Lord of all mouths,
He whom [mouths] have never spoken? A thing which can
Be exhaustively uttered is like us—
Its nature is our equal. There is only one who is not made,
Because his father is Lord.

   The End.[22]

20. That is, God's Fatherhood and God's Being.
21. Syr., *w-'ên dāršān 'akḥad*. This should probably be taken to mean "being debated."
22. C omits.

HYMN FIFTY-SIX

{8},[1] *According to the same melody.*[2]

[m] [56:1] Who would not imitate those fathers
Who believed simply? They neither investigated nor discussed.
They utterly rejected the debates of the subtle one,[3]
Who has hardened our heart. It has become heavy, brought
    down
From divinity's side. [Divinity] has rejoiced at the innocent
Who believed and excelled.

> REFRAIN: *To you, praises from all!*

[m] [56:2] Who could comprehend Noah's immense silence?
For one hundred years he subdued his debating within his
    heart,
While fools reviled him [asking], "Where is the flood?"
He did not ask or discuss where the deluge was
Which would slay the wicked. Indeed, it was not revealed
For one hundred years.[4]

[m] [56:3] Who would look upon Abraham and not be silent?

---

1. B. See note 1 attached to 50:1.

2. See note 1 attached to melody of hymn 49.

3. Syr., *qaṭṭînâ*, which is the same word Ephrem applied to Aetians in *CH* 22:4. While here the singular suggests Ephrem has Satan in mind, it is hard not to hear echoes of these fourth-century debates.

4. Ephrem's reading of Noah depends upon details found in Gn 5.32 and 7.6: in 5.32, just before God announces his plans to destroy the earth, Noah is said to be five hundred years old. Then, following the Lord's commandment to Noah in Gn 7.1–4 to enter the Ark, the text specifies that Noah is six hundred years old. Ephrem takes this basic data, and from it develops the portrait of the silent Noah, who endured the ridicule of "fools" for one hundred years.

He bound his beloved—the son of the promise—
And placed him on the altar. He did not ask or discuss,[5]
Nor did he debate and demand, "Where is [our] agreement?
Where is the promise?" He put away his tongue
And unsheathed his knife.[6]

[m] [56:4] Who would not marvel at how silent Abraham was,
When there was an opportunity for his word and his question?[7]
If that elder was silent and did not ask a question
About his son who was going to die, who will cut off his own
    hope
By presumptuously debating about the Son of God,
By whom Isaac was delivered?[8]

[m] [56:5] So that you will not erroneously think Abraham
Irrational, you will find that he was talkative,
And see that he was a debater: when, on the Sodomites'
    behalf,
He was not ashamed to be bold, he brought the Judge of all
    down from
Fifty to ten: his talking was helpful,
And his [eventual] silence heroic.[9]

[m] [56:6] He spoke when it was helpful, and grew silent when
    it was appropriate.
He guarded[10] [himself] with discernment, [...][11] what was
    beneficial.
So that you would not think him weak,
Unwilling to avenge himself, he conquered four kings,[12]

---

5. Note that this line is repeated verbatim from 56:2:4, thus functioning as a verbal refrain to unite Noah and Abraham.

6. Gn 22.9–10.

7. A misspells as *šwylh*, but BC corrects as *šû'ālâ*.

8. Reading Gn 22.13 christologically.

9. Gn 18.22–33.

10. A has "he kept" (*nāṭar*) before "he was silent" (*w-šāteq*), but this line division upsets the 5+5 rhythm. Following C, Beck suggests moving "he kept" (*wa-nṭar*) to the beginning of the following line, which I have also done.

11. AB very clearly have *pw'*, which is not an identifiable Syriac word. This same term appears again in *HF* 63:5:2, and is equally ambiguous there. C changes it to *pnî*, "turned to," though this leaves the stich short one syllable. Moreover, at 63:5:2, C does not substitute *pnî*.

12. Lit., "four kings were conquered."

And went to save them.[13] They had seized the son of his
  brother,
But [Abraham] endured to become victorious.
[m] [56:7] From that Old Testament, let us learn
How the children of truth listened to him with a love of
  discernment.
{They}[14] believed [truth's] giver and affirmed its writer,
While the children of error listened to every aid
With an ear for controversy, and mouths for derision.
[Yet] they who mocked him have been rejected.
[m] [56:8] Therefore, the two Testaments instruct us
That the faithful never debate or discuss,
For they have faith in God. But the scribes and the crooked
Debaters never keep silent. The Books are full of peace,
But they are full of rage. Their debating has aged them,
And their rust consumes them.
[m] [56:9] Who would not be threatened by Moses: when
  he slipped
Only a little and doubted, the rock could not
Produce water, and he was forbidden to enter
The Promised Land.[15] Who [then] could enter
The land of the living[16] without believing
In the Son of Greatness?
[m] [56.10] From craftsmen learn well,
That [it is] neither permitted[17] nor allowed for an ignorant
  party
To judge their [own] works, nor can they be
A crucible for [testing] their wisdom. Though all the wisdom
Of the weak be extended, it [still] cannot arrive
At a place greater than itself.

13. I.e., his nephew, Lot, and his family. Gn 14.1–16.
14. BC. A, "he."
15. Cf. Ex 17.6 and Nm 20.9–12. In both accounts water *does* come out of
the rock. In Nm 20.9–12, however, Moses has to strike the rock twice before
water comes out, and then he is informed by God that, on account of his dis-
belief, he will not enter the Promised Land. It thus seems that Ephrem is referencing the imagined first striking of the rock in Nm 20.11.
16. Cf. Ps 27.13.
17. Syr., *d-lâ šārê*, following DJBA, sub. *šry*, #1.

[m] [56:11] Who could judge the words of the Judge of all?
Who could reproach the voice of the One who reproaches all?
Though someone blind cannot investigate, he puts faith in
     medicine
And trusts that the iron will ease his pain.
Though it utterly tears him apart, he trusts the branding iron,
Even as it torments him.
[m] [56.12] Who would not marvel: everyone has faith
In the medicine-book from which a doctor reads
And repeatedly teaches us, so that we will trust his words
And agree to his medicine without judging or questioning.
But God's Books: can {they}[18] not persuade
That the Son is his Begotten?[19]

        {*The End.*}[20]

    18. BC. A, "he."
    19. See also *HF* 53.
    20. B.

HYMN FIFTY-SEVEN

{9},[1] *According to the same melody.*[2]

[m] [57:1] Who has investigated himself? Whose hand
    has ever explored
How and where he collects and stores
A reservoir of teaching? Through repetition, he empties
The writings into his heart: he gathers in memory,
Increases through study, and diminishes [them] through
    idleness.[3]
All of these things are astonishing!

    REFRAIN: *Praises to your kingdom!*

[m] [57:2] Who can enter himself and observe
Whether there is an empty place for teaching,
And [whether] the soul is lacking?[4] And if memory
Increases much, it is a wonder that it receives without
    filling up,
And gives without decreasing. Everything is in the heart,
Yet there is nothing in it.
[m] [57:3] Who can gaze upon memory's splendor—
An image of its Creator? What it is cannot be comprehended:
Without laboring, it holds the names of created things,
And though it has no place, every place is within it.

---

    1. B. See note 1 attached to 50:1.

    2. See note 1 attached to the melody of hymn 49.

    3. In terms of Ephrem's anthropology, here and in the following stanza he clearly locates memory in the heart, though in 57:2:3 he seems to identify the soul and the heart, while in 57:4:3 he appears to equate memory and mind.

    4. I.e., lacking in teaching.

Just like names,[5] all things are suspended inside it,
Though its power never grows weary.
[m] [57:4] Who could enter within memory
And explore how the names of created things exist,
Since neither it nor they can be explored? Within the mind
And within Being everything dwells. So within the Father of
    truth
There is the Son of truth. And neither he nor they[6]
Can be explored—how they are.
[m] [57:5] Who does not recognize that the soul does not
    leave,
But when it does leave, the body dies because [the soul] has
    passed?
For this reason, the memory flies to every region,[7]
And there is no place where you can say, "Look: here it is."
Though it is inside the body, creation is smaller than it,
For [memory] exists within everything completely.
[m] [57:6] Who has examined a sleeper running even while
    sleeping?
If the soul wanders in a dream,
Why would the mind wander with it, when, look, it is awake?[8]
Who has slept, yet been able to see? Who has been awoken and
    remembered [a dream]?
How does one who is asleep see? How does one who is awake
    forget [a dream]?
Look: all of it is a wonder.[9]

5. That is, in addition to the names that are stored in memory.

6. This could refer either to the "the names of created things" (from line 2), or the Father and the Son. The former seems more likely, with Ephrem drawing a parallel between the Son, who dwells in the Father, and names, which dwell in the mind.

7. That is, while the soul is bound to the body, the memory can be everywhere.

8. Or, "it watches" (i.e., the dream). There is a passivity implicit in Ephrem's use of the word "wander" (*pāhyâ*). Thus it can be juxtaposed with the vigilant mind, which is not passive, and so does not wander.

9. As is clear here, and will be assumed in the following stanza as well, Ephrem conceives of dreams as produced by cooperation between the mind and the soul: dreams reside in the soul, yet are controlled, and later remembered, in the mind.

[m] [57:7] Without the mind, how has the soul by itself
Seen the dream in front of it? And if it did see [such a dream],
    {how}[10]
Did it not perceive it had seen [it]?[11] With what memory
Did it keep everything that it saw, until its [other] half awoke
And helped it remember? How can it remember
What was submerged alongside of it?
[m] [57:8] Who would not marvel at [the fact that] the sun is
    without feet,
Though its path[12] [extends] above it? And how would it walk
    on [its path]?
It does not have feet, and it does not have wings.
It is in motion, yet does not move. No one walks,
Flies, or swims [upon it].
Look: all of these things are a marvel!
[m] [57:9] Speak and explain to us, O mortal word,
Where your treasure dwells,[13] and in what part
Of the mind you reside. Are you a small part of the soul?
Does [your][14] end ever come? You are born of that which
    produces you—
It gives birth, yet is not diminished. How, within the heart,
Do your movements vibrate?
[57:10] From this humble word of yours[15]
May you admirably learn the glorious word—
The Word of God. For if your own word
Can never know [how] to tell of itself,
With silence honor your Creator's Word,
Whose silence[16] is unsearchable.

10. Syr., *'aykan*, BC. A, *'ûhdânâ*, "memory," which it mistakenly copies from
the following line.

11. That is, without the mind.

12. That is, presumably, the sun's rays.

13. Treasure here stands as a metaphor for that hidden place from which a
word comes and in which its meaning dwells.

14. Syr., "its."

15. Speaking here to his audience, who have been asked to contemplate
their own powers of speech.

16. C, "glory."

HYMN FIFTY-EIGHT

{*10*},[1] *According to the same melody.*[2]

[m] [58:1] Who has noticed water inside trees[3]
Changed there into a multitude of things,[4]
When the water transforms itself by a command,[5]
Taking the shape of wood for things to be built?
And from that very [wood], a ships' planks come,
So that by [water] itself we overcome [water].[6]

> REFRAIN: *Praises to your wisdom!*[7]

[m] [58:2] Who has seen wood destroyed by smoke?
All of it dissolves and floats off in the air,
So that even the feel of it changes because of fire,
Becoming impossible to hold?[8]
It began as a plant, ends in flame,
And is concealed in wonder!

1. B. See note 1 attached to 50:1.
2. On this melody, see note 1 attached to the melody of hymn 49.
3. Lit., "in the womb of trees," by which Ephrem could be referring to the water feeding the roots of a tree, or the presence of water within the tree itself.
4. Lit., "a multitude of numbers" (*sûg'â menyānê*). *Menyānê* could also be vocalized *mannînâ*, "insect," a reading which could make an allusion to Gn 1.20.
5. Beck (*HF [G]*, 155) reads as "command [of God]," but it seems to me this could also refer to the command of the builder referenced in lines 4–6.
6. The Syriac of this passage represents Ephrem at his most ambiguous. It is not clear to me if he is referring to the presence of water in wood generally, or if he is speaking of the role water plays in making trees to grow. Either way, his final rhetorical point is fairly clear: water is a part of wood, ships are built from wood, and thus, by extension, water helps us to travel upon water.
7. B, "your truth."
8. Lit., "it becomes un-holdable for the hand of holders."

[m] [58:3] Who can investigate to where the vapor
Of spices, the smell of sacrifices,
And the breath and smoke of wood burning ascend?
Is it kept inside something,[9] so that it can come to something
    else?[10]
Or has it dissolved into nothing, that the Lord of everything
Might be magnified in everything?
[m] [58:4] Whenever a thing-made investigates he finds his
    equals.
If he investigates creatures, he finds neighbors of himself,
For the Lord is hidden from him. However much lower the
    name
"Dust" is than "God," lower still is debating about [dust]
In order to [understand] the Maker. In name and in reality:
In both he is scorned.[11]
[m] [58:5] Who would not accept this without controversy:
Just as the name "thing-created" or "thing-made"
Will never fare well in comparison
With the name "Creator," so also disputing about him
Weighs little balanced alongside the glory
Of him by whom all was created.
[m] [58:6] Who would reach out to that which is greater than
    himself,
Without wing for his weak soul,
To come to the great height of the one so short?[12]
He lowered himself to Zacchaeus. The short one in the height
Of a tree dwelt. And the Exalted One gracefully
Walked beneath him.[13]
[m] [58:7] Speak what is profitable and explain the teaching.

9. I.e., the thing on earth, from which it ascends.
10. I.e., the thing in the sky, to which it ascends.
11. Syr., *šîṭ*, which shares a root (*š-w-ṭ*) with the word translated "lower" in lines 3 and 4. This passage implies a connection between divine names and the realities which these names represent: misnaming God, or applying names to him in a disordered way, lead ultimately to a misunderstanding of his nature. Ephrem explicates this further in the following stanza.
12. Syr., *mkîkâ* (lit., "down low"), which carries the sense of "humble," but here describes the physical stance of Christ *vis-à-vis* Zacchaeus.
13. Lk 19.4–5.

Interpret what is beneficial and discuss what builds-up.
Question the deniers and repudiate the crucifiers.
Investigate their Books and refute their arguments.
Teach innocence, increase {simplicity},[14]
And bring ignorance to enlightenment.
[m] [58:8] Speak of [his] goodness, for he freely nourishes you.
Proclaim [his] righteousness, for he will repay you and
    increase you.
Bless his existence, for when you were not, he made you.
Magnify his fatherhood, for he has numbered you among his
    children.
Await his kingdom, for, look: he has invited you—even you—
And has called you to his table.
[m] [58:9] What has he not given you? Yet, everyday you draw[15]
    against him
Your debating[16] and your tongue. The Books are true,
The seas are rich, meals are beloved,
And fasts are illuminating. He who is weak has grown fat[17]
Upon the things at your banquet. Do not trouble yourself to
    teach
Torturous debating![18]
[m] [58:10] Whenever the king's son has not opened to his
    laborers
The treasure of the kingdom, a dangerous thought
Takes shape there: those presumptuous
Do not wish to acknowledge the king's son.
They call[19] him an equal, [saying] "the crown he has received
Has magnified him by grace."[20]

---

14. Syr., pšîṭṭûtâ, BC. A, pšîṭṭâ, "a simple thing."

15. Lit., "is unsheathed."

16. B, "your head."

17. Syr., 'et'arreš. B, 'etra''eš, "to be trampled," though the lexica do not attest r-'-š in any extended forms. C, 'etdarreš, the meaning of which is not clear in this context (e.g., "has grown learned," "has been instructed").

18. Or, "debating about torments."

19. Ephrem uses the verb kannî, from which comes the noun kûnāyâ, "title," on which see pp. 36–37.

20. Cf. Mt 21.33–41.

[m] [58:11] Our King and our King's Son opened the treasure
    and scattered
The good things of the Kingdom. Two worlds he has given us,
[One] that passes, and [one] that will remain. And because his
    mercy
Has surpassed his gift, the King has lifted up
And given to us his Son—a gift for his beloved—
And killed him and saved us through him.
[m] [58:12] What has cast {among us}[21] strife and torment,
Harmful debate, destructive musing,
Abundant blaspheming, the extremes of hateful things,
Envy instead of love, and jealousy instead of truth?
The Evil One saw the Good One—how he was good to us
    without cause.
He put on jealousy, to destroy us unexpectedly.
[m] [58:13] Let us therefore say to Satan, who troubles us
When we investigate our Savior: "Leave. Go and investigate the
    demons
So you will find your equals. From there, investigate the [evil]
    spirits,
So you will know your neighbors. Investigate Gehenna,
For its fire is your keeper. Explore the darkness,
For it is wholly prepared for you!"

    {*The End.*}[22]

21. BC.
22. B.

{*11*},[1] *According to the same melody.*[2]

[m] [59:1] The waters of our forgiveness and the floods
  of our reconciliation
Have come unto quarreling.[3] In them, two parties
Pursue their debates. The People quarreled in the desert
And in the Church the peoples dispute over the waters.
[First] in the Red Sea, my brothers, and now they dispute
In the waters of the sanctuary.

  REFRAIN: *Praises to your forgiveness!*

[m] [59:2] Who does not quarrel? Who does not ask
His friend, "Who baptized you? Where
Did you receive baptism?"[4] Who has not warned,
"Do not let his hand baptize you, for he is a schismatic priest"?
Thus they have become controversial waters
For the controversial parties!
[m] [59:3] Who is the Holy Spirit,[5] that she did not receive
  a body,
And in no place did the Prophets introduce her weakness,
[Nor] the Apostles her want? Maiden and handmaid,

---

1. B. See note 1 attached to 50:1.
2. On this melody, see note 1 attached to the melody of hymn 49.
3. This stanza, along with 59:2, hints at practical consequences that followed from debates about Trinitarian belief and baptism. On the role of baptism in the fourth-century debates, see note 8 attached to 13:6. Ephrem's polemic here, however, seems to depend upon a shared baptismal practice, emphasizing especially a Trinitarian invocation. See also *HF* 28:12 and 51:7.
4. Lit., "Where was your baptism received?"
5. Or, "What is … ?"

Creature and thing-fashioned they never proclaimed her,
As they proclaimed him "Son."[6] She is exalted above the body,
She is exalted above everything.[7]
[m] [59:4] Let us debate about her in particular: if it were
    necessary
For [the Books][8] to describe for us the natures of the Father
    and the Son and the Spirit,
And reveal, concerning the Maker, that, though unmade,
    he makes,
And (as they say) dictate concerning the Son, that he is
    Creator,[9]
Why did they not reveal to us the Trinity—
The nature of how it exists?
[m] [59:5][10] Who does not recognize that he has arranged and
    enumerated them,
Ordered and numbered them—the threefold names
Of the Father, Son, and Spirit? And it is fitting that insofar as
He enumerated their names, he revealed their natures.[11]
If it is written, let us proclaim [it]. If it is not written, let us
    confess
That their nature is hidden.[12]

6. Grammatically, it is awkward in English for Ephrem to connect a negative and positive assertion with "as," but his meaning is clear: in the same way
that they *did* call Jesus "Son," they did *not* call the Spirit "created."

7. On the role of the Holy Spirit in fourth-century controversies, see Introduction, pp. 40–41.

8. While the subject here is not specified, I am taking it as "the Books" on
the basis of 59:5:5.

9. Syr., *bry',* which could be vocalized as *bāryâ* ("creator," as I have taken it),
or *baryâ* ("created"). While the Syriac of this stanza and the previous stanza
is obscure, Ephrem appears to be rehearsing a hypothetical argument of one
who accepts the divinity of the doctrine on Father and Son (thus calling the
Son "creator"), but is skeptical about the full divinity of the Holy Spirit. On
this aspect of the debates, see Introduction, pp. 40–41.

10. Now begins Ephrem's answer to the hypothetical questions posed in
the previous two stanzas.

11. Ephrem again articulates the idea that names are indicative of natures.

12. Thus humans can proclaim an identity of natures based on the fact
that, as names, they are grouped together in Scripture. At the same time, humans cannot investigate these natures (as Ephrem will state in 59:6).

[m] [59:6] Because it[13] has not revealed to us the Three,[14]
It has shown clearly that we must not
Investigate the natures of the Father, Son, and Spirit.
But the care of that Good One is such that
In all ways, and with all means,
He shows mercy on humans.

[m] [59:7] Therefore, without arguing, accept that everything
Written and spoken—both names and titles[15]—
He wished to provide fullness to the life of humanity.
Neither for debating or arguing
Should we investigate their nature,[16] but to understand
How great is their love.

[m] [59:8] Because the Holy Spirit did not receive a body,
She is exalted above voices and above the words
Spoken about the divinity
Of our Lord, and his humanity.[17] Meanwhile, the scribes, with
    controversy,
Disturb and then fling these words
Into the ears of humanity.

[m] [59:9] Because they did not know the will of [these
    words],[18]
Each one, through controversy, invoked them according to his
    own will.
He clothed them in judgment, and debating made them
A weapon for war, and a shield for controversy.
Look: peaceful words have quarreled with debaters,
Though their peace has not suffered.

[m] [59:10] The peaceful, peace-giving word of our Lord:
We have made war with it, and plotted battle with it.

---

13. That is, Scripture. This could also be taken as "he," in reference to
God.

14. That is, the nature of the Three.

15. On these two terms, see pp. 36–37.

16. Note how in this stanza Ephrem moves seamlessly between the singular
and plural of "nature" (*kyānâ/ê*).

17. That is, the words that apply to Christ's humanity, such as "thing-made,"
do not apply (and in Scripture are not applied) to the Spirit. Therefore, her
divinity should not even be at issue.

18. See 59:8:3.

We have hated charity because of it, and we have loved envy
    because of it.

We have driven tranquility away with it. We have banished
    peace with it.

We have murdered ourselves with it, and desolated each other
    with it,

Hating one another because of it.

[m] [59:11] The clear font, never troubled,

That proceeds from the Clear One: debaters have disturbed it,

And the peaceful flock has drunk troubled waters,

And has become troubled, because impurity has come in.

It has rendered serenity troubled, and the flock has gone mad,

Along with its shepherds.[19]

[m] [59:12] Because those fat among the flock have grown fat
    and resistant,

The son of Buzi[20] testified that they have gored the weak,

Cast down the sick, scattered those gathered,

And lost those who had been found.[21] Because this narrative

Is greater than my mouth, the Prophet who was introduced
    by it[22]

Will also complete it.[23]

> {*The End.*}[24]

19. Ephrem is echoing Ezek 34.18, as he does also in *HF* 35:3–9. See the
comments in note 15 attached to 35:3.

20. I.e., Ezekiel.

21. Ezek 34.4.

22. I.e., because Ephrem alluded to the parable before mentioning its author by name.

23. As suggested in note 15 attached to 35:3, Ephrem uses this passage
from Ezekiel to critique subtly the religious leaders of his own day. With this
in mind, the conclusion of this hymn is made all the more dramatic: Ephrem
acknowledges the weight of the critique he is making, but coyly points back to
Ezekiel, as if all he has done is to repeat the biblical words, merely letting his
audience spell out their implications.

24. B.

HYMN SIXTY

{*12*},[1] *According to the same melody.*[2]

[m] [60:1] Who would not refute the presumptuous? Why,
If he did not beget,[3] did he wish to write for us?[4]
And if he did wish [to write it], they have condemned his wish,
Since he wished to speak.[5] But if he truly begot,
They have opposed his truth. In both of these [cases], defeat
   falls
To the side of the presumptuous.

   REFRAIN: *Praises to your Kingdom!*

[m] [60:2] What would compel the Father of truth,
Though he had begotten no child, to identify[6] "Father," or
   "Son"?
Did he want to deceive us? Did he want to adorn us?[7]

---

   1. B. See note 1 attached to 50:1.
   2. On this melody, see note 1 attached to the melody of hymn 49.
   3. Lit., "him not begetting ..."
   4. Ephrem presumably has in mind the Father's words at Christ's Baptism
(Mt 3.17) and Transfiguration (Mt 17.5), as well as the words, christologically
understood, of Ps 2.7. It is possible as well that Ephrem has in mind an older
reading of the baptismal account, in which the words of Ps 2.7 are integrated.
On this, see G. Winkler, "The Original Meaning of the Prebaptismal Anointing and its Implications," 71.
   5. All these instances of "wish" in this passage derive from the root ṣbâ,
and could also be translated, in its passive form, as "to be pleased." Ephrem
is likely echoing the Father's words at the Baptism and Transfiguration, in
which, after proclaiming Christ his "Son," he states that he is "well pleased"
with him, using this same verb.
   6. Syr., *nšammeh*, lit., "to name."
   7. Syr., *lan kay ṣbâ d-našpar*. This could also be vocalized as *ṣbâ d-nešpar*, according to which it would be translated, "did he wish to please us." I have opted

Did he wish to slander himself?[8] If this were the case[9]—
God forbid!—these things[10] would be ill-fitted
To the mouth of One who is true.[11]
[m] [60:3] Let us resolve this on its own [terms]: if it seemed
good to him,
Though he had not begotten, to slander himself, [by saying]
he was a Begetter,
Then, because of this concealed reasoning—
Hidden from every nature—who would be harsher than he,
Who [yet] uncovered himself and revealed his mystery, to the
point that even children
Conversed with him in the marketplace?
[m] [60:4] Speak now for the side of the presumptuous:
"He has not slandered himself, so let us [only] say that he is a
Begetter."[12]
But why are people tripped up by the birth
Of a Son who is not one in truth, who though [in reality] our
companion,
Assured us that he was the Son? And that so-called[13] Father
Told us he was [Father] in truth.
[m] [60:5] Because the presumptuous proclaim that he does
not beget,

---

for the first reading, taking it as a reference to Ephrem's idea of the "borrowed
names." "Father" and "Son," of course, are names he classifies as "true," thus
belonging rightfully to God, and to us only nominally. Here, Ephrem rhetorically reverses his actual position, wondering if God has "borrowed" human
names to elevate human language.

8. That is, by calling himself "Father," even though he had never begotten
(see also *HF* 60:3:2 and 60:4:2).

9. That is, that he did not beget.

10. That is, names implying he had begotten.

11. On the one hand, Ephrem's logic is not entirely clear here: logically
speaking, why would the names "Father" and "Son" be any more deceitful than
other names Ephrem takes as borrowed (e.g., God repenting or growing weary,
etc.)? On the other hand, this passage indicates the degree to which, within
Ephrem's mind, the names "Father" and "Son" occupy a unique status within
Scripture, due to the fact that they are spoken intimately, between Father and
Son, at the Baptism, Transfiguration, and Crucifixion.

12. That is, let us call him "begetter," but understand it metaphorically.

13. Syr., *šʾîlâ*, the term elsewhere translated as "borrowed."

A thing [they say is] found in the Prophets and in the Apostles,
If the presumptuous are found to be true,
Then the Prophets have gone astray. But if the Apostles of the
     true one
Are true, they mock the presumptuous,
Who have gone astray and led [others] astray.
[m] [60:6] Who, then, has refused this,[14] which the
     presumptuous
Proclaim with every mouth, though not altogether agreeing,[15]
But which he has proclaimed for us with a mouth [full] of true
     things,
Things the Spirit has sung, and [about which] their Books
     agree,
United in their words? Those true are silent,
But those presumptuous babble.
[m] [60:7] Who would not sing the praise of Leah and Rachel?
The names that they gave were pleasing to God.[16]
He has affirmed our children, and confirmed for us that our
     child
Is the child of our womb. Let us not refuse his love.
Let us—all of us—affirm his Child, that he is the Child of his
     womb,
And the fruit of his hiddenness.
[m] [60:8] The all-knowing Lord asked the demon
About his name—what[17] it was. And he did not deny the name
Of the defiled demon, just as none of the demons
Denied his name. The scribes were ashamed and called
Our Savior a creature, but the demon scorned them,
For he is the Son of God.[18]
[m] [60:9] From himself Legion had learned how

14. That is, the truth of the name "Son."
15. That is, they proclaim that he is "begetter," even as they interpret it
differently.
16. Referring to the etymologies of their children's names, in Gn 29.32–
30.24.
17. Taking the Syriac 'aykan-(h)û as "what," following Mk.5.9 (P), in which
'aykannâ renders τί.
18. Mk 5.1–20; Lk 8.26–39.

His [own] name corresponded to his legion in its
    interpretation.[19]
Thus, he cried out when he perceived that [Christ] was the
    Son of God,
For his name corresponded to his Father. If the impure name
Of the Evil One—our enemy—corresponded to his evil,
How much more [the name] of our God?
[m] [60:10] Who will compare the names of the Holy One,
Which correspond to [one another] in every way: "He who is,"
    to his essence,[20]
"Just One," to his justice,[21] and "Good One," to his goodness?[22]
In these things, he agrees [with himself]. How different his
    Fatherhood,
And out of sync with itself, if he has no glorious
Child, who is from his womb!
[m] [60:11] Who will not rejoice? For if these titles
Correspond to one another—earth to Adam,[23]
Eve to life,[24] Peleg to division,[25]
And {Babel}[26] to confusion[27] (for they came to confusion)—
Let us quiet the disorder. Receive in order
The threefold names!
[m] [60:12] From Babel learn: there
Three went down and confused [the tongues], for he said,
    "Come! {Let us}[28] go down,"
And this no one could say to only one.[29]
To one, [he would say] "Come![30] Let us go down." The Evil

19. Ibid.

20. Syr., *'îtyâ* (here Ephrem intends a connection with the divine name of
Ex 3.14) and *'îtûtâ*.

21. Syr., *kînâ* ("Just One") and *kînûtâ* ("justice").

22. Syr., *ṭābâ* ("Good One") and *ṭaybûtâ* ("goodness").

23. Syr., *'âdamtâ* ("earth") and *'âdām* ("Adam").

24. Syr., *ḥawwâ* ("Eve") and *ḥayyûtâ* ("life").

25. Syr., *pelleg* ("Peleg") and *pûlāgâ* ("division").

26. B. A misspells as *balbel,* anticipating *bûlbālâ*.

27. Syr., *bbl* ("Babel") and *bûlbālâ* ("confusion").

28. B. A mistakenly changes the verb form to third-person plural ("Come!
They went down …").

29. Gn 11.7.

30. The distinction cannot be conveyed in English. In 60:12:2, Ephrem has

One, with the tongues
That were confused, has babbled in our day—
[In] the Church instead of Babel.
[m] [60:13] Who would not marvel? Now, since there is an
    opportunity
For error to grow strong because of our sickness,
It has grown sicker.[31] If the power of our unity
And the love of our harmony will return to us,
Who will resist us? For on earth and in heaven
Our Truth can loose and bind.[32]

    {*The End.*}[33]

---

taw ("come!"), a plural imperative. In 60:12:4, he has *tâ* ("come!"), the singular imperative.

31. "It" could refer either to "error" or to "sickness."

32. Cf. Mt 16.19; 18.18.

33. B.

{13},[1] *According to the same melody.*[2]

[m] [61:1] Who would not be afraid? Our Lord promised a
 millstone
For the neck of whoever caused one of the children of light to
 stumble.[3]
Those who trouble the simple with questions,
Their investigation is a millstone for them, for they are mired
 in debate,
Unable to emerge from it, for they cannot keep quiet,
So their musing is detested.

>   REFRAIN: *Praises to your coming!*

[m] [61:2] A patient word, to teach
About the Father and the Son, that they are mingled with one
 another:
Either [the Son] lowered his Father down along with himself,
 to become allied
Even with creatures, or [the Father] lifted up the Son
Along with himself, so that he became a stranger to creatures.
For the Son is like the Father.[4]
[m] [61:3] A word with power, unwilling to be silent,
Unwilling to deceive: if the name "Son"

----

1. B. See note 1 attached to 50:1.
2. On this melody, see note 1 attached to the melody of hymn 49.
3. Mt 18.6; Mk 9.42; Lk 17.2.
4. Ephrem here offers two hypothetical misinterpretations of the unity of
the Father and the Son: either the Son's Incarnation brought the Father down
to the level of creatures, or the Father's exalted state raised the Son up to the
point where he could have no connection with creatures.

Is related to "creatures,"[5] then the name "creatures"
Is related to "Creator."[6] Yet if the name "creatures"
Is foreign to "Creator," then it is also foreign
To the Son of the Creator.[7]
[m] [61:4] What occurs with the nature of the Begetter
Can occur with the Child of the Begetter.
[He is] the splendid ray of his splendid Begetter.
He is not cut-off, because he is like his root.
He is not confined, since he is bound [only] in his title.
He is like him in everything.
[m] [61:5] From the Father learn the Son: if the Begetter
Is akin to creatures, his Son would also be found
Equal to creatures. But if the Father is a stranger [to them],
Would his Fruit be akin to [them]? Or, would he distance
    himself from him,
And say, "He is not my Son"? But if he has called out, "He is
    [my] Son,"
He has silenced the controversy.
[m] [61:6] Who will not marvel at the pair of roots
Which have destroyed their natures and changed their
    names?[8]
Both are concealed from their fruits:
The root of freedom [bears] the fruit of servitude,[9]

5. Referring to the Arian argument that Christ, God's Son (*brâ*), is nevertheless a "creature" (*brîtâ*, given here in its plural form, *baryātâ*), based upon Prv 8.22.

6. Thus, etymologically speaking, "creatures" (*baryātâ*) is related to "creator" (*bārûyâ*), even though in terms of Being they are fundamentally distinct. Linguistically, Ephrem's point is that two words derived from the same root (*br'*) can nevertheless carry opposite meanings.

7. Throughout the remainder of this hymn, Ephrem is concerned with establishing "begotten" as a necessary corollary of "Son." Much of his argument depends upon the Syriac version of Prv 8.22, in which the verb for "to create" (*brâ*) forms the root of "creature" (*brîtâ*), "Creator" (*bārûyâ*), and "Son" (also vocalized as *brâ*). Ephrem argues that if one is to determine the identity of the Son on the basis of the root *b-r-'* ("to create," Prv 8.22), then one must admit this range of meanings. Additionally, if one accepts the name "Son," one must accept its semantic corollary "begotten."

8. I.e., freedom and servitude.

9. That is, divine freedom accepts the servitude of the Incarnation.

And the tree of servitude [bears] the fruit[10] of Greatness.[11]
Though hidden, they have blossomed.
[m] [61:7] In this alone [is] the weapon [to defeat it]: if the
    Son of truth
Is not reckoned a thing-begotten, then also a thing-made
Should not be considered a creation.[12] It must be one of the
    two:
Either the two sides stand with one another stably,
Or they change. Either their names stand firm,
Or their natures dissolve.
[m] [61:8] Who would not ask: if the name "Son"
Can become "creature"[13] in debating about it, then can
    "creature" also
[Become] "begotten one" through questioning it,[14] since his
    name need not
Correspond to him?[15] Has he abandoned his own truth
And fled to "begotten," just as the name "Son"
He has joined to "creatures"?
[m] [61:9] Therefore, since "creature" is not like "creature,"
As "begotten" is not like "son,"[16]
The confusion has only grown. If the Son of truth

10. "Fruit" in line 4 is *pîrâ,* and in line 5 is *'âdšâ.*

11. That is, through the servitude of the Crucifixion, Christ is revealed as "great."

12. That is, by definition a son must be begotten, just as a thing made must be a creation: the two words (though etymologically different) mean the same thing. Ephrem is trying to catch his opponents in an exegetical error: why must *'bādâ* ("thing-made") be taken literally, while *brâ* ("son") can be taken metaphorically?

13. That is, if *brâ* ("Son") morphs to "creature" (*brîtâ*), the two both being derived from the root *b-r-'* ("to create").

14. "Son" (*brâ*) and "creature" (*brîtâ*) are both derived from the root *b-r-'* ("to create"), while "begotten one" (*yaldâ*) is derived from the root *y-l-d* ("to beget" or "to give birth"). While the latter is unrelated morphologically to the former, Ephrem's underlying question remains: if "creature" can be derived morphologically from the name "Son," why can "begotten" not be derived from it semantically?

15. According to Ephrem's opponents.

16. That is, if one does not take "begotten" as implicit in "Son," then the meaning of "creature" is equally less certain.

Had stripped off and destroyed his name—God forbid!—
Who could justly call out his names?
They would pass beyond what is proper.[17]
[m] [61:10] Look: why did Moses receive the divine name[18]
And the heavenly glow,[19] and yet not presume
To say that he was God, nor lead the people astray,
Even though the children of the People have always thirsted
To stray in every way? (Look: their calf cries out[20]
And their Book bears witness!)
[m] [61:11] Why did that blessed Apostle and his companion,
When people began to offer them sacrifices
And set incense before them (they called them gods,
For they saw marvelous things), [why did] they rend their
    hidden heart
And their visible clothing, and undertake to preach,
Rather than be worshiped?[21]
[m] [61:12] Why did John refuse, [saying] "I am not
The messiah whom you seek?"[22] And if the servant[23]
    understood
His Lord to be his equal,[24] that Nazirite who does not lie
Has turned to serious deceit [by saying], "he is the Son of
    God."
He signified that "He is,"[25] and, look: the preacher's word
Cries out through the world.
[m] [61:13] Why did Gabriel not deceive Daniel
And say that he was God,[26] or the Seraph deceive
Isaiah and say that he was the Son of God?[27]

---

17. That is, humans would be calling Christ things that he is not.

18. Ex 3.14.   19. Ex 34.29–35.

20. Ex 32.   21. Acts 14.8–18.

22. Jn 1.20.   23. That is, John.

24. That is, not really God.

25. Syr., *d-'îtaw(hy)*, probably echoing the divine name at Ex 3.14 (P, *'ahîyyah*).

26. Dn 8.16–17. Ephrem probably means that Gabriel did not call Daniel "God," but the reverse could be true as well (a reading strengthened by the fact that, in the following line, it is the Seraph who refuses to call Isaiah "God").

27. Is 6.6.

Watchers[28] do not lie. Prophets do not deceive.
Apostles do not stir up trouble. Yet, he who is greater than all
Would completely lie?
[m] [61:14] Listen to me: if [the name] were not true,
It would be rebuked and be done. His truth alone can
Spread to the East, expand to the West,
Seize the North, and conquer the South.
It descended into the deep, and emerged victorious. It
   ascended to the height, and dwells [there].
It has ruled over all, in all.

   {*The End.*}[29]

28. On "watchers," see note 6 attached to 3:5.
29. B.

HYMN SIXTY-TWO

{*14*},[1] *According to the same melody.*[2]

[m] [62:1] From the beginning, our equal[3] has seduced and
    bound us
To worship our equals. His Son has freed us from all [this].
And because we have escaped [slave] labors, our Lord is [now]
    our equal.
And because {we have}[4] abandoned our [own] inventions, our
    portion is creation.
We have offered our worship to the venerable Father,
With the venerable Son.

    REFRAIN: *Praises to your admonition!*

[m] [62:2] Who could not understand? Adam gave names
To the animals, and they seemed good to the Lord of all—
The names the servant gave—and [thus] they were written and
    believed.[5]
But Adam's children experience no fear when their debating
    battles
The name "Son," which the mouth of God
Proclaimed in their ears.[6]

---

1. B. See note 1 attached to 50:1.
2. On this melody, see note 1 attached to the melody of hymn 49.
3. That is, Satan, who, unlike Christ, is created.
4. B. A, "he has ..."
5. Gn 2.19–20, but also echoing the Lord's words in response to his own creation throughout Gn 1.
6. This passage suggests a two-tiered process of naming: on the one hand, Adam names the animals, which represents a purely human phenomenon, albeit approved by God. On the other hand, God himself names his own Son. If we map this onto Ephrem's understanding of "true" and "borrowed" names

[m] [62:3] Our Lord is represented as a "way,"[7] for he has
carried us to his Father.

He is represented, again, as a "door,"[8] for he has led us into
his Kingdom.

Even as a "lamb"[9] has he been represented, for he was
slaughtered for our propitiation.

And just as he has been named, so has he fulfilled his
commandments.[10]

How much his name agrees with and corresponds to his
Begetter:

If he is Son, he is Begotten!

[m] [62:4] By the name alone, [a name's] meaning[11] can be
perceived.[12]

A name can interpret itself for us:

"Made" [suggests] its maker,[13] "created" its creator,[14]

"Fashioned" its fashioner,[15] "begotten" its begetter:[16]

They proclaim without controversy—a weapon which, in
debating it,[17]

(on which, see pp. 36–37), we could perhaps suggest that borrowed names are
ultimately Adamic, whereas true names are ultimately divine (though inevitably limited according to human understanding).

7. Jn 14.6   8. Ibid.

9. Jn 1.29

10. B, *pûrqānaw(hy)* (i.e., "prices of ransom?"). Ephrem's meaning here
is similar to that articulated in *HF* 30:6, where he draws a parallel between
Christ telling his disciples to turn the other cheek, and then himself doing so
in his Passion.

11. Or, "power" (*ḥaylâ*).

12. Ephrem states clearly one aspect of his understanding of language:
"names" suggest (whether morphologically or just semantically) their meanings. Elsewhere, of course, when Ephrem references "borrowed" names, he
argues for a divide between a word and its meaning (see pp. 36–37).

13. *'bādâ* ("thing-made") and *'ābûdâ* ("maker"), both of which derive from
'bad, "to make."

14. *Brîtâ* ("created") and *bārûyâ* ("creator"), both of which derive from *brâ,*
"to create."

15. *gbîlâ* ("fashioned") and *gābûlâ* ("fashioner"), both of which derive from
gbal, "to fashion."

16. *yaldâ* ("begotten") and *yālûdâ* ("begetter"), both of which derive from
iled, "to beget."

17. B, "in its truth."

Can never be defeated.

[m] [62:5] By this confusion the one causing trouble is
    rebuked.

Clearly, every name corresponds to its root:

"Thing-made" to "maker," "creature" to "creator,"

And "begotten" to "begetter."[18] Is every name fixed,

Yet the name "son" is lost? It is not lost, for the lost

Are found and return within it.

[m] [62:6] On the terms of [this argument], and against it:
    as "creature"

Means "creature" without controversy, in name and in reality,

It is fitting to claim also that "son"

Means "son," since he is "Son" in name and in reality.[19]

If his name is false, the names of everything,

In everything, are false.

[m] [62:7] Who would be named "begotten," with his begetter
    nowhere found?

Are the names "Begotten" and "Begetter" borrowed,

And thus "Father," in his name, divided against his name,[20]

And likewise "Son" [divided] against his "begotten"? The fruit
    and its tree

Are undivided, for the taste of truth

Proclaims their names.

[m] [62:8] Who can perceive[21] "thing-made" in the name
    "Begotten,"

Or "creature" in the name "Son"?[22] By the fruit alone[23]

Can its taste be perceived. Yet if sweetness has

A bitter taste, the names of everything

18. See notes 13, 14, and 16 to 62:4.

19. That is, one cannot read "creature" literally and "Son" figuratively.
Moreover, as Ephrem argues in *HF* 53, if "Son" is read literally, it will necessi-
tate a reinterpretation of "creature."

20. B, "against himself."

21. Syr., *ṭā'am*. Lit., "taste," following from 62:7:5–6.

22. The first two are unrelated on both a semantic and a morphological
level (*'bādâ* vs. *yaldâ*). "Creature" (*brîtâ*) and "son" (*brâ*), are related on a morphological level, but Ephrem aims to distance them on a semantic level.

23. Syr., *d-menneh w-beh d-pîrâ*, which B has as *d-menneh w-breh d-pîreh*, "by
the son of the fruit."

Are misheard.[24] But who can change
The names of the Lord of all?
[m] [62:9] Because they let themselves be called "human"
    according to grace,
They did not destroy their natures with the title.[25]
The precise names of humanity they put on,[26]
And their name became a crucible for [testing] them:[27] if the
    Son is a thing-made,
He is found [to be] our equal, but if the Son is Lord,
He is truly our God.[28]
[m] [62:10] Who would not marvel? If his Son were a thing-
    made,
His Begetter's womb would make him equal to all,
And he would be found more honorable in the birth from
    Mary,
Who made him a true brother to humanity,

24. That is (extending the metaphor to "begotten"), if Christ is called "Son" and "Begotten," yet is not so, then this is like a fruit being called sweet when it is actually bitter.

25. That is, "human," when applied to God, is a borrowed name, which does not reflect God's nature.

26. B, "were put on" (Syr., *lbîšîn*).

27. I.e., in which they could be tested.

28. The first four lines of this stanza can be read differently (following Beck, *HF [G]*, 168): "Because humans have been titled (gods) according to grace, / Their natures have not become lost through the title. / They are clothed in the accurate names of humans, / And their names are a crucible for them." While this reading in some ways reflects the sentiment Ephrem articulates in *HF* 63:8, I have translated it differently for the following reasons: (1) The surrounding context is concerned with the names "begotten" and "begetter," and the correct understanding of names as they apply to God. Ephrem is not here concerned with human names, and the way divine names apply to humans. (2) *'nāšâ* ("human," or "humans") is not pointed as plural, yet the verb *'etkanni(w)* is. While we could take *'nāšâ* as collective, in that case one would expect the verb to be singular. (3) If "humans" is the subject of *'etkanni(w)*, line 3 makes little sense, because Ephrem nowhere speaks of humans being clothed in human names, only humans being clothed in divine names, or God being clothed in human names. (4) Line 4a reflects an idea similar to what we see in 44:1: there Ephrem speaks of the books being a crucible in which God's names can be tested. Nowhere do we see him speaking similarly of human names (applied to humans).

Than in the womb which made him a common companion[29]
To reptiles and beasts.[30]

[m] [62:11] Who can deny the names of the True One?
Hear the truth in his name. If the name "Son" or "Begotten"
Is found untrue, then deny
Also the name "creatures." And if it is found true,
Is then every name meaningful[31] and sound, while that
    name "Son" is tasteless?
We are tasteless, so we have made him tasteless.

[m] [62:12] Who would render tasteless the accurate names
Of Father, Son, and Spirit, through which the tasteless
Scribes have acquired taste? The strength of everything that
    exists
Can be rendered tasteless through mixture, while Father,
    Son, and Spirit
Are alone steadfast. Their power
Is not associated with mixture.

[m] [62:13] Who can be baptized with borrowed names?
Who can give thanks with borrowed names?
We are divided in the truth, whose power
Can never can be torn apart, for the Father's love
Can never be separated from his Begotten. Who can rend
    asunder
Unified names?

[m] [62:14] Who would not mock [this]? If the Creator
Has magnified his creatures over himself,
Since their names agree [with one another], is the name
    "Father" in doubt?[32]
Everyone is clothed with his names. The Father and
    Son alone
Have stripped off their names. The names of everything

---

29. B, "... a companion to every / reptile and beast."

30. That is, if he were born from Mary, he would at least have the distinction of being human. If he is simply created by the Father, according
to Ephrem's rhetoric, his status and identity would occupy no clearly distinguished space.

31. Lit., "tasty."

32. That is, it makes no sense to read human language literally (with signs
and signified aligning), but not to do the same with divine language.

Are deceitful in everything.[33]

[m] [62:15] Who would let the presumptuous both
Go his own way, and according to his own will? He has heeded
  and affirmed
The names of creatures, but turned and cast off the names
"Begotten" and "Begetter." With his own will
Bind him to his schism. However much he turns,
Confine him within truth.

    {*The End.*}[34]

33. Ephrem's point here is that language—especially divine names—applies
accurately to God, and metaphorically to humans. From Ephrem's perspective,
however, his opponents are getting it backward: they are overconfident in their
ability to assess the meaning of language, while overly metaphorizing divine
language (i.e., names that God has applied to himself).

34. B.

HYMN SIXTY-THREE

{*15*},[1] *According to the same melody.*[2]

[m] [63:1] Who does not perceive, my son, that whoever has
    been given a title,
His titles have been given for a reason?[3]
And wherever the need has grown, they are permitted to
    remain.[4]
[Yet] at the time [for signing] a treaty, there are deeds and
    inquiries.
True names are sought in that time
To seal the truth.[5]

    REFRAIN: *Praises to your Begetter!*[6]

1. B. See note 1 attached to 50:1.
2. On this melody, see note 1 attached to the melody of hymn 49.
3. Lit., "a reason has called his titles into being."
4. Lit., "they remain, permitted."
5. This stanza is working on two levels. On one level, Ephrem is speaking
merely of the human context of language and communication (particularly
economic communication). Yet the theological overtones are clear, beginning
especially in line 4. While on one level "treaty" (*dîyyatîqâ*) refers merely to the
document signifying an agreement between two people, on a theological level
it signifies Scripture, a context in which it would be best translated "Testament." In the context of Scripture, "deeds" refers to the names that God has
"borrowed" to communicate himself to humanity. "Inquiries" shares a root
with *š'îlâ*, "borrowed," and it may be that, coupled with "deeds," Ephrem intends it as a synonym. Finally, on a human level, "true" names refer to the
precise language of a treaty, which aims to make the agreement as clear as
possible. On a theological level, however, the phrase suggests the revelation,
from the midst of borrowed names, of the true names "Father" and "Son."
6. B, "to the Son of life!"

[m] [63:2] Who does not recognize that when our Lord was
    crucified,
He called out to his Father and handed over his orphans and
    his disciples,
[Saying], "My Father, receive and protect them."[7] And when he
    was resurrected
He sealed, by means of his death, that he was the Son of that
    Father
And caused his name to pass through a crucible, to be
    believed
Throughout the whole world.
[m] [63:3] Who would not give thanks? On the cross
He called out to his Father and handed over the body of his
    humanity.[8]
And so that that they would confess him "Son," his voice tore
    open the tombs,
And tore open the [curtain of] the sanctuary.[9] He wrote to
    send away the People,
And called out to receive the peoples. And as the Son of truth,
He sealed the treaty.[10]
[m] [63:4] Who would not marvel? This word perished
With the mouth of our Savior when his body fell asleep:
"My Father, into your hands."[11] That voice, whose word
All voices anticipate,[12] as a great witness
Gave thanks, then negotiated and wrote, to seal that he is not
    a thing-made.[13]

7. Jn 17.11.   8. Lk 23.34.
9. Mt 27.51–53.

10. Harking back to the treaty language of 63:1, Ephrem presents Christ's
Crucifixion and Resurrection as the signing of a legal document, which ne-
gates a relationship with one people (the Jews) and establishes the relationship with another (the Gentiles).

11. Lk 23.46.

12. Syr., *qāla-(h)w d-kul qālîn / qdîmîn l-ba(r)t qāleh*. Ephrem's meaning here
is not entirely clear to me (note that Beck leaves the words untranslated, *HF
[G]*, 171). The basic sense of *qdîmîn*, of which "all voices" must be the subject,
is "to precede," and, by extension, "to anticipate" (*LS*, 1317, sub. *qdm*, #3). The
sense, then, would be that all words typologically point to Christ's words on
the cross, which is how I am taking it here.

13. Still using the language of treaty, now Christ's dying affirmation of

For, as the Son, he represented his Father.[14]
[m] [63:5] Because the guard—he of the division
Called centurion—guarded so diligently,[15]
When the words of our Savior, calling out loud to his Father—
The last of all the words shook the earth below,
And darkened the sun above—[the centurion] too cried out and sealed
That he is the Son of God.[16]
[m] [63:6] From the Lord of all learn how sweet he is:
He did not call himself by the name "Essence,"[17]
Since the name of being[18] is greater and higher according to its righteousness
Than [the name] related to grace.[19] And his height did not bend down
To put on creatures his name and his title,[20]
For his name is "Essence."[21]
[m] [63:7] Who will not marvel at his name and at his mercy?
His name {surpasses}[22] all, yet his love is bent down to all.
And since he has other names that are sweet,
Poured out on creation, and that have bent down to magnify
His works with his titles, he came down into them and put on

---

himself as "Son" functions as a "document" to refute a subordinationist reading of Prv 8.22.

14. That is, as one who can rightfully sign off on the agreement his Father established.

15. I have left *pw'* untranslated. See also note 11 attached to 56:6.

16. Mk 15.39.

17. Syr., *'îtûtâ*.

18. Syr., *'îtyâ*, which is derived from the same word (*'ît*) as *'îtûtâ*.

19. That is, Christ called himself "Son of God," rather than YHWH (of which both *'îtûtâ* and *'îtyâ* serve as equivalents), since "son" can be applied to created things, while *'îtûtâ* cannot. On this point, see Beck, *Die Theologie,* 11.

20. Note that here "name" (*šmâ*) and "title" (*kûnāyâ*) are synonyms.

21. Here Ephrem suggests a hierarchy of names: at the top sits those names which relate to God's existence and which ultimately are derived from the divine name of Ex 3.14. At a slightly lower level are those names—Father, Son, etc.—which belong properly to God, but which God shares with humanity. At the lowest level are those terms which relate properly to humanity, but with which God clothes himself.

22. Syr., *mrîd*, B. A misspells as *mrîr*, "more bitter than all."

His names as his possessions.[23]
[m] [63:8] The heavenly King called his works kings.
And though he is God, he also called them gods.[24]
And though he is judge, look: his works act as judge.[25]
And since they walk around, he called himself weary.[26]
And because of [humans'] vehicles, he made for himself a
    chariot,[27]
To become like us in everything.
[m] [63:9] Who, therefore, is so foolish and stubborn
To think—even a little—that because humans
Are called by his names, then there is one nature
Of a human and of God? Because the Lord
Is called by the name of the things he has made, "made" and
    "maker"
Balance in a single comparison.
[m] [63:10] Whenever he has called us by his own name
    "King,"
It is true for him and a metaphor for us.
And whenever he has called himself by the name of his works,
It is nature for us, and a title for him.[28]

23. Ephrem suggests a threefold hierarchy of language: at the top are
the names of God that denote his being (words derive from *'it*, connected
to Ex 3.14). The "true names"—Father, Son, King, Good, Just, etc.—occupy
a step below these, in that they belong properly to God, yet can be shared
with humans. Then, a step below these are the "borrowed" names, which belong properly to humans but which God puts on mercifully. (On this linguistic
division, see pp. 36–37.) While Ephrem typically speaks of God putting on
borrowed names, this passage is unique in that it is the "true" names that God
clothes himself in. In this way, the Incarnation has a revelatory effect on human language: certain commonplace terms—Father and Son, primarily—are
shown to signify God most properly.

24. Ps 82.6.

25. The first three lines of this stanza provide instances of God clothing
humans in his true names. Now, beginning in line 4, he will address instances
in which God took on himself human, "borrowed" names.

'26. Cf Is 1.14 and parallels.

27. Beck (*HF [G]*, 172, n.13) takes this as an allusion to Mt 21.7, but it could
also refer to Ezek 1.

28. Here we have the idea that "title" (*kûnāyâ*) can refer to a borrowed name
(see pp. 36–37).

The name of truth is known and a borrowed name is known,
For us and for him.
[m] [63:11] Thus, for the discerning, he has given his names
To his possessions, by means of his mercy—not for discussion,
But for sweetness. Investigation, my brothers, fails.
Let us increase prayers. For though he is not related {to us},[29]
He is like our kind. And though he is different from all,
He is over all, in all.
[m] [63:12] Because if he had [totally] separated himself,
He would have been unable to clothe his possessions in his
    names.
And if, according to our wickedness, he had completely
    despised us,
He would have made a chasm impossible to cross
By the scribes, who have destroyed walls with questions,
And borders with discussions.[30]
[m] [63:13] Who would not be astounded at what evil and
    deceitful
Slaves have done? Instead of praising
Their good Lord, who has come to us in his Son,
Explained his heart to us, himself dwelling with us,
And has spoken with us with trust—[instead of] them tasting
    his love,
He has tasted their bitterness.

    {*The End.*}[31]

29. B. A, *leh*—"to him"—taken reflexively with *mḥayyen*.
30. On walls and borders, see *HF* 37:24.
31. B.

HYMN SIXTY-FOUR

{*16*},[1] *According to the same melody.*[2]

[m] [64:1] O our Lord, uproot the thorns, for the Evil One has
   sown them.[3]
Plough up the weeds. They[4] have seen us investigating,
And have rejoiced as we quarrel. They are united in our
   division,
And collected around our scattering. They have rejoiced, for
   our crucible[5]
Has not rebuked their falsehood, nor our light their sores,
Nor our voice their debating.

    REFRAIN: *Praises to your righteousness!*[6]

[m] [64:2] Who would not weep? We are backwards:
Wherever it is right to be silent, we incite trouble.
Wherever it is fitting to rebuke, we are muzzled.
Before humans, we take [what we need] and then move on.
In front of God alone we stand
To investigate how he is.
[m] [64:3] Who could even investigate Satan,
Who terrifies and incites us? [Who could investigate] whether
   he has senses,
Or how he is put together? Where are the holes
For ears and eyes, and whether there is a mouth,

1. B. See note 1 attached to 50:1.
2. On this melody, see note 1 on the melody of hymn 49.
3. Lit., "the Evil One is their sower."
4. While "thorns" and "weeds" both presumably refer to groups within the
Christian community, "they" here switches to those outside.
5. Referencing the baptismal font.   6. B, "to the Son of righteousness."

Since, look, he has no body? Or whether he has limbs,
Since, look, there are no joints?
[m] [64:4] Regarding accursed Satan, who teaches us
To investigate hidden things: who has investigated whether
He is entirely in every person, or how he can mix
His thought with our mind, and his words with our words,
Or how he inspires his will in our heart?
He is astounding in his foulness![7]
[m] [64:5] Who would not be ashamed? The Evil One enters
The body and scoffs at the soul dwelling within it.
How has [the soul] not felt Satan's clinging,
Dwelling and housed within it? Nor can [the soul] feel
The touch of the one settled within it. While it investigates
    its Lord
It should be investigating its murderer.
[m] [64:6] Who has investigated the earth? Though its
    measurement can be observed,
It stretches out measurelessly. From where have ears [of corn]
    produced
Whole harvests? Date-palms, sweetness?
Grapes, wine? Olives, oils?
From where have blossoms brought colors and fragrances,
Along with spices?
[m] [64:7] Someone could say to us, "Water causes the seed
To grow, and makes it big." On the basis of [water], ask
About [its] source: what causes it to swell,
For it flows without fail? The Good One, who increases
The treasure of springs, increases all,
For he gives life to all.
[m] [64:8] Who has seen and investigated the Behemoth on
    dry ground,
Or the Leviathan in the sea[8]—how they are fat
And happy without food? And who has explored the dreadful
Insides of their nests?[9] How much more hidden than all

---

7. B, "foul things."
8. Jb 40.15–41.34; Ps 104.26.
9. Lit., "the wombs of their reeds," reflecting Jb 41.21, where the Behemoth is said to "lie in a covering of reed."

Is the Child of the Lord of all? And who could explore the
   great
Womb of his Begetter?
[m] [64:9] Who could count how many natures
Are far from us, in the sea and on dry ground?
And our soul knows not how to depict them.
Look, they are all difficult [to understand], crying out
   together:
"Do not approach the air! Let your debating cease,
O weak humans!"
[m] [64:10] Someone may say to me, "From where do you know
The nature of the Lord of all?" It is anathema if I ever
Avow that I myself know. [Rather], his Books have uncovered
   him.
And because it is right to affirm God,
I have listened and affirmed him. And because of my faith, I
   have abstained from
An investigation [born out] of my presumption.
[m] [64:11] I have never wandered after people
Saying, as they say, "I have seen that they call
Our Savior other names, unwritten."
I have left what is unwritten and turned to what is written,
Lest on account of those unwritten things,
Someone destroy what is written.[10]
[m] [64:12] The waters he created and gave to the fish for their
   use.
The Books he inscribed and gave to humans as an aid.
The [two] testify to one another: if the fish pass beyond
The border of their path, their jerking is painful.
And if humans pass beyond the border of the Books,
Their dispute is deadly.

   {*The End.*}[11]

10. On this passage, see *HF* 52:14, and pp. 37–39.
11. B.

HYMN SIXTY-FIVE

{*17*},[1] *According to the same melody.*[2]

[m] [65:1] Who has ever been crazy enough to look around
   without light,
Investigate without shining, or explore without brightness?
Yet the foolish scribes have gone out of the Books,
To wander around in a wasteland, and have neglected the
   Testament—
The way of the kingdom. Its milestones are the Prophets,
Its resting-places the Apostles.[3]

   REFRAIN: *Praises to your comeliness!*

[m] [65:2] Speak for your party: nature is before your
   hands,
And the Books before your eyes. Nature is hard for us
   [to understand],
But the Books are easy for us. It is not from nature
That we have learned Christ. It is fitting that wherever
We have learned his humanity, from there we should
Seek his divinity.[4]
[m] [65:3] From the place we learned about Mary's child,
It is right that from there we should learn about his glorious
Former Birth. And although nature

1. B.

2. On this melody, see note 1 attached to the melody of hymn 49.

3. At the conclusion of *HF* 64, Ephrem mentioned this idea of unscriptural discourse. In 65:1 and 2, he begins to dramatize this idea, depicting subordinationist rhetoric as a wandering away from the language of Scripture.

4. Unlike *HPar* 5:2, where nature and Scripture seem to provide equally valid sources of revelation, Ephrem here subordinates nature to Scripture.

Stands before us in everything,[5] {the Book}[6] can teach

About the Father and the Son and the Spirit—whether in
truth

They baptize and enliven us.

[m] [65:4] By himself he is defeated:[7] either he recants, and
the baptism

Of the presumptuous is [thereby] false,[8] or he affirms his
baptism,

[And] becomes like Marcion, who partook of the Maker,

Yet denied the Maker, rejecting marriage,

Even as he was conceived and born.[9] Bitter is the fruit

That has denied its root.

[m] [65:5] Who, {once}[10] baptized, could debate and destroy

The thing into which he was baptized? He could not destroy
[it],

Because he could not be baptized without the names

Of the Father, Son, and Spirit. And the word,[11] sustaining

Itself in everything, can accept the testing

Of those who presume.

[m] [65:6] Who could investigate creation's inner parts[12] and
secret places—

The tastes of different things, natures that change,

Some of which stand alone, and some of which procreate?

Marvel at the trees that mate, my brothers!

[Give] glory to their Creator, since disputing about them falls
quiet,

And debating is silent.

---

5. Syr., *maqbel*. Ephrem's meaning is that, though nature is more immediately apparent, when speaking of the birth of Christ, it is Scripture which
should provide models for our understanding.

6. B. A, "nature."

7. I.e., Ephrem's opponent, who holds a subordinationist Christology, yet
still practices a Trinitarian baptism.

8. That is, option one is to renounce belief in the Trinity, thereby nullify-
ing baptism.

9. On Marcion, see note attached to 22:10.

10. B (A supplies in the margin).

11. I.e., the Trinitarian baptismal formula?

12. Lit., "wombs."

[m] [65:7] Who has investigated the olive tree? Though it
    seems unified,
It bears distinctly—leaves that are unlike
The branches in their color, sinews that are different
From the fruits in their tastes. And in one single fruit,
Three are conceived, so that when [the olive] is pressed, it
    produces
Water, juice,[13] and oil.[14]
[m] [65:8] Who has investigated fire—how it is conceived
Within a womb of wood, and the friction, like {labor pains},[15]
Provides a resistance, and it produces [fire]? But for our
    purposes, let us imagine
A man[16] who has never seen fire,
But only heard reports of it, and thus cannot investigate
What it is, or how it is.
[m] [65:9] From [the report] alone, can he understand
And mentally depict the image of a flame,
Or how two natures come from it—
The glow and its heat, one of which is seen by the eye,
And one felt with the hand? Neither can we who see
Comprehend disputing about him.
[m] [65:10] Therefore, if a blind man investigates the light,
Yet cannot depict the sun and its rays
In his heart {or}[17] his thought, he can in no way
See the ray and the child of that sun,
But can only believe
What someone has told him.
[m] [65:11] If a blind man wants to resist
What he hears and not believe [it], he will fall into a host of
    evils,
For he has investigated without understanding, wishing to be
    found
Blind in both the eye and the mind.

---

13. Syr., *ḥalbâ*, which can also mean "juice" or "sap."
14. On olives, see also *HVir* 4–7.
15. Syr., *ḥeblâ*, B. A, *ḥalbâ*, on which, see previous note.
16. Lit., "Let us place / something like a man ..."
17. B. A, "of ..."

If he wanted to believe, the teaching of righteousness
Would have illumined his blindness.
[m] [65:12] How we suffer under questions!
How we are troubled by debates!
Our mind is blind, as it considers that Child
And investigates how he is. There is no other way
Except to simply believe
The voice of truth.
[m] [65:13] Who will not fear? If a blind man is blamed
For hearing yet not believing the word of a person
Who wishes to tell him how the light is,
How much more deserving of judgment is one who has heard
    and not believed
The voice of God, for the voice of his Begetter
Proclaimed "This is my Son."

Completed are the {seventeen}[18] hymns according to the
    melody "The Herd of Bardaisan."

18. B. A, "sixteen."

HYMN SIXTY-SIX

According to the melody: "If you dispute Being ..."[1]

[']² [66:1] Woe to the one³ who has presumed and led himself
  astray,
Wishing to limit his Fashioner,
Even though he is dust.

REFRAIN: *Glory to the Son!*

['] [66:2] Whoever perceives that he is dust,⁴
Will give thanks to the finger that has fashioned him
And set him upright!
[b] [66:3] Schism has fallen among the debaters,
In the midst of the great sea,⁵ which they measure
As if it were a pond.
[b] [66:4] With a great mountain, he has brought them to
  naught.⁶
Look: they are crushed, for with a scale
They investigate his height.
[b] [66:5] With a {hidden}⁷ sun he⁸ provoked them

---

1. This melody comprises hymns 66–78, and carries a meter of 4+4 / 4+4 / 4.
See 69:1, where this line is repeated.
2. Hymns 66 and 67 form an acrostic on the Syriac alphabet, albeit with
several letters repeated.
3. B, "whoever."
4. Cf. Gn 3.19.
5. On the metaphor of the sea, see note 36 attached to 4:13.
6. On the metaphor of the mountain, see note 10 attached to 1:3.
7. B. A, "With the sun he hid ..."
8. That is, "the Evil One" (see 66:10). Ephrem's meaning is that the Evil
One made them think that they could see, when in reality they were in the
dark.

And made them dark. They do not see,
But they investigate.
[b] [66:6] Though they were washed in the Three,
Look: they have become defiled, because they have become
    divided
Over their names.
[b] [66:7] In the Church [there is] investigation, and before
    the holy place,[9]
A heart divided by the perversity
That [comes] through disputation.
[b] [66:8] In the Church envy bites a person.
In the Ark, [there was] a peaceful muzzle
For a wild animal.[10]
[b] [66:9] Under the pretext of truth, they have become
    archers:
They have made a quiver for investigation,
Full of arrows.
[b] [66:10] The Evil One seduced the simple
And introduced his arguing into the questions,
So that he cut off hope.
[g] [66:11] He provoked humans
With unnecessary things, so they would forsake
The things given.
[d] [66:12] Becoming drunk, they put on schism
Like a breastplate. They tore apart the truth
Like a garment.
[h] [66:13] But that truth cannot be divided:
It has split the factions and cast [them]
From the kingdom.
[h] [66:14] Look: as if in war, they have put on armor
[To protect] against victory,[11] for in it is hidden
[Their] defeat.

9. B, "truth."

10. Typically, Ephrem views Noah's ark as a type of the church (see *HF* 49:5). Here, however, he uses the ark to shame the church. In *CGen.* 6:10, Ephrem chastises the people of Noah's day for their failure to be moved by the animals' love for one another.

11. Syr., *zākûtâ*, which can also be rendered "innocence."

[w] [66:15] Though it seems that they are engaged in war
Because of truth, it is because of [a desire for] praise
That they are engaged in the struggle.
[z] [66:16] They prevail and boast. They are defeated, yet grow proud,
Seduced [into thinking] that because of truth,
They must die.
[ḥ] [66:17] Their controversies have urged them
To say something not permitted
For the tongue.
[ṭ] [66:18] They float like waves among the waves
In a flood, inconceivable
To the mind.[12]
[y] [66:19] Day comes, bringing debate:
It never wanes. [There is] a new transgression
On account of pride.
[k] [66:20] They have broken up the Book, not to read,
But to wander off. But how could they investigate?
How could they dispute?
[l] [66:21] They are clothed on the inside with secret rage.
Yet they are proven guilty when the serpent hisses
In their words.
[m] [66:22] Who can silence them?
Though they seem to seek truth,
[In reality] they seek to quarrel.
[m] [66:23] Mile-markers are placed on the King's road.
Fools have abandoned it, fleeing to a wasteland,
And, look, wandering around in it.[13]
[m] [66:24] Whoever has walked on the King's road,
Has walked to meet the King
And his gift.

{*The End.*}[14]

12. While it is difficult to represent in English, in the Syriac "inconceivable" clearly modifies "waves." On the metaphor of the "sea," see note 36 attached to 4:13.
13. On the metaphor of "mile-markers," see note 14 attached to 2:13.
14. B.

HYMN SIXTY-SEVEN

{2},[1] *According to the same melody.*[2]

[n][3] [67:1] The sign of truth is placed in the Books.
Fools have abandoned it and have begun to cast-off
The Lord of the sign.[4]
[n] [67:2] Let us investigate whether there are archers
Who have abandoned the target[5] and directed arrows
At their king.
[n] [67:3] This is the sign: the Father is one
Without division, and the Son is one
Without disputing.
[n] [67:4] The revealed sign sits in the light,
While the fool shoots arrows in the night,
In the dark.
[n] [67:5] May quiet be a boundary for words,
And silence a boundary for investigators,
[Marking off] hidden things.
[n] [67:6] May the mouth learn how to speak,
And {then}[6] speak, lest it regret
Once it has spoken.
[n] [67:7] May [the mouth] first learn, then[7] teach,
Lest it become like a passage

---

1. B. The latter numbers hymns 67–70 as 2–5 (with the assumption that 66 is number 1), and hymns 75–78 as 10–13. Hymns 71–74 are not numbered.
2. On this melody, see note 1 attached to the melody of hymn 66.
3. On the acrostic, see note 2 attached to 66:1.
4. On "sign" (*nîšâ*), see note 4 attached to 1:1.
5. This is the same term (*nîšâ*) translated as "sign" in the previous stanza.
6. Syr., *'aken*, B. A, *'aykan,* "how."
7. Syr., *'aken.* B *'ayken,* "how to."

For what is useless.

[s] [67:8] The Books are set up like a mirror:[8]
The one whose eye is clear sees there
An image of truth.

[s] [67:9] Placed there is the image of the Father.
Depicted there is the image of the Son,
And the Holy Spirit.

[w] [67:10] Placed are the three names,
One after another, with faith,
For baptism.

['] [67:11] An excuse has entered to cause trouble:
"It is necessary to investigate them[9]
In order to accept them."

['] [67:12] Debating has entered. Controversy has entered.
Strife has entered, and truth has fled.

[....][10]

[p] [67:13] It would be better for them to accept the truth
Without debating, than, with debating,
To forsake everything.

[p] [67:14] It would be better for them to acquire life
Simply, than without wisdom
To acquire death.

[p] [67:15] It would be far better to drink water
When thirsty than, instead of drinking,
To measure the fountain.

[p] [67:16] It would be much better for a child
To know his father by seeing
Than by investigating.

[p] [67:17] It would much better, therefore, that in the ways
Of faith we learn truth
Without debating.

[ṣ] [67:18] In all these things, desire a blessed assembly.
Strip off controversy, put on love,
And proclaim the truth.

[q] [67:19] He first opened the treasure of his mercy

---

8. On the metaphor of the mirror, see 3 note attached to 2:1.

9. The names or the persons they represent or both.

10. Stich missing in ABC.

And fashioned Adam, when he did not exist,
From dust.
[r] [67:20] He hastened to open the gate of Sheol,
And sent forth[11] Adam's body,
Which was dust.
[r] [67:21] He hastened, too, to open the gate of Paradise,
On account of the promise,[12] and he made Adam to dwell
By the tree of life.
[š] [67:22] Glory to the One who forged this key.
Though it is one, it has opened
Every treasury.
[š] [67:23] Glory to the Father, hidden in his essence.[13]
Glory to the Son, whose Birth is hidden
Under a seal of silence.
[š] [67:24] Praise to the unlimited Father.
Praise to the inscrutable Son,
Together with the Holy Spirit.
[t] [67:25] Increase in me, Lord, silence and word,
That I might live through them, that I might hide your
    investigation
But speak your glory. Glory to your Name![14]

>   {*The End.*}[15]

---

11. C, "raised up."   12. Cf. Lk 23.34.
13. Syr., *'îtēh*. B, "being" (*'îtûteh*).   14. Final hemistich omitted in BC.
15. B.

HYMN SIXTY-EIGHT

{3},[1] *According to the same melody.*[2]

[?][3] [68:1] The Books agree, but humans are divided:
Over the one truth schisms have come
From freedom.

>   REFRAIN: *Praise to you, my Lord!*

[b] [68:2] Under the pretext of truth, the weak have desired
Control, so humans
They could call to their side.

[g] [68:3] They have gathered assemblies, and become lords
   [of them]—
Lords of thousands and hundreds,
Lords of ten.

[d] [68:4] When peace had ended, many robbers—
All the thieves of the thieving parties—
[Arose], one against another.

[h] [68:5] In debating, they mused as if in a contest,
While brothers shot their arrows at brothers—
Great lamentation!

[?][4] [68:6] The weak unsheathed their tongues.
They smote and were smote. And since there was no blood,

---

1. B. See note 1 attached to hymn 67.

2. On this melody, see note 1 attached to the melody of hymn 66.

3. Hymn 68 forms an acrostic on the Syriac alphabet. The first stanza, however, begins erroneously with the letter *k*. A possible solution, which Beck suggests (*HF [S]*, 209, n. 2), is to switch the first and second hemistiches of line 1, since 1b begins with the necessary ʾ. Either way, the sense of the passage is the same.

4. Following the acrostic, this stanza should begin with *w-*, but begins with *l-*.

There was also no fear.

[z] [68:7] Wrathful is the sword, though it is weak.
Sweet is the tongue, though it is a murderer,
Due to blindness.

[ḥ] [68:8] Vain pride has stirred up the debaters,
As [desire] for a crown makes athletes, who strike
    and are beaten,
Willing to suffer.

[ṭ] [68:9] They are totally conquered even in their victory,
Because their motivation is presumption
And great woe.

[?]⁵ [68:10] Where is the one who won? Even though he won
He was defeated utterly, because [his own] pride
Defeated him.

[k] [68:11] How the debtor's⁶ loss has doubled,
For he has come into debt through debating and envy—
A complete loss!⁷

[l] [68:12] Whoever has taken his companion captive through
    investigation,
Pride has taken him captive, as if [trapped] in a pit—
Great humiliation!

[m] [68:13] One is full of rage, another schism:
There are ten thousand evils. What is the hope
That has cut off that hope?

[n] [68:14] Let us weep: they have attacked God
And a human being with speech,
In order to conceal him.

[s] [68:15] On earth there is arguing against heaven.
The earth is troubled. Debating rises up
Like smoke.

['] [68:16] Heaven and the highest heaven are barren
On account of disputing. The caves of the earth
Are full of blasphemy.

---

5. This stanza begins with ', where one would expect ṭ or k.

6. The term here translated as "debtor" (ḥayyābâ) is from the same root, ḥāb, as the term translated "defeated" in the previous stanza.

7. On economic metaphors generally, see note 39 attached to 5:15. For their negative application, see also *HF* 38:4.

[p] [68:17] The heavens have provided for those below
Dew and rain—floods full
Of all good things.
[ṣ] [68:18] The earth {has bound}[8] all questions
To heavenly things—a debating full
Of every blasphemy.
[q] [68:19] Mud[9] fought its companions
With disputes. It fell to the earth
And became dust.
[r] [68:20] Ten thousand of ten thousand watchers[10] sat quiet.
Two examiners, body and soul:
See how they roar!
[š] [68:21] Michael sat quiet with Gabriel.
Dust debated with dirt—
Great injustice!
[t] [68:22] The sickness has grown worse, and their words have
  failed
On account of their debating
And their disputing.
[t] [68:23] Thank you, Lord, for sparing me
From the disputing of all the presumptuous,
That I might live before you!

　　　{*The End.*}[11]

8. Syr., ṣemdat, B. A, ṣemrat, "to suffer from."
9. Syr., *qûlā'â.* Here a metaphor for humans, who are derived from dirt.
10. On watchers, see note 6 attached to 3:5.
11. B.

HYMN SIXTY-NINE

{4},[1] *According to the same melody.*[2]

[69:1] If you dispute Being,[3] it is error.
Where would you begin? Where would you end,
Frail one?

    REFRAIN: *Glory to the Father!*

[69:2] Between the beginning and the end
There is rest for the one who travels
On the King's road.
[69:3] For Being, there is neither beginning
Nor end. It is therefore difficult
For the one who investigates him.
[69:4] If you are divided over the truth which you have held,
You will pour yourself out. Error will give you as a drink
To the parched earth.
[69:5] If you are troubled by a secret thought,
Debating it will become a great sea,
And it will overcome you.
[69:6] With faith like a boat,
Travel with his Books like a sailor
Into [safe] harbors.
[69:7] Without his Books, do not travel on [the sea].
Give thanks to his name, so he will increase his harbors
Among his floods.
[69:8] In his love he has turned aside, becoming small, though
    he is great.

1. See note 1 attached to hymn 67.
2. On this melody, see note 1 attached to the melody of hymn 66.
3. See the melody to hymn 66.

He has become a spring, for whoever is too weak
To travel [on the sea].
[69:9] And in his love he became a sea,
To acquire thereby the one in need
Of treasures.
[69:10] But if he were to use his nature,
Neither those above or those below
Could travel on it.
[69:11] What thing-made can investigate
Divinity? There is a chasm between it
And the Creator.[4]
[69:12] Divinity is not far removed
From [its] possessions, for love stands between it
And creatures.
[69:13] No one among investigators
Can approach God. But he is very near
To the discerning.
[69:14] One who is impure cannot share
In that Holy One, all of whom dwells
Within holy things.
[69:15] No one crafty can come
To that Knower, whose love is
For the guileless.
[69:16] One who is puffed-up cannot come
To that Exalted One, for his love bends down
To the humble.
[69:17] That God cannot be limited
By a human, though he has mercy
Upon humans.
[69:18] That Maker cannot be limited
By things-made, though very great is
His work.
[69:19] That living Son[5] cannot be voiced
By mortals, nor his birth
By debaters.

4. On this notion of "chasm" (*peḥtâ*), see Brock, *The Luminous Eye*, 26–27.
5. C, "one."

[69:20] What could overcome that Greatness?
A weak spirit? A diminished soul?
A frail body?
[69:21] Whoever has believed himself capable of investigating
    him,
His word wanders, his heart drifts,
All of him presumes.

>   {*The End.*}[6]

6. B.

HYMN SEVENTY

{5},[1] *According to the same melody.*[2]

[70:1] With what eye could a thing-made look
Upon the Maker? [The eye] is a creature,
And he is the Creator.

　　REFRAIN: *Glory to your name!*

[70:2] Who could gaze and look upon the soul within us?
It cannot be seen by the mind,
Nor by the eye.
[70:3] If someone were to investigate the mind,
One would confess it, and another deny[3]—
Great scandal!
[70:4] The blind soul, which itself
Cannot see: how could it gaze
Upon divinity?
[70:5] Neither can it explore itself.
By which senses will it presume to investigate[4]
That Creator?
[70:6] Travel in [safe] harbors, frail one.
For when the sea gains force, the harbor nearby
Is like a refuge.
[70:7] Draw near to investigation in accordance with your
　　strength.
And if your heart wanders off and perishes,
Keep quiet.

　　1. B (see note 1 attached to hymn 67).
　　2. On this melody, see note 1 attached to hymn 66.
　　3. B adds "it" (*bāh*), which, however, upsets the meter.
　　4. B, "to look upon."

340

[70:8] Quiet is not far-off,
Nor must your mouth purchase silence
For a costly fee.
[70:9] Silence is easy. Debating is hard.
Investigation is not imposed with force
Upon the presumptuous.
[70:10] And though the commandment[5] seems
To compel absolutely, it is not compulsory
But free.
[70:11] And if the law[6] is not one of force,
What debate can compel us
To discuss?
[70:12] He gave the commandment and denied debating.
In his Testaments, there is neither investigation
Nor inquiry.
[70:13] He gave the law instead of disputing.
And instead of investigation, [he gave] faith,
On account of our weakness.
[70:14] The natures[7] he has made are incomprehensible.
How much more his nature, hidden within itself
And unspeakable?
[70:15] The Child who is from him knows him
Without controversy, without going astray,
So how would he investigate him?
[70:16] All that is made wanders far off
When it investigates, for it is insufficient
For that Maker.
[70:17] And if his love makes us great,
Let us understand ourselves, that our nature cannot
Investigate his nature.
[70:18] Every created thing errs greatly
If it thinks it can investigate
That Creator.
[70:19] Whatever is made should not forget[8]
That in its discussion it is very far

---

5. Cf. Mt 22.37; Jn 13.34.   6. Ibid.
7. Here referring to created things.   8. B, "Let [it] not forget."

From its Maker.
[70:20] There cannot be, among creatures,
A vessel so great that in it is contained
That Greatness.
[70:21] There cannot be among minds
A space[9] capable [of containing] the knowledge
Of divinity.

9. Lit., "womb" (*'ûbâ*).

HYMN SEVENTY-ONE

According to the same melody.[1]

[71:1] He is a discerning maker,
Who has not toiled thoughtlessly
In how he creates.[2]

    REFRAIN: *Blessed is his glory!*

[71:2] If he made a vessel[3] within which he could
Be contained, the thing-made would be greater
Than its Maker.
[71:3] It would be foolish for a thing-made to be
Exceedingly great, yet its Maker
Less than it.[4]
[71:4] And if that Creator is great,
How could the thing he has made increase
To the level of his knowledge?
[71:5] If [you say that] what he has made can
Increase to his level, this is wandering
Beyond belief.
[71:6] Since everything he has made is a wonder,
The Maker[5] being great, his creatures too
Are glorified.
[71:7] Creation is great because its Creator is great.
It [can become] small, too: inasmuch as it magnifies
Itself, it becomes weak.
[71:8] What he has made is not small

---

1. On this melody, see note 1 attached to the melody of hymn 66.
2. See *HF* 71:9.   3. B, *'bādâ* ("thing").
4. Lit., "not greater than it."   5. B, "Creator."

When it comes to his love, but it is small
When it comes to praise of him.
[71:9] The Creator has not troubled
Himself to create something
That could contain him.
[71:10] Nor has that Maker fought
Against himself to make a thing
That would limit him.
[71:11] Neither is there envy between the Creator
And {his}[6] creatures, for his love is put on
By his possessions.
[71:12] One who is created cannot
Be compared to his Creator
With respect to his knowledge.
[71:13] Concerning creation, the Books call out
That, as great as it is, [it is] much smaller
Than its Creator.
[71:14] None[7] has thought these
Or similar things regarding the fruit
Or regarding its Begetter.[8]
[71:15] The Prophets have called out, the Apostles have
    confessed,
Those exalted and those lowly:
He is the Son of the Exalted One.[9]
[71:16] And his glory, crowded together[10]
In all creation, can convince
Even those who are blind.
[71:17] Who would neglect the great thundering
Of all his preachers, besides the ear
Of all the presumptuous?

6. B.

7. That is, none of "prophets and apostles," following 71:16.

8. Up to this point, Ephrem has articulated a firm distinction between Creator and created, especially with respect to knowledge. Here he affirms that
this distinction does not apply to the distinction between Christ (the fruit)
and his Begetter.

9. Syr., 'ellāyâ. B, 'ābûdâ, "the Maker."

10. On this expression, see note 10 attached to 4:4.

[71:18] Look: though his preachers are many,
He testifies that his work is greater
Than the one who preaches him.[11]
[71:19] Look: all our eyes, along with our minds,
Are very weak next to the strength
Of divinity.
[71:20] The splendor that has shone forth from him
Comprehends him. The light that he has begotten
Knows him.

11. "He testifies" could be read with line one as its object.

HYMN SEVENTY-TWO

According to the same melody.[1]

[72:1] Bound yourself with great wonder,
O hearer! Collect your thought
From scattering!

> REFRAIN: *Glory to the Firstborn!*

[72:2] Through faith he draws near to you.
But through investigation, you grow far
From {his}[2] help.
[72:3] Great debating cannot
Touch him. He is more luminous
Than investigators.
[72:4] Remain with him in faith.
Though you despise it, you will come to it
When you have worn yourself out.
[72:5] Nor can your effort [help you] comprehend this,
For without him you cannot know
That he is.
[72:6] If you debate on and on,
He has [still] given you this: you can know
Only that he is.
[72:7] As much as one may labor,
This is what he knows. Outside of it,
There is nothing that he knows.
[72:8] He reveals much to the one who seeks him,
And hides much from the one who investigates him.[3]

1. On this melody, see note 1 attached to the melody of hymn 66.
2. B.
3. These two lines provide one example of Ephrem drawing a clear distinc-

346

Be quiet, presumptuous one!

[72:9] He was not concealed from you only on high:
He is above and below. He was lost by you,
Yet is present to you.

[72:10] Look: between the two, who can understand him?
He is concealed from you, O investigator,
And present to you, O worshiper!

[72:11] He is revealed in his goodness and hidden in his
    essence.
Instead of his greatness, seek his goodness,
Which is present to you!

[72:12] His treasure is open, but his substance[4] is concealed.
This is for you: instead of discussing him,
Seek his help.

[72:13] Look: his great compassion beckons you,
Weak one, to know his treasure,
Full of mercy.

[72:14] His great strength will not {allow}[5] you
To look and see, according to your own will,
How and how great he is.

[72:15] If you presume to go before [him],
How far can you go before the One who is before all?
He cannot be surpassed.

[72:16] There is no place to pass beyond him.
You are far from him. Beyond him
There is nothing.

[72:17] It is not only that you cannot pass
Beyond him. You will not even
Reach him.

[72:18] There is no going before and no passing beyond.
There is no arriving and no remaining:
He is a wonder within all.

[72:19] And if you could arrive at every [place],
He would meet you, without changing

---

tion between *b'ā* (here translated as "to seek"), which here carries a positive
valence, and *bṣā* ("to investigate"), which carries its standard negative valence.

4. Syr., *qnûmeh.*

5. Syr., *šābeq*, B. A, *sāpeq*, "to comprehend, be able."

Where he is.

[72:20] Your size is too small, too short.

[He is] far from you. Were he near to you,[6]

How would you investigate him?

[72:21] He is not like fire, which though far away,

Is so near that the body is too weak

To approach it.[7]

[72:22] Nor is he like the sun, for though he does not hold
   back

His strength from the eye, he can be diminished

In his weakness.

[72:23] The Lord is mingled with his possessions.

[He is] both near and far. Look: they investigate him

And lead themselves astray.

[72:24] Look: they think about him, as though far away—

At a great distance—while they are placed

As in the palm of his hand.

[72:25] The great sea—spacious vessel—

They cannot measure it,

How great it is.

[72:26] Yet even the sea is a drop

Next to Greatness. You will not fall into him

Without wandering off inside him.

---

6. B, "Since he is not near ..." (*kad lâ naqqîp*).

7. That is, while fire is entirely unapproachable, God can be approached.

HYMN SEVENTY-THREE

According to the same melody.[1]

[73:1] Look at these metaphors: the sun and the Father,
The shining and the Son, the heat
And the Holy Spirit.[2]

> REFRAIN: *Blessed is your Sender!*

[71:2] And though he is One, a Trinity
Is seen in him incomprehensibly.
Who could explain?
[73:3] One is many: one is three,
And three are one. Great aberration,[3]
Revealed wonder!
[73:4] The sun is distinct from its beam,
Yet mingled with it,[4] so that its ray
Is still the sun.
[73:5] No one claims [that there are] two suns,
Even though [the sun's] ray is the sun
To those on earth.
[73:6] We do not call upon two gods,
Even though our Lord is God
To creation.
[73:7] Who could investigate how and where

---

1. See note 1 attached to the melody of hymn 66.
2. On the Trinitarian imagery in this hymn, see Beck, *Ephräms Trinitätslehre,* 75–99.
3. The term Ephrem uses for "aberration" is *pehyâ,* derived from *phâ,* which he usually intends negatively (e.g., "to wander errantly"). Here, however, it simply suggests the unexpectedness of the Trinity.
4. BC, "distinct, yet equal" (*prîšîn w-šāwîn*).

[The sun's] ray is joined, [and where] its heat
Is joined and dwells?
[73:8] They are neither separate nor confused.
They are distinct [yet] mingled, joined and dwelling
    together[5]—
Great marvel!
[73:9] Who could touch and explore them,
Even though it seems they are simple
And plain?
[73:10] Touch the sun for me, apart from its ray!
Look and see its heat,
If you can.
[73:11] Divide the sun from its ray for me.
[Divide] the heat from both of them,
If you can.
[73:12] Though the sun [dwells] among heavenly beings,
Its {heat}[6] and its shining [dwell] among earthly beings:
[This is] a revealed symbol!
[73:13] [The sun] inclines its beam to the earth.
It dwells in the eye, clothed with it
As with a body.[7]
[73:14] And whenever [the eye] closes in sleep,
[The sun] strips off [its ray], like one dead,
Who will rise again.
[73:15] How the light penetrates the eye,
No one can tell, like our Savior,
Who dwelt in the womb.
[73:16] Inside the eye the light clothes itself
With beautiful sight. It goes forth to inspect
All creation.
[73:17] [It is] just like our Savior, who put on a frail
Body and went forth to sow himself[8]

5. B, "and equal."

6. Syr., ḥûmeh, B. A, ḥûbeh, "love."

7. That is, the sun is clothed with the eye; the eye becomes like the sun's body.

8. The verb here is šdâ, with a third-person masculine singular subject. Its basic meaning is "to throw down," "to drive away," or "to cast out" (see LS,

Through all creation.

[73:18] Whenever the ray has departed
From the side of its source, it is still not separate
From its begetter.

[73:19] It leaves here its heat,
Like the Holy Spirit, whom our Lord left
To his disciples.

[73:20] See the images in creation.
Do not become divided over the Trinity,
Lest you be destroyed.

[73:21] Because it was difficult for you, I have shown you:
One is three: Trinity,
One Essence.[9]

1512, col.2–1513, col. 1). Beck (*HF [G]*, 193) leaves the verb untranslated, and suggests the possibility that the manuscripts should be corrected to read *šrâ*, "to loose, unbind," but admits that such a meaning makes little sense within the context. *DJBA* suggests another possible meaning for *šrâ*, "to sow seeds, to plant" (*DJBA*, 1111, col. 1, sub. *šr'*, no. 1:13), which I have followed here. This meaning makes sense within the context of the hymn, for Christ, like the light, enters through the body, and spreads out to creation.

9. On Ephrem's use of "one Essence" (*hdâ 'îtûtâ*), see pp. 37–39.

HYMN SEVENTY-FOUR

According to the same melody.[1]

[74:1] Who will render me fit to gaze and look
Upon you, O light, in whom the mysteries
Of your Lord are crowded together?[2]

> REFRAIN: *Blessed is your Begetter!*

[74:2] Who could investigate its heat?
For though it is divided, it is not separated,
Just like the Holy Spirit.
[74:3] The power of its heat dwells
In everything—all of it with all,
All of it with one.
[74:4] It is not cut off from the ray
That is mingled with it, nor from the sun
That is mixed with it.
[74:5] As it extends to creatures,
Each one bears the power of its heat,
Insofar as it is able.
[74:6] By it, one who is naked becomes warm,
Clothed in it like Adam,
Who was [yet] exposed.
[74:7] It is loved by all who have been stripped,
As it sends[3] them prepared

1. On this melody, see note 1 attached to the melody of hymn 66.
2. On this expression, see note 10 attached to 4:4. On the Trinitarian imagery in this hymn, see Beck, *Ephräms Trinitätslehre,* 99–116.
3. Ephrem is making a pun on the word *šlaḥ,* which can mean "to strip" (as in line 1, connected with the nakedness mentioned in the previous stanza), or "to send" (as in line 2). Further, the term "apostles" (*šlîḥê,* lit., "those who are

For all things.

[74:8] The Spirit has put on the Apostles[4]
And has sent them to the four regions
For [their] work.[5]

[74:9] In [the light's] heat everything becomes ripe,
As in the Spirit everything becomes holy—
A revealed symbol![6]

[74:10] By it the cold within the body
Is overcome, like impurity
By the Holy Spirit.

[74:11] In it, fingers,[7] which the cold had bound,
Are freed, like the souls
The Evil One has bound.

[74:12] In it, the calves of spring rejoice,[8]
Just as the disciples [rejoice] in the Holy Spirit,
Who has dwelt in them.

[74:13] In heat, the bonds of winter,
With which it impedes fruits and blossoms,
Are severed.

[74:14] In the Holy Spirit, too, are severed
The bonds of the Evil One, with which he keeps back
All beneficial things.

[74:15] Heat awakens the womb[9]
Of the silent earth, as the Holy Spirit
The holy Church.

[74:16] A single frail person: how he wanders!

---

sent), which Ephrem will use in the following stanza, derives from this same verb.

4. See note 3 attached to previous stanza. Note as well here the language of "putting on" (*lebšat*). Typically, Ephrem speaks of Christ "putting on" a human body (see, e.g., *HF* 4:2, 17:5, 19:7, etc.). Here, however, it is the Spirit who "puts on" or "is clothed in" the apostles.

5. Lit., "works," or "actions" (*sû'rānê*).

6. That is, the sun's heat forms a "revealed symbol," i.e., one that can be seen and grasped by humans, and which points to the hidden reality of the Spirit's working.

7. Syr., *ṣeb'ātâ*. B, *ṣebwātâ* ("things").

8. Cf. Mal 4.2.

9. Syr., *raḥmēh*, lit., "bowels, intestines."

How he investigates the great, limitless
Treasure!
[74:17] How he wanders! For he measures against himself
That which extends to the four regions,[10]
Yet are still too small for it!
[74:18] Heat loosens the onerous, cold
Bridle—the silence of frost
Upon the lips.
[74:19] The mouth and tongue [can then] speak,
Like the tongues of the Spirit,[11] which rested
Upon the disciples.[12]
[74:20] With its heat, with tongues,
The Holy Spirit drove silence
From the disciples.
[74:21] Silence onerous and cold,
As in winter, was terrified
To speak.
[74:22] That People—a symbol of winter,
An image of cold—grew completely dark
On account of[13] the disciples.
[74:23] The Holy Spirit, through the tongues
Of fire that came, thawed the power[14]
Of the cold.
[74:24] She drove fear from the disciples.
Silence fled [their] tongues
By means of tongues.
[74:25] Satan has been conquered like winter.
The People have grown angry, altogether dark[15]
Like February.

10. Beck (*HF [G]*, 195, n. 4) translates this as "heavenly regions" (*Himmels-gegenden*), but Ephrem referred in *HF* 74:8 to the "four regions" of the earth, to which the apostles were sent. It seems likely that he has that same meaning in mind here.

11. Syr., *rûḥâ*. B, "fire" (*nûrâ*).

12. Acts 2.3.

13. Or, "against."

14. Spelled incorrectly in A as 'z', but corrected in BC (*'ûzâ*).

15. C, "angry."

[74:26] There the sparrows on high spoke
With a new voice, despising
The hawk and winter.
[74:27] These things heat has done.[16]
These things the Holy Spirit has fulfilled.
Who can understand?

   {*The End.*}[17]

16. Syr., *sa'ret*. C, *ṣārat*, "has depicted."
17. B.

HYMN SEVENTY-FIVE

{*10*},[1] *According to the same melody.*[2]

[75:1] The sun has illumined you. Look, it has caused
   you to wonder,
O weak one, yet you do not know
How to investigate it.

   REFRAIN: *Praise to you!*[3]

[75:2] How will you investigate that Creator
As a human being? Know your humanity,
O human!
[75:3] The subtlety of that light
Cannot be touched; it is not concealed
By things that hold it.[4]
[75:4] The heat from that ray
Cannot be seen by the eyes—
It is [too] fine.
[75:5] It has conquered the eyes with its heat
And the hands with its subtlety,
For they cannot touch or see [it].
[75:6] The mouth, the ears, and the nose,
Three senses: they cannot sense
The Three.
[75:7] No mouth has ever tasted
That light, nor a nose

1. B. See note 1 attached to hymn 67.
2. On this melody, see note 1 attached to the melody of hymn 66.
3. B, "Glory to the Hidden One."
4. Ephrem is here emphasizing the transcendence and immanence of the
sun: humans cannot touch a sunbeam.

Inhaled [its] scent.[5]
[75:8] Nor has the ear ever heard
The light's voice, as it moves
Across creation.
[75:9] And if the three senses
Are useless beside this tiny sun
Which is in the firmament,
[75:10] Then your whole body [is useless], if the senses
Cannot meet the divinity
Hidden from all.
[75:11] The three useless senses,
Along with the Trinitarian symbols
Within the sun,
[75:12] Call out that they are alien
To the discussions of the Father, Son,
And Holy Spirit.
[75:13] Lift up the waters opposite the sun.
See there an image of the Holy One's
Begotten.
[75:14] Without separation and without emission,
Fire births a child, splendid
Like its begetter.
[75:15] [Fire arises] neither through a division of the sun's side,
Nor is it a small part from within water.
[This is] a great mystery!
[75:16] Though the waters and the sun remain complete,
There is one begotten,[6] in which one can see
The begetting of the Son.
[75:17] He has depicted difficult things with simple things
Because of our weakness, so that simply
We may know that he is Son.
[75:18] With every image that Sweet One
Has approached our sickness
In order to heal it.
[75:19] And if he who is a great and imageless
God had not drawn near
To our humanity,

5. B, "rising" (denḥâ).   6. I.e., fire.

[75:20] Then that human, who is weak,
Would seek, through his own weakness, paths
Toward Greatness.

[75:21] Be not lazy, O mind!
Build bridges of the Spirit and cross over
To your Creator!

[75:22] O son of a thing-made,[7] make for yourself wings—
The holy Books.[8] How [else] would you arrive
At the Son of your Lord?

[75:23] The soul, too, must be diligent
In all means. How will it arrive
At the Holy Spirit?

[75:24] And you, O body, do not slack!
Fly like the eagle to the body
That gives life to all!

[75:25] And since human senses are weaker
Than the discussion of divinity,
Do not debase yourself!

[75:26] Look: the senses of the sons of the High One,
Though subtle and spiritual,
Are yet insufficient.

[75:27] Therefore, cease from discussion,
O dense senses of the fat body,
Causing pus to flow!

[75:28] Let us leave such things as are pure.[9]
Speak to us of the impure things
Of the impure demons.

[75:29] Your body's senses can speak to us
About the spiritual senses
Of the stinking demons:

[75:30] With these nostrils Legion breathes.
With these feet, the Evil One runs
Over all creation.

{*The End.*}[10]

7. Or, "son of a slave."
8. Or, "make the books of the Holy One your wings."
9. Lit., "such things … are left."
10. B.

HYMN SEVENTY-SIX

{11},[1] According to the same melody.[2]

[76:1] Look: [trees'] fruits are called
By the name of the trees, whether [the fruits] are sweet
Or bitter.

    REFRAIN: *Blessed are you, with your Father!*

[76:2] The names of both trees and fruits
Are the same.[3] They are different, yet the same—
A great mystery!
[76:3] A fruit is different from its tree,
Yet the same as it, since one title
Is given to both.
[76:4] Sweet is the root and sweet is its fruit.
With the same name, call upon both—
It and its fruit.
[76:5] Differentiate between the names "trunk" and "fruit,"
But make them the same, too. Call the fruit
By the name of its tree.
[76:6] For if [the tree] is sweet, they call the fruit
Sweet as well, and its root,
Even though it is pungent.

---

1. See note 1 attached to hymn 67.
2. On this melody, see note 1 attached to the melody of hymn 66.
3. Syr., *šāwîn*. A more literal translation of the latter term would be "equal"
or "of equal worth." The metaphor provides Ephrem with a language for
speaking about the sameness and difference between Father and Son. In the
same way, for example, that an olive tree and an olive fruit both carry the
name "olive," both "Father" ("tree") and "Son" ("fruit") share the name "God"
(see 76:7).

[76:7] Differentiate between the names "Father" and "Son,"
But make them the same, too: the Father is God,
And the Son is God.
[76:8] For the Father's name is God
And the Son's name is God—
Just as it is written.
[76:9] He is distinct in name, because he is Son,
And the same in name, because he is God—
Glory to his name!
[76:10] And if they are true—both trees
And their fruits—then the Father and the Son,
How much truer!
[76:11] He has depicted hidden things with revealed things,
In order to show what is unseen
By what is seen.
[76:12] He has inscribed his symbols in trees,
To explain what is incomprehensible
With what is comprehensible.
[76:13] He has interpreted for us difficult things
With easy things, that with ease
We will understand him.
[76:14] And difficult things with simple things
He has explained to us, that simply
We will know that he is Son.
[76:15] That he is our Lord and God
The righteous perceive, but the deniers
[Do] not even [perceive] his Father.
[76:16] The Books call out that the Father is God
And the Son is God. The People who deny
Are without God.

      {The End.}[4]

   4. B.

HYMN SEVENTY-SEVEN

{*12*},[1] *According to the same melody.*[2]

[77:1] "That hour, he does not know."[3]
The foolish weigh [the hour][4] next to the Son:
How it is exalted!

REFRAIN: *Blessed is your knowledge!*

[77:2] If the Firstborn knows the Father,
What is above the Father,
Which the Son does not know?[5]
[77:3] [They say]: "No one knows that hour,[6]
Not even the Firstborn, for the Father alone
Knows it."
[77:4] If, as they think, he does not know it,
On account of which [they say] he is a creature, look: they
    depart from[7] him
In their disputing.
[77:5] Come marvel: if [they think that] our Lord,
Because he is a creature, does not know
That hour,

---

1. See note 1 attached to hymn 67.
2. On this melody, see note 1 attached to the melody of hymn 66.
3. Mt 24.36; Mk 13.32. This verse, and the issue of Christ's knowledge, will form the theme of the next three hymns. On the context of Ephrem's use of this verse, see pp. 32–33.
4. That is, the Son's ignorance of the hour.
5. That is, if the Son knows the Father but not the hour, then something (i.e., the hour) must be above the Father.
6. Mt 24.36; Mk 13.32.
7. Syr., *'ābrîn*. C, *'ābdîn*, "they make him."

[77:6] Those who were created by his own hand,
Have presumed to investigate
The Lord of hours, instead of the hour!
[77:7] Therefore, let them stand by their word:
Everything created should keep silent
Beside the Creator.
[77:8] Inside the knowledge that knows his Father,
That hour is contained[8] too—
Inside[9] his knowledge.
[77:9] If [the Father] let [the Son] know his glory,
Yet hid from him the temporal hour,
The hour would be greater than [the Son].[10]
[77:10] Consider the hour that he does not know
Alongside the Father, whom he does know. Weigh and see
Which is better.
[77:11] "The Son, who alone knows the Father,"[11]
Knows all of him, not just a measure,
For he is not lacking.
[77:12] The root that is true
Truly knows
The fruit it has begotten.
[77:13] That fruit that [supposedly] knows less
Than its root is yet mingled
Altogether with all of it.
[77:14] For if [the fruit] falls short in its knowledge
Of its tree, it also falls short in its name,
So that it is not its fruit.
[77:15] But if the fruit resembles in its name
The root, it resembles it
Also in knowledge.
[77:16] The sweetness within both of them is one.
The knowledge within both of them is one,
For they are mingled.
[77:17] Fruit is mingled inside its tree,
And in fruit, there is its root as well:

---

8. Syr., *'eṭhebšat.* C, *'eṭhešbat,* "to be reckoned."
9. B, *ṭhêt* ("beneath"). 10. Or "greater than [the glory]."
11. Cf. Mt 11.27.

Who will separate [them]?
[77:18] They are indivisible in that sweetness.
They are indivisible in knowledge.
Perfect[12] truth.
[77:19] The fruit's love is in its root,
And in the fruit is [love] of the tree:
Who will divide [them]?
[77:20] The names of Father, Son, and Spirit
Are equal and united in the hovering
At baptism.[13]
[77:21] United names, an equal procession.
One will, like one yoke,
They come bearing.
[77:22] And as they are equal in the hovering
At baptism, so they are equal
Also in agreement.
[77:23] The fruit, however, bent down and put on a body.
Along with it, he put on the weak names
Related to it.
[77:24] Just as he put on our humanity,
He went further and put on our knowledge
For us.
[77:25] The Knower-of-all became ignorant.
He asked and listened like a human being,
For humanity.
[77:26] If those who are weak have yet searched into his
    essence,
Can the Son not
Comprehend the hour?[14]
[77:27] They should either keep quiet, if he does not know,
Or if they investigate, they should confess that the Son
Knows all.
[77:28] If they investigate, even though it is not permitted,
It is presumption. If it is permitted,

12. B, "knowledge / *of* perfect truth."
13. On "hovering," see note 13 attached to 38:12.
14. That is, if they think they can understand God, do they not think the
Son can understand the hour?

It is [permitted only] as a gift.[15]
[77:29] He who has allowed dust to debate,
How does [that dust] hinder his Son from knowing
The temporal hour?
[77:30] "That hour, he does know."
The reason for this ignorance
Is the body he put on.

      {*The End.*}[16]

15. As elsewhere in the *HF*, Ephrem opens a small loophole for investigation: here it can be done, provided one has the right orientation toward it.
   16. B.

HYMN SEVENTY-EIGHT

{*13*},[1] *According to the same melody.*[2]

[78:1] Never {wish}[3] to say
About that hour, "The Son does not know it."
He discerns it.[4]

> {REFRAIN: *Blessed is the One who knows all!*}[5]

[78:2] The hour that comes from counting
He knows, for in him all numbers
Are formed.
[78:3] If it relates to the year, he discerns it,
For in him the months of the year are formed
Like limbs.
[78:4] If it relates to months, he knows it,
For in him the days of the month are arranged
Like joints.
[78:5] If it relates to days, he does not err,
For hours and Sabbaths and weeks
Have been arranged by him.
[78:6] If it relates to the sun, he knows it,
For he has cleared the paths of winter,
And the steps of summer.
[78:7] If it relates to the moon, again, he discerns it,

---

1. See note 1 attached to hymn 67.
2. On this melody, see note 1 attached to the melody of hymn 66.
3. Syr., *teṣbê*, B. A, *tebṣê*, "to seek."
4. The words for "know" and "discern" are *'ida'* and *ḥkam*, which Ephrem uses synonymously throughout this hymns.
5. B.

For he has made full moons the markers[6] [of seasons],
Along with the new moon.
[78:8] Whether he is on high or in the deep,
All creation is suspended in his hand,
By his finger.
[78:9] Compare the hour that he does not know
To the Holy Spirit, whom he knows,
Though she is great.
[78:10] Please explain to us what the reason is:
How and why has [the Father] concealed from him
The hour of his triumphal coming?
[78:11] If he concealed [it] from him for this reason,
[Namely,] so that [the Son] would be diminished, lest he
    be compared
Mistakenly to him,
[78:12] That construction is very weak.
See how its refutation[7] will come
In a single moment.[8]
[78:13] When that hour has been revealed,
And the trumpet has sounded, and the triumphal coming
    has occurred,
[The hour] will be complete.
[78:14] [The Son], therefore, has been compared with it,[9]
And inequality has become equality,
According to their [very own] word.
[78:15] It must be one of the two: if he is smaller than [the hour]
Because he does not know it, he will be like it
When he has perceived it.
[78:16] {But if, when he has perceived it, he is no greater,}[10]
What will be gained? Look: he will know it,

---

6. Syr., *kess'â mile* ("full moons the markers"). B, *kess'â mallê*, another way of saying "full moons" (*kess'â*, "full moons," *mallê*, "full"). In this case, it would simply read, "He has made full moons, / along with ..."

7. Syr., *šrāyeh*, BC. A, *šûrāyâ*, "conclusion."

8. Syr., *šā'â*. B, *mellâ*, "word."

9. I.e., the hour (but see *HF* 78:11 where Ephrem uses the same phrase to speak of comparing the Father and the Son).

10. BC. Missing in A.

Yet be smaller.

[78:17] Even Satan can know
That hour, since when it is revealed
He will be destroyed.

[78:18] So great is the hour which he has concealed
From his Beloved that even Satan
Can know it!

[78:19] Come, then, and hear the reason he is glorified:
He is the Lord of all. He is greater than all.
All is suspended in him.

[78:20] The reason that God is glorified
Is his goodness,
Which is eternal.

[78:21] And the reason for his glory compared with his
    Begotten
Is his fatherhood, which is
Everlasting and eternal.

[78:22] O holy reasons,
Which with creatures and {with the Firstborn
Are never ending!}[11]

[78:23] Therefore, it is a temporal hour, and a temporal
    reason,
And a temporal word. And along with what is temporal,
Its time passes.

[78:24] Great is the reason behind his making,
For a thing-made can never be greater
Than its Maker.

[78:25] Great is the reason behind his fatherhood,
For his Begotten can never be
The Begetter.

[78:26] Let us therefore seek another explanation
For that hour, since the first
Has been clarified.

[78:27] Since he has been refuted,[12] he acknowledges and
    reveals

11. BC.
12. That is, Ephrem's imagined disputant.

"That hour, our Savior
Does know,"
[78:28] While whispering to us, as in secret,
"The controversy has contrived and spoken this,
To conquer through it."[13]
[78:29] The controversy has been vanquished and truth is
   victorious.
Debating has perished, and a crown has come
To the victor.

{Completed are the thirteen hymns [according to the melody]
   "If you investigate Being."}[14]

---

13. While it is not entirely clear who is speaking this line, the sense of it is
clear: Ephrem voices his suspicion that this debate over the Son's knowledge
of the hour has arisen as a ruse for his opponents' real concerns, namely, to
destroy the church's unity.
   14. B.

HYMN SEVENTY-NINE

According to the melody "God in his mercy..."[1]

[79:1] My son, which is more laudable by comparison?
Which surpasses [the other] on a scale:
That he does not know the hour, or that he knows
The Father who is greater than the comparison?
He showed that he did not know, and he showed that he would
    not rush
To investigate the hour, to impede [you] through the hour,
So that even the hour would rebuke you:
Do not investigate the Lord of all hours![2]

REFRAIN: *Glory to you, Son, Messiah, Knower-of-all!*

[79:2] Through your very self know that he is the Knower,
Who, look, has gone ahead and bound your knowledge,
For your freedom is an unclean maiden,
Who, because of wine, let her master's treasures be plundered.
He has prepared fetters for her, and readied chains for her.
Look: barriers encircle her. Walls surround her.
Even if these have not kept her back,
From them recognize her madness!
[79:3] He knew that clans and tongues

---

1. On this melody, see note 1 attached to the melody of *HF* 26.
2. This hymn, compared with 77 and 78, provides an interesting test case
in the hermeneutics underlying the collection of this hymn: clearly, 77–79
all aim to refute subordinationist readings of Mt 24.36. At the same time, 79
differs from 77 and 78 in meter, style, and vocabulary. Given that 79 shares a
meter and melody with hymns 26–30, it is reasonable to wonder whether it was
originally a part of that "collection," but was later re-edited, and placed beside
77 and 78 on the basis of a shared theme.

And Greek musings upon hidden things[3]
Were ready to come to his teaching,
For it is a net that has gathered all peoples.
His {leaven}[4] has drawn forth and led the {wild-asses}[5] to his
   teaching.
So they would not be confused in their practices,[6]
With one yoke of truth
He taught one unified practice.
[79:4] He has given no place to the quick,
Who runs around by himself, doubtful.
He has given no place to the investigator,
Who has taken off the yoke of faith.
The scribes and the simple; the clever and the guileless:[7]
There is a single harmonious yoke for all of them.
The chariot's yoke shows
That things divided find agreement under it.
[79:5] To eat or drink, sleep or get up
[Belongs to] freedom's unbound authority.
Even {horses}[8] possess the freedom
[To do] what they wish, and however much they wish.
But they do not have the same power under a yoke:
When love is placed upon them and truth is bound to them,
They can neither stray nor lead astray,
For they obey the charioteer's will.
[79:6] If there is no freedom
In the stock of wild animals,[9]

3. Cf. *HF* 2:24. On Ephrem's distrust of "Greek" thought, see note attached
to 2:24.
   4. Syr., *ḥmîra*, B. A, *ḥamrâ*, "wine."
   5. Syr., *'rādê*, following ms B. A, *'dr'*, "aid, help." On "wild-asses," see Gn 16.12
(P), which Ephrem further references in *HNat* 13:17, and *CH* 8:10:6.
   6. Syr., *rehṭâ*. Lit., "course; effort."
   7. Syr., *tmîmâ*, which can also mean "perfect, upright."
   8. Syr., *rākšê*. C has *regšê*, "senses." Either reading is possible, for Ephrem is
literally speaking of a horse-drawn chariot, but using it as a metaphor to articulate a spiritual anthropology.
   9. Lit., "If, where there is no freedom, / look: it is among the family of the
wild animals." Though confusedly worded, Ephrem's sense is clear: of all the
places one would expect to find freedom, the domain of wild animals would

How will it be found in one's [own] house[10]—
A human—the vessel of the soul's movements?
[The human] is confined by truth,[11] yet free in behavior.
Through conversion, he passes to things that are good,
[Stepping up] on truth's stairway,
After having fallen down to debased error.
[79:7] He stays up,[12] then goes to sleep. Once asleep,
He guards the wages [acquired while] awake.[13]
Likewise, he fasts and eats at the appropriate time,
And does not negate his fast with eating.
The meal and the fast are both pure and fair.
Truth is one and error is right next to it.
If you barely turn from its side, quickly, like a beam [of light],
It quickly [becomes] like a chasm.
[79:8] In one assembly there are different wills.
They are never at fault for being different,
But they are at fault for being altogether divided,[14]
For they walk against the yoke of faith.
If even horses[15] can be unified under a single yoke,
And David wrote that a human being
Is like the wild animals,[16]
It is a wonder he cannot [at least] be like them!
[79:9] Look: there are confused practices[17] among the
    assemblies,
Dissenting wills within houses,[18]
Divided questions in the churches,

---

seem to be the likeliest of candidates. Yet, even here, there is no freedom. As
line 3 will make clear, this is part of an argument against the absolute freedom of human beings.

10. I.e., the human body, the house of the soul.

11. B, "by one truth."

12. Syr., *šhar*, which can refer to keeping vigil.

13. Lit., "the wages of his waking are kept by him."

14. Ephrem is drawing a distinction between two similar words, *prîš* ("distinct") and *plîg* ("divided").

15. Syr., *rākšê*. C, *regšê* (see note 8 attached to 79:5).

16. Ps 49.21 (P).

17. Syr., *rehṭâ*, lit., "course, effort" (*LS*, 1441, sub. *rehṭâ*, no. 1 and 3).

18. Syr., *dayrātâ*, almost certainly referencing monastic houses.

And sickly minds in the congregations.
As a result, whose is the woe? There is anger in the sea,
And an earthquake on the land, because they have
 investigated the Creator
By whose hand they were created.[19]
Look: through investigation of him, {creation has become
 troubled}.[20]
[79:10] Look: teaching is like a mirror,
Fixed between the Lord and his servants.
His creation and its computations show
That they[21] cannot hide from the Creator.[22]
Whenever they go to investigate him, they see his
 abasement.
He was depicted at that hour[23] so that they would
 immediately feel shame,[24]
So that, by his humble {image}[25]
They would be kept back from his powerful Birth.
[79:11] With the eye of thought, look upon
Creation—all of it, entirely:
Like a body it is put together by the Fashioner-of-all,
And it cannot hide itself from its Creator.
My brothers, how can an image be depicted
So that its parts are hidden from its craftsmen?
No hour can be
Hidden from the wisdom of its Creator.
[79:12] My brothers, look at a number:
It is constructed like a body by the Knower-of-all.
Its sums are like its limbs,

---

19. Lines 6 and 7 of *HF* (S) should be rescanned as follows: *w-zaw'â b-gaw yabšâ da-bṣaw l-bārûyâ* (5+5) / *da-b-'îdê 'ettaqqen* (3+3).

20. Syr., *meštagšān baryāteh*, BC. A, *meštagšîn b-brîteh*, "they are troubled by creation."

21. Lit., "it."

22. That is, the component parts of creation (including the hour when the Son of Man will return, following Mt 24.36) cannot be inaccessible to the Creator.

23. Ephrem now returns to the theme of the "hour" of Mt 24.36.

24. I.e., for investigation. *'etkḥad* can also be "to stand in awe."

25. Syr., *ṭûpseh*, BC. A, *ṭûpeh*, "voyage."

The seasons and times[26] are like its joints,
The hours are like its forms, the years are like its figures,
And that hidden hour is like its thought.
Like the rest of its parts
Are its months, its weeks, and its days.
[79:13] {Who has}[27] wandered off, crazed,
Destroying his thought and becoming like
Those drunks who have destroyed their mind?
What fool has until now thought
(Regarding the image adorned by the Father of truth
By the finger of his beloved), that there is any way
That {glorious}[28] hour
Would be hidden from the finger that depicts all?
[79:14] So even if [the hour] is not named,
His foreknowledge has not forgotten it.
He has prepared a place in which it is fixed,
And from where it will emerge, {from}[29] hidden to revealed.
Though not present, it is present to its Lord
Now, for look: it is kept in the treasury {of}[30] his knowledge.
If it is hidden within his root,
It is not hidden from the fruit [that dwells] within his womb.

   {*The End.*}[31]

26. Syr., *zabnê*, which Beck mistakenly prints as *zb'*.
27. Syr., *'aynaw*, BC. A, *'w*, which could be *'aw* ("either, or"), *'â(w)*, "O!," or *'û*, "woe!"
28. Syr., *mšbaḥtâ*, B. A, *maḥšabtâ*, "thought."
29. Syr., *w-men*, BC. A, *tammān*, "there."
30. B.
31. B.

HYMN EIGHTY

According to the melody {"The whole creation has given you birth ..."}[1]

[80:1] Ask and listen with discernment:
Faith is a second soul.
As much as the body exists through the soul,
The life of the soul is supported
By faith. If [the soul] renounces
Or falls into doubt,[2] it will become a corpse.

> REFRAIN: *The time of trial [brings]*
> *Rejoicing among athletes,*
> *For, look: [there is] an opportunity to receive*
> *Victory!*[3]

[80:2] The body, thus, is mortal.
Look: it depends upon the soul. The soul depends
Upon faith. Faith
Depends upon divinity,
For from the Father, through his Son, proceeds
The truth that gives life to all in the Spirit.
[80:3] With this truth a person can
Gird himself[4] with exalted things,
Within a living soul. By means of the body,
He sees and hears. Through faith,

---

1. BC. Hymn 80 is the lone example of this meter and melody, made up of six-line stanzas, with a meter of 4+4 per line. This melody appears also in *CH* 12.

2. Syr., *'etpalleg;* lit., "becomes divided."

3. This appears to be a metered refrain. Beck divides it 5 / 5 / 8. I have divided it 5 / 5 / 5 / 3.

4. Syr., *napšeh,* which could also be rendered, "his soul."

Love, and wisdom, he is mingled
With divinity, and depicted in its image.
[80:4] Let us not abolish this marvelous
Arrangement. Let faith
Not be emptied from our souls,
Lest there come to us hidden dead—
Those about whom Life spoke:
"Let the dead bury their dead."[5]
[80:5] This air—the soul of everything,
Living breath—gives life to the body.
Whoever presumes to sever himself from
[This] living current, becomes a manifest dead man.
Whoever severs himself from the speech
Of Truth, his soul becomes a hidden corpse.
[80:6] "I desire not the death of a mortal,"[6]
Life—he who gives life to all—has testified.
As the True One has sworn,
Without deceit, the font of life
Has revealed his will and poured out his love,
For he thirsts greatly to kill our death.
[80:7] The Book has determined that the one who is righteous
Can live by faith.[7]
He has made the truth like a
Splendid root, and way of life
Like fruit. With faith
He has lifted them up and hung them on a branch of truth.
[80:8] In the revealed type, look: hidden things
Appear to you, as before [your] eyes.
The body is needy, like a merchant
[Longing] for possessions. And the mind
Gathers its treasures like a sailor,
For faith, the ship of life.
[80:9] And though the body exists
Through the life of the soul, it exists [also] through bread.
And the soul, though it is living,

---

5. Mt 8.22; Lk 9.60.   6. Ezek 18.32.
7. Hab 2.4; Rom 1.17.

Even though it does not live without training,
Through faith's help[8]
It can live. And the Books testify.
[80:10] He spoke to faithful Lazarus, and [Lazarus] came
    forth,
And his scent was sweet because of the voice that called him.[9]
The peoples have come to life in the symbol of Lazarus—
Hidden life. And as a symbol of the People,
The thief died—he who strangled himself
And bequeathed his destruction[10] to the scribes who paid
    him.[11]

> {*The End.*}[12]

---

8. Syr., *'ûdrānê.* C. *sû'rānê* ("actions").

9. Jn 11.1–44, esp. v. 39.

10. Syr., *ḥbālâ.* From this same root is derived *ḥeblâ,* "rope," and Ephrem is playing with the ambiguity.

11. Mt 27.3–5.

12. B.

HYMN EIGHTY-ONE (HYMN ONE "ON THE PEARL")

On the Pearl, according to the melody: "Who is able?"[1]

[81:1] One day, I took up
A pearl, my brothers. I saw in it symbols,
Things of the Kingdom, images and types
Of that Greatness. It became a fountain
And I drank from it symbols of the Son.

> REFRAIN: *Blessed is the One who compares the high
> kingdom to a Pearl!*[2]

[81:2] I placed it, my brothers, in the palm of my hand
To observe it. I began to look at it:
On one side, it had a face.
On every side, [it offered] examination of the Son,
Who is incomprehensible, because he is entirely light.
[81:3] In its beauty, I saw the Pure One,
Who is not moved. In its purity [I saw]
A great mystery: the body of our Lord,
Unsullied, without division.
I saw the truth that is undivided.
[81:4] It was Mary that I saw there—
Her pure conception. It[3] became the Church,
And the Son was inside it.[4] [It took on] the likeness of
    a cloud,

---

1. On the five hymns "On the Pearl," see pp. 15–16. This melody, which will
continue through the end of the *HF*, consists in five lines of 4+4.

2. This is the only refrain given for hymns 81–83.

3. Or, "she."   4. Or, "her."

That one which carried him,[5] and a heavenly mystery,
That shone forth his fair splendor.
[81:5] I saw in it his signs—of his triumphs
And of his crownings. I saw in it his aids,
Along with his profits. [I saw the signs of] his secrets
And his revelations. It became larger to me
Than an Ark, so that I roamed around inside it.
[81:6] I saw in it rooms without shadows,
Because it is born from light. [I saw] rational types
Without tongues; the speech of mysteries
Without lips. A silent lyre,
Voicelessly gave forth song.
[81:7] {A trumpet}[6] sounded, and thunder whispered:
"Do not be rash! Abandon hidden things,
Take up what is revealed!" I saw in a clear sky
Some rain—a fountain, from which my ears,
As from a cloud, were filled with interpretations.
[81:8] Like that manna, which alone
Filled the People in place of meals,[7]
It filled me with its tastes—
The pearl—in place of Books
And their readings and interpretations.
[81:9] But if I should ask whether there are
Other mysteries, it has no mouth
With which I could hear it, nor ears
That it might hear me. Nor [does it have] senses,
That [pearl] from which I have acquired new senses.
[81:10] She responded and said to me—the child of the sea[8]—
"I am infinite. As for that sea
From which I ascended, it is a great treasury
Of the symbols which are in my bosom. Inquire into the sea,
But do not examine the Lord of the sea.

---

5. Cf. Acts 1.9.
6. Syr., *šīpurâ*, BC. A misspells as *špûrâ*.
7. Ex 16.1–36.
8. Here begins a direct speech by the pearl, which will continue through the rest of hymn 81 (81:16).

[81:11] "I saw divers[9] descending after me.
{Terrified}[10] of what was in the sea,
They returned to dry land. They could not wait
Even a brief moment: 'What is it we see?
Let us examine the depth[11] of divinity!'
[81:12] "The waves of the Son fill benefits
With harmful things. Do you not see
The sea's waves? If a ship resists,
[The waves] will break {it.}[12] But if it {yields},[13]
And does not resist, it is preserved.
[81:13] "In the sea all the Egyptians were drowned,
Even without investigating.[14] And without examination
The Hebrews were swallowed up on dry land.[15]
How will you be saved? The Sodomites
Were licked with fire, so how will you be found innocent?[16]
[81:14] "[Seeing] these atrocities, the fish in the sea
Shake beside us. Do you then have
A heart of stone, that you read these things,
And [yet] are unmindful of them? Great fear!
Even righteousness was very silent.
[81:15] "Examination is mingled with praise:
Which will win? Glory and
Investigation rise up from the tongue.
Which shall he heed? Examination and prayer

9. Ephrem makes a pun on 'āmûdê ("divers"), which in 2:10 will translate
as "ones to be baptized." This stanza thus represents a subtle critique of those
who are recently baptized and immediately wish to wax theological about
their new faith.

10. Syr., metbalhîn, BC. A, metbahlin, "at ease."

11. Syr., 'ûmāqâ. B, "womb" ('ûbâ).

12. BC. A, "him."

13. Syr., metramyâ, BC. A, metrāymâ, "to be lifted up."

14. Ex 14.23–25.

15. Nm 16.31.

16. Gn 19. Ephrem's argument is this: even without impious examination
and questioning, the Egyptians, Hebrews, and Sodomites were all destroyed.
Thus, the person that investigates divinity inappropriately is much worse than
all of these groups that were destroyed. Essentially, Ephrem is positing investigation as worse than the sins of the Egyptians, Hebrews, or Sodomites.

From one mouth, which shall he hear?
[81:16] "For three days, Jonah was
Our neighbor in the sea.[17] Creatures inside the sea
Shook, saying, 'Who is it that flees
From God?' Jonah fled
And [still] you dare to investigate him?"[18]

{*The End.*}[19]

17. Jon 1–2.
18. That is, God (as opposed to Jonah).
19. B.

HYMN EIGHTY-TWO (HYMN TWO
"ON THE PEARL")

{2},[1] *According to the same melody.*[2]

[82:1] What are you like?[3] Your silence will speak
To the one who listens to you. With a silent mouth.
Speak to us. Whoever listens to
The whisper of your silence, your symbol will call out
Silently regarding our Savior.
[82:2] Your mother is the virgin of the sea.[4]
Without his marrying her,[5] she fell[6] into his bosom.
Without his knowing her, you were conceived at its side.
Without realizing it, Jewish women
Slay your image when they hang you up.[7]
[82:3] You who are begotten alone:
Of all jewels you resemble
The high Word that uniquely
The High One begot. Jewels that are fashioned
Resemble the symbol of exalted things-made.[8]

1. B, which numbers hymns 82–85 of "On the Pearl."
2. On this melody, see note 1 attached to the melody of hymn 81.
3. A adds "pearl," which upsets the meter of this line.
4. According to R. A. Donkin (*Beyond Price, Pearls and Pearl-Fishing: Origins to the Age of Discoveries* [Philadelphia: American Philosophical Society, 1998], 1–16), there were three ancient theories for how pearls were made: first, that pearls were drops of rain that crystallized within the oyster; second, that they resulted from lightning striking the oyster; third, that oysters conceived the pearl virginally. Ephrem suggests the third option here, but at 84:14 suggests the second option. Thanks to Joshua Lollar for directing me to this source.
5. I.e., in marriage.
6. Syr., *neplat.* B, *nāpat,* "she bent down."
7. I.e., as earrings.
8. That is, among jewels, the pearl is unique in that it can serve as a symbol

[82:4] The manifest begetting of a hidden womb
Is a great mystery.[9] Your luminous conception
Was without seed. Without seed was
Your pure begetting. Without brothers [was]
Your nativity, which is unique.
[82:5] Our Lord had brothers, and yet was without brothers,
For he was single. O solitary one!
Great is the mystery that is uniquely
Your type: in the crown of a king
You have brothers and sisters!
[82:6] Precious jewels are your brothers.
Along with beryl and pearls,
[They are] like your companions. Gold is
Like your family. The crown
Of the king of kings comes from your friends.
[82:7] When you ascended from the sea—
A living tomb—you acquired this
Fair assembly of brothers, relatives,
And kin. The wheat is on the stalk
And you are on the crown with many others.
[82:8] Therefore, repayment is made to you
As is right, when from that depth
{You are exalted}[10] to a fair height. The stalk bears
The grain in a field, but you, the king's
Head carries upon a chariot.
[82:9] O daughter of the waters,[11] who abandoned the sea
In which you were born![12] You ascended to dry ground,
And were cherished upon it. Lovingly, they took you
And adorned themselves with you, just like that Birth
Which the peoples have loved and, with it, been crowned.

---

of Christ, the Only-Begotten. Other jewels, which must be cut and shaped, can
still serve as symbols of exalted things, but exalted things that nevertheless
have come into being.

9. Syr., *râzâ,* which could also be translated as "symbol," referring to its
signification of Christ's birth.

10. C, though it adds four extra syllables to the meter.

11. Syr., *mayyâ.* B, *yammâ,* "sea."

12. Ephrem switches from second to third person ("in which *she* was born").
I have retained the second person for the sake of consistency with what follows.

[82:10] In a true symbol,[13] Leviathan is trampled down
Among mortals.[14] The ones to be baptized[15] stripped
And put on oil.[16] In the symbol of the Anointed One,[17]
They took you, [pearl], and ascended. The apostles[18] stole
The soul from [Leviathan's] mouth, who was embittered.
[82:11] Your nature is like the silent lamb
In its sweetness.[19] For, if one should pierce it,
And take and hang it on {his}[20] ear,
As [Christ on] Golgotha, it casts all of its rays
All the more upon those who see it.
[82:12] The beauty of the Son is depicted in your beauty:
He clothed himself with suffering, {to the point that}[21] nails
    passed through him.
A prick passed through you: they pierced you,
Just as [they pierced] his hands. Because he suffered, he
    reigned,
Just as in your suffering, your beauty increases.
[82:13] If they had spared you, they would not have loved you.
For when you suffered, you reigned. Simon "the Rock"[22]
[Wished]{to spare}[23] the rock,[24] so that he who struck it
Was struck by it.[25] Because of his pain,
His beauty adorns the height and the depth.

    {*The End.*}[26]

13. B, "In symbol and in truth."
14. Here, baptism is the "truth" to which the biblical symbols of Leviathan
(Jb 41.1–34; Ps 104.26) refer.
15. Syr., *'āmûdê.* See note 9 attached to 81:11.
16. Syr., *mešḥâ.* On the pre-baptismal anointing in Syrian rites, see Winkler,
"The Original Meaning of the Prebaptismal Anointing and Its Implications."
17. Syr., *mšîḥâ,* "Messiah."
18. Ephrem is punning on *šlîḥê,* which can mean "apostles" or "those who
have stripped" (i.e., for baptism).
19. Ephrem is speaking to the pearl.
20. B.   21. BC.
22. Syr., *šem'ôn kîpâ.*
23. Syr., *ḥās,* B. A, *ḥašš,* "to feel" or "to suffer."
24. Mt 16.22.
25. Cf. Mt 21.42–44, but also referring to Christ's reprimand of Peter in
Mt 16.23.
26. B.

HYMN EIGHTY-THREE (HYMN THREE "ON THE PEARL")

{*3*},[1] *According to the same melody.*[2]

[83:1] You were blameless in your nakedness,
O pearl. Even the merchant
Who stripped off your robe was drunk with love for you,
Though he did not expose you: your garment is your light,
Your cloak is your brightness, O naked one!
[83:2] You resembled Eve, who was clothed
In her nakedness. That cursed one deceived her,
Despoiled and abandoned her. But the serpent could not
Strip your glory. In your symbol
Women are clothed with the light of Eden.
[83:3] He has made the pearls of Ethiopia
Shine greatly, as it is written.[3] How, O pearl, did he give you
To Ethiopia of the Nubians—he who gave
Light to the People? For his rays have reached
The Ethiopians and the Indians.
[83:4] The believer from Ethiopia,[4] [while sitting] on the
    chariot,
Saw Philip. The lamb of light
Met the black man as he was reading
From among the verses [of Scripture]. The Ethiopian was
    baptized
And clothed with light. He glistened as he drove away.

1. See note 1 attached to hymn 82.
2. On this melody, see note 1 attached to the melody of hymn 81.
3. Cf. Jb 28.19.
4. Acts 8.28–40.

[83:5] He converted and taught. From black men
He has made white men. And Ethiopian women—
Black women—have become pearls
For the Son. He lifted up to his Father,
From among the Ethiopians, a crown that glistens.
[83:6] The Queen of Sheba [was] a lamb who came
To the place of the wolf.[5] Solomon, inspiring her,
Gave her a lamp of truth.
Though he himself turned to paganism, she was enlightened
     and left.[6]
But they became dark, as is their custom.[7]
[83:7] The light that descended with that
Blessed woman into the house of darkness,
Its effulgence lasted until a new light
Came.[8] The [former] light found
The Dazzling One, and the place was enlightened.
[83:8] In the sea there are many fish,
For many miles. And in their vastness
They are actually quite small. Through your smallness,
     O pearl,
A crown has become great. The likeness of the Son—
Adam—has become great in his smallness.[9]
[83:9] Your crown upon the head, your beauty before the eye,
Your ornament upon the ear. Ascend from the sea,
Neighbor of {dry land},[10] and come to dwell
Upon the ear. The ear loves
The word of life, just as it loves you.
[83:10] In the ear is the word, and outside of it
The pearl. When [the ear] is attentive[11] to you,

5. 1 Kgs 10.1–10.

6. 1 Kgs 11.4–8.

7. That is, "The [Jewish] People." On Ephrem's characterization of Jews as "dark," see Shepardson, *Anti-Judaism*, 53–62.

8. That is, the Queen of Sheba's Judaism paved the way for an Ethiopian conversion to Christianity, through the eunuch.

9. That is, Adam has become great in Christ's smallness.

10. Syr., *yabšâ*, BC. A repeats *yammâ*, "sea."

11. Syr., *zhîrâ*, which can mean "to be attentive to," or "to be illumined by." Ephrem draws on both of these meanings in this and the following line.

It becomes wise {through you}.[12] It will be illumined[13]
By the word of truth. {Be}[14] his mirror!
See the beauty of the Word in your beauty!
[83:11] By yourself you teach how honorable
The High Word is. The earlobe
Is a tree of the flesh, and you are upon it,
The fruit of light. Would one not see your symbol
In the womb that bore the light?
[83:12] In you, O pearl, {is the parable}[15]
Of that kingdom, and the virgins
Five who entered it bearing the light
Of their lamps.[16] They are like you—
Shining, clothed with light.
[83:13] Who would give a pearl
To a poor woman? For when she had put it on,
It would seem ill-fitted to her. [But] you freely provide
Faith, all of which is fitting
For all humanity's parts.
[83:14] A woman would not exchange her pearl
Even for gold. Great shame
That you willingly cast your pearl
Into the mire! In the temporal
Pearl we see that which is eternal.
[83:15] What is in a purse, is also on a signet ring,
As well as in a treasure. Beyond one gate,
[There are] other gates, with locks
And keys. You, pearl,
The High One has sealed, as he has sought [to seal] all.

   {*The End.*}[17]

---

12. BC.   13. See note 11 above.
14. Syr., *hwî*, B. A, *hî*, "it is."
15. Syr., *matlāh*, BC. A, *mtalnāh*, "we have compared."
16. Mt 25.1–12.
17. B.

HYMN EIGHTY-FOUR (HYMN FOUR "ON THE PEARL")

{4}, *According to the same melody.*[1]

[84:1] The thief possessed faith—
That [faith] which possessed him—and it raised him up and
　placed him
In paradise.[2] He saw in the cross
The Tree of Life. That [faith] was a fruit,
And he took the place of Adam as an eater.

> REFRAIN: *Blessed is the one who believed like Simon—who*
> *inherited your blessing!*

[84:2] The fool who has faith
Alongside all [kinds of] questions, irritates [that faith]
In the same way that poking the eye with a finger
Blinds the eye. Worse than this is
The one who investigates faith.
[84:3] A diver will not examine
A pearl. All merchants
Rejoice in it without examining
From where it came. Nor does a king
Study it while being crowned with it.
[84:4] Because foolish Balaam had become
A foolish beast, through an ass
[God] spoke with him—him who despised the God
Who spoke with him.[3] He reproves you

---

1. On this melody, see note 1 attached to the melody of hymn 81.
2. Lk 23.43.
3. Nm 22.9–12, 28–30. See also *HF* 41:7.

With a pearl, instead of an ass.
[84:5] The People who had acquired a heart of rock,
He refuted with a rock. For, look: the rock
Obeys words.[4] He made it a witness
To reprove them. You who are dumb
In our day, the pearl reproves.
[84:6] With a swallow and a heron he rebuked
Humanity.[5] With an ox he rebuked [them],
And with an ass.[6] Now, a pearl
Reproves. Look at the flying birds,
The things in the middle, and those below!
[84:7] Your light[7] is not like the moon, waxing
And waning. The sun, whose rising
Is greater than all, its type is depicted
In your smallness—a symbol of the Son
Whose single brightness is greater than the sun.
[84:8] Fullness itself, full of light
Is the pearl. There is no craftsman
Who can steal from her, for her beauty is her fortification,
As well as her guard. She lacks nothing:
Wherever she is, she is entirely whole.
[84:9] If someone wants to break off and take
A piece of you, you become like
The faith that has perished among unbelievers,
Who have denigrated and mangled it. Yet faith
Recovered is greater than [recovering] you.
[84:10] Faith is a complete nature,
Indestructible. The disturber[8]
Suffers because of it. The denier
Is destroyed by it. Whoever expels the light
From his eyes becomes blind.
[84:11] Fire and wind are divisible,
Though they are strong. Light alone,
Of all things created, is indivisible,
Like its Creator. Nor is it barren,

---

4. Ex 17.6.   5. Jer 8.7.
6. Here referring to Is 1.3.   7. That is, the pearl's light.
8. I.e., the devil.

For it also begets without suffering loss.
[84:12] If someone thinks that you are created,[9]
He errs greatly. Your nature declares
That it is not created through skill,
Like all [other] stones. [It is] like[10] the Child
Whom construction did not make.
[84:13] Your rock has fled comparison
With the rock of the Son, for your own birth
[Was] inside the deep, while the Son of your Creator
[Was begotten] in the highest heights. He is like you
And not like you, for he is like the Father.
[84:14] According to the story, two wombs
Bore you: an unbound nature
Descended from on high,[11] while a fixed body
Ascended from the sea. In the other[12] birth[13]
You manifested your love for humanity.[14]
[84:15] Hands fastened you[15] when you took on a body
For those who would hold you. [They fastened you] on a
    crown,
As on a cross; on a wreath,
Like a victory [wreath]; on the ears
Like words. You are spread over everything.

    {*The End.*}[16]

---

9. Ephrem is still speaking to the pearl, though obviously referring to the Son as well.

10. Syr., *b-'rāz-(h)û yaldâ*. Literally, "in a symbol is the Child."

11. Probably lightning, but possibly rain (see note 4 attached to 82:2).

12. C, "the last," or "latter."

13. That is, the birth from the oyster.

14. Ephrem is still addressing the pearl, as evidenced by the second-person feminine pronouns.

15. Syr., *qab'ek*. The verb *qba'* can also convey "to pass a nail through."

16. B.

HYMN EIGHTY-FIVE (HYMN FIVE "ON THE PEARL")

{5},[1] *According to the same melody.*[2]

[85:1] O gift that freely ascended
With the diver:[3] you are similar to this manifest
Light that freely shines
Upon all humans: a parable of the hidden [light]
That freely gives hidden brightness.
[85:2] The painter depicts you in an image
With paints. In you is depicted
Faith with types and symbols,
As with paints. Instead of an image,
In you and in your colors, your Creator is depicted.
[85:3] O you who lack scent: the odor of symbols
Rises up from you. You are inedible,
Yet you gladden those who hear.
You are undrinkable, yet in a story
You are made into a font of symbols for ears.
[85:4] O pearl, you who are great
In your smallness: your size is diminished,
Your extent small, along with your weight.
But your glory is great! There are none like
That crown, yet upon it you are placed.
[85:5] Who has not perceived how great you are
In your smallness? If someone scorns you
Or destroys you, that one is blamed

1. See note 1 attached to hymn 82.
2. On this melody, see note 1 attached to the melody of hymn 81.
3. C missing from here to hymn 87:9:1.

For his ignorance. Whenever he sees you
In a king's crown, he is drawn to you.
[85:6] Those naked[4] dove down and drew you out
O pearl! Kings were not
The first to give you to humanity,
But the naked[5]—the symbol of the poor,
The fishermen, the Galileans.
[85:7] Indeed, clothed bodies could not
Come to your side. The naked came
Like infants. They buried their bodies
And came down to your side. You rushed toward them
And took refuge with them. How they have desired you!
[85:8] Before the poor[6] opened their pockets
And brought forth a new wealth,
Their tongues announced you.
They set you among merchants,
In the palms of humans, as a medicine of life.
[85:9] The symbolic naked ones[7] saw your resurrection
On the seashore. On the lakeshore[8]
The true[9] apostles[10] saw the resurrection
Of the Son of your Creator in you and in your master.
Both the sea and the lake have been adorned.
[85:10] The diver ascended from within the sea
And put on clothes. Simon Cephas,
While swimming, came up from the lake
And put on his clothes.[11] Just like their clothes,
Both places[12] have put on love of both of you.
[85:11] Since, look, I have wandered within you, pearl,

4. Syr., *šlîḥê,* "naked" or "apostles." See note 18 attached to 82:10.
5. Syr., *šlîḥâ.* See previous note.
6. That is, the apostles, following 85:6.
7. Syr., *šlîḥê.* See p. 352, n. 3.
8. See Jn 21.1.
9. Here, Ephrem juxtaposes "symbol" (*rāzâ*) and "truth" (*qûštâ*), in a way similar to "shadow" and "fulfillment": divers, who search for pearls, represent the "shadow," and the apostles the "fulfillment."
10. Syr., *šlîḥê.* See n. 4 above.   11. Jn 21.7.
12. I.e., the sea and the lake.

May I collect my mind. Since I looked upon you,
May I become like you. Since you are entirely collected
Within yourself, and since at every moment
You are one, may I become one in you.
[85:12] I have collected a pearl to make
A crown for the Son. Instead of stains
Upon my limbs, receive my offering.
It is not that you have need. Rather, my need
I have offered to you. Cleanse my stains!
[85:13] That crown is completely [full] of eloquent
Pearls: instead of gold,
It is girded with love. Instead of leather,
With faith. Instead of hands,
Praise lifts it up to the One who is lifted up.

Completed are [the hymns] on the pearl.[13]

13. B, "The End."

HYMN EIGHTY-SIX

Another, according to the same melody.[1]

[86:1] May the memory of the fathers breathe
Within our words.[2] They were exceedingly lucid,
Wise and subtle,
Guileless, without discussion.
They cleared[3] and then came down the road of life.

> REFRAIN: *Blessed is the one who has you called by the
> name your Father called you!*[4]

[86:2] And though their revelations were new,
They were neither difficult nor strange,
As [false][5] teachings are. And they did not rebel
Like the investigators. In every flood
Their faith acted as their ship.
[86:3] {He}[6] gave the law. They were [its] keepers.
When he annulled [a law], they annulled it. With
    impure ravens
He fed Elijah,[7] and from a carcass,

---

1. On this melody, see note 1 attached to the melody of hymn 81.

2. Or, "The memory of the fathers breathes/within the words [of Scripture]" (see Beck, *HF [G]*, 224).

3. Ephrem makes a pun here: the word "to clear [a path]" is *draš*, from which the noun *drāšâ*, "debating," is derived.

4. B, "Praise to you, Son of the Creator, who gives life to all!"

5. While Ephrem simply has "teachings" (*yûlpānâ*), and will use this word elsewhere in a positive sense, especially in the singular (though see *HF* 38:4 for a positive sense of the plural), it can also signify "false teachings," as it does in the title of his *CH* (albeit there modified by *ṭʿāyê*, "false, wandering").

6. B, A, "they."

7. 1 Kgs 17.6.

There was honey for Samson.[8] They did not go around
   debating
Why it was impure, or why it was pure.
[86:4] And when he annulled Sabbaths among sick People,
They clothed themselves in health.[9] Samson took
A foreign woman as a wife, and there was no debating
Among the righteous ones.[10] The prophet received
An adulteress, and the just ones kept quiet.[11]
[86:5] He reproached the righteous, calling forth and reciting
Their crimes. He showed mercy to sinners,
And freely gave life, flattening the mountains
Of their sins. They discerned that God
Should not be corrected by a human.[12]
[86:6] [He is] the Lord of truth, and his works have become
His shadow, so that wherever
His will has looked, they too have directed
Their wills. Since he is light
In him their shadows have become light.
[86:7] How wretched are all the deniers
Of clear things! Although he has engraved
This New Testament
Alongside that of the Prophet,[13] as from sleep
The vile have arisen, calling out, troubled.
[86:8] The path that the just have straightened out and gone
   down
With truth,[14] they themselves[15] hated it,[16]

---

8. Jgs 14.9.

9. Cf., *inter alia*, Mt 12.9–13.

10. Jgs 14.1–11. Note, however, that Samson's parents *do* debate with Samson regarding the marriage (v. 3).

11. Hos 1.2.

12. Ephrem does not seem to have a specific biblical passage in mind here. Rather, what he gives is a general, and idealized, reading of salvation history: the righteous go astray, God has mercy, and they recognize the error of their ways.

13. Here, "that of the prophet" seems to refer to the entirety of the Tanakh.

14. Lit., "their truth."

15. I.e., "the vile," carried over from the previous stanza.

16. The verb given in both manuscripts is *zaqrûh*, "they have woven it." *PS*

Because they were drunk. They have left it and gone out,
Because they have investigated. Evil debating,
An evil guide, has led them astray.
[86:9] They saw a ray [of light]. They made it dark,
So they could explore it. They saw beryl—
Faith. Upon investigating it,
They fell down and perished. A pearl
They made into a stone, and were tripped by it.
[86:10] O Gift, which fools have made
A deathly treasure! The People severed
Your luminous foundation from your source.
Though they have not severed [false] teachings,[17]
They have separated your beauty from your root.[18]
[86:11] Those who wished to separate you
Have been separated by you. By you, fools
Are severed and cast away. The tribes that germinated
On Zion have been severed and cast away.
Look: they have sprouted, but they are dry.
[86:12] The circumcised grew dirty, for in your font
They did not wash. They reeked and stank,
For the scent of your aromas did not waft
From their garments. Odious are the [false] teachings.[19]
Since they have not {been whitened by you},[20] they do not
     shine.
[86:13] Limit yourself to our smallness,
O Gift! For until it has explored you
On all sides, love cannot
Be still, or keep quiet. Diminish yourself,
O Greater-than-all, you who have come to all!

(vol.1, 1150, sub. *zqar*), however, provides one passage that corrects *zqar* to *sqar*,
"to hate" (see also Beck, *HF [G]*, 225, n. 9), which I have followed here.

17. On "teachings," see note 5 attached to 86:2.

18. Ephrem here attributes fourth-century subordinationist ideas—divid-
ing the Son from the Father, his source—to "the People," a rhetorical plot that
he will intensify in hymn 87 (see note attached to top of hymn 87). On the
conflation of biblical Jews and fourth-century subordinationists, see Shepardson, *Anti-Judaism*.

19. On "teachings," see note 5 attached to 86:2.

20. Syr., *ḥwar(w) b-ek(y)*, B. A, *ḥār(w) b-ek(y)*, "looked upon you."

[86:14] The investigators can be blamed for this,
O our pearl:[21] instead of love
Schism has come in, presuming to investigate,
To expose your beauty.[22] It is not an idol,[23]
It is your beauty,[24] which cannot be explained.
[86:15] Manifest your beauty among the deniers!
To what can you be likened? The whole of you is a face,
O pearl! Onlookers wander off,
Disturbed by you. The divided have divided you,
Yet are divided by you. You are entirely unified.[25]
[86:16] They did not notice your beauty, because they lacked
The eye of truth.[26] That veil
Of prophecy, and the glut of symbols
That [stand] before your brightness, is for them a covering.
They thought you were something else,[27] O Mirror!
[86:17] Therefore, the blind faction fouled
Your pure beauty.[28] The circumcised despised you,
For they did not think they had seen
Even a lowly prophet in you. Rather, alien
Teachings they thought they saw in you. [29]

21. Even though the five "Hymns on the Pearl" concluded with *HF* 85, the imagery continues here.
22. Syr., *d-neglûg šûpārek(y)*. While this phrase sounds innocuous in English, Ephrem intends to convey an egregious exposure of something that should remain hidden. For a similar idea, albeit using different vocabulary, see *HF* 9:2.
23. Or, "statue" (*glîpâ*). B, *glāpâ*, "sculpture."
24. B, "the birth" (*yaldâ*).
25. The verb here is *šwâ*, which more literally means, "to be even, equal." I have translated it as "unified" because it is juxtaposed with "divided." Yet the image undoubtedly plays on the features of a smooth pearl, as opposed to Ephrem's opponents, who are uneven and jagged, or even separated.
26. As will be revealed in the final stanza, Ephrem's object of inquiry has shifted from "pearl" to "mirror." On ancient mirrors, see n. 3 attached to 2:2.
27. Syr., *'ḥrîtâ*, lit., "another." This could mean either "they think you are something you are not" (as I have taken it), or "they think you are *an other*," i.e., a reflection of themselves.
28. Throughout the remainder of this hymn, the pronouns remain second-person feminine singular. Thus, grammatically speaking, the remainder of the hymn is addressed either to the mirror or the pearl (both of which are grammatically feminine). On the basis of 86:22, "pearl" seems more likely.
29. Ephrem associates the term "alien" (*nûkrāyâ*) with Marcion in *CH* 48:1. Thanks to Rob Morehouse for pointing this out to me. On Marcion, see note

[86:18] Fools have set you above the height
Of that Maker.[30] The circumcised have thrown you down,
Like some fraud, below the Creator,
To the great deep. Since in you they have become dirty—
Both parties—they must be cleansed in you.
[86:19] Because they have elevated you too high, and brought
    you too low,
Level the two sides:[31] come down a little
From the height of denial
And strangeness,[32] and ascend from the depths
Of Judaism (even though you are in heaven).
[86:20] Our Lord is set between God
And humans. The prophets are
Like his heralds. The Just One rejoices
Like his child. This word has conquered
Jews and deniers!
[86:21] Come, O Gift of the holy Church:
Rest inside of it. The circumcised have tormented you
Because they are gossips, and [they have tormented] the
    teachings
Because they quarrel. Blessed is the One who has given you
A lovely assembly to extol you!
[86:22] In Moses's Testament you depicted
Your splendors, while in the New
Testament, through readers, you revealed
The shining of your light. Blessed is the One who has given us
Your rays and your splendors.

   {*The End.*}[33]

---

20 attached to 21:10. He will refer to Marcionism, along with Judaism, in the
following two stanzas.
   30. See previous note.
   31. Lit., "them."
   32. Referencing Marcion's "strange god" (see note 29, above).
   33. B.

HYMN EIGHTY-SEVEN

According to the same melody.[1]

[87:1][2] As in a contest, I saw debaters,
Prideful.[3] They were worn down
From [trying to] taste fire,[4] see the wind,[5]
Touch the light. On the basis of [just] a beam,
They strained to make distinctions.

> REFRAIN: *Glory to the Father and to his Son Jesus,*
> *and to his Holy Spirit.*

[87:2] The Son, who is more subtle than the mind,
They wanted to explore. The Holy Spirit,
Who cannot be touched, they thought they could touch
With their questions. And the Father, who is eternally
Inexplicable,[6] his debaters [tried to] explain.
[87:3] A good example of our faith

---

1. On this melody, see note 1 attached to the melody of hymn 81.
2. This vivid hymn depicts the fourth-century controversies in a synoptic and dramatic fashion, emphasizing episcopal intrigue and ambition as surface manifestations of deeper Satanic plots. It is here, as well, that Ephrem explicitly depicts the thought of his subordinationist opponents as a "Judaizing" tendency. On this, see Shepardson, "'Exchanging Reed for Reed': Mapping Contemporary Heretics onto Biblical Jews in Ephrem's *Hymns on Faith*," *Hugoye: Journal of Syriac Studies* 5:1 (2002), at http://www.bethmardutho.org/index.php/hugoye/hugoye-author-index/137.html, which also provides a complete English translation of the hymn. While the *HF* as a whole has referred to ecclesial strife, and at times cast this in an anti-Jewish light, the hyperbolic quality of this rhetoric is unique to this hymn. See also note 18 attached to 86:10.
3. B, "schismatic" (*bnay ḥeryānâ*).   4. Ms B omits *d*-prefix from *nûrâ*.
5. Or "spirit."
6. Syr., *mettargam*. B, *met'aqqab*, "indisputable."

[Is that] of Abraham,[7] of our repentance,
The Ninevites,[8] and the house of Rahab,
Our hope.[9] For us there are the Prophets,
For us there are the Apostles. The Evil One grows envious.
[87:4] The evil custom of the evil calf
Of the Egyptians; the hateful appearance
Of the hateful idol of the four faces
Of the Hittites;[10] the accursed disputation,
The hidden worm[11] of the Greeks.[12]
[87:5] That bitter one saw good order
And upturned it. He saw hateful things[13]
And sowed them. He saw hope
And suppressed and severed it. The debating that he planted,
Look: it has yielded the fruit of the poison of [the serpent's]
    teeth.
[87:6] Satan saw that the truth had strangled him
And his weeds, and he went off
To devise [new] plots and lay snares
For the faith. He shot at priests
The arrows that those in authority[14] love.
[87:7] Upon the throne,[15] they struggled
[To see] who would be first. One secretly
Desired it, but concealed [the fact]. One openly
Fought for it. One acted shamefully
And one acted with guile: they are the same.
[87:8] Even one who is young thinks
It his time.[16] One who is old
Does not consider that the beyond is near.
[It is] a grievous illness: the old, the young,

---

7. Cf. Gn 15.6. See also *HF* 21:6.   8. Jon 3.5–10.
9. Jos 6.25.   10. 2 Chr 33.7 (P).
11. Cf. Mk 9.48.
12. On "Greeks," see note 24 attached to 2:24.
13. Syr., *sanyātâ*. Ephrem is making a pun: *sanyâ* is "thorn bush."
14. Syr., *rîšānûtâ*, which Beck translates as "episcopacy" (*Bischofsamt*) (*HF* [G], 228).
15. I.e., the bishop's throne.
16. Lit., "does not think that it is not his time."

Even infants[17] seek office!
[87:9] Satan stripped off the first scribes
And put on others.[18] The People, worn out,
The worm and the locust had gnawed and consumed them,
Then abandoned and left them. The worm has come
To the new garment of the new People.
[87:10] He saw the crucifiers, that they were rejected and cast
    away
As strangers. From among those of the same family,[19]
He made investigators. From worshipers
There came debaters. From that garment
He brought forth the worm and placed it all around.
[87:11] He brought forth the locust in a wheat granary,
And sat and watched. A pure storehouse,
Look: it was desolated. Look: the garments of glory
Have been eaten. He mocks us,
And we [mock] ourselves, for we are drunk.
[87:12] He sowed weeds and planted brambles
In a pure vineyard. He defiled the flock
And leprosy spread. Lambs upon lambs
Became his possessions.[20] He began among the People,
But came to the peoples to finish.
[87:13] Instead of that reed[21] which the first People
Held out to the Son, the last [peoples], presuming
In their treatises, have written with a reed[22]
That he is [only] human. The Evil One has exchanged
A reed for a reed against our Redeemer.
[87:14] Instead of the garments of many colors

---

17. Syr., *yallûdâ*. This could also be vocalized as *yālûdâ*, "parents."

18. Syr., *ḥrānê*. BC, *'ḥrāyê*, "latest," or "most recent."

19. I.e., Christians (thus, those of the same family as Ephrem's own audience).

20. Lit., "his land."

21. Syr., *qanyâ*. Ephrem is playing on the double meaning of this term: it refers initially to the "reed" by which, according to Mt 27.48, Jesus was offered vinegar, but it will take on a second meaning in reference to the "reed-pen," with which Ephrem's opponents have written their tracts.

22. See previous note.

In which [the People] clothed him,[23] they[24] have dyed a title
Falsely.[25] Many names
He has put on, whether creature
Or thing-made, though he is the Maker.
[87:15] While [the People] {braided}[26] a crown for him from
        mute,
Quiet thorns, wordy thorns
Of the mind he[27] has woven together out loud
As hymns.[28] And he has hidden unnoticed
Briars inside songs.
[87:16] Satan saw that he had been exposed
In the former things, when he manifested the spitting,
The vinegar, the thorns, the nails, the cross,
The garments, the reed, and the lance which smote him.
They were despised and obvious, so he changed his plans.[29]
[87:17] He introduced error,[30] instead of the slap
That our Lord received. Instead of spitting,
Disputing arose, and instead of garments,
Hidden schisms. Instead of the reed
Controversy arose to afflict all.

---

23. Mt 27.28 and Lk 23.11.

24. At this point, ms B switches to a third-person masculine singular subject, in reference to "the Evil One" from the previous stanza. I have retained ms A's plural verb form, because it suggests the close connection Ephrem sees between his opponents and the Satanic forces undergirding their activity.

25. Ephrem uses the language of dying clothes to draw a connection between the Passion scenes and the subordinationist controversies.

26. Syr., *da-gdal*, B. A, *da-gāl*, "to pour out."

27. Here ms A switches to a third-person singular subject, referencing "the Evil One." On this, see note 24 attached to 87:14.

28. Syr., *madrāšê*.

29. This stanza could be taken in two ways: as I have taken it, Ephrem refers to two phases of Satanic activity: first, that involving the life of Christ; second, that involving Ephrem's own time. Lines 1 and 2a, however, could be taken as a complete thought, referencing Gn 3. Line 2 would then be translated: "... in the first things. Then he manifested ..." I have kept it as it is, however, because thus far Ephrem has only been emphasizing two periods of deception.

30. Syr., *pahyâ*, which I have elsewhere translated as "wandering off," but have used "error" here to make its implications explicit.

[87:18] Pride called out to anger, her sister.
Envy and wrath, arrogance and guile
Replied and came along. They have taken counsel[31]
Against our Savior, just as on that day
They took counsel,[32] when [our Savior] suffered.
[87:19] Instead of the cross, controversy is
A hidden cross. Instead of nails,
Questions have entered. Instead of Sheol,
Denial. A second passion[33]
Satan wished to renew.
[87:20] Instead of the sponge moistened with vinegar,[34]
He has given arrows[35]—investigation, utterly
Soaked with death. The gall that he[36] gave,
Our Lord spit out.[37] The fraudulent investigation
That the bitter one gave has pleased fools.
[87:21] Though in that time there was a judge
Against them, look: judges
[Stand] as if against us. And instead of an inscription,[38]
Their ordinances.[39] The crown is absolved,
For priests have placed stumbling blocks before kings.
[87:22] Instead of the priesthood praying
On behalf of the kingdom that wars would cease
From humanity, they have urged them[40]
Toward a perverse war, so that kings begin

31. Syr., *melkâ šqal(w)-(h)waw*. There is a double meaning here: if we vocal-
ize the first word as *malkâ*, the meaning would be "they have stirred up the
king," referring to the role of the Roman government in Christ's death and
the role of the emperor in fourth-century controversies.
32. See previous note.
33. C, "sign," presumably referring to the cross.
34. Mt 27.48.
35. Syr., *gîrê*. See also *HF* 1:3. Ms C, *geddê* ("wormwood").
36. Ms B, "they." On this switching between singular and plural, see note
24 attached to 87:14.
37. Mt 27.33.
38. Lk 23.38.
39. Syr., *pûqdānê*. It seems that this refers to anti-Nicene laws enacted by
Constantius or Valens. On this period, see pp. 25–27.
40. I.e., kings.

To fight against their cities.
[87:23] O our Lord, reconcile priests and kings.
In one Church, let priests pray
For their kings, and kings show mercy
To their cities. And the quiet within,
Through you, may it be for us a wall without.

Completed are the hymns on faith
Of Mar Ephrem,
Eighty-seven in number.[41]

41. Ms B, "Completed is the copying of the hymns on faith, which are 87,
of Mar Ephrem, Saint and Teacher." Ms C, "Completed is the copying in this
penqîtâ of the hymns on faith, which in number are 87, spoken by the glorious
Mar Ephrem."

GENERAL INDEX

Aaron: priesthood of, 108; sons of, 108, 185

Abraham, 87, 123, 158, 285–87, 399

Abraham of Nisibis, 8

abyss, 74, 162, 243

Adam, 69, 93–94, 97, 107n21, 165, 180, 190n9, 197, 201, 205–6, 221, 251, 263, 303, 310–11, 333, 352, 385, 387

Aetius, Aetians, 20–21, 24–26, 31–32, 35–36, 42–44, 47, 73n13, 190n11, 285n3

air: as breath, 375; and Christ's Ascension, 277; as element, 240; as metaphor for God's Being, 85–86; as object of debate, 323; the soul as, 59

Aithallaha of Edessa, 19, 22

Amar, Joseph P., 6n13, 7n20, 10n41, 12n50, 20n83, 26n115

Amos, Prophet, 216

angels. *See* Cherubim, Gabriel, Michael, Seraphim, watchers

animals: Adam giving names to, 310; on the Ark, 329; compared with humanity, 61, 201–2, 209, 213, 218, 370–71; language of, 128; in the vision of Daniel, 110–11

Antioch, 26, 42–43

Apostles: as fishermen, 391; as title for New Testament books, 65, 67–68, 160, 276, 296, 302, 309, 344; general, 92, 148, 207, 231, 253, 399

Apostolic Constitutions, 136n8

Arius, Arianism, 19–20, 24, 32–33, 42–44, 46. *See also* Nicaea, Council of

Ark, of Noah. *See* Noah

Ark, of the Covenant, 109–10, 113, 158

arrogance, 161–62, 216, 402. *See also* pride

arrows, 58, 179, 216, 329, 331, 334, 399

assembly: of investigators, 178, 334; as title for the Church, 256, 332, 371–72, 397

Athanasius, 23, 32, 41, 46

audacity (*ḥṣap*): general, 185; in first-person statement, 143; of love, 143; of investigators, 183. *See also* debate, discussion, error, investigation, presumption, wandering

Audians, 20

Babel, Tower of, 303–4

Babu of Nisibis, 8

Babylon, 253

Balaam, 166, 230, 387

baptism: and the Apostles, 231, 383; of Christ, 92, 102, 124–25, 249, 267; of Ethiopian eunuch, 384–85; in Ephrem's community, 124, 223–24, 231, 269, 296, 325; anointing, baptismal, 92n12, 260, 136n7, 383; and names of the Trinity, 136, 161, 164, 184, 241, 267, 314, 325, 332, 363

Bar Dayṣān, 7, 145n5, 161n9, 259, 327

405

181, 183, 187, 215, 230, 237, 241, 253, 271, 272, 280, 331, 338, 346, 383, 396, 400; as a millstone, 305; in the Church, 109, 329; into angels, 173; into the Creator, Maker, 60, 62, 111, 252, 356, 362, 372; into the demons, 295; into the divine Being, 337, 368; into divine birth, 88, 140, 221, 247, 262–63; into the divine Essence, 217, 283; into divine knowledge, 112, 188; into the divine fatherhood, 246, 284; into divinity, 338; into the Father, 70; into the Firstborn, 82, 86, 99, 108–9, 118–19, 183, 187, 327, 341; into God, 321, 380; into hidden things, 109, 271, 322; into the Holy Spirit, 187; into the Knower-of-all, 140; into Moses, 106; into the Sabbath, 231; into Scripture, 270, 294, 330, 369; into the Trinity, 239, 251, 262, 298; compared to arrows, 402; compared to a mirror, 66; compared to a sword, 163, 216; general, 23–25, 41–51, 61, 64, 71–73, 74, 76–78, 86–87, 102–3, 106–8, 110, 114–17, 119–20, 126, 129, 141, 162, 172–73, 177–78, 180–82, 183–84, 218, 230, 234, 238, 242–44, 253–54, 283, 320, 323–24, 328–29, 332–33, 335, 340–41, 346, 348, 354, 363–64, 372, 379, 395–96; present, juxtaposed with past, 113; strange, 109, 258; understood positively, 66, 67n19, 80. *See also* audacity, controversy, debate, discussion, error, faith, presumption, schism, wandering

Isaac, 286. *See also* Abraham

Isaiah, Prophet, 123, 173n7, 213, 308

Israel, 213

Jacob of Nisibis, 6n19, 8, 19, 20n83

Jacob of Serugh, 12, 14n58

Jerome, 12n48, 13n54

Jerusalem, 241, 279. *See also* Jews

Jesus, 97, 138, 160–61, 279, 398. *See also* Christ, soul

Jethro, father-in-law of Moses, 81

jewels, 178, 381–82

Jews, Judaism: and Jerusalem, 241; and the Messiah, 242; and Scripture, 241; as the People, 105, 118, 119, 174, 241–42, 277, 296, 308, 317, 354, 360, 376, 378, 384, 388, 395, 400, 401; general, 147n9, 149, 176n17, 317n10, 385n7, 396n18; Judaism, 397. *See also* chasm, deniers, Pharisees, scribes, Son, symbol

Job, 115

John, Evangelist, 199, 203–4, 206

John of Ephesus, 49n184, 143n9

John of Persia, 19

John the Baptist, 117n27, 122, 125, 158, 249, 308. *See also* Zechariah

Jonah, 155, 380

Jordan, river, 100, 110, 113, 267

Joseph, husband of Mary, 146–47, 165

Joseph, son of Jacob, 139

Joshua, son of Nun, 82

Jovian, emperor, 7

Judah, 249

Judaism. *See* Jews, Judaism

Judas Iscariot, 376

Judas Thomas. *See* Thomas

Julian, emperor: general, 7; *Hymns against*, 42n173, 45, 83n22

Just One. *See* God

justice, 130, 131, 205, 259, 273n5, 275, 279, 303. *See also* grace

Kaufhold, H., 19n82

king, kings: and priests, 27, 82, 402; biblical, 286; emperor as, 20–21; of Greece, 43n173; in Ephrem's own context, 223, 402–3; Pilate as, 139; general, 143, 155, 382, 387, 391, 402n31; mind as, 178. *See also* Christ, David, God, Son

Rachel, 302

Rahab, 399

Red Sea, 110n38, 296

rennet, 88, 171

resting-places ('âwwânâ), 66, 80, 324.
See also mile-markers, path, road,
way

resurrection, 150, 182, 226, 317n10,
391

road: divine, 76, 130, 239; general,
101n16, 274, 281; toward investigation, 128, 239; of the King, 330,
337; of life, 393. See also mile-
markers, path, resting-places, way

robber. See thief

rooster, 150

root: as metaphor for Christ's lineage,
132; of linguistic terms, 312; marriage as, 325; of organic material,
235, 238; truth as, 375. See also
Christ, Father, fruit, Son, tree

Russell, Paul, 7n20, 24n105, 28n125,
28n127

Sabbath, 231, 365, 394

Sabellians, 20

sacrifice, 92, 123, 176, 264n8, 293,
308

Samson, 205, 394

Satan: and the hour of Christ's return, 367; and internal Christian
division, 129, 213, 399–402; and
investigation, 295, 321–22; and the
temptation of Jesus, 102; as mocking, 274; as subtle, 285; defeat of,
354. See also demons, Evil One,
nature, serpent

scale, 88n46, 131, 132, 219, 259,
328, 369

schism, schismatics, 52, 58, 64, 101,
184, 205, 213, 223, 271–73, 296,
315, 328, 329, 334–35, 396,
398n3, 401

Scott, James C., 44n175

scribes (sāprē), 69, 102, 204n9, 224,
231, 242, 266, 267–68, 270, 274–

75, 287, 298, 302, 314, 320, 324,
370, 376, 400

sea: as metaphor for divinity, 75, 77,
120, 187, 217, 237, 328, 338; as
incomprehensible, 84, 221, 323,
348; debating as, 337; general,
134, 149, 155, 229, 258, 274, 340,
372, 378–79, 382, 385, 389, 391;
of hidden things, 162, 255; Jonah
within, 380; Jesus walking upon,
100–101, 125, 277; Red Sea, 112,
296, 379

seed, 83, 134, 142, 150, 154, 158,
169, 211, 224, 322, 382

Seraph, Seraphim, 69, 79, 123, 146,
173, 186, 308. See also Cherubim,
Gabriel, Michael, watchers

serpent, 141, 190, 330, 384, 399. See
also Satan

sheep, 134, 136, 206, 209. See also
Christ, flock, lamb

Sheol, 333, 402. See also Gehenna

Shepardson, Christine, 23n99,
69n10, 204n10, 385n7, 398n2

shepherd (general), 206–7, 209, 299.
See also Christ.

ship ('elpâ), 101, 134, 149, 260–61,
337, 375, 379, 393

sickness, 205, 219, 233, 255, 304,
336, 357, 399. See also drugs, healing, medicine

sign (nîšâ), 57–58, 99, 150, 200, 213,
260, 331, 402n33. See also image,
symbol, type

silence: and faith, 101, 136, 144, 148;
and praise, 77, 79; and prayer,
154–55; and speech, 219–220,
333; angelic, 69, 71; as refuge, 77;
of Abraham, 286; of the Father,
127–28, 278; general, 23–24, 62,
64, 67n22, 86, 107, 115, 140, 162,
202, 216, 218, 226, 254, 272, 306,
330, 341, 354; of Noah, 285; of the
pearl, 381; regarding the Trinity,
68, 79, 106, 117, 121, 158, 161,
164, 234, 247, 251, 284, 291, 331,

silence: regarding the Trinity (*cont.*) 333; regarding hidden things, 221, 224, 271. *See also* faith, prayer

Simon Peter, 261n16, 383, 387, 391

sinful woman, 122

Socrates Scholasticus, 26n112

Sodomites, 286, 379

Solomon, king, 123, 275–76, 385

Son (divine): and the Books, 200; and creation, 93–94, 96, 251; and divine names, 86, 161, 187, 267–69, 271, 275, 301, 312–13, 319n23, 360, 363; and investigation, 120, 141, 217, 253, 357; and the Jews, 241–42; and the soul, 149; as Begotten, 28–29, 34–37, 41, 58n12, 90, 92, 158, 161, 183, 248–49, 270, 272, 276, 284, 288, 306n7, 307, 311–15, 357, 367, 381, 389; as Child (*yaldâ*), 60, 64, 71, 86, 91, 95, 97–99, 113, 117, 128, 150, 162, 178n6, 180, 183, 187, 191, 199, 200, 211, 214, 219, 223, 230, 234, 239, 242, 244, 252, 254, 261–63, 267, 269, 281, 300, 302, 303, 306, 323, 324, 326–27, 341, 389, 397; as Creator, 252; as Firstborn, 71, 86, 93, 95, 97, 99, 101, 108–9, 112, 114n8, 115, 117–19, 172, 346, 361; as hidden, 276, 333; as Lord, 313; as treasure, 87, 112n48; beauty of, 383; begetting of, 58, 90, 245, 248; beloved, 68; compared to the sun, 349; of the Creator, 146, 169, 204, 264, 306, 389, 391, 393n4; of David, 166; of the Exalted One, 344; of the Father, 317; general, 81, 97, 103, 114, 128, 135, 148, 157, 164, 175, 177, 189n5, 198, 208, 216, 230, 239, 249, 250, 263, 270, 297, 300, 310, 318, 320, 325, 328, 331, 359n3, 361–62, 364–66, 374, 379, 385, 392, 398, 400; of God, 68–70, 223, 280, 286, 302–3, 308, 360; of Greatness, 287; image of, 332;

of Joseph, 146; of the King, 155, 277–78, 294–95; of life, 146, 167; likeness of, 385; of the Lord, 277; of the Maker, 209; mingled with the Father, 305; nature of, 88, 99, 298; of the Promise, 286; of righteousness, 321n6; symbols of, 377, 388; in Trinitarian controversies, 23, 26, 28–42, 57n4; of truth, 290, 307; of the womb of the Father, 183; voice of, 127n8. *See also* Christ, Father, God, Lord, types

soul: and debate, 244; as invisible, 199–200, 340; and the body, 149, 235, 266, 290, 322, 336, 339, 371n10, 374–75; and suffering, 135, 149; eye of, 88; general, 102, 136, 140, 149, 152, 178, 196, 256, 264, 293, 323, 358, 383; of Jesus, 138; nature of, 58–61, 289, 291. *See also* discussion, dreams, Evil One, eye, explore, faith, fire, freedom, God, nature, Son, wandering

Sozomen, 6n18, 48n26

sun: and investigation, 83–84, 91, 173, 181–82, 184–85, 221, 291, 326, 328–29, 348, 350, 352, 356–58; as Trinitarian metaphor, 225–28, 229, 234, 349–358; at the Crucifixion, 139, 318; Christ's knowledge of, 365; worship of, 216. *See also* Christ, eye, Father, heat, light, Son

symbol (*râzâ*): and baptism, 135; of the cross, 147–48, 150; of the Firstborn, 118–19; of Jews, 354, 376; lamb as, 150; of the Lord, 75; in the natural world, 235, 350, 353; in Scripture, 258, 260; of the Savior, 149; of Scripture, 159, 203n5; true, 383. *See also* image, pearl, sign, treasure, type

synagogue, 139. *See also* Jews

talents, 89, 133n23, 170n15, 279. *See also* credit, debt, deposit, gift, interest, treasure

INDEX OF HOLY SCRIPTURE

Old Testament

421

CPSIA information can be obtained
at www.ICGtesting.com
Printed in the USA
BVOW03s1922020917
493714BV00001B/66/P